D1162839

Philosophy and Politics – Critical Explorations

Volume 1

Series editors
David M. Rasmussen, Boston College, Chestnut Hill, Massachusetts, USA
Alessandro Ferrara, University of Rome 'Tor Vergata', Rome, Italy

More information about this series at http://www.springer.com/series/13508

Johannes Drerup • Gunter Graf
Christoph Schickhardt • Gottfried Schweiger
Editors

Justice, Education and the Politics of Childhood

Challenges and Perspectives

 Springer

Editors
Johannes Drerup
Institute of Educational Science
WWU Münster
Münster, Germany

Gunter Graf
Centre for Ethics and Poverty Research
University of Salzburg
Salzburg, Austria

Christoph Schickhardt
National Center for Tumor Diseases (NCT)
University Hospital Heidelberg
Heidelberg, Germany

Gottfried Schweiger
Centre for Ethics and Poverty Research
University of Salzburg
Salzburg, Austria

ISSN 2352-8370   ISSN 2352-8389   (electronic)
Philosophy and Politics – Critical Explorations
ISBN 978-3-319-27387-7   ISBN 978-3-319-27389-1   (eBook)
DOI 10.1007/978-3-319-27389-1

Library of Congress Control Number: 2015960930

© Springer International Publishing Switzerland 2016
This work is subject to copyright. All rights are reserved by the Publisher, whether the whole or part of the material is concerned, specifically the rights of translation, reprinting, reuse of illustrations, recitation, broadcasting, reproduction on microfilms or in any other physical way, and transmission or information storage and retrieval, electronic adaptation, computer software, or by similar or dissimilar methodology now known or hereafter developed.
The use of general descriptive names, registered names, trademarks, service marks, etc. in this publication does not imply, even in the absence of a specific statement, that such names are exempt from the relevant protective laws and regulations and therefore free for general use.
The publisher, the authors and the editors are safe to assume that the advice and information in this book are believed to be true and accurate at the date of publication. Neither the publisher nor the authors or the editors give a warranty, express or implied, with respect to the material contained herein or for any errors or omissions that may have been made.

Printed on acid-free paper

This Springer imprint is published by Springer Nature
The registered company is Springer International Publishing AG Switzerland

Contents

Contributors

Alexander Bagattini Department of Philosophy, University of Düsseldorf, Düsseldorf, Germany

Nicole Balzer Institute of Educational Science, University of Münster, Münster, Germany

Mar Cabezas Centre for Ethics and Poverty Research, University of Salzburg, Salzburg, Austria

Johannes Drerup Institute of Educational Science, WWU Münster, Münster, Germany

Elizabeth Edenberg Department of Philosophy, Fordham University, USA

Allyn Fives UNESCO Child and Family Research Centre, National University of Ireland, Galway, Ireland

Gunter Graf Centre for Ethics and Poverty Research, University of Salzburg, Salzburg, Austria

International Research Centre for Social and Ethical Questions, Salzburg, Austria

Philip D.Th. Knobloch Department of Comparative Education, Ruhr University Bochum, Bochum, Germany

Lars Lindblom Department of Historical, Philosophical and Religious Studies, Umeå University, Umeå, Sweden

Colin M. Macleod Department of Philosophy and Faculty of Law, University of Victoria, Victoria, BC, Canada

Nicholas John Munn Department of Philosophy and Religious Studies, University of Waikato, Hamilton, New Zealand

Josephine Nielsen Department of Philosophy, Queen's University, Kingston, Canada

Christoph Schickhardt National Center for Tumor Diseases (NCT), University Hospital Heidelberg, Heidelberg, Germany

Christina Schües Institute for the History of Medicine and Science Studies, University of Lübeck, Lübeck, Germany

Gottfried Schweiger Centre for Ethics and Poverty Research, University of Salzburg, Salzburg, Austria

Clemens Sedmak Department of Theology and Religious Studies, King's College London, London, UK

Centre for Ethics and Poverty Research, University of Salzburg, Salzburg, Austria

Introduction to Justice, Education, and the Politics of Childhood: Challenges and Perspectives

Questions concerning the moral, legal, and political status of children and childhood are widely debated in a variety of academic disciplines, ranging from moral and political philosophy to jurisprudence, educational science, and medical ethics. This volume is intended to contribute to these ongoing interdisciplinary controversies by developing new perspectives on the diverse theoretical and practical challenges posed by political and ethical issues related to children and childhood. It comprises essays by scholars from different disciplinary backgrounds on diverse theoretical problems and public policy controversies that bear upon different facets of the life of children in contemporary liberal democracies. The book is divided into three major parts that are each organized around a common general theme. The *first* part ("Children and Childhood: Autonomy, Well-Being, and Paternalism") focuses on key concepts of an ethics of childhood. Part *two* ("Justice for Children") contains chapters that are concerned with the topics of justice for children and justice during childhood. The *third* part ("The Politics of Childhood") deals with issues that concern the importance of childhood as a historically contingent political category and its relevance for the justification and practical design of political processes and institutions that affect children and families.

The *first* part of the volume comprises essays on ethical questions concerning children and childhood. Among the most widely discussed systematic problems in the contemporary debate on the ethics of children and childhood are the following three topics. The first topic concerns the status of children as developing and not yet fully autonomous agents and rights holders. While it is widely acknowledged today in the philosophy and sociology of childhood that children are not to be regarded as mere passive and entirely non-autonomous agents, the specific theoretical, normative, and institutional implications of this insight still remain disputed. To what extent and in which domains can children be regarded as at least locally autonomous agents? What are the specific differences between the agency of children and the agency of adults? How can the fact that children are developing and not yet fully autonomous agents be reconciled with their status as rights holders?

The debate about children as partially and locally autonomous agents is closely related to the second topic that concerns the systematic normative function of different conceptions of autonomy in conceptions of children's well-being (Schickhardt 2012; Bagattini and Macleod 2015), of the specific vulnerability of children (Giesinger 2007; Andresen et al. 2015), and of a good and flourishing life for children (Brighouse 2006; Andresen et al. 2010). While it is usually agreed upon that some conception of autonomous agency is to be regarded as central for children's well-being, the exact normative place and function of autonomy in competing theories of childhood are still controversial. Is the facilitation or promotion of autonomy constitutive for a good life for children in modern liberal societies? How is the partial autonomy of children related to their vulnerability? What are the specific differences between the well-being, vulnerability, and the good life of children and of adults?

A considerable part of children's lives takes place in the context of asymmetrically structured interaction orders and institutions (e.g., in the family, educational institutions) in which the value and principle of respect for autonomy often comes into conflict with other values and principles (e.g., well-being). Many of the value conflicts that pervade educational interactions and institutions raise questions concerning the justifiability of different forms of paternalism toward children (Drerup 2013). Problems of the justification of paternalism as the third topic discussed in many debates on the ethics of childhood can be either addressed in more general terms or with a specific focus on a particular field (e.g., medical contexts, the family, social work). Most theoreticians would agree that some form of paternalism toward children is both inevitable and justified. But there are still ongoing controversies about the criteria and principles that should guide our normative assessment of different forms of paternalism toward children. How do these criteria differ with regard to different institutional contexts and professions? How should conflicts between different forms of paternalism (e.g., between familial paternalism and legal paternalism) be resolved? These and other questions and problems of ethical theories of childhood are addressed in part *one* of this volume.

In Chap. 1 ("Constructing Children's Rights") Colin Macleod analyzes problems concerning the ascription of rights to children. Moral rights are often characterized as having a special relationship to agency. But the link between agency and rights is often thought to pose an obstacle to the attribution of rights to children. Since children are not mature agents, they cannot be proper bearers of rights or at least of rights grounded in agency. In his paper Macleod provides a way around this obstacle. Drawing on a form of constructivism, he argues that some rights can be attributed to children in virtue of their status as juvenile agents. To substantiate this claim he develops a characterization of the specific agency of children and indicates how it provides a justificatory basis for distinctive rights of children.

Paternalism is a salient feature of rearing and caring for children. In Chap. 2 ("Future-Oriented Paternalism and the Intrinsic Goods of Childhood") Alexander Bagattini discusses a specific version of paternalism, namely, future-oriented paternalism. Future-oriented paternalism is directed to presumed valuable goals for the child's later life as an adult. Bagattini analyzes the normative implications of future-oriented paternalism. In a first step he points out that future-oriented paternalism is often understood as entailing what can be called the "instrumental conception of childhood". In a second step he critically examines and rebuts this conception of childhood. In a third step he argues for a refined version of future-oriented paternalism that does not make use of the instrumental conception of childhood.

One area of social life with outstanding importance for the clash of children's self-determination with the exercise of power over children is informed consent. The question posed by Allyn Fives in Chap. 3 ("Who Gets to Decide? Children's Competence, Parental Authority, and Informed Consent") is whether children should be permitted to make decisions that authorize their participation in research and/or their receipt of medical care or whether someone else should make those decisions on their behalf, namely, a parent or someone charged by the state with acting in a parent's absence. Fives explores children's competence to make informed consent decisions. In defining competence, some authors give priority to the capacity for autonomous self-determination, while others prioritize the capacity to make decisions that will promote one's well-being. However, conflicts may arise between the idea that we ought to respect children's autonomy and the idea that we ought not do so but rather promote children's well-being. Fives argues that forms of authoritative parenting can provide opportunities for joint decision-making between parents and children and in that way can promote the development of children's competence. The implications for the laws and policies of the state are significant. His argument suggests that the state should support children's rights to make informed consent decisions and also should require that parents support their children's free and informed decision-making.

Nick Munn begins Chap. 4 ("Capacity, Consistency, and the Young") by observing that young citizens in modern liberal democratic societies are subject to various limitations on their rights and responsibilities that other citizens are exempt from. In particular, their criminal liability is lessened comparative to other citizens, and their entitlement to make medical and political decisions is reduced. In each of these domains, the justification for the differential treatment of the young refers to lacking capacities. However, the time and methods with which capacity is attributed to young people differ between the medical, criminal, and political domains. Munn then argues that modern liberal democratic states owe to young citizens a consistent recognition of their capacity for autonomous decision-making and that this recognition requires the legal status of young citizens to be updated and standardized over the domains under consideration. This requirement is not commonly satisfied by democratic societies, as the way in which their capacities are judged is inconsistent between the three domains under consideration.

In Chap. 5 ("Eating Disorders in Minors and the Role of the Media: An Ethical Investigation") Christoph Schickhardt proposes an ethical analysis of the role of the media for the development of eating disorders such as anorexia nervosa and bulimia nervosa and related issues such as unhealthy weight control behavior of children and adolescents. Eating disorders are highly severe mental diseases and relatively common among minors. Although their pathogenesis is complex, there is considerable evidence suggesting that the idealizing presentation of very slim bodies in the media, to which many children are exposed intensively for years since early childhood, might contribute to minors' risk of developing eating disorders. This raises ethical questions concerning the well-being and rights of children and adolescents as well as the rights and responsibility of the media. Applying a liberal-egalitarian point of view, Schickhardt argues that while using seductive presentations of thin bodies is no core element of the freedom of the media, it jeopardizes central elements of children's well-being. Putting susceptible and vulnerable young people at risk for eating disorders is ethically inacceptable. Thus, according to Schickhardt, measures to protect minors and foster their media literacy and resilience are due. In his conclusion, the author proposes some concrete measures which might be suitable.

Part *two* of this volume ("Justice for Children") focuses on topics of justice for children and justice during childhood. There is a growing debate within philosophy about the specific content of justice for children, compared to justice for adults, the respective rights and duties of different stakeholders, and the criteria to evaluate justice and injustices in the context of childhood. One can analyze this debate by separating three central questions: What is the adequate currency of justice for children (e.g., primary goods, capabilities)? What principles should guide the distribution of the relevant currency of justice among children and in relation to adults? Who or which institutions are responsible for the protection and preservation of justice for children? In the following we provide a general overview of the most important theoretical positions in this debate.

The debate about the currency of justice for children is mainly driven by the insight that children differ from adults in important ways and that hence a currency that is adequate for adults could be inadequate for children (Macleod 2010). Maybe the most prominent example are primary goods in the Rawlsian sense, which are widely endorsed in theories of justice. The adequate use of these goods depends on certain competencies that children, at least younger ones, lack such as reflecting one's preferences and making reasonable choices. The Rawlsian primary goods of basic liberties and rights, income and wealth, or the social basis of self-respect are all conceived against this background of rational agents and seem to be inadequate for children. Children do have rights but they are usually restricted (e.g., they are not able and not allowed to exercise certain liberty rights when they are very young).

But also many other theories of justice that put much normative weight on autonomy have to cope with difficulties when it comes to the case of children. Another example for such a theory is the capability approach of Martha Nussbaum and Amartya Sen, which emphasizes that as a matter of justice people are entitled to certain capabilities, substantial freedoms, in order to realize a life they have reason to value (Nussbaum 2011). With respect to many aspects of their lives, children are not autonomous agents and cannot make much use of such substantial freedoms because they are heavily dependent on others who care for them and protect them from harms. Think of the example of health: While it seems reasonable to allow adults to choose for themselves whether or not they want to realize their life plan by letting their health deteriorate, we would not want to grant children the same freedom and choice. That is why some theorists within the capability approach have argued that in the case of children, we should view functionings, in the sense of actually realized capabilities, as the adequate currency of justice (Dixon and Nussbaum 2012; Graf and Schweiger 2015).

The second important question concerns the principles that should guide the distribution of goods between children, but also between children and adults. Obviously it is not enough to know the kinds of goods children are entitled to. We also need to identify how we should distribute them among children. Is a society only just if it provides an equally good education for all children or is it enough to have all of them educated to a sufficient level and allow inequalities above that threshold level? Do we need to identify the worst-off and help to improve their situation? To what extent are inequalities between the worst-off and the best-off acceptable? The answers vary vastly. Elizabeth Anderson, for example, develops a theory of justice (Anderson 1999, 2010) which suggests that it is enough if all children have sufficient education to have an equal standing as democratic citizens but that there is no need to equalize education. As long as all are sufficiently educated, it would not violate justice if some go to elite private schools and others to public schools. A similar argument can be found in the capability approach of Martha Nussbaum. She also claims that we should define sufficiency levels and not aim for strict equality at least in some dimensions (Dixon and Nussbaum 2012). Egalitarians object that all children should have the same of at least some goods or chances. Inequalities above the threshold level should not be ignored, especially since such inequalities during childhood translate into inequalities later on when it is very hard, if not impossible, to "level the playing field" (Macleod 2013).

In question is not only the distribution among children but also between children and adults. We can identify here two contradictory tendencies in most societies that are also reflected in the literature. On the one hand children have far fewer goods or far less power than adults, and they have far fewer rights. Children are not on an equal level with adults. For example, Harry Brighouse has argued that children's views are seen as only consultative in contrast to adult's views that are authoritative in respect to decisions that affect them (Brighouse 2003). This view corresponds to a widely implemented practice also in family courts, where judges decide whether or not a child is competent enough to have a say in decisions that affect them. On the other hand children are viewed as particularly needy, deserving special attention and protection. For many people it seems intuitively reasonable, for instance, to save the child and let the old man die, if both cannot be saved – which has important implications for healthcare (Anand 2005). This seems to imply that the distribution of goods, capabilities, or chances between adults and children is not straightforward. In some cases adults are granted more; in other children deserve priority treatment. The reasons for that are again located in the particular nature of childhood: Children lack some competencies and are particularly vulnerable, and being a child normally implies having a longer life ahead.

Finally, the third question is concerned with the distribution of responsibilities, rights, and duties among particular agents of justice for children. Most theories of justice are concerned with the design of the state and its institutions, but agent-centered approaches have shown that the state is not the only and, in some cases, not the most important agent. One of these agents that is most prominently discussed in philosophical approaches to justice for children is the family, especially the parents (Archard 2003; Austin 2007; Brighouse and Swift 2014). In liberal societies we can find a deeply rooted conviction that parents are responsible for their children, their well-being, education, and provision and that they have far-reaching rights with regard to them. Parents are allowed to make a wide range of decisions for their children that have important consequences for the course of their life. This liberal standard has often been criticized, for example, because of the inequalities that it allows (Brecher 2012). Children from wealthier families have more opportunities, and they usually fare better in life. The state has to be concerned with justice for all children, and the aim of the reduction of inequalities consequently often comes into conflict with the autonomy of the family. The distribution of responsibilities is intertwined with the distribution of rights and duties of parents in relation to their children as well as with the rights, and maybe duties, of the children themselves. It is still in question to what extent the state is allowed to interfere in family life in order to protect children's claims of justice or children's rights and how to balance the costs and benefits that are usually attached to such interferences (Macleod 2007). Another issue concerns obligations that are of particular importance for children: children's claim to be loved. While it is uncontroversial that it is good for children to be loved, it is less clear whether parents are obliged to do so and whether and how the state has to compensate children in the case of failure (Liao 2006; Ferracioli 2015).

But also other agents of justice can be seen as relevant: In the case of weak states and global poverty, neither the families nor the states seem to have the power to protect children and to distribute goods, capabilities, or chances fairly. In such cases other agents can be held accountable: international institutions and organizations that are more powerful and keep up global structural injustices that hurt children in poor countries. The responsibilities of people living in affluent countries toward these children are also debatable. Some have even argued that an obligation to adopt can be defended to ensure justice for children (Friedrich 2013). In the following we give a short overview of the chapters of part two:

In Chap. 6 ("Equality of What for Children") Lars Lindblom revisits the equality of what-debate and asks whether previous conclusions hold if we analyze the arguments from the perspective of children. He makes and defends three claims. First, that even if welfare cannot be justified as an equalisandum for adults, it remains a reasonable position for the case of children. This claim is argued for by showing that Dworkin's rejection of equality of welfare relies on an idea of responsible agency that is inappropriate for the case of children. This route cannot reject equality of welfare with regard to children. Second, we owe children welfare rather than opportunity for welfare. Lindblom argues that Richard Arneson's move from equality of welfare to equality of opportunity for welfare relies on the same kind of problematic assumption about responsible agency as Dworkin's argument for resources. However, the assumption about responsible agency still holds for adults, and for them we need an equalisandum that takes responsibility into account. Moreover, since children will grow up to be adults, they will need preparation for this stage in life.

Therefore, both welfare and the appropriate responsibility-sensitive equalisandum will be relevant for children. Lindblom's third claim is that a general theory of the equalisandum of justice should have a structure like Cohen's (1989) equality of access to advantage. Advantage is understood as consisting of both welfare and resources, and access is comprised of both actually having something that is an advantage and having the opportunity to achieve a good.

In Chap. 7 ("Social Policy and Justice for Children") Gunter Graf and Gottfried Schweiger argue that the systematic protection and advancement of the well-being of children, and hence the reduction of child poverty, is a key task of social justice, which should therefore guide policy design and implementation. However, they also discuss the special composition of the well-being of children and point out some of the difficulties for state action in this regard. In particular, they argue that the importance of love and affection for a child's well-being limits considerably the possible political measures to provide fair life chances to all children. This again reflects the insight that poverty should not be reduced to economic inequality.

In Chap. 8 ("The Politics of the Level Playing Field: Equality of Opportunity and Educational Justice") Johannes Drerup provides an analysis of some of the most important criticisms of equality of opportunity as a principle of educational justice. In a critique of the critique, the author shows that the apparent plausibility of recent non-egalitarian criticisms can be traced back to tensions between particular interpretations of autonomy as an aim of education and equality of opportunity as a principle of educational justice. Drerup argues that in contrast to adequacy conceptions, conceptions of equality of opportunity are better able to take into account the educational dimension of educational justice, both in terms of the justification of autonomy as an educational aim and in terms of the specific structure of educational practices and constellations. Finally, he shows that based on the theoretical and normative framework of liberal perfectionist accounts of the politics and ethics of education, a "responsibility-sensitive egalitarianism" can reconcile and resolve some of the tensions between equality of opportunity and autonomy as an educational aim.

In Chap. 9 ("Child Psychological Abuse, Public Health, and Social Justice: The *Cinderella Law* Debate") Mar Cabezas analyzes the problem of intra-familial psychological or emotional abuse of children. Based on a discussion of the "British Cinderella Law Project," she points out that psychological or emotional child abuse is to be regarded as a problem of social justice. Furthermore, she reconstructs and criticizes different attitudes toward mental and physical health that can be found in current debates on physical and emotional abuse. Finally, Cabezas argues for the necessity of a specific legal recognition of emotional and psychological abuse as a threat to children's health and well-being.

In Chap. 10 ("Epistemic Injustice and Children's Well-Being") Christina Schües criticizes conceptions of justice that are focused merely on the offender and dismiss the experiences of the affected. In order to discuss children's lives, it is necessary to include their experiences and perspectives and to give them a voice of their own. By addressing ethical and epistemic injustice, her approach enfolds the sense of injustice itself; it poses the question of how to describe injustice as a phenomenon on its own and depicts prejudices due to ageism, racism, or sexism that may exclude the testimony of particular persons, namely, children. Children belong to the group that is particularly vulnerable to be affected by ethical and epistemic injustice because their testimony is dismissed quite easily. They are born into and live in relations they did not choose. Based on these relations children experience the surrounding world, they feel trust or mistrust, and they face injustice or justice occurring toward themselves or others. Thus, according to Schües, ethical and epistemic injustices violate children's well-being.

Children live their childhoods embedded in social contexts, which are shaped by the way a society is organized and structured and by the different norms and values present in its political culture. Childhood is a period of time, which interlinks in many respects with the sociocultural institutions of society. Therefore, the sociological study of childhood often speaks of "childhoods" in the plural: Depending on how and where a child lives, her experience of this phase and her accessible life chances can be very different (James and Prout 1997; Goddard et al. 2005). This is certainly true in a historical and cross-cultural perspective, but also in modern societies, which are characterized by pluralism, sociocultural differences, and often enough dividing lines between different societal groups along gender, race, and ethnicity. Thus, it is difficult to look at childhood as a uniform phenomenon. How it is lived and experienced depends on a variety of factors that connect to the broader societal framework and political regulations. It is here that the idea of "the politics of childhood" comes into play, which is the central topic of the *third* part of this book. With this term we would like to emphasize the importance of childhood as a historically contingent political category and its relevance for the practical design and the justification of political processes and institutions that affect children and families. Childhood is not a "natural" category (although some biological and psychological facts are of great importance to understand human development) that necessary belongs completely to the private realm, but it is interwoven with social and cultural practices that are changeable and open for reinterpretations (for a historical overview on different modern conceptions of childhood: Baader et al. 2014).[1] A good example of this is the case of the family, which is intertwined with what can be understood as childhood, since growing up typically happens to a large extent in this environment. The family is often considered to be an exemplary case of a

---

[1] Especially since Ariès' (1960) influential study on the history of childhood, it has been disputed whether the concept of childhood is to be regarded as an exclusively modern idea that did not emerge until the late seventeenth century or if also earlier societies possessed a concept of childhood. Archard draws on the Rawlsian distinction between concept and conception and distinguishes between a basic concept of childhood, which "requires that children be distinguishable from adults in respect to some set of unspecified attributes", and a conception of childhood that "is a specification of those attributes" (Archard 2015, p. 32). Contrary to Ariès, he argues that even though past societies did not share our modern *conception* of childhood, it is rather questionable that they completely lacked any *concept* of childhood. Instead there are "good reasons for thinking that all societies at all times have had the concept of childhood." (ibid., p. 35). Analogously, especially in the sociology of childhood, it is debated whether the categories of "childhood" and "children" constitute historically contingent social constructions or if they are also grounded in anthropological facts (ibid. p. 29f.).

private institution that can be separated from the public sphere. But as has been convincingly argued, such a view is untenable (Olsen 1985; Nussbaum 2000). The state, for instance, already plays a central role when it comes to the question which forms of human communities are defined as families. There is no family form that exists by nature. It is rather a political decision which unions legally count as families at all and enjoy the privileges and duties connected to this status. Furthermore, it must be acknowledged that the family is a unit in which power structures and inequalities are reproduced, an issue central to feminist approaches to justice (Okin 1989). And depending on how the state supports or monitors the family or some of its members through social regulations (e.g., gender-sensitive labor market policies; restrictions with regard to the comprehensive doctrines parents may teach to their children), the political status of the family can be influenced in significant ways. In turn, this directly influences children's lives. The politics of childhood and the politics of the family are therefore deeply connected.

Addressing the politics of childhood from a normative perspective, the approach taken in this book does not simply analyze the status quo of the position of children in a given society, but it draws on considerations of social justice, well-being, responsibilities, and other normative ideas to develop a critical perspective on how children should be treated and respected within a political community. Understood in such a broad way, the politics of childhood involves many different questions and certainly overlaps at some points with issues discussed in part one and two of this book. It raises questions about the scope and limits of state power in the lives of children and about the values children should be taught and how this relates to the ideas and form of lives of their parents. Education is therefore a central category which has received considerable attention in the literature in political philosophy (Brighouse 2002; Anderson 2007).

In any case, the politics of childhood has to scrutinize current political priorities and analyze whether they do justice to the specific moral status of children. The category of vulnerability (a concept that is certainly crucial for a proper understanding of childhood) opens up, in the political practice, many doors for misinterpretations and abuses. It can be used to disempower children, to overprotect them, and to completely isolate them from the public domain. In such cases, the politics of childhood has to identify the respective injustices and work on viable alternatives.

A related point concerns the status of children as political actors. How far and in what way can or should children themselves be political agents who are able to represent and defend their own interests and points of view within the political community? This is a highly debated issue in many academic disciplines devoted to the study of childhood, and many commentators argue that many societies, including modern western democracies, have been reluctant to view children in such a way (Mayall 2002). They perceive children rather as recipients of services or passive beneficiaries of adults' care or of care provided by the state but not as participants in matters affecting them. Such an attitude is definitely still prevalent in many political contexts. Typically, children do not have strong political powers and are not organized politically to bring in their own point of view in public debates. Rather, adults have to speak and decide for them. Such an attitude toward children is still widespread. However, it has been challenged already in 1989 by the most important political document on the entitlements of children: the United Nations' Convention of the Rights of the Child (UCRC). There, children are portrayed as active agents with politically relevant voices that must be heard and taken seriously, a fact that political institutions have to respect and promote (Lansdown 2001). Since then, there have certainly been important initiatives to empower children politically and to involve them in different levels of decision-making (Percy-Smith and Thomas 2010). Nevertheless, in their political role as active participants and decision-makers, children remain marginalized in the politics of most nation states.

There are definitely good reasons why children are not given full political power, reasons that overlap with arguments in favor of a justified paternalism toward children. However, an ethical theory needs to work out in detail what weight should be given to children's voices in decisions affecting them – a right specified in the URCR under Article 12. As Harry Brighouse has argued, it is reasonable to consider children's voices mainly as consultative. This means that they have the right to state their point of view but that their voices do not automatically determine what is in their interests for the purpose of decision-making (Brighouse 2003). Rather, children's views have to be evaluated against other values and reasons, something that is usually done by adults. Given the developing nature of children and the inexperience that is connected to their young age, such a view seems reasonable. However, for a practically applicable politics of childhood, this argument has to be developed further and connected to the political practice. On the one hand, children are a very heterogeneous group with different competencies, experiences, and capabilities. Giving weight to their views is therefore a complex issue that demands attention and guidelines that can be applied in practice. On the other hand, one must be careful not to underestimate the capacities children have from a young age on. Often, adults do not treat children's voices adequately, and there is certainly a lot of work to be done until it can be said that our society shows equal concern and respect for children as fellow citizens.

The five chapters that deal with these and related issues that concern the politics of childhood will be briefly summarized below:

In Chap. 11 ("Cultural Minorities and the Lives of Children") Josephine Nielsen argues that liberal multiculturalists should recognize a minority right to raise and keep children within particular cultural communities. She begins by expounding why children should be acknowledged within theories of multiculturalism and political philosophy more generally. She then argues that if minority members value their culture, then they consequently have an interest in the continued existence of their cultural communities. Along these lines, she defends the position that in order for cultural communities to exist in the future, children, as potential community members, should be brought up in the cultural and normative context of these communities. This is her argument for the secondary interest held by members of minority communities. She is convinced that if her arguments hold for the primary and secondary interests of minority members, a defeasible right to children being raised and kept within cultural communities can be justified. Nielsen concludes by considering three possible objections to her proposal.

In Chap. 12, entitled "Civic Education: Political or Comprehensive?", Elizabeth Edenberg considers the problem children, conceived of as future citizens, pose to understanding the scope and limits of Rawls's *Political Liberalism* by focusing on the civic education of children. Can a politically liberal state provide all children the opportunity to become reasonable citizens? Or does the cultivation of reasonableness require comprehensive liberalism? In considering these questions, Edenberg shows that educating children to become reasonable in the way Rawls outlines imposes a demanding requirement that conflicts with Rawls's aim of including a wide constituency in the scope of political liberalism. Rawls's aim of making reasonableness broadly inclusive for political purposes is in tension with his goal of using reasonableness as the standard that delineates the scope of liberal legitimacy. Edenberg argues that political liberalism can and should try to cultivate the reasonableness of its future citizens through the civic education of children. However, a defensible version of political liberal civic education requires introducing a bifurcation within Rawls's conception of reasonableness. A political liberal form of civic education should aim toward the inclusive scope of reasonableness by cultivating reasonableness in only two of what appear to be three senses that Rawls emphasizes. Teaching children that legitimacy requires embracing public reason demands more than may be justifiably required by a state that seeks to be broadly inclusive.

In Chap. 13 ("'I Can't Tell You *Exactly* Who I Am ...': The Creation of Childhood and Adulthood in F. Scott Fitzgerald's Short Story *The Curious Case of Benjamin Button*") Nicole Balzer provides some theoretical impulses for contemporary debates about childhood. The major part of her paper consists of a discussion of F. Scott Fitzgerald's short story *The Curious Case of Benjamin Button*. She shows that the Button case not only puts into question common ideas of human development. In fact, it also gives insights into what it requires to live one's life in accordance with the socially and culturally established differentiation between children and adults. Balzer argues that the crucial characteristic of the development of Benjamin Button's life is to learn to adapt to other's expectations by means of performing in particular ways, if necessary in neglect of his feelings and needs. Finally, she suggests that any theoretical approach to childhood is intimately connected with the ways in which we refer to and conceive of *adulthood*. Thus, if we want to address political and ethical questions in the terrain of childhood, according to Balzer, the study of the meanings and significations of "adulthood" is indispensable.

In Chap. 14 ("Education for Autonomy in the Context of Consumer Culture") Philip Knobloch provides an analysis of the concept of education for autonomy in the context of consumer culture. Analyzing the international debates about education for sustainable development, Knobloch argues that concepts of critical consumer education seem to offer possibilities to support the development of autonomy in relation to the sphere of consumption. Therefore, he introduces a concept of critical consumer education that works explicitly with the specific concept of consumer culture and that focuses on sustainable product communication. Although education for critical consumption seems to be a privileged option today, the specific and somehow problematic esthetic dimensions of critical consumption and sustainability, which play an important role in some related educational concepts, indicate that also forms of general consumer esthetic education should be taken into consideration to clarify the concept of education for autonomy. Therefore, he additionally presents such an esthetic concept, also explicitly related to the concept of consumer culture. Discussing also the problematic aspects of both concepts, Knobloch concludes that approaches of consumer esthetic and critical consumer education should be integrated into a wider concept of education for autonomy in the context of consumer culture.

In the final chapter ("*My Place*; Catholic Social Teaching and the Politics of Geborgenheit"), Clemens Sedmak analyzes the concept of *Geborgenheit,* a German term that expresses a sense of being nested within a sheltering space to which one can open up. He argues that *Geborgenheit* is a key component of a good childhood and discusses it in relation to political questions from the perspective of Catholic Social Teaching. In the first section, he draws on Sally Morgan's influential autobiography *My Place* to motivate how crucial "belonging" and "feeling safe" are for a child's life. In the second section, he formulates a definition of *Geborgenheit*, based on six aspects, and suggests that it can serve as a valuable hermeneutical and analytical tool for the discourse on the politics of childhood. In the third section, Sedmak presents some fundamental aspects of Catholic Social Teaching and its relationship to the concept of *Geborgenheit.* He concludes that Catholic Social Teaching can contribute to a deeper understanding of *Geborgenheit* as a category to approach normative issues in the politics of childhood.

Most of the essays in this volume were first presented at the MANCEPT Workshop in Political Theory in Manchester in September 2014. We would like to thank all of the participants for many fruitful discussions and for their continuous commitment to this project. Special thanks go to Anna Blundell for the proofreading.

Münster, Germany	Johannes Drerup
Salzburg, Austria	Gottfried Schweiger
Salzburg, Austria	Gunter Graf
Heidelberg, Germany	Christoph Schickhardt

References

Anand, Paul. 2005. Capabilities and health. *Journal of Medical Ethics* 31(5): 299–303. doi:10.1136/jme.2004.008706.
Anderson, Elizabeth. 1999. What is the point of equality? *Ethics* 102(2): 287–337.
Anderson, Elizabeth. 2007. Fair opportunity in education: A democratic equality perspective. *Ethics* 117(4): 595–622. doi:10.1086/518806.
Anderson, Elizabeth. 2010. Justifying the capability approach to justice. In *Measuring justice: Primary goods and capabilities*, ed. Harry Brighouse, and Ingrid Robeyns. 1st ed, 81–100. Cambridge/New York: Cambridge University Press.
Andresen, Sabine, Isabell Diehm, Uwe Sander, and Holger Ziegler (eds.). 2010. *Children and the good life. New challenges for research on children*. Dordrecht: Springer.

Andresen, Sabine, Claus Koch, and Julia König (eds.). 2015. *Vulnerable Kinder. Interdisziplinäre Annäherungen*. Wiesbaden: Springer.

Archard, David. 2003. *Children, family, and the state*, Live questions in ethics and moral philosophy, 1st ed. Aldershot/Burlington: Ashgate.

Archard, David. 2015. *Children. Rights and childhood*, 3rd ed. London/New York: Routledge.

Ariès, Philippe. 1960. *L'enfant et la vie familiale sous l'ancien régime*. Paris: Libraire Plon.

Austin, Michael W. 2007. *Conceptions of parenthood: Ethics and the family*, Ashgate studies in applied ethics, 1st ed. Aldershot/Burlington: Ashgate.

Baader, Meike, Florian Eßer, and Wolfgang Schröer (eds.). 2014. *Kindheiten in der Moderne. Eine Geschichte der Sorge*. Frankfurt/New York: Campus.

Brecher, Bob. 2012. The family and neoliberalism: Time to revive a critique. *Ethics and Social Welfare* 6(2): 157–167. doi:10.1080/17496535.2012.682503.

Brighouse, Harry. 2002. Egalitarian liberalism and justice in education. *The Political Quarterly* 73(2): 181–190. doi:10.1111/1467-923X.00455.

Brighouse, Harry. 2003. How should children be heard? *Arizona Law Review* 45(3): 691–711.

Brighouse, Harry. 2006. *On education*. London/New York: Routledge.

Brighouse, Harry, and Adam Swift. 2014. *Family values: The ethics of parent–child relationships*, 1st ed. Princeton: Princeton University Press.

Dixon, Rosalind, and Martha Nussbaum. 2012. *Children's rights and a capabilities approach: The question of special priority*. Chicago Public Law & Legal Theory Working Paper, no. 384. http://papers.ssrn.com/sol3/papers.cfm?abstract_id=2060614.

Drerup, Johannes. 2013. *Paternalismus, Perfektionismus und die Grenzen der Freiheit*. Paderborn: Schöningh.

Ferracioli, Luara. 2015. The state's duty to ensure children are loved. *Journal of Ethics & Social Philosophy* 8(2): 1–20.

Friedrich, Daniel. 2013. A duty to adopt? *Journal of Applied Philosophy* 30(1): 25–39. doi:10.1111/japp.12003.

Giesinger, Johannes. 2007. *Autonomie und Verletzlichkeit. Der moralische Status von Kindern und die Rechtfertigung von Erziehung*. Bielefeld: Transkript.

Goddard, Jim, Sally McNamee, Adrian James, and Allison James (eds.). 2005. *The politics of childhood: international perspectives, contemporary developments*, 1st ed. Basingstoke/New York: Palgrave Macmillan. http://site.ebrary.com/id/10262994.

Graf, Gunter, and Gottfried Schweiger. 2015. *A philosophical examination of social justice and child poverty*. 1st ed. Basingstoke: Palgrave Macmillan.

James, Allison, and Alan Prout (eds.). 1997. *Constructing and reconstructing childhood: Contemporary issues in the sociological study of childhood*. London/Washington, DC: Falmer Press

Liao, S. Matthew. 2006. The right of children to be loved. *Journal of Political Philosophy* 14(4): 420–440. doi:10.1111/j.1467-9760.2006.00262.x.

Lansdown, Gerison. 2001. *Promoting children's participation in democratic decision-making. Innocenti insight*. Florence: UNICEF International Child Development Centre.

Macleod, Colin M. 2007. Raising children: Who is responsible for what? In *Taking responsibility for children*, ed. Samantha Brennan, and Robert Noggle, 1st ed, 1–18. Studies in childhood and family in Canada. Waterloo: Wilfrid Laurier University Press.

Macleod, Colin M. 2010. Primary goods, capabilities and children. In *Measuring justice – Primary goods and capabilities*, ed. Harry Brighouse, and Ingrid Robeyns, 174–192. Cambridge/New York: Cambridge University Press.

Macleod, Colin M. 2013. Justice, educational equality, and sufficiency. *Canadian Journal of Philosophy* 40: 151–175.

Mayall, Berry. 2002. *Towards a sociology for childhood: Thinking from children's lives*. Buckingham/Philadelphia: Open University Press.

Nussbaum, Martha. 2000. *Women and human development – The capabilities approach*, 1st ed. Cambridge/New York: Cambridge University Press.

Nussbaum, Martha. 2011. *Creating capabilities: The human development approach*, 1st ed. Cambridge/London: Belknap Press of Harvard University Press.

Okin, Susan Moller. 1989. *Justice, gender and the family*. New York: Basic Books.

Olsen, Frances E. 1985. The myth of state intervention in the family. *University of Michigan Journal of Law Reform* 18(4): 835–864.

Percy-Smith, Barry, and Nigel Thomas (eds.). 2010. *A handbook of children and young people's participation: Perspectives from theory and practice*. London/New York: Routledge.

Schickhardt, Christoph. 2012. *Kinderethik. Der moralische Status und die Rechte der Kinder*. Münster: Mentis.

Part I
Children and Childhood: Autonomy, Well-Being and Paternalism

Chapter 1
Constructing Children's Rights

Colin M. Macleod

> *"No political theory is adequate unless it is applicable to children as well as to men and women."*
>
> Bertrand Russell

Abstract Moral rights are often characterized as having a special relationship to agency. But the link between agency and rights is often thought to pose an obstacle to the attribution of rights to children. Since children are not mature agents, they cannot be proper bearers of rights or at least of rights grounded in agency. This paper provides a way around this obstacle. Drawing on a form of constructivism, I argue that some rights can be attributed to children in virtue of their status as juvenile agents. I offer a characterization of the agency of children and to indicate how it provides a justificatory basis for distinctive rights of children.

Keywords Children's rights • Agency • Intrinsic goods of childhood • Constructivism

Introduction

In her essay 'Children's Rights and Children's Lives' (1988), Onora O'Neill draws our attention to the importance for moral theory of considering distinctive features of the lives of children. In my view, a great deal of contemporary work on theories of justice, especially theories of distributive justice, has not adequately grappled with O'Neill's insight. Of course, everyone recognizes that children have moral standing. Everyone also acknowledges that social and political institutions along with more informal social practices should acknowledge and respond suitably to this standing. However, the dominant theoretical devices and strategies relied upon for the articulation of the demands of justice are generally insensitive to full and

C.M. Macleod (✉)
Department of Philosophy and Faculty of Law, University of Victoria,
PO BOX 1700 STN CSC, Victoria, BC V8W 2Y2, Canada
e-mail: cmacleod@uvic.ca

© Springer International Publishing Switzerland 2016
J. Drerup et al. (eds.), *Justice, Education and the Politics of Childhood*,
Philosophy and Politics – Critical Explorations 1,
DOI 10.1007/978-3-319-27389-1_1

proper consideration of the distinctive moral claims of children. For instance, the hypothetical contractors in Rawls's original position are characterized in terms of developed rational, moral and emotional capacities that children lack (Rawls 1971). The imaginary participants in the auction and hypothetical insurance markets that are used to generate Dworkin's theory of justice are assumed to be fully responsible and competent economic agents (Dworkin 2000). And Gauthier's more Hobbesian contractors are depicted as shrewd and sophisticated rational maximizers (Gauthier 1986). These influential approaches to justice are not designed with the lives of children directly in view and it is not surprising, consequently, that Rawls, Dworkin, Gauthier and other leading theorists have said so little about justice and children. In O'Neill's work, however, there are some useful resources that provide a partial corrective to this serious problem. In this paper I will draw upon these resources in developing an approach to the identification and justification of children's rights. I hope that the account offered here defuses some puzzles about the attribution of fundamental moral rights to children.

Three themes of O'Neill's work figure in my account of children's moral rights. First, the view draws upon aspects of O'Neill's constructivism. Constructivism comes in different varieties and has different philosophical motivations but I follow O'Neill in invoking a fairly loose construal of the idea.[1] As she puts it, "to construct is only to reason with all possible solidity from *available* beginnings, using *available* and *followable* methods to reach *attainable* and *sustainable* conclusions for relevant audiences" (1996: 63). She invites us to treat agency as a point of departure for this kind moral constructivism. According to O'Neill, constructivism provides a feasible way of developing an authoritative theory of moral reasons. Constructivism is attractive from a metaethical point of view because it both avoids relativism and steers clear of the more controversial metaphysical and epistemological commitments of those varieties of moral realism that seek to anchor moral objectivity in real, and causally efficacious, moral properties. To be sure, I do not think constructivism, especially of a broadly Kantian variety, can entirely avoid making claims about how certain natural properties have value and are sources of moral reasons. Most obviously, Kantians seem committed to affirming the inherent value of rational nature and insisting that proper appreciation of its value involves treating and responding to it in distinctive ways. (Acknowledging the 'real' as opposed to merely the conventional or stipulated value of rational nature in this sense strikes me as compatible with some kinds of moral realism. The analysis I develop does implicitly make some assumptions about the relation between facts and values. I assume, for instance, that recognition of certain 'facts' about the presence or absence of

---

[1] Since the strategy I follow does not rely upon a highly structured procedure for the identification of moral principles, its status as a type of constructivism might be questioned by those who view constructivism as requiring precisely defined and perhaps even formal procedures. I am less concerned with the propriety of the label than with the general idea of moral reasoning as closely bound to a determination of the prerequisites and prerogatives of agency.

capacities gives us reason to act in certain ways and to make value judgements.[2] But this kind of metaethical assumption is, I think, relatively uncontentious and is consistent with a wide variety of approaches to normative theory.) But I think O'Neill's instinct to ground at least some basic moral principles in reflection on features of agency is plausible and helpful.[3] As she puts it: "The art is to use minimal and plausible assumptions about human rationality and agency to construct an account of ethical requirements that is rich and strong enough to guide action and reflection" (1988: 452).

Second, in developing an agency grounded constructivist moral theory O'Neill cautions us against reliance on idealized depictions of agency. Idealized accounts of agency that attribute to persons "comprehensive cognitive capacities and powers to act" (O'Neill 1996: 35) can generate distortions in ethical reasoning. Reliance on idealized conceptions of agency can lead to principles for action that are not relevant or accessible to real persons with finite capacities and real human vulnerabilities. Ethical theory may reasonably abstract from the particular features of specific individuals but the abstractions, as opposed to idealizations, it invokes must track salient features of actual human agency, including its collective dimensions and its limitations. "If human beings are assumed to have capacities and capabilities for rational choice or self-sufficiency or independence from each other that are evidently not achieved by many if any actual human beings, the result is not mere abstraction; it is idealization" (O'Neill 1996: 41). Our theorizing must give suitable recognition to the fact that human agents are: "*vulnerable* and *needy* beings in the sense that their rationality and their mutual independence – the very basis of our agency – is incomplete, mutually vulnerable and socially produced" (O'Neill 1988: 457). As I explain below, I think the concern about distorting idealizations applies with particular force to many understandings of the relation between children's rights and agency. So the view of children's rights I develop builds upon a characterization of agency that highlights distinct and salient features of the agency of children. Children's rights should fit children's agency and this requires attention to children qua children and not merely children as potential adults with mature moral powers.

Third, although she does not pursue it herself, O'Neill describes a general strategy for the construction of rights that I find fruitful and worth developing. En route to arguing against the fundamentality of rights, O'Neill notes the possibility of treating rights as "entitlements to whatever goods and services, as well as forbearances may be needed to nurture and sustain the possibility of agency" (O'Neill 1988: 455).[4] The idea is that we can distinguish between social and material conditions

---

[2] Consider the familiar example about the relation between sentience and moral judgements. The fact that a being can feel pain seems morally salient. It gives a person a reason to judge pain as bad and provides a moral reason to avoid causing pain to sentient beings.

[3] I place less emphasis on testing principles via some variety of Kantian universalization test. But I do accept that sound moral principles and claims must be universalizable in the sense that they must be able to be endorsed by all reasonable persons.

[4] O'Neill rejects this approach on the grounds that we have no reliable way of determining "which accommodation of various welfare (or welfare and liberty) rights would be maximal" (1988: 455).

that play a highly valuable, and perhaps indispensible, role in fostering agency and letting it flourish and those conditions that, however desirable or valuable along other dimensions, are less intimately connected to the sustenance of agency. Developing this strategy in detail depends on articulating a conception of agency and providing an account of the ways in which the meaningful development and sustenance of agency can be shaped and influenced by material and social conditions. There are likely to be some controversies about both dimensions of the approach since the precise nature of human agency is contested. Although I try to identify and interpret some features of the agency of children, I do not offer a detailed comprehensive conception of agency. I do assume that the agency of adults is constituted, at least partly, by rational capacities that permit adults to understand their circumstances and make authoritative choices about how to respond to their circumstances. That is a loose but reasonably familiar depiction of adult agency and I think it is relatively uncontroversial that we have reason to value the development and exercise of rational capacities by persons. The strategy for the articulation of children's rights that I explore depends both on accepting that agency is valuable and that the agency of children is interestingly different from the agency of adults.

Assuming we adopt the substantive normative claim that the facilitation and protection of agency is morally urgent (and perhaps even morally paramount), we can view rights as entitlements to those social and material conditions that are *integral* to the sustenance of meaningful agency. Other material and social conditions that persons reasonably value but which are not integral to the sustenance of agency fall outside the main ambit of moral rights. Of course, since the conditions most conducive to the development and flourishing of one person's agency may not entirely coincide with maximal promotion of the agency of others, we will have to find a scheme of rights that gives due attention to the *equal* claim of all persons to sustenance of their agency. This may involve tricky questions about how best to harmonize the agency-based claims of different persons. Negotiating these kinds of potential tension can be particularly important in the context of reconciling the rights of adults, especially parents, with those of children. I confess that I have no comprehensive account of how the requisite balance is to be effected. But I am optimistic, especially under conditions of moderate scarcity, that there is a feasible and stable assignment of rights that adequately honours and protects the agency of both children and adults. In this paper, however, my main objective will be to offer a characterization of the agency of children and to indicate how it provides a justificatory basis for distinctive rights of children.

I think O'Neill is misled here by a mistaken assumption that a constructivist account of rights must attempt to identify a set of co-possible rights that is, in some difficult to specify sense, maximal (or perhaps 'most basic'). Talk of maximization is tempting but misguided. We should instead see the construction of rights as a matter of first, identifying the important prerequisites and prerogatives of agency and second, determining how, with attention to the gravity of different dimensions of agency, the protection and support of the agency of all persons can be harmonized such that the agency of all of is equally sustained. The construction process is complex, interpretative and qualitative, not simple and quantitative.

Although my argument is inspired by O'Neill's work in many ways, it will quickly become apparent that my view departs from her conception of a sound moral theory in some important respects and it may be helpful to flag two important differences between her view and mine at the outset.

First, O'Neill argues that reflection on the lives of children provides a justification for developing a theory in which obligations rather than rights are assigned theoretical primacy. In particular, she emphasizes the importance of imperfect obligations in tracking the kind of moral consideration children are owed. This is not to say that O'Neill rejects the idea that children have rights. But she is sceptical that rights are morally fundamental and she thinks we can get a clearer view both of what we owe children generally and how we should conceive their rights by focusing, in the first instance, on obligations. I agree that the recognition of imperfect obligations is important to moral theory but I am not persuaded that there is a genuine dichotomy between recognizing imperfect obligations and acknowledging the fundamentality of rights, including children's rights. At any rate, the account of children's rights I offer here does not diminish or distort the point that imperfect obligations matter. I suspect, however, that I have a more expansive view of the rights of children than O'Neill and I do not think that children's rights are corrosive to intimate family relationships of the sort integral to nurturing children.

Second, O'Neill has a distinctive view of the relation between certain kinds of rights and their institutional recognition that I reject. O'Neill contends that rights to goods, services and opportunities can only be meaningfully asserted or claimed (or waived) if there are institutional arrangements in place that identify the agents who are responsible for ensuring that the rights are respected.[5] In the absence of determinate institutional arrangements, so-called 'welfare rights' (so often referred to in international charters of rights) become mere 'manifesto rights' and this leaves the "content of these supposed rights wholly obscure" (O'Neill 1996: 132). O'Neill claims that universal economic, social and cultural rights "*must* be institutionalized: if they are not there is no right" (O'Neill 1996: 132). I strongly disagree. In my view, the content of the moral rights of persons, including rights to resources and opportunities, can be fixed prior to determining the precise institutional arrangements that are best suited to ensuring that the rights in question are respected. We can insist, for instance, that all persons have a fundamental right to access the social and material resources that are essential conditions of human dignity even if no existing institution has been charged with the responsibility of fulfilling this right.

---

[5] O'Neill seems to have two concerns about universal welfare rights. The first, and the one I focus on here, is a putative conceptual point linking the content of welfare rights to existing institutional agencies who can be identified as having violated a right should they fail to act in the ways specified by the right. The idea seems to be that there cannot be rights violations without clearly specifiable rights violators. The second concern that I do not take up is a speculation about the way in which a "premature rhetoric of rights can inflate expectations while masking a lack of claimable entitlements" (O'Neill: 133). I accept that persons engaged in political activity may abuse the language of rights and represent political demands as rights claims when there are, in fact, no entitlements. This phenomenon may fuel hostility to rights discourse in some contexts. However, where genuine moral rights are at stake, it is entirely appropriate for those whose rights are not recognized by institutions to believe that they have been unjustly denied that to which they are entitled.

When existing institutions fail to recognize and respond adequately to a (genuine) fundamental right we have reason to criticize and reform institutions or to create new ones. Poor or defective institutional design should not ground scepticism about the existence of rights.

Agency, Rights and Children: Puzzles

Justification for the idea that persons have fundamental moral rights is often located in claims about the nature and value of rational agency.[6] Rights are seen as universal moral entitlements to which all persons can lay equal claim simply in virtue of their status as rational agents. Of course, controversy sometimes surrounds both how best to characterize the specific content of rights and how the link between agency and rights is best understood. But when it comes to fundamental rights, all persons are supposed to have the same rights. Interest theories of rights tend to treat rights as securing and protecting crucial interests of agents. These theories seek to identify the morally weighty interests that all agents have and assign rights protections to those interests deemed to be essential to successful functioning as an agent. Choice theories of rights, by contrast, view rights as protecting the authority of agents to make decisions about the conduct of their own lives.[7] Although choice theories tend to emphasize liberty rights, they need not be hostile to 'welfare' rights since meaningful exercise of liberty has various material conditions and requires that agents have reliable access to the resources and opportunities that make free action possible. Similarly, although interest theories are very hospitable to 'welfare' rights in virtue of the evident basic interest agents have in accessing resources and opportunities that secure and promote their welfare, interest theories can also accommodate familiar liberty rights by appealing to Millian observations about the reliable connection between basic liberties (e.g., speech, association, conscience) and individual wellbeing. These observations suggest that the contrast between choice and interest theories need not be as great as is sometimes assumed.[8]

---

[6] I set aside sophisticated varieties of consequentialism that treat rights as devices that we must usually rely upon in order to maximize goodness. In such theories, rights are not morally fundamental but are useful, perhaps even indispensible, devices for the maximization of overall human welfare.

[7] For discussions of these models of rights in relation to the rights of children see Griffin 2002; Brighouse 2002; Brennan 2002.

[8] The proposal I develop about the relation between children's moral rights and juvenile agency need not be hostile to recognition that some rights of children (or adults) serve to protect fundamental interests that are independent of agency. My main objective is to motivate the idea that an important range of children's rights can be articulated and defended by appeal to distinctive and normatively valuable features of their agency. One could express this point by insisting that children have a fundamental interest in enjoying goods accessible via juvenile agency and this might suggest that my approach is committed to an interest model of rights. For my part, I do not think a lot hangs on this matter. As I say above, I think the contrast between interest and choice models of rights can be overblown. For my purposes, the important point is the suggestion that children

However, both strategies, insofar as they rely upon a static and idealized conception of agency have difficulty providing a satisfactory theory of children's moral rights. In order to determine what rights persons have simply qua rational agents we need first to provide a characterization of rational agency and then determine how rights can be grounded in this characterization. Standard characterizations of rational agency often take as their paradigm a mature, autonomous self with developed cognitive and moral capacities. Rights are then conceptualized in relation to this model of agency.

We can see this kind of idealizing approach at work in Rawls's influential account of basic liberty rights and the allied theory of primary goods. Both these elements of Rawls's theory of justice depend crucially on conceiving the participants in social cooperation as free and equal citizens. The conception of citizens as free and equal persons that animates Rawls's view is itself explained in terms of two moral powers: the capacity for a sense of justice and the capacity for a conception of the good. The former power is "the capacity to understand, to apply, and to act from (not merely in accordance with) the principles of political justice that specify the fair terms of social cooperation" (Rawls 2001: 19). The latter power is "the capacity to have, revise, and rationally to pursue a conception of the good" (Rawls: 2001:19). According to Rawls, the fundamental interests of participants in social cooperation lie in securing conditions favorable to the development and exercise of the moral powers. An important dimension of characterizing persons in terms of the moral powers is that persons can assume responsibility for their ends. In other words, each person is assumed to have the ability and authority (over the course of a life) to develop, reflect upon and to pursue a conception of the good. Consequently, the advantages of social cooperation with which justice is appropriately concerned are those that provide persons with the conditions of and means to exercise and develop the moral powers. It is not the role of justice to supply persons with particular ends much less a comprehensive conception of the good for persons to implement. Similarly, justice is not concerned with ensuring that persons succeed in implementing the plans and projects they elect to pursue or that they are happy.

The selection of primary goods as the appropriate metric of individual advantage proceeds against this background. The idea is to identify resources that are suitably connected to the exercise and development of the moral powers and which are compatible with assigning the responsibility for ends to persons. So in drawing up the list of primary goods, Rawls seeks to establish a credible link between particular primary goods and the moral powers. For example, the basic rights and liberties that top the list of primary goods "are essential institutional conditions required for the adequate development and full and informed exercise of the two moral powers" (Rawls 2001: 58). Similarly, income and wealth are viewed as all-purpose means "generally needed to achieve a wide range of ends whatever they may be" (Rawls 2001: 59). In effect, a good is eligible for inclusion on the list of primary goods if it can be shown that it contributes significantly to either: (1) the development of the

---

display a distinct form of agency that merits recognition and protection. One, though perhaps not the only, function of rights is to mark certain claims of persons as meriting special recognition and protection.

moral powers, (2) the conditions conducive to exercising the moral powers in reflection and deliberation or (3) to the exercise of the moral powers in pursuing chosen ends.

Rawls's strategy for the identification of basic rights arguably relies on an idealized conception agency. But as O'Neill warns idealization in moral theory "can easily lead to falsehood" (1996: 41). As she explains, "an assumption, and derivatively a theory, idealizes when it ascribes predicates – often seen as enhanced, 'ideal' predicates – that are false in the case in hand, and so denies predicates that are true of that case" (1996: 41). It is perhaps debatable whether the two moral powers model of persons invoked by Rawls is an apt description of adults involved in mutually beneficial social cooperation. But it is clear children are not agents in Rawls's sense and hence his idealization introduces distortions of the sort O'Neill highlights. Even if Rawls's model of agency can be harnessed to yield plausible conclusions with respect to the rights of adults, it will yield problematic conclusions concerning the rights of children.

Idealized models of agency, such as Rawls's, create puzzles about attribution of rights to children. Because children do not fully display the features of ideal agency, arguments linking rights to features of agency will not directly apply to children. Without abandoning an ideal model of agency for the articulation of rights, there are three possible responses to this lacuna. First, we can simply deny that children are proper bearers of moral rights (Griffin 2002). Second, we can claim, following the so-called the child liberationists, that children sufficiently approximate the model of ideal agency for us to be warranted in extending (more or less) the same set of rights to children as to adults (Farson 1974; Holt 1974). Third, somewhat more subtly, we can identify children's rights solely in relation to their status as potential rational agents. On this last approach, children's rights can be different from adults' rights but are understood exclusively in terms of the conditions that are necessary to secure the full development of mature rational agency.

All three of these responses strike me as unsatisfactory. Denying that children have any moral rights whatsoever generates very unpalatable implications. Consider the right not to be tortured. Surely a children's rights skeptic does not really want to deny that it is wrong to torture children and that children have a fundamental, enforceable moral entitlement not to be tortured. Recognition of this entitlement is not optional, negotiable or dependent on the rights or claims of other interested parties (e.g., parents of children). But accepting that children have a basic moral entitlement not to be tortured just is to accept that they have a moral right not to be tortured. It is also implausible to deny that the rights of children and (mature) adults are different in important respects. Credible attributions of moral rights to persons depend, I suggest, on establishing some resonance between the putative right and the agency of the person to whom it is attributed. The only way the would-be child liberationist can establish a suitable resonance between the standard autonomy rights of mature adults and the agency of children is to exaggerate the moral competencies and cognitive capacities of children. The agency of children is not unrelated to that of adults and there is, of course, a developmental process through which children develop the moral and cognitive capacities on which the assignment of some rights to adults depends. A theory of rights should try to interpret and respond the developmental character of agency rather than ignore it or gloss over it.[9]

The third response is more adequate but offers an incomplete picture of children's rights. The underlying potential of most children to become mature adults with the cognitive and moral capacities constitutive of autonomy figures in the identification of *some* of the distinctive rights of children. The development of meaningful autonomy in children can be obstructed or subverted by neglect, abuse, inattention and material deprivation. Given their vulnerability and dependency, children, qua future mature agents, need secure access to nutrition, medical care, shelter, and education. If rights serve "to nurture and sustain the possibility of agency" then it is plausible to maintain that all children are entitled to the social and material conditions that facilitate the development of mature agency. The content of these rights will in some respects overlap with the rights of adults but will differ in some respects. So whereas the right to security of the person protects both children and adults against assault, adults have liberty rights that children lack. Similarly, children arguably have welfare rights that protect the development of agency (e.g., equal rights to excellent educational resources) that adults either do not have or only have in more limited ways. However, an account of children's rights that is focused entirely on the development of mature agency is incomplete because it fails to consider what respect for the agency of children qua children requires. The lives of children have aspects that are normatively important in ways that are not directly linked to the development of mature agency. By identifying and characterizing distinctive facets of the agency of children, we can identify some children's rights whose function is not to facilitate the development of mature agents but rather to protect the agency of children. The rights so identified will be different both from the rights that adults and children have in common and from the rights of children that reflect a concern for the development of agency. Or so I shall argue. To make good the claim, I will try to illuminate some dimensions of what I'll call *juvenile agency* and then I will suggest ways in which we can attribute rights to children in virtue of facets of juvenile agency.

Juvenile Agency

In order to shed light on the character of juvenile agency, it may be helpful to identify some paradigmatic dimensions of mature agency. Autonomous adults have cognitive and moral capacities to reflect upon ends rationally. They can understand the options available to them and deliberate, in a variety of ways, about the value of

---

[9] For the purposes of this discussion, I do not take up the interesting question of what rights can be attributed to adults who, due to cognitive impairments, never develop or lose rational capacities requisite to mature agency. Such adults can be 'childlike' in some respects and thus their rights to make authoritative decisions about their own lives may be constrained in important ways. However, it also seems likely the rights of such adults will not be simply identical to children with similar rational capacities.

different ends. They can also adopt and pursue ends in a way that reflects their authority and responsibility as end setters. Where there is a range of morally permissible ends available to an agent, a mature agent has the unique authority to determine which one to adopt and pursue. To an important degree, the success or failure of the agent in pursuing freely selected ends is the responsibility of the agent who adopted them. If I freely decide to play hockey instead of soccer, then, provided others treat me fairly, I must accept responsibility for how well or poorly it works out for me. (This does not mean that I can or should be expected to pursue my ends entirely independently from others. Acknowledging the authority and responsibility of mature agents is compatible with recognition of the vulnerability and interdependency of human rational agency.) Similarly, if mature agents freely adopt and pursue morally impermissible ends, then they are reasonably subject to blame, disapprobation and punishment.

The agency of children is interestingly different. Children do have preferences, often very strongly held preferences, and they adopt ends in the sense that they choose both what activities they wish to pursue and how to pursue them. However, they are novice end-setters in a variety of ways. They cannot always understand the options that are available to them, they cannot fully deliberate about possible ends and, as a consequence, they lack full authority to set ends and they do not bear full responsibility for the ends they set.[10] Of course, if we focus on the rational capacities that children lack we will perhaps be inclined to follow Tamar Schapiro and view childhood as a "predicament" (Schapiro 1999: 728): a normatively regrettable state from which children need to be saved by helping them develop the capacities of mature agency. Viewing childhood as a predicament fits with the conception of children's rights in which rights are identified solely in relation to the development of autonomy.

However, I want to suggest that there is a kind of integrity internal to juvenile agency that merits respect on its own terms. Consider the following two related facets of childhood agency[11] that are connected to the way in which children are novice end setters. First, childhood is characterized by a degree of innocence that lends itself to spontaneity and unchecked creativity in the choices of children. Children, especially young children, are receptive to very diverse activities and experiences. They can be amused, engaged, scared, and puzzled by things that strike adults as banal or familiar. This allows the exercise of agency, through making various childhood choices, to be accompanied by a sense of wonderment and confidence. But innocence of this sort involves a kind of ignorance of or unfamiliarity with the workings of the world. In adults innocence can be an obstacle to agency

---

[10] Robert Noggle argues that children are 'special agents' because they do not display the same degree of "temporal extension" as adults (Noggle 2002: 102). This helps to explain why children's ends often involve very short-range plans and why there can be a degree of instability in the preferences of children.

[11] The suggestions I make about distinctive features of juvenile agency are related to the idea that there are intrinsic goods of childhood that matter from the point of justice. See Brennan 2014; Gheaus 2014; Macleod 2010, 2014.

precisely because it involves epistemic errors that bear on prudent and successful planning. Innocent adults are naïve and they are less able to set their ends rationally. But the innocence of children does not seem like an encumbrance to meaningful childhood action, at least when viewed on its own terms. Part of the distinctive activity of children involves rapid shifts in plans and preferences and receptiveness to new options. Moreover, new preferences are adopted and pursued without much concern about potential obstacles to the satisfaction of preferences.

Second, children's agency is fuelled by remarkable imaginative powers. Children can imaginatively transform ordinary household items into the elements of a complex make-believe world. Similarly, they can ascribe personality and agency to inanimate toys and include these imaginatively animated creatures in wonderful adventures and narratives. From a perspective of mature agency, many of these exercises of imagination present themselves as errors – a failure to see and appreciate the world as it really is. However, it seems clear that the lives of children are enriched by their imaginative participation in make-believe worlds and, at a suitable age and stage, it does not seem regrettable that children make choices and embark on projects that are predicated on false or distorted views of the world. Moreover, even if the playful exercise of imagination contributes crucially to the development of mature agency, I do not think its normative significance should be viewed entirely in instrumental terms. Play has value as an expression of juvenile agency independently of its hedonic value. Of course, a child who 'chooses' to be a dragon slaying knight has fun but the creative expression of agency involved in play has, I believe, significance in its own right. Thus often it is appropriate for adults to respect the choices of children about how to play, even when they know that the choices made by children will lead to frustration rather than to pleasure. Similarly, what constitutes appropriate play need not be gauged solely in relation to a developmental standard.

Rights and Juvenile Agency

There may be other distinctive dimensions of juvenile agency that merit attention but the innocence and imagination aspects that I have sketched above provide materials for constructing an account of children's rights that goes beyond the development of mature agency account. We can begin simply by noting the special vulnerability of juvenile agency. Children can be easily robbed of their innocence and they can be denied adequate opportunities for imaginative expression and play. As highly dependent beings, they are unable to secure for themselves the social and material conditions of juvenile agency. Rights, I have suggested, can be identified as entitlements to the social and material conditions integral to the sustenance of agency. So we need to consider, with due attention to the attributes of real persons rather than idealized agents, how resources and opportunities should be distributed and institutions structured in order to facilitate the flourishing of juvenile agency.

Consider first what is plausibly required to protect and sustain the innocence of children. Innocence can be threatened or undermined by exposure to some of the harsher realities of the world. So even when young children are sufficiently cognitively developed to grasp information about certain subjects – e.g., violence, sexuality, the pain and suffering of others – it often makes sense to insulate them from such information or to present it in ways that are not fully accurate. So often we restrict the material children can read or view not because they literally cannot understand it but because exposure to the material would be upsetting or jarring. In the case of mature agents, it is usually disrespectful of agency to block access to or to distort information. But respect for juvenile agency seems different. Honouring the innocence of children arguably depends on reliably providing them with a safe, secure and loving household in which their parents (or caregivers) can shield them from the potentially corrosive dimensions of the world. We can capture the entitlement at stake here by saying that children have a right to a protective family, that is to care and affection by parents that both shields children from corrosive elements of the adult world and which affords them opportunities to manifest and experience a period of innocence.[12] This does not mean that parents have unlimited prerogatives to monitor and control the information and influences to which children are exposed (Macleod 1997, 2003). Although honouring childhood innocence is, I believe, important, its character and what is involved in respecting it changes as children mature. Parents and others can wrong children by infantilizing older children in the name of preserving their innocence. Respecting the rights of children involves attention to the dynamic and developmental aspects of agency, too. Nonetheless, the normative importance of childhood innocence provides, I believe, a sufficient basis for constructing a distinctive children's right.

A similar constructivist strategy can be deployed in relation to the imaginative facet of juvenile agency. It might initially sound trivial but sustaining the imaginative capacities of children involves providing them with diverse opportunities for fun and games. Children who, from a very young age, are forced to work and who have little time or opportunity to exercise their imaginative capacities in a satisfying fashion are deprived not only of pleasurable experiences but also of dignity.[13] Treating children with respect, I contend, involves recognizing a right to play. Play has many different dimensions and there are diverse ways in which children can be furnished with opportunities for play. So what is required in order to respect the right to play will vary from context to context. For instance, the games and sports children play vary from culture to culture but facilitating play always involves allocation of both adequate time and resources. Advocates of the right to play often emphasize various

---

[12] Roberto Benigni's film *Life is Beautiful* arguably provides a poignant illustration of the importance protecting the innocence of childhood. In the film, the main character shields his son from the full horrors of a Nazi concentration camp by inventing an elaborate ruse according to which the prisoners are involved in an elaborate game. Whereas it would be objectionably deceitful to trick adults in this way, I think Benigni's character can be interpreted as struggling valiantly to respect the rights of his son.

[13] Even though she expresses doubts about attributing this kind of right to children, O'Neill seems sympathetic to the basic point I am making here. "Cold, distant or fanatical parents and teachers, even if they violate no rights, deny children the "genial play of life": they can wither children's lives" (O'Neill 1988: 450–51). On my view, of course, such parents and teachers do violate children's right to play.

developmental benefits of play. In a similar vein, Schapiro sees play as contributing something important to the process of self-development through which the predicament of childhood can be overcome (1999: 732). The contribution of play to the development of agency is, of course, important but I think we should also value play as expression of juvenile agency that merits respect. This point can be important when we turn our attention to the way institutions should be designed in order to respect the right to play because if we value play only in developmental terms then we may undersupply opportunities and resources for play. Similarly, we can underestimate the importance of play, and consequently the importance of opportunities for play, if we think of its non-developmental value in exclusively hedonic terms.

Conclusion

The foregoing remarks do not, of course, provide a comprehensive account of children's rights. Once we recognize the dynamic dimension of agency along with the distinction between juvenile and mature agency, the task of constructing a complete account of children's rights becomes very complex. Not only must we determine the basic content of rights that sustain the development of mature agency and those that protect facets of juvenile agency but we must also determine how these different kinds of rights should be integrated. Moreover, the content and integration of both of these kinds of rights needs to be responsive to the dynamic character of children's agency. Just as the kind of nurturing that is likely to promote the development of mature agency in a 4 year old will be different from the developmental attention needed by a 12 year old, what is involved in respecting the innocence of a toddler will be different from respecting the innocence of a teenager. This means that, especially with respect to its institutional implications, a detailed account of children's specific rights will be graduated in the following sense: Both children's entitlements to social and material resources and their prerogatives to set and pursue ends will be adjusted in relation to the cognitive, psychological and moral capacities they have at different stages. Put more simply, respecting the agency of children means different things at different ages.[14]

By way of conclusion, I should note that I doubt that O'Neill would endorse my strategy for constructing children's rights. As I noted above, O'Neill's constructivism treats obligations as fundamental and deploys Kantian tests of universalization as a part of the constructivist methodology. The form of constructivism deployed in this paper is much more interpretative in character: constructing rights is a matter of interpreting the character and sustaining conditions of agency. However, I hope the way in which the argument draws inspiration from O'Neill's work is now clear. Rights theory must take the actual lives of children seriously. In addition to acknowledging

---

[14] To complicate matters even further, it is possible that there will be some variation between cultures or national communities about how children's rights are specified. To some degree, differences in cultural conventions may have a bearing on how the content of some rights, such as the right to play, is interpreted.

their dependency, vulnerability, and cognitive immaturity, this involves grappling with real and different aspects of the agency of children. Idealized accounts of agency employed in contemporary contractualist and contractarian theory are particularly unhelpful when we try to understand children's rights. By offering some reflections on the special character of juvenile agency and its relation to rights, I have tried "to reason with all possible solidity from *available* beginnings, using *available* and *followable* methods to reach *attainable* and *sustainable* conclusions for relevant audiences" (O'Neill 1996: 63).[15]

References

Brennan, Samantha. 2002. Children's choices or children's interests: Which do their rights protect. In *The moral and political status of children*, ed. David Archard and Colin Macleod. Oxford: Oxford University Press.

Brennan, Samantha. 2014. The goods of childhood and children's rights. In *Family-making: Contemporary ethical challenges*, ed. Françoise Baylis and Carolyn McLeo. Oxford: Oxford University Press.

Brighouse, Harry. 2002. What rights (if any) do children have? In *The moral and political status of children*, ed. David Archard and Colin Macleod. Oxford: Oxford University Press.

Dworkin, Ronald. 2000. *Sovereign virtue: The theory and practice of equality*. Cambridge, MA: Harvard University Press.

Farson, R. 1974. *Birthrights*. London: Collier Macmillan.

Gauthier, David. 1986. *Morals by Agreement*. Oxford: Oxford University Press.

Gheaus, Anca. 2014. The intrinsic goods of childhood and the just society. In *The nature of children's well-being: Theory and practice*, ed. A. Bagattini and C. Macleod. Dordrecht: Springer.

Griffin, James. 2002. Do children have rights? In *The moral and political status of children*, ed. David Archard and Colin Macleod. Oxford: Oxford University Press.

Holt, J.C. 1974. *Escape from childhood: The needs and rights of children*. Hammondsworth: Penguin.

Macleod, Colin. 1997. Conceptions of parental autonomy. *Politics and Society* 25(1): 117–140.

Macleod, Colin. 2003. Shaping children's convictions. *Theory and Research in Education* 1(3): 315–330.

Macleod, Colin. 2010. Primary goods, capabilities, and children. In *Measuring justice: Primary goods and capabilities*, ed. Robeyns Ingrid and Brighouse Harry. Cambridge: Cambridge University Press.

Macleod, Colin. 2014. Agency, authority and the vulnerability of children. In *The nature of children's well-being: Theory and practice*, ed. A. Bagattini and C. Macleod. New York: Springer.

Noggle, Robert. 2002. Special agents: Children's autonomy and parental authority. In *The moral and political status of children*, ed. David Archard and Colin Macleod. Oxford: Oxford University Press.

O'Neill, Onora. 1988. Children's rights and children's lives. *Ethics* 98: 445–563.

O'Neill, Onora. 1996. *Towards justice and virtue: A constructive account of practical reasoning*. Cambridge: Cambridge University Press.

Rawls, John. 2001. *Justice as fairness: A restatement*. Cambridge, MA: Harvard University Press.

Rawls, John. 1971. *A Theory of Justice*. Cambridge: Harvard University Press.

Schapiro, Tamar. 1999. What is a child? *Ethics* 109(July): 715–738.

---

[15]I would like to thank Johannes Drerup, Gunter Graf and Gottfried Schweiger for helpful feedback on this essay. I also acknowledge Baroness O'Neill of Bengarve for the reply she gave to an earlier version of this essay at a conference in her honour at the Royal Society in London.

Chapter 2
Future-Oriented Paternalism and the Intrinsic Goods of Childhood

Alexander Bagattini

Abstract Paternalism is a salient feature of most children's lives. This paper explores a specific version of paternalism, namely future-oriented paternalism. Future-oriented paternalism is directed to presumed valuable goals for the child's later life as an adult such as autonomy and education. This paper analyses the normative implications of future-oriented paternalism. In a first step it is pointed out that future-oriented paternalism is often understood as entailing what can be called the 'instrumental conception of childhood'. In a second step this conception of childhood is critically examined and rebutted. Hence the paper asks in a third step for a refined version of future-oriented paternalism that doesn't make use of the instrumental conception of childhood.

Keywords Paternalism • Childhood • Equality • Intrinsic goods of childhood

Introduction

Parents want their children to live good lives. Some parents may do better than others, but all in all this assumption seems to be warranted. Usually parents care for their children and they accept many, emotional as well as economic, hardships to accomplish this task. On the other hand, children need the care of their parents (or of other responsible adults) to live good lives. Most people believe that this reciprocal relatedness of interests entails paternalism. *Paternalism* is the view that the state or a Person A interferes with another Person B against B's will, whereby the state or A have to be motivated by the aim that B will be better off than without the paternalistic action (Dworkin 1972). The background-assumption is that the person acting paternalistically is more competent concerning the well-being of the paternalized person than him/herself and acts in his/her *best interest*. The concept of best interest will be addressed in the next section. In what follows, two assumptions will be

A. Bagattini (✉)
Department of Philosophy, University of Düsseldorf, Düsseldorf, Germany
e-mail: bagattini@phil.hhu.de

© Springer International Publishing Switzerland 2016   17
J. Drerup et al. (eds.), *Justice, Education and the Politics of Childhood*,
Philosophy and Politics – Critical Explorations 1,
DOI 10.1007/978-3-319-27389-1_2

made: first, paternalism concerning children is justified *in principle*. This means that it will be assumed that children are in need of adults making decisions in their best interest (in general). Yet this is compatible with further restrictions about the content of paternalism concerning children. Second, it will be assumed that parents typically are the right persons to make decisions in the best interest of their children. The following considerations depend on this assumption which is taken to be captured in our Common Sense idea of child-rearing.

Paternalism is a salient feature of most children's lives. In many cases parents try to prevent *immediate* harm to their children. Where immediate harm is concerned, most people endorse that parents should overrule their children's decisions. Yet not all paternalistic actions are motivated by the idea of preventing immediate harm. Sometimes, parents want their children's to live good *lives in the future* and overrule their decisions in this regard. We may call this *future-oriented paternalism*. We can distinguish at least three forms of future-oriented paternalism concerning children: first, future-oriented paternalism motivated by the future of the child as a child, second by the youth the child is supposed to become, and finally by the adult the child is supposed to become. Let us consider the case in which parents want their child to prepare for a school test. In the first case they might warn her that she runs the risk of not passing the grade. In the second case they might argue that it will be difficult, later on, to find a job trainee position after school. In the third case they might point out that her whole career depends on passed exams.

This paper will for the most part focus on future-oriented paternalism of the last kind, when parents justify their paternalistic actions by reference to the child's future life as an adult. Hence, when the term 'future-oriented paternalism' is mentioned, it is always related to the child's later life as an adult. Different usages of the term will be made explicit.

The *first section* of the paper develops a first definition of future-oriented paternalism. It will be pointed out that it presupposes a specific conception of childhood, namely the instrumental conception of childhood. The instrumental conception of childhood will be criticized in *section two* because it does not pay proper attention to the moral status of children as equals among equals. Section two, furthermore, develops the idea of an alternative conception of childhood, according to which there are intrinsic goods of childhood. *Section three* of the paper examines the ethical implications of this conception of childhood for future-oriented paternalism.

Future-Oriented Paternalism

For a start, consider the famous first verse of Cat Stevens' song *Father and Son*:

> It's not time to make a change, just relax take it easy. You're still young, that's your fault. There's so much you have to know. Find a girl settle down, if you want, you can marry. Look at me, I am old, but I'm happy. I was once like you are now and I know that it's not easy to be calm when you've found something going on. But take your time, think a lot,

why, think of everything you've got. *For, you will still be here tomorrow but your dreams may not.*

Stevens' song captures the idea of future-oriented paternalism very nicely. The father contemplates the ideas of his son (about a change) which, from his perspective, are not adequately connected to the necessities of life. Describing them as dreams, he proclaims to have the clearer view on what matters (and what not), due to his greater experience. Finally, the father does not seem to argue in an authoritative way. Rather, he seems to be deeply driven by his opinion that the son's later self will suffer from what is planned right now.

In other words: the father makes use of the notion of *best interests*. It means that persons make decisions on behalf of the interests of other persons because they assume to be (and may be) more competent to do so. In some cases this concerns the relation of adults when, for example, physicians or lawyers act in the best interests of their clients. The case of children is more specific because paternalism towards children seems to be justified by default. This does not mean that parents do not have to care about their children's opinions. It just means that, in the end, parents have the last word in vital matters concerning the child's life. The best-interest-principle is controversial for many reasons. However, it seems that future-oriented paternalism needs this principle in the one or other version. Hence, for the sake of argument, let us assume it is a valid principle. In order to work with the best-interest-principle we need to make two distinctions: first, the distinction between actual and future interests of a person, and second, the distinction between internal and external interests. Internal interests are the subjective interests of the child while external interests are the interests of the child from a mere objective perspective.[1] Future-oriented paternalism entails that children's actual interests are subordinated in relation to their later interests as a matter of principle. Further, parents have their own views about education and how the later self of the child should be constructed. Most people believe that parental authority in matters of education is warranted at least to some degree. This is enough to make the following claim: Children need the guidance of their parents (or of other adults) to become persons capable to act in favor of their own interests. Bearing these distinctions in mind, we can define future-oriented paternalism as follows:

> *Future-oriented paternalism*: (i) The subordination of its actual interests in relation to its future interests is in the best interest of the child. (ii) In order to meet this condition (i) children need the guidance of adults (external interests).

The father in Stevens' song proclaims to know better what is good for his son. Further, he makes clear that, from his perspective, real life is yet to come ("you will still be here tomorrow"), while the actual interests of the son are less important or even idle ("but your dreams may not"). At the end of the paper the definition of future-oriented paternalism will be critically discussed. However, first we have to

---

[1] Another way to make this point is the following: external interests are the interests that the child should have. Hence external interests require a third-person-perspective that is typically taken by the parents of the child.

examine the normative implications of future-oriented paternalism in more detail. The vital question for now is: how is claim (i) justified? A tentative and plausible answer is that goods such as autonomy, education and even happiness are hard to acquire for adults if they were not paternalized as children. Nonetheless, the question still remains why it is a good thing, or even a morally good thing, to do? Why should the later interests count more than the actual interests of the child?

Several plausible answers are at hand. To begin with, the interests of the later person (of the adult the child is supposed to become) simply count *per se*. Hence, and because this later person cannot represent her interests now, future-oriented paternalism is justified. However, this argument does not justify the claim that the interests of the later person are always overriding, according to the above-mentioned definition of future-oriented paternalism. We would need a separate argument in order to reach this conclusion. Such an argument could be derived from the fact that, at least statistically, the later part of the life of the child is longer. In this respect there would at least be a quantitative reason to prefer the future interests of the child. However, to *justify* future-oriented paternalism we need more than quantitative reasons.[2] Further, we would need a qualitative reason why the interests of the future person count more. Such a reason is captured in what Anca Gheaus calls the instrumental conception of childhood (Gheaus 2014).

Conceptions of Childhood

The Instrumental Conception of Childhood

The instrumental conception of childhood is the preferred conception of the modern era. It is driven by the idea that childhood is a *transitory state* that must be overcome by means of education. According to this idea, the value of childhood depends completely on its contribution to what all modern philosophers have considered as the vital part of human life – the autonomy of the person the child is supposed to become. Accordingly, in the instrumental conception of childhood the very value of childhood consists in its contribution to fostering the later autonomy of the child. Hence, for qualitative reasons future-oriented paternalism can easily be justified in this conception of childhood. Concerning childhood, the instrumentalist would argue in the following way: The end of human life is autonomy. Because children are not yet autonomous they are, so to say, on their way towards (full) humanity. One of the first modern authors who contemplated this position was John Locke. In a famous passage of his *Second Treatise of Government* he writes:

Children [...] are not born *in this full state of equality* (which consists of the equal right to natural freedom), though they are *born to it*. Their parents have a sort of rule and justification over them when they come into the world, and for some

---

[2] I am skeptical that even the aggregation of quantitative reasons (like the aggregation of pleasurable experiences) would have the normative weight to justify future-oriented paternalism.

time after, but 'tis but a temporary one. [...] *Age and reason* as they grow up, loosen them till at length they drop quite off, and leave a man at his own *free disposal*" (Locke 1988, V/55).

To be sure, this passage is not fully clear and certainly open to different interpretations. The important things to note for the moment are Locke's cryptic expressions "not born in this full state of equality" and "born to it". Locke makes clear that there is a relation of children to the principle of equality. Being one of the founders of modern liberalism, in Locke's philosophy the principle of equality is basically a principle concerning the moral status of persons, namely that all persons have equal rights. As it does not seem to be appropriate to grant children equal rights, Locke claims that they are not born in the full state of equality. But, as he claims, they are born to it. Making this point, Locke deviates from what can be called the proprietarian conception of childhood, according to which children are the property of their parents. The proprietarian conception of childhood was the default model for child rearing in the classical world (Gardner 1998). Some authors combined it with the doctrine of *patria potestas* (Aristotle 2009), while others (Plato 2008) claimed that the state (and not fathers of families) owns the children. Locke seems to endorse the very doctrine of *patria potestas,* but he rebuts the proprietarian conception of childhood (Archard 2004). He does so by mentioning that children belong to the category of persons, at least in the sense that they pass through a process that leads to full equality. But if full equality is a property of the future person (the child is supposed to become), parents cannot be owners of their children. They cannot be owners of their children because they have a duty to make sure that the adult person's equality as a rational and free agent is respected. The "rule and justification" of parents over their children is, then, confined by the principle of equality, and it entails duties that are oriented at the development of the capacities that are vital for becoming a rational and free agent. Being such an agent is the political quality that modern philosophers where so fond of because it entitles persons to be autonomous parts of society in the full-blooded sense. This means that one shares all the rights and duties of citizenship. Kant forcefully expresses this point in the following passage from his work *The Metaphysic of Morals*:

> The only qualification for being a citizen is being fit to vote. But being fit to vote presupposes the independence of someone who [...] wants to be not just a part of the commonwealth but also a member of it, that is, a part of the commonwealth acting from his own choice in community with others. This quality of being independent, however, requires a distinction between *active and passive citizens*. (Kant 1996, 314)

The distinction between active and passive citizens is directly connected to the capacities that are necessary to be "fit to vote", which in turn is related to the person's independence. Only independent (meaning autonomous) persons are fit to vote and, by that token, full-blooded members of the liberal society. According to Kant, children belong to the same group as women at that time: they were excluded from society's economic contexts and, hence, dependent. Analogous to Locke, Kant accepts that children have to be subsumed under the principle of equality. This is why Kant declares children to be citizens. But they are considered individuals with different moral status than full-blooded citizens, which is captured by the expression "passive citizen".

For Kant as well as for Locke, children are persons. This is a new and, for this time, quite radical perspective of childhood. But the value of childhood is completely derived from its contribution to proper adolescence. And proper adolescence is defined by means of becoming an autonomous person, a rational and free agent, or, in Kant's words, an active citizen. Because the value of childhood is defined by reference to the value of autonomy, this conception can be called the instrumental conception of childhood. The instrumental conception of childhood must not be confused with the proprietarian conception of childhood. The crucial difference is that the former sets limits for parental authority and parental paternalism, while the latter does not. Yet it is not childhood per se that sets the limits but the instrumental value of childhood for proper adolescence. Childhood *per se* is rather seen as a vehicle than as something of intrinsic value. Hence, according to modern philosophers, childhood must be respected, but not for its own sake. In the light of this traditional way of considering the condition of childhood, Tamar Schapiro calls childhood a predicament.

> [C]hildhood is a predicament. [T]he condition of childhood is one in which the agent is not yet in a position to speak in her own voice because there is no voice which counts as hers. (Schapiro 1999, 729)

The "voice which counts as hers", the child's "own voice", is the voice of reason – the essential component of autonomy. According to Schapiro, children do not count as moral agents because they lack the relevant status – autonomy – that in turn is dependent on specific capacities such as emotional stability, a stable identity and the faculties of reason. That children lack full moral status does not mean that they have none at all. Following Locke and Kant, Schapiro considers children to be on their way towards autonomy and full equality. These goals define the value of childhood, which, in turn, confines parental prerogatives. This instrumentalist view of childhood is clearly expressed in the next passage:

> There is [...] a concept which [...] sheds some light upon the liminal status of children. This is the concept of ‚play‘. It may make sense to see play as a strategy – perhaps the strategy – for working through the predicament of childhood. By engaging in play, children, more or less deliberately ‚try on‘ selves to be and worlds to be in. This is because the only way a child can ‚have‘ a self is by trying one on. [...] Play is children's form of work, for their job is to become themselves. (Schapiro 1999, 732)

Again, Schapiro considers children to be on their way through the predicament of childhood. The games children play are one of the things that most people consider to be essential for talking about children at all. According to Schapiro, the value of these games is completely derived from its contribution to adolescence – the outdistancing of the predicament of childhood. This passage exemplifies a further point, namely that the instrumental conception of childhood is not necessarily hostile towards childhood. The instrumentalist can perfectly grant children many of the things that are important to them from their perspective, e. g. time to play. But in the end, the goods of childhood are only good insofar as they contribute to the goods of adulthood. This is so because the goods of adulthood are derived from that latter person's moral status as an autonomous being.

The instrumental conception of childhood has a clear bias in order to prefer the future interests of the child (as an adult person). Hence the instrumental conception of childhood provides the normative framework for the justification of future-oriented paternalism. The argument runs as follows: Because children are not yet capable of making their own decisions, because adults are better in this regard, and because children's later lives (as adults) have more moral weight, future-oriented paternalism is justified. However, many authors have criticized the instrumental conception of childhood.

Escape from the Predicament

The most radical criticism of the instrumental conception of childhood comes from the so-called child-liberationists. Child-liberationists typically start from the premise that the unfair exclusion of people from enjoying equal rights is incompatible with political liberalism. Stressing this point, authors like John Holt and Richard Farson argue that competence-criteria would not only justify the discrimination of children but of adults as well. However, age seems to be a rather arbitrary criterion. Following this line of thought, child-liberationists argue that children should enjoy equal rights (Holt 1974; Farson 1974). Child-liberationism has been thoroughly criticized and, in my point of view, successfully refuted (Archard 2004). Yet it entails an important message, namely that the leading assumption of the instrumentalist conception of childhood is in need of justification. In other words, we need to give a sensitive answer to the question of why children should enjoy different moral status than adults. I will follow Anca Gheaus who argues that there is no such answer.

In her paper "The Intrinsic Goods of Childhood and the Good Society" Anca Gheaus calls the predicament view of childhood into question. She writes:

> The normative belief that rationality is *the* source of personhood and hence of (full) moral status, combined with a descriptive belief that children are insufficiently rational, yields the conclusion that childhood is a predicament. If both the descriptive and the normative elements of this view on childhood are correct, then children's moral status is indeed derivative from the expectation that they will reach adulthood. (Gheaus 2014, 41)

Gheaus mentions two claims or elements that are entailed by the predicament view: first that only rationality and autonomy are legitimate sources of full moral status, second that children are insufficiently rational. According to the first, normative claim, Gheaus argues that it is contentious. There are other accounts of moral value. While most people would accept that autonomy and rationality are necessary for conferring moral value to a person, it seems far less clear that it is sufficient. Consider, for example, the recent debate about the moral value of vulnerability (Mackenzie 2013). In my point of view, the vulnerability of persons is an excellent reason to justify moral duties towards them. This is, in turn, only feasible if we accept that those persons have moral status. According to the second, descriptive, claim, Gheaus mentions the work of developmental scientist Alison Gopnik that suggests that the rational capacities of children have been largely underestimated. I think that Gheaus overstresses this point because her aim is to show that the predicament view is wrong. However, what Gopnik's work entails is that children live according to different rational principles than adults rather than being autonomous persons. Hence, as it seems there is leeway in the instrumental conception of childhood to endorse Gopnik's theses about children's development. By any means it would be necessary to bring in more details from both accounts to make a case against the descriptive claim of the predicament view.

Nonetheless, Gheaus' criticism does not lose its grip. The instrumentalist needs to say far more about his claim that *only* rationality and autonomy confer moral status to persons. If this were true, future-oriented paternalism would be justified in principle. However, there are other values, such as aiding the vulnerable, that confer moral value as well. If this were not the case, it would be perfectly justified to make children's lives worse as long as this contributes to proper adolescence in the sense of becoming an autonomous agent later in life. Gheaus mentions the example of considerable economic duties (child labor for example) (Gheaus 2014). As many people would hesitate to endorse that this is the right treatment of children, examples like this intuitively bring in more evidence against the instrumental conception of childhood.

The Intrinsic Goods of Childhood

What is the alternative to the instrumental conception of childhood? The child-liberationists seem to overstress their point when they claim that there is no vital normative difference between adults and children. In their conception, future-oriented paternalism (like any form of paternalism) does not seem to be justifiable at all, which seems to be an extremely implausible result. Yet it is one thing to claim that childhood is not only instrumentally valuable and quite another thing to dissolve the normative distinction between adults and children. This is not necessary for conferring the same moral status to children as to adults. What we need is the distinction between "treating as equal" and "treating equally" (Dworkin 1977). The distinction allows considering children under the principle of equality (treat them as equals) while not granting them equal rights (treating them not equally). Using this distinction, we can refute the instrumental conception of childhood but still allow for (at least some) future-oriented paternalistic actions like compulsory schooling.

But in which sense are children equals? One part of the answer is that we have to consider children as persons in the full-blooded sense. Calling them equals says nothing more or less than this: children are persons and enjoy basic rights. These rights may in many cases differ from the rights of adults. Still they are rights and have to be protected by the respective authorities. Furthermore, if the instrumental conception of childhood is wrong, there has to be some value of childhood that is not reducible to its contribution to proper adolescence. In other words: childhood must be good in itself. It is important to keep in mind that this claim does not entail that childhood is not (instrumentally) good for proper adolescence. This means that accepting that there are intrinsic goods of childhood does not force us to the much stronger claim that the value of childhood is *only* defined by those intrinsic goods of childhood. Nonetheless, if childhood is good in itself, there have to be intrinsic goods of childhood, which means: goods that render a childhood good irrespective of their contribution to proper adolescence (Gheaus 2014; Macleod 2010).

As Colin Macleod notes, those intrinsic goods of childhood "[...] are not accorded sufficient attention [...]" in normative disputes concerning children (Macleod 2010, 188). Macleod develops his account of intrinsic goods of childhood in the light of an elaborated criticism of two accounts of justice: the primary-goods-account of John Rawls and Nussbaum's capability-approach. According to Macleod, both accounts consider questions about what we owe to children in relation to their future agency as moral persons. Macleod refutes this "agency-assumption" (Macleod 2010, 179) because it is unfair towards children *as children*. In the light of this criticism Macleod reaches the same conclusion concerning the goods of childhood: namely that respecting children as children means accepting that one owes them goods for their own sake. Those goods that are owed to children as children are called intrinsic goods of childhood. Concerning these, goods Macleod writes:

> [I]ntrinsic goods of childhood should not be understood in purely welfarist terms. Having a happy childhood with plenty of fun and amusement is, of course, a good thing, but not all elements of a good childhood need be pleasant. Indeed a valuable childhood will have its share of frustration, difficulties, and even emotional and physical pain. Instead, we should think about the goods as emerging from various forms of creative stimulation of distinct human faculties. To realize the goods, we engage and activate the physical, emotional, aesthetic, cognitive, and moral faculties of children by exposing them to circumstances in which they can experience and give expression to their faculties and face challenges involved in using these faculties. [...] But these forms of such engagement need not yield contentment nor must they contribute to the development of agency to be worthwhile. (Macleod 2010, 187)

Macleod claims that the primary goods of childhood must not be defined exclusively in terms of children's welfare. He seems to think that welfare is equivalent to happiness. While he accepts that happiness constitutes a vital part of childhood, he points out that there are valuable experiences for children that are not happy but rather can be frustrating as well. What Macleod means is that children need to be challenged in many ways to fulfill their potentials *as children*. Sometimes parents are too motivated to prevent their children from unpleasant experiences. Such cases of overprotective behavior might be a problem if the child does not learn how to deal with difficult situations and to cope with negative feelings like frustration. It is not clear that all welfarists would accept this hedonic reduction of their theory.

However, for the sake of argument, let us focus on the basic point expressed in the last quote, namely that a good childhood is not always pleasurable. This means at least that the intrinsic goods of childhood are more robust, so to say, than mere opinions of parents or children. This point is decisive. Contrary to the goods of adulthood (where liberalism forces us to accept that people know best what is good for them), the goods of childhood are not completely belief-dependent. They are related to what Macleod calls "distinct human faculties". This is by no means a clear or self-evident term. Furthermore, one has to be aware of several threats when using it. The first threat is falling back to the agency-assumption and the instrumental conception of childhood. Talking about distinct human faculties is semantically very close to understanding the value of childhood in terms of goods like autonomy or happiness. Yet if we want to define *intrinsic* goods of childhood, they must be conceptually independent (meaning: not derived) from external or instrumental goods such as autonomy or happiness. The second threat is what can be called the ideological threat. This concerns the question of who has the authority to define what is typically human. Some religious communities might bring their normative views to the table while, for example, physicians are prone to medicalized conceptions of humanity.

In my point of view, we have to consider evidence from the relevant sciences as well as normative issues to come to grips with this idea of distinct human faculties. To be clear, such faculties have to be specific to children if we want to show that they are related to intrinsic goods of childhood. Hence, in what follows we have to address two questions: First, what are specific child-like (human) faculties? Second, which goods are related to them?

In order to make a first step towards a clearer grasp of the idea of specific child-like faculties, consider Franz Kafka's short story *The Top*, which is about a philosopher trying to understand the principles of a moving top while children are playing with it. While the children are happily running around the top, full of curiosity, imagination and playfulness, the philosopher is completely focused on his thoughts and observations and not even aware of the playing children (Kafka 1995). The philosopher is so interested in the mechanics of the top that he does not recognize the complex analogue picture of the situation. In this way the story expresses a sharp contrast between the mind-sets of the playing children on the one hand and the philosopher on the other. The philosopher is much more motivated by his inner plans, motives and thoughts than the children are. In this sense, the short story expresses a difference between children and adults in general: namely the difference between playing and planning, or between playing and future-oriented action.

As Allison Gopnik explains in her book *The Philosophical Baby*, there are two facts about the mind-sets of babies and young children that help us to understand this difference. The first is attention; the second can be called pretension. As Gopnik notes: "For babies, *attention* is much more likely to be captured by interesting external events than directed by internal plans and goals." (Gopnik 2009, 117, my Italics) A baby's attention is, in a word, not focused on conceptual plans but affected by external objects. This thesis is supported by a number of experiments like the one in which babies are confronted with changing mobiles and where they are only focused when new mobiles are hung up in front of them (Gopnik 2009, 31ff). The same thesis seems to hold in the case of young children. In the case of young children, Gopnik cites experiments with questionnaires as evidence for the same thesis: namely that they are not focused in the same way as it is the case with adults in general and that their attention is much more fine-grained and affected by external objects than by internal plans.

The second difference between children and adults mentioned by Gopnik is related to children's *pretension*. When children play, they typically pretend to act certain characters like shopkeepers, cowboys, astronauts, princes and princesses. What Gopnik points out is, firstly, that children take their roles very seriously, and that they, in a way, live their roles. However, she claims secondly that children know the difference between their fictional world and the real world perfectly.

From the adult perspective, the fictional worlds are a luxury. It's the future predictions that are the real deal, the stern and earnest stuff of adult life. For young children, however, the imaginary worlds seem just as important and appealing as the real ones. It's not, as scientists used to think, that children can't tell the difference between the real world and the imaginary world. [...] It's just that they don't see any particular reason for preferring to live in the real one (Gopnik 2009, 71).

In other words: the way children play is very much affected by children's mind-set which is not biased in order to distinguish the real world and the imaginary world. This is one of the major resources of the intensity, authenticity, and joy of children's games. Gopniks insights into children's minds are relevant for the current purpose of this paper. On the one hand they support what is sometimes called the modern conception of childhood (Archard 2004). According to the modern conception of childhood, children are, on the one hand, categorically separated from adults. However, on the other hand they clearly exceed the modern conception of childhood, insofar as children are considered to be much more self-sustained and competent in their own 'environments' than has been thought (both in science and in common sense) for so long.

In what follows I will take for granted that there are distinct child-specific faculties such as imagination, curiosity, playfulness and open-mindedness, and that these faculties are basically grounded in children's mind-sets. This leads to our second question, namely why we should consider such capacities as goods of moral weight. Because it is easy to fall back into the instrumental conception of childhood, it is important to bear in mind that those goods are goods for their own sake. This means that their goodness is not derived from 'external' goods such as autonomy or happiness. Fostering the just mentioned faculties in children will, of course, have an impact on their later autonomy and happiness. But if they are intrinsic goods of childhood, we must not derive their value exclusively from this contribution. So, why should we call such goods intrinsic goods of childhood? There is an indirect answer to this question. It depends on the assumption that children enjoy the same moral status as adults, which in turn entails that they count as equals. Counting as an equal person means that one's interests count equally. It does not seem to be a farfetched assumption that children's interests are closely related to their specific faculties. In other words: respecting children as equals means accepting that children's interests *as children* count.[3] This entails that interests coming from children's engagement motivated by child-specific faculties such as imagination and playfulness have to be protected. In some cases those interests have to be protected even against the will of children, for example when children seem to lack drive or if they want to eat too many sweets. The more decisive lesson for this paper is that those interests have to be protected against anyone, including adults that make plans for their children's future.

Future-Oriented Paternalism Revisited

If the considerations of the last sections are correct, future-oriented paternalism is under pressure. We have seen that for conceptual reasons the instrumental conception of childhood provides a straightforward justification for future-oriented paternalism. If the future interests of the child have more normative weight than its actual interests, the child should subordinate its current interests in cases of conflicting interests. Because I have presupposed that children need the guidance of adults or their parents respectively, the ingredients for the justification of future-oriented paternalism are at hand for the adherent of the instrumental conception of childhood. However, this argument in favor of future-oriented paternalism is invalid because one of its premises is wrong, namely that the future interests of the child have in principle more normative weight than its current interests. It has been pointed out that the radical shift of the child-liberationists is not adequate because it neglects vital parts of the nature of children, especially children's vulnerability. Children are particularly vulnerable concerning goods that might be relevant for them as adults. Abandoning future-oriented paternalism altogether would mean to neglect this vital developmental part of children's lives, such as education and moral or social development. This comes close to a dilemmatic situation: on the one hand, future-oriented paternalism is morally flawed because its underlying rationale is invalid. On the other hand, we need future-oriented paternalism to do justice to the child's future interests as an adult. What is needed is a revised definition of future-oriented paternalism that is not biased toward the future interests of the child and that respects, in other words, the intrinsic goods of childhood. Consider again the definition of future-oriented paternalism as it has been introduced in section "Introduction" of this paper:

> *Future-oriented paternalism*: (i) The subordination of its current interests in relation to its future interests is in the best interest of the child. (ii) In order to fulfill proposition (i), children need the guidance of adults (external interests).

---

[3] Jean-Jacques Rousseau arguably started out taking this position (Rousseau 1979). Rousseau literally invented the concept of `negative education' which seems to entail the idea that childhood is valuable per se. However, to elaborate on this interesting aspect would clearly exceed the limited scope of this paper.

Because the general legitimacy of paternalism in relation to children has been accepted in this paper (see section "Introduction"), the major failure of this definition of future-oriented paternalism has to be in proposition (i) demanding the general subordination of children's current interests in relation to children's future interests as adults. It is proposition (i) of the definition of future-oriented paternalism which neglects children's interests in the intrinsic goods of childhood. The adherent of the instrumental conception of childhood may say that proposition (i) is compatible with respecting the goods of childhood, but only insofar as they contribute to the goods of adulthood, such as autonomy and rationality. There is no leeway in the instrumental conception of childhood for respecting the goods of childhood as intrinsic goods of childhood. If this is morally flawed, as I have argued, then we need a revised version of proposition (i) that takes proper account of the current and the future interests of the child. However, and by means of our analysis, not all interests of children matter equally. As has been pointed out in the previous section, what gives children's current interests value is that they are intrinsic goods of childhood. Consider the following suggestion for a revised version of proposition (i):

(i*) The subordination of its current interests in relation to its future interests is in the best interest of the child if those of his/hers current interests are considered which are related to the intrinsic goods of childhood.

Proposition (i*) does not neglect children's interests in intrinsic goods of childhood. It does not neglect children's future prospects either. It simply demands that those later goods, such as autonomy and education, have to be balanced against children's interest in purposeless play, imagination and joy. However, there is still a fundamental problem to solve: namely the fair consideration of the child's current *and* future interests. There will be cases of conflict between what we may call a good childhood and the child's later interests as an adult. In order to test our intuitions concerning proposition (i*), let us consider the three following cases:

Normal Norman: Norman is a normally talented child when it comes to music. His parents want him to become a virtuous piano player later in life. Driven by this idea, Norman's parents urge him to attend piano lessons several times a week. This frustrates Norman because he is more interested in playing soccer with his friends.

Talented Ted: Ted is a highly talented child when it comes to music. His parents want him to become a virtuous piano player later in life. Driven by this idea, Ted's parents urge him to attend piano lessons several times a week. This frustrates Ted because he is more interested in playing soccer with his friends.

Handicapped Hannah: Hannah is physically handicapped in her hand-motoric, and piano lessons help her to train her fine-motoric skills. Hannah's parents want her to take piano lessons several times a week because this is considered the most effective way to overcome her condition. However, this frustrates young Hannah because she is more interested in playing soccer with her friends.

In Norman's case, the parents might be driven by their own ambitions. For the sake of argument, let us assume that Norman's parents truly believe that becoming a virtuous piano player later in life is in their son's best interest. However, most people would not accept their doing so if their son ends up full of frustration. This seems to be a strong intuition and it is forcefully supported by the above mentioned conception of childhood, according to which there are intrinsic goods of childhood. This conception entails that childhood is valuable because it is full of joyful, playful and imaginative activity. Accordingly, Norman's parents simply do not pay proper respect to Norman's right to having such a childhood if they pressure him to take piano lessons. There is a default-disclaimer to this line of thought. One might argue that children need pressure, at least sometimes, because they usually lack the stamina for long-term projects such as learning an instrument. However, this even supports the idea of a childhood constituted by intrinsic goods of childhood. Accepting the relevance of those goods does not mean a laissez fair attitude towards children. Quite on the contrary: parents are demanded to figure out what is their particular child's interest. Listening to children's opinions is as vital in this context as the parent's more experienced perspective. In some cases it might be better to support children's inclination to stop their musical training, while in others it might be evident that this inclination is a rather passing mood. Hence in Norman's case the parents should try to figure out together with Norman which future-oriented projects could be compatible with his current interests in joyful play and imaginative activity. This is the deeper meaning of treating Norman as an equal. To be clear, the parents neglect their future-oriented educational duties if they allow every mood of their son to put an end to long-term projects such as learning an instrument. But they also neglect their duties if they are only oriented by future-oriented considerations. In doing so, they would not be considering Norman's interests on a fair level.

Things become more complicated in Ted's case. To make the point as clear as possible, let us assume that Ted is a superior musical talent. Let us further assume, for the sake of argument that Ted's parents believe to be acting in Ted's best interest. They might argue in the following way: "If we don't push Ted in such a way that we urge or even force him to practice several hours a day, he won't be able to realize his talent. This, in turn, will make him unhappy later in life. He might even be angry with us later because we didn't push him enough." There is something to be said for this line of argument. Unusual talent needs special care. Further, the assumption that undeveloped talent will be a source of frustration later in life seems to be justified. However, even making this point does not entail that Ted's parents are entitled to neglect their son's interest in joy, imagination and play. They have special duties that are related to Ted's unique musical talent. It might be the case that balancing those duties against Ted's interest in the intrinsic goods of childhood is more complicated than in other cases. Nonetheless, they are not entitled to ignore their son's interests even if they sometimes might be in conflict with their aspirations. As in Norman's case the parents could, firstly, try to engage Ted in a playful way in his piano lessons. However, what if this is not enough to develop Ted's unique talent? Probably Ted's talent is a normative reason to push him more than, say, Norman's parents should push their son. It could be considered as a normative reason if we assume that self-fulfillment is of normative weight and that the training of talent is a vital part of this. However, even if this is acceptable, even if we justify future-oriented paternalism in this way, it is not sufficient for ignoring Ted's interests in joyful play and imagination completely.

The case of Hannah seems to be somewhat similar to Ted's. Again, let us assume that Hannah's parents are only motivated by what they believe to be in Hannah's best interest. They might have seen the best experts in the field of fine motoric development that gave them the advice about the piano lessons and that only daily training would help. What is similar in the cases of Hannah and of Ted is that in both cases there is a strong rationale, a highly justified prediction that the adult person will be extremely frustrated if the parents do not do what they can to make sure that their children make the best out of their condition. In the same way it seems to be rational to predict that they might even address reproaches toward their parents when they are grown up. However, there are differences between both cases. In Ted's case the full development of talent is at stake. In Hannah's case the parents want to surmount their daughter's illness. Hence, in Hannah's case we have to balance Hannah's health (especially later in life) against her current interest in intrinsic goods of childhood. And again, surely Hannah's parents have a much more complicated business in making such decisions. But they still have to be aware of their child's interest in goods such as purposelessness play and imagination. There might be unpalatable situations when treatment and specific therapies are so vital that there are good reasons to neglect such interests. However, such reasons have to be considered carefully, and this is exactly what good parents have to do.

What these examples help to see more clearly is that proposition (i*) cannot be applied to all cases without paying attention to the specific situation of the case. When weighing children's current and future interests, we always have to ask which goods are at stake in the future. In some cases future-goods such as self-fulfillment and autonomy might justify the subordination of children's current interests in the intrinsic goods of childhood such as joyful play and imagination. However, even if the former are only accessible if the latter are neglected, parents should be careful with their judgment. Firstly, they do not treat children as equals if they do not pay adequate respect to their interest in the intrinsic goods of childhood. As I have argued in section "Conceptions of childhood" of this paper, children should be considered equals from a moral point of view. Secondly, there might be cases of conflict, and in some cases such as Hannah's or Ted's it might be difficult to find an exact solution that is fair to the child's current and future interests. However, even if it is difficult the parents should at least try to find a way that comes close to such a solution. Thirdly, it should be clear that children are dependent on their parent's judgment. Whatever parents decide, in the end the children will have to live with the consequences of these decisions. If parents should have the right to make decisions on behalf of their offspring, and if children's interests count equally, parents should be aware of their roles as (good) parents. If this is true then future-oriented paternalism cannot be defined in general, furthermore we would have to accept that proposition (i*) can only function as a so called "rule of thumb" which provides orientation in similar situations.

Conclusion

Future-oriented paternalism is a salient feature of most children's lives. AS in the quoted song by Cat Stevens, many parents think it to be in their children's best interest if they subordinate their current interests in relation to their future interests as adults. In this paper it has been argued that this is morally questionable. It is morally questionable because children as equals are not mere instruments of their parent's educational aims. Rather, as equals they are ends in themselves and have to be respected in their interests. It has been pointed out that children have an interest in the intrinsic goods of childhood such as joy, play and imagination and that this interest represents a normative reason against future-oriented paternalism. Because children have developmental interests that require future-oriented paternalism we ended up in contemplating the following dilemma: On the one hand future-oriented paternalism is in the child's developmental interest, on the other hand future-oriented paternalism seems to neglect children's interest in the intrinsic goods of childhood. As a solution a revised definition of future-oriented paternalism has been suggested. This definition of future-oriented paternalism entails the basic idea of future-oriented paternalism, namely that it is legitimate if parents paternalize their children in order to make sure that later educational aims such as autonomy, happiness or self-fulfillment are attainable. However, it adds the requirement that paternalistic action has to address the child's interest in goods such as joy, imagination and play. It has been pointed out at the end of this paper that there is no 'clinical' metric for any consideration of children's current and future interests because the situations of parents and of children are too different to bring them under one general principle. However, as a "rule of thumb" the revised definition of future-oriented paternalism seems to capture the relevant ideas to solve the dilemma.

References

Archard, D. 2004. *Children. Rights and childhood.* London: Routledge.
Aristotle. 2009. *Nicomachean ethics.* Oxford: Oxford University Press.
Dworkin, G. 1972. Paternalism. *The Monist* 56: 64–84.
Dworkin, G. 1977. DeFunis v. Sweatt. In *Equality and preferential treatment: A "Philosophy and Public Affairs" reader,* ed. M. Cohen, 63–84. Princeton: Princeton University Press.
Farson, R. 1974. *Birthrights.* London: Macmillan.
Gardner, J.F. 1998. *Family and familia in Roman law and live.* Oxford: Oxford University Press.
Gheaus, A. 2014. The intrinsic goods of childhood and the just society. In *The nature of children's well-being,* ed. A. Bagattini and C. Macleod, 35–53. Dordrecht: Springer.
Gopnik, A. 2009. *The philosophical baby.* New York: Picador.
Holt, J. 1974. *Escape from childhood. The needs and rights of children.* New York: Penguin.
Kafka, F. 1995. *The complete stories.* New York: Shocken Books.
Kant, I. 1996. *The metaphysic of morals.* Cambridge: Cambridge University Press.
Locke, J. 1988. *Two treatises of government.* Cambridge: Cambridge University Press.
Mackenzie, C. 2013. *Vulnerability. New essays in ethics and feminist philosophy.* Oxford: Oxford University Press.

Macleod, C. 2010. Primary goods, capabilities, and children. In *Measuring justice. Primary goods and capabilities,* ed. I. Robeyns and H. Brighouse, 174–193. Cambridge: Cambridge University Press.

Plato. 2008. *The republic.* Oxford: Oxford University Press.

Rousseau, J.J. 1979. *Emile: Or on education.* New York: Basic Books.

Schapiro, T. 1999. What is a child? *Ethics* 109(4): 715–738.

Chapter 3
Who Gets to Decide? Children's Competence, Parental Authority, and Informed Consent

Allyn Fives

Abstract One area of social life with considerable importance for the exercise of power over children is informed consent. The question posed here is whether children should be permitted to make decisions that authorize their participation in research and/or their receipt of medical care, or whether someone else should make those decisions on their behalf, namely a parent or someone charged by the state with acting in a parent's absence. Adults are permitted to make informed consent decisions when they are judged competent to do so, and this paper will explore children's competence to make informed consent decisions. In defining competence, some give priority to the capacity for autonomous self-determination while others prioritize the capacity to make decisions that will promote one's well-being. However, conflicts may arise between the judgment that we ought to respect children's autonomy and the judgment that we ought not do so but rather promote children's well-being. If such moral dilemmas can arise in deciding whether children are competent, it follows competent persons are able to perceive when moral judgments come into conflict and when such a conflict presents as a moral dilemma, and are prepared to deal with, and are capable of dealing with, such a conflict. It is also argued that competence is not an all-or-nothing category but rather admits of differences in degree and, in particular, children's capacity for competence evolves and develops. Also, although the exercise of parental authority in most cases is a limit on children's voluntariness, it can be exercised in such a way as to promote children's competence. It will be argued here that authoritative parenting can provide opportunities for joint decision-making between parents and children and in that way can promote the development of children's competence. The implications for the laws and policies of the state are significant. The argument of this paper suggests the state should support children's rights to make informed consent decisions and also should require that parents support their children's free and informed decision making.

Keywords Children • Competence • Dilemmas • Informed consent • Medical research • Parenting

A. Fives (✉)
UNESCO Child and Family Research Centre, National University of Ireland, Galway, Ireland
e-mail: allyn.fives@nuigalway.ie

© Springer International Publishing Switzerland 2016
J. Drerup et al. (eds.), *Justice, Education and the Politics of Childhood*,
Philosophy and Politics – Critical Explorations 1,
DOI 10.1007/978-3-319-27389-1_3

Introduction

One area of social life with considerable importance for the exercise of power over children is informed consent. The question posed here is whether children should be permitted to make decisions that authorize their participation in research and/or their receipt of medical care, or whether someone else should make those decisions on their behalf, namely a parent or someone charged by the state with acting in a parent's absence. This paper addresses one element of informed consent, the competence required to make informed consent decisions. Every day, health care providers, researchers, and relatives are tasked with deciding whether *adult* patients and *adult* subjects are competent to make decisions about their medical treatment and/or their research participation (Buchanan 2004). Such decisions must be made concerning *children* when they are entitled by law to provide autonomous consent. In many jurisdictions, children aged 16 and above are entitled to provide autonomous consent for health care provision, and a minority of jurisdictions has introduced adolescents' ability to consent to research as well (Felzmann et al. 2010). This paper examines some of the ethical issues that arise in situations where children are entitled by law to provide autonomous consent. As adults are permitted to make such decisions when they are judged competent to do so (Beauchamp and Childress 2009), it may be argued that, if children have the competence to make an informed consent decision then, in the first instance at least, they should be permitted to make those decisions. However, there is considerable controversy concerning both what capacities are required for competence and whether we should think of competence as a threshold.

In defining competence, both in respect of children and adults, some give priority to the capacity for autonomous self-determination (Feinberg 1971; Berg et al. 1996; Beauchamp and Childress 2009) while others prioritize the capacity to make decisions that will promote one's well-being (Buchanan and Brock 1986; Buchanan 2004). However, in this paper it shall be argued that we may be faced with a moral dilemma in deciding whether or not children are competent, that is, a conflict between two moral judgments that we are disposed to make relevant to deciding what to do (Williams 1965). In particular, conflicts may arise between the judgment that we ought to respect children's autonomy and the judgment that we ought not do so but rather promote children's well-being. If such moral dilemmas can arise in deciding whether children are competent, it follows competence itself entails more than *merely* either the capacity to make decisions that best promote one's well-being or the capacity to autonomously pursue one's aims and objectives. Competent persons in addition are able to perceive when moral judgements come into conflict and when such a conflict presents as a moral dilemma, and are prepared to deal with, and are capable of dealing with, such a conflict.

In the literature on informed consent, both in respect of children and adults, competence is a threshold dividing those whose decisions we should respect from those whose decisions we need not respect (Beauchamp and Childress 2009). Voluntariness also is thought of as a threshold dividing those who are free from the influence of others from those who are not (Hawkins and Emanuel 2005). One approach to children's informed consent is to lower the competence and voluntariness thresholds, which is the case with the status of a "mature minor" (Partridge 2014). An alternative approach is to argue that competence is not an all-or-nothing category but rather admits of differences in degree and, in particular, children's capacity for competence evolves and develops. Also, although the exercise of parental authority in many cases is a limit on children's voluntariness, it can be exercised in such a way as to promote children's competence. Of particular relevance is the psychology literature on *authoritative* parenting, which is a parenting style that strikes the optimal balance between responsiveness and demandingness (Baumrind 1996). It will be argued here that authoritative parenting can provide opportunities for joint decision-making between parents and children and in that way can promote the development of children's competence. The implications for the laws and policies of the state are significant. The argument of this paper suggests the state should support children's rights to make informed consent decisions and also should require that parents support their children's free and informed decision making.

Competence and Children

Informed consent has a number of necessary elements (Beauchamp and Childress 2009: 120–121). First, those consenting must have sufficient competence to understand and to decide, and sufficient voluntariness in deciding. In addition, those seeking informed consent are responsible for the full disclosure of material information and (in therapeutic procedures) the recommendation of a plan, while those whose consent is being sought must have sufficient understanding of both of these. Finally, there are two consent elements, both the decision in favor of a plan and the authorization of the chosen plan. According to Beauchamp and Childress these elements of informed consent apply to adults as well as children (ibid.: 116). Therefore, if children are to provide informed consent, for research participation and/or medical provision, they must consent and also understand the information provided, but also the children themselves must be sufficiently competent and their behavior sufficiently voluntary. It should be noted that competence refers to "the ability to perform a task," in this case the task of making a decision, and a person, in this instance a child, may be considered competent "relative to the particular decision to be made" without being considered competent relative to other tasks or other decisions (ibid.: 112, 116).

There are rival standards of competence, ranging from the very weakest to the strongest. A *weak* standard defines competence "exclusively as an ability to carry out certain mental tasks: to understand the information relevant to making the decision; to appreciate how this information applies to oneself in one's current situation; and to realize that one is being asked to make a decision about the treatment(s) being suggested" (Culver and Gert 1990: 622). As this weak standard does not include any requirement of rationality, on this account, a competent individual may nonetheless make irrational decisions. In contrast, the *strong* standard requires not only "the ability to state a preference" and the ability to "understand one's situation and its consequences" and to "understand relevant information," but also the ability to "give a reason," to "give a rational reason," to "give risk/benefit-related reasons," and to "reach a reasonable decision (as judged, for example, by a reasonable person standard)" (Beauchamp and Childress 2009: 114–115). It should be noted that proponents of the weak standard accept that the rationality of people's decisions *is* relevant to whether they should be permitted to make those decisions. For instance, an adult judged competent by the weak standard can still make irrational decisions, and when a refusal of medical treatment is "seriously irrational, as when the consequences are death or serious and permanent injury," "the refusal should be overruled" (Culver and Gert 1990: 623). That is, even those who propose a weak standard include all the elements of the strong standard in deciding whether or not to permit individuals to make choices. Therefore, although there is disagreement over whether irrational decisions are by definition also incompetent decisions, there is consensus that we are not required to respect seriously irrational decisions, and this is the case for adults and children.

The *strong* standard, discussed above, is informed by both the value of individual well-being and the value of individual autonomy. Competent individuals can provide informed consent because they have the capacity to make decisions about how to govern their lives generally and also how to promote their well-being specifically (Appelbaum et al. 1987; Appelbaum 2007). However, those who have attempted to conceptualize the moral foundations of competence acknowledge that the values of individual well-being and individual autonomy "can sometimes conflict" (Buchanan and Brock 1986: 30). While the value of well-being requires that we sometimes protect individuals from the consequences of their own decisions, autonomy is of value as people want to make decisions about their own life, and the desire to make such decisions "is in part independent of whether they believe that they are always in a position to make the best choice" (ibid.: 29). This conflict of values can also be represented a clash of moral doctrines. While on the one hand the utilitarian position is that an act is right insofar as it promotes happiness or well-being (Mill 1861), on the other hand the Kantian position requires that we always respect the autonomy or humanity of persons and it is this and not the consequences for well-being that is to be prioritized (Ross 2006; see Berg et al. 1996).

In the two examples presented below the possibility for value conflict is demonstrated when parents and physicians were required to make judgments about children's competence. In both examples, parents and physicians concluded that the decision to enroll in research should be taken out of the children's hands. Can these moral judgments be justified and if so how?

Two Examples

Example (a): Mary is 16 years old, recently diagnosed with cancer, and wishes to participate in a Phase I oncology trial. As the purpose of such trials typically is to determine the safe dose range and the possible side-effects of an innovative cancer treatment, they "expose patient-subjects to significant risks of harm without a reasonable expectation of direct therapeutic benefit" (Jansen 2009: 28). Mary knows that it is not in her best medical interests to enroll, but wishes to do so so as to contribute to the scientific and medical efforts to cure cancer. Agreeing to participate in a trial "out of a concern for the good of future patients" is an altruistic decision (ibid.: 27). Mary is not suffering from a "therapeutic misconception" as she does not misconceive her participation in a trial as therapeutic in nature (Beauchamp and Childress 2009: 129). Rather, she is primarily motivated by altruism.

Mary's wish to enroll seems to be in accord with her autonomous pursuit of her own, altruistic, values. If this is the case, and if Mary's parents give priority to the value of autonomy they will conclude that, in respecting her autonomy, Mary should be free to make this decision herself. However, in our example, her parents judge Mary to be incompetent, and take the decision out of her hands. Their moral judgment is in line with Buchanan and Brock's position, which gives priority to the value of individual well-being. In a position worked out for elderly and incompetent adults but also applied to the case of children, Buchanan and Brock argue that incompetent decision-making just is decision-making that leads to harmful consequences for the decision-maker. Although we should respect the autonomy of those who are competent, this is so because competent individuals are less likely to make decisions that will harm their own interests: a patient's choice "should be respected" when there are grounds for believing that such a choice "is reasonably in accord with the patient's good and does reasonably protect or promote the patient's well-being" (Buchanan and Brock 1986: 36). In deciding whether or not Mary is competent to make this decision, we make a consequentialist calculation of the effects of Mary's decision on her own well-being.

Example (b): The second example is a randomized controlled trial (RCT) comparing hypericum (St. John's Wort), sertraline (Zoloft), and placebo in the treatment of major depression (Miller and Brody 2003). In RCTs, treatments are withheld and treatments are assigned to patients not on the basis of therapeutic need but instead by a random process (Altman 1991; Jaded 1998). We say that the medical community it is out of *equipoise* when it takes the view that the deal offered to participants in a trial is bad or not in their interests (Fried 1974; Marquis 1983; Freedman 1987; Jansen 2005), and in such a case the attending physician should advise against enrolment in the trial (Miller and Weijer 2006). In our example, the researchers wish to recruit John, a 16 year old boy suffering from depression. The attending physician has advised that this trial offers a *bad deal* for John, and while his parents accept this advice John does not. John is not suffering from a therapeutic misconception: he is aware that his participation in the trial is not therapeutic in nature. Although John is aware that the medical community is not equally poised between the relevant treatment arms, in contrast he believes that his depression will be equally well treated by hypericum, placebo, or sertraline. While he rejects his physician's view that sertraline is the *better* treatment, he believes that each of the three treatments is equally effective. Unlike Mary in our first example, John is not motivated by altruism, but rather has attempted to make a decision about how best to promote his well-being. It should be noted the results of the trial found no statistically significant differences between hypericum and placebo or between sertraline and placebo (Miller and Brody 2003).

Were John's parents justified in taking the decision out of his hands? As we saw, one approach to the conceptualization of competence is to give priority to autonomy. For instance, Joel Feinberg rejects the view that protecting "a person from himself is always a valid ground for interference in his affairs" but concedes that such interference is valid under certain conditions, namely, when the person's risky behavior is *substantially nonvoluntary* (1971: 106, 124). If the risks have been taken on the basis of an autonomous, deliberate choice, which requires "time, information, a clear head, and highly developed rational faculties" (ibid.: 111) then we are not justified in preventing that risky behavior (see Beauchamp and Childress 2009: 113). However, if we follow Feinberg in giving priority to autonomy we can arrive at two incompatible moral conclusions about what to do. Even if John can be shown to have sufficient time, information, clarity, and rationality, it may be decided that his decision was not sufficiently voluntary. Let us assume John has done a considerable amount of research and is aware for instance that there is an honest null hypothesis at the start of the trial (the hypothesis that there would be no significant difference in effect between placebo and either hypericum or sertraline). He may believe this justifies his decision to enroll. Yet, the views of the medical community could be used to support the conclusion that John is deciding in a way that is rash or ill-considered or ill-informed and therefore not fully voluntary.

Moral Dilemmas

Kantian and utilitarian positions claim to provide ways to arrive at moral conclusions about what is right all things considered. Whenever there seems to be a tension or conflict between values, it is nonetheless always clear what is right. For the Kantian, we should respect autonomy, and for the utilitarian we should promote well-being. However, what our two examples suggest is the possibility that, in some instances, we do not have the resources to resolve conflicts between moral conclusions and that we are faced with moral dilemmas.

A moral conflict or dilemma is a case "where there is a conflict between two moral judgments that a man is disposed to make relevant to deciding what to do" (Williams 1965: 108). Therefore, a moral dilemma is "a situation in which the agent morally ought to do A and morally ought to do B, while he cannot do A as well as B" (de Haan 2001: 269). More precisely, there are two basic forms the dilemma can take. The first is where "it seems I ought to do each of two things, but I cannot do both" (Williams 1965: 108). Such a dilemma can arise when considering the decision-making of adults, and such a dilemma arose in our first example concerning a 16 year old girl. It is equally correct to say of Mary's parents that they ought to promote her well-being *and* they ought to respect her autonomy. However, because it was not possible to do both, they were faced with a moral dilemma. If they promote her well-being, they are doing the right thing, but for that reason they are not doing what they ought to do, namely respecting her autonomy. The second form a dilemma can take "is that in which something which (it seems to me) I ought to do in respect of certain of its features also has other features in respect of which (it seems) I ought not to do it" (ibid.). Once again, this type of dilemma can arise in respect of adults, and it arose in our second example concerning a 16 year old boy. It is equally correct to say of John's parents they ought to respect John's autonomy in the decision he has made about how to promote his well-being *and* they ought not to do so but rather protect him from the consequences of his poorly-made decisions. Once again, as these are mutually exclusive options, they cannot do both and are faced with a moral dilemma.

A dilemmatic conflict is one where even when we do what we ought to do we are forced to do something that morally speaking we should not do. Crucially, we should feel regret in these situations, even if we are confident that we have acted for the best in trying to resolve the conflict. This is the case because there is a "moral remainder of disagreeableness" in the form of obligations unfulfilled (Williams 1978: 63). For instance, if we take a decision out of a child's hands so as to promote her well-being and in so doing fail to respect her autonomy, as in Mary's situation, then it is correct to feel regret for the fact that we have violated her autonomy even if we believe that all things considered we have done the right thing in promoting her well-being. If we should feel regret in dilemmatic situations, then it seems to follow that our dominant philosophical systems, utilitarianism and Kantianism, are inadequate to the task of resolving these conflicts. Because it is assumed as a philosophical and moral truth that we should always prioritize the fundamental value, whether well-being or autonomy, both the utilitarian and the Kantian will conclude that any conflict of values is only apparent rather than real, and therefore there is no call for regret when we resolve the apparent conflict by giving priority to the fundamental value (see Hare 1981; Veatch 1995).

What is to be avoided is a moral philosophy that claims to provide a criterion of moral judgment that, when it is applied, removes what were only apparent moral conflicts and therefore removes the justification for moral regret when we have done what is right. What is required instead is an awareness of the plurality of moral values and the possibility for conflict between those values, and yet also an approach whereby we may hope to arrive at moral conclusions about what ought to be done. All of this is possible in a form of practical reasoning guided by the requirement of reasonableness. On one definition, *reasonableness* "involves a readiness to politically address others of different persuasions in terms of public reasons" (Freeman 2000: 401); and *public* reasons are considerations "we might reasonably expect that [others], as free and equal citizens, might also accept" (Rawls 1997: 579; see also Scanlon 2002; Fives 2013). Public reasons do not presuppose the truth of any one moral doctrine, such as utilitarianism or Kantianism, or the truth of any one moral value, such as well-being or autonomy. So public reasons are considerations that you and I can share, and you and I can arrive at a shared decision on the basis of those considerations, even while acknowledging the plurality of sometimes conflicting value commitments.

Competence and Reasonableness

So far I have argued that when making moral judgments about children's competence we may be faced with a dilemmatic conflict of values. Therefore, in judging
children's competence we must be reasonable and engage in public reasoning. A
further implication is that, if decisions about health care provision and research
participation can generate moral conflicts, for children to be considered competent
they also must have the capacity to address moral dilemmas and so they too must be
reasonable. We can look at how the person capable of reaching a reasonable decision, the person who satisfies the highest standard of competence, might do so in
Example (a) and Example (b). In both examples, as a basic requirement, the reasonable person must be aware of the moral dilemma's presence.

In Example (a), Mary wished to enroll in the trial even while knowing that to do
so would not promote her well-being. If she is fully reasonable, she will be aware
that different values are promoted in different ways by the decision. She will be
aware also that the decision presents a conflict of values, as choosing to enroll in the
trial promotes the autonomous pursuit of her good but does not promote her own
well-being. She must also understand the severity of the risks for her well-being and
the odds of those risks. In addition, her adherence to her own altruistic values must
not be such as to impair her reasoning, as it must be compatible with a willingness
to give full consideration to how this altruistic behavior will affect her own well-
being. If this is true of Mary, she is well placed to make a decision that can be presented as an attempt to resolve a moral dilemma. In contrast, if she is unable or
unwilling to gauge the severity of the risks to her well-being, or if she is unaware of
a conflict of values this would suggest that Mary does not possess the competence
required to make this difficult decision.

In Example (b) John wished to enroll in a trial so as to promote his own well-
being. If he is fully reasonable he should be aware that others disagree with him
about the severity and the likelihood of the risks associated with the trial. He should
be aware that such disagreement was understandable given the scientific evidence
and the views of the medical profession. In addition, he should appreciate the
importance of this decision within his own life, including how central and far reaching the choice is within his plan of life (Brock 1988: 551). At the same time, if John
shows clear signs that he does not appreciate that it is understandable for others to
believe his decision-making will lead to significant risks for his well-being, or an
inability to judge the significance of the decision within his overall plan of life, once
again this would suggest he does not possess the required competence.

Making Children Competent: Lowering the Threshold

So far I have focused on the capacities of individuals who are competent to make
informed consent decisions. I now ask are children competent in this way? When
and how do children become competent? In the literature on informed consent,

some have argued that judgments of competence are of an all-or-nothing quality. Although competence is relative to a specific task, nonetheless it is argued that the function of competence judgments is to distinguish two classes of persons: "persons whose decisions should be solicited or accepted from persons whose decisions need not or should not be solicited or accepted" (Beauchamp and Childress 2009: 111). Voluntariness, like competence, also is thought of as a threshold. A "person acts voluntarily if he or she wills the action without being under the control of another's influence" (ibid.: 133). Just as informed consent cannot be sought from those who are incompetent, it is not possible to coerce or to infringe the autonomy of those who are incapable of voluntariness: "Coercion subverts real choice and so cannot meaningfully be said to occur when real choice is not even an option" (Hawkins and Emanuel 2005: 17). Taken together, the threshold criteria of competence and voluntariness would suggest that if children do not meet the thresholds, morally speaking there are no reasons why they should make decisions in informed consent procedures and instead those decisions should be made by the relevant responsible adults, usually parents.

A recent development in both law and medical practice has been to lower, or bring forward in time, the thresholds of competence and voluntariness. In this way a substantial minority of adolescents are re-categorized as being entitled by law to provide autonomous consent. The *mature minor* is a legal construct that "considers adolescents, as far as possible, as equivalent to adults for the purpose of medical decision-making" (Partridge 2014: 2; Hunter and Pierscionek 2007). Once the adolescent has passed the new, lower threshold, in many cases the age of 16, they are considered entitled to consent to medical treatment, and this has been implemented in a number of jurisdictions (Felzmann et al. 2010). The rationale for lowering the thresholds of competence and voluntariness is that many adolescents have the capacities required to make informed consent decisions. For instance, it is argued that many adolescents have developed past the stage of *autonoetic consciousness* (Metcalfe and Son 2012), which involves the ability to understand their own situation and its consequences and the relevant information, and have attained fully developed agency, "a notion of self that is partly constructed out of our descriptions and some articulated sense of our lives" (Baker 2013: 317).

The lowering of the thresholds for competence and voluntariness has been criticized, however. Some have argued that many adolescents will not be ready to take on this responsibility. The empirical data on adolescents' decision-making capacity provides evidence of "faulty perceptions of risk, inadequate capacities to gauge the long-term outcomes of their decisions, and more limited control of their impulses" (Partridge 2014: 2; see Taylor 2013). However, empirical studies have returned mixed findings in regard to how the competence of adolescents compares to that of adults (Halpern-Felsher and Cauffman 2001; Miller et al. 2004). For instance, no differences were found between 10th grade adolescents and adults in terms of their "comprehension of the research procedures, risks and benefits, voluntary nature of participation, and confidentiality protections" (Bruzzese and Fisher 2003: 13; see Weithorn and Campbell 1982).

Therefore, the data do not seem to establish with certainty whether adolescents do or do not have sufficient competency for decision-making in research and medicine. In any case, even if adolescents are considered equivalent to adults for the purpose of decision making, it does not follow that each and every adolescent is competent. As is the case with any adult, any adolescent can still be considered incompetent based on an examination of their capacity to make the relevant decision. Therefore, lowering thresholds cannot provide the final word on whether any one adolescent is considered competent to provide informed consent. Rather, when we lower the thresholds, we commit ourselves to treat adolescents and adults alike, but what we already know is that many adults are judged incompetent to make informed consent decisions.

Helping Children Become Competent: Joint-Decision Making

There is a second argument against the lowering of thresholds. Although a lower threshold may grant many adolescents a right to make decisions they did not previously enjoy, nonetheless, even when we lower thresholds we still treat competence and voluntariness as all-or-nothing qualities and it is a mistake to do so. An alternative approach is to acknowledge that adolescents have competence in a formative state, and also this is a state that can be nurtured and developed by parents and other adults. In particular, it is argued that making decisions in collaboration with their parents can help nurture the decision-making capacities of adolescents (Partridge 2014: 6). Research has shown that parent-child engagement in decision making has a positive impact on adolescent affective decision making as well on the reduction of risky behavior such as binge drinking (Xiao et al. 2011).

A collaborative approach to decision-making fits with what Diana Baumrind (1996) refers to as "authoritative" parenting style, which has the optimal combination of responsiveness and demandingness. Authoritative parenting is characterized by high levels of both parental interest and active participation in the child's life, open communication with the child, high levels of trust, encouragement of psychological autonomy, but also high levels of monitoring and high levels of awareness of what the child is doing, with whom, and where (Aunola et al. 2000: 207). In sharp contrast, authoritarian parents are unlikely to let children have any say in decisions that affect their lives, and permissive and neglectful parents are more likely to let children do whatever they wish however risky it may be. Authoritative parenting provides a way for children's autonomy to be nurtured through collaboration in decision-making with their parents. In authoritative parenting, parental authority is exercised over children and therefore this counts as a restriction on their voluntariness. Nonetheless, as with Vygotsky's (1978) account of the Zone of Proximal Development, parental authority is employed in a supportive manner (as a proximal outcome) to empower children (as a distal outcome).

If we conceptualize children's competence as something parents can nurture and enhance we do away with a threshold view of both competence and voluntariness.

This allows us to appreciate that some are partly competent, that their competence can be enhanced through collaborative decision-making, and that parental authority can be used so as to promote children's competence (Fives 2015). How should we assist children to become competent? As Joseph Raz argues in regard to the related concept of "the capacity sense of autonomy," the capacity to control and create one's own life, to promote autonomy we must create an adequate range of options for people to choose from as well as "help in creating the inner capacities required for the conduct of an autonomous life" (1986: 408). What is involved in promoting both the inner capacities and the external opportunities for children's competent decision-making in informed consent procedures? The answer to this question may lie in the notion of proximal and distal outcomes.

Conclusions

The argument of this paper has a number of implications for the power exercised by parents over children. On the one hand, it has been argued that children must meet a high standard of competence before they can be free to make informed consent decisions. Competent decision-making requires not only the capacities to express or communicate a preference or choice, to understand his/her own situation and its consequences or the relevant information, and to give a reason, or a rational reason, or a benefit-related reason, or reach a reasonable decision. In addition, the competent individual must be prepared to address a conflict of values and able to attempt to resolve such moral conflicts. It has also been argued that competence and voluntariness are not all-or-nothing thresholds, and that in many cases what is required is joint decision-making involving both parents and their children. This is the case as parents can play an important role in helping their children develop so as to become capable of independent decision-making, but also because parents continue to enjoy rights as parents and continue to be bound by their parental duties of care towards their children.

On the other hand, this paper has argued for considerable limits on parental authority. If we accept that joint decision-making is required for many situations, then parental authority should be exercised so as to promote children's competence and voluntariness. This has import implications for the laws and policies of the state. For it follows that the state should support children's rights to make informed consent decisions, but also the state should require that parents support their children's free and informed decision making.

The implications of this paper will be unsettling to many. If parents are expected to promote competent decision-making among their children through joint decision-making, this is a significant and weighty responsibility. Parents are required not only to encourage their children to reason well about how decisions might affect their well-being as well as how those decisions align with their children's values. Parents also are required to foster the awareness in children that even if they reason adequately in these ways they may be left with moral regrets. And parents in addition are required to guide their children as they try to find a path through moral dilemmas that seem most satisfactory from the point of view of reasonable decision-making.

References

Altman, D.G. 1991. Randomization: Essential for reducing bias. *British Medical Journal* 302(6791): 1481–1482.
Appelbaum, P.S. 2007. Assessment of patients' competence to consent to treatment. *The New England Journal of Medicine* 357: 1834–1840.
Appelbaum, P.S., C.W. Lidz, and A. Meisel. 1987. *Informed consent: Legal theory and clinical practice*. New York: Oxford University Press.
Aunola, K., H. Stattin, and J.E. Nurmi. 2000. Parenting styles and adolescents' achievement strategies. *Journal of Adolescence* 23(2): 205–222.
Baker, J. 2013. Children's agency, interests, and medical consent. *HEC Forum* 25(4): 311–324.
Baumrind, D. 1996. The discipline controversy revisited. *Family Relations* 45(4): 405–414.
Beauchamp, T.L., and J.F. Childress. 2009. *Principles of biomedical ethics*, 6th ed. Oxford: Oxford University Press.
Berg, J.W., P.S. Appelbaum, and T.G. Griso. 1996. Constructing competence: Formulating standards of legal competence to make medical decisions. *Rutgers Law Review* 48: 345–396.
Brock, D.W. 1988. Paternalism and autonomy. *Ethics* 98(April): 550–565.
Bruzzese, J.-M., and C.B. Fisher. 2003. Assessing and enhancing the research consent capacity of children and youth. *Applied Developmental Science* 7(1): 13–26.
Buchanan, A. 2004. Mental capacity, legal competence and consent to treatment. *Journal of Royal Society of Medicine* 97(September): 415–420.
Buchanan, A., and D.W. Brock. 1986. Deciding for others. *The Milbank Quarterly* 64(2): 17–94.
Culver, C.M., and B. Gert. 1990. The inadequacy of incompetence. *The Milbank Quarterly* 68(4): 619–643.
De Haan, J. 2001. The definition of moral dilemmas: A logical problem. *Ethical Theory and Moral Practice* 4(3): 267–284.
Feinberg, J. 1971. Legal paternalism. *Canadian Journal of Philosophy* 1(1): 105–124.
Felzmann, H., J. Sixsmith, S. O'Higgins, S. Ni Chonnachtaigh, and S. Nic Gabhainn. 2010. *Ethical review and children's research in Ireland*. Dublin: Office of the Minister for Children and Youth Affairs.
Fives, A. 2013. Non-coercive promotion of values in civic education for democracy. *Philosophy and Social Criticism* 39(6): 577–590.
Fives, A. 2015. Parents, children, and good leadership: Is parental authority compatible with children's freedom? In *Ethics and leadership*, ed. Jacqueline Boaks and Michael Levine. London: Bloomsbury.
Freedman, B. 1987. Equipoise and the ethics of clinical research. *New England Journal of Medicine* 317(3): 141–145.
Freeman, S. 2000. Deliberative democracy: A sympathetic comment. *Philosophy and Public Affairs* 29(4): 371–418.
Fried, C. 1974. *Medical experimentation: Personal integrity and social policy*. New York: American Elsevier.
Halpern-Felsher, B.L., and E. Cauffman. 2001. Costs and benefits of a decision: Decision-making competence in adolescents and adults. *Applied Developmental Psychology* 22: 257–273.
Hare, R.M. 1981. *Moral thinking: Its levels, method, and point*. Oxford: Oxford University Press.
Hawkins, J.S., and E.J. Emanuel. 2005. Clarifying confusions about coercion. *Hastings Center Report* 35(5): 16–19.

Hunter, D., and B.K. Pierscionek. 2007. Children, Gillick competency and consent for involvement in research. *Journal of Medical Ethics* 33(11): 659–662.

Jaded, A. 1998. *Randomised controlled trials: A user's guide*. London: BMJ Books.

Jansen, L.A. 2005. A closer look at the bad deal trial: Beyond clinical equipoise. *Hastings Center Report* 35(5): 29–36.

Jansen, L.A. 2009. The ethics of altruism in clinical research. *Hastings Center Report* 39(4): 26–36.

Marquis, D. 1983. Leaving therapy to chance. *Hastings Center Report* 13(4): 40–47.

Metcalfe, J., and L. Son. 2012. Anoetic, noetic and autonoetic metacognition. In *The foundations of metacognition*, ed. M. Beran, J.R. Brandl, J. Perner, and J. Proust. Oxford: Oxford University Press.

Mill, J.S. 1861. Utilitarianism. In *Liberty and other essays*, ed. John Gray. Oxford: Oxford University Press [1991].

Miller, F.G., and H. Brody. 2003. Therapeutic misconception in the ethics of clinical trials. *Hastings Center Report* 33(3): 19–28.

Miller, P.B., and C. Weijer. 2006. Fiduciary obligation in clinical research. *Journal of Law, Medicine & Ethics* 34(2): 424–440.

Miller, V.A., D. Drotar, and E. Kodish. 2004. Children's competence for assent and consent: A review of empirical findings. *Ethics and Behavior* 14(3): 255–295.

Partridge, B. 2014. *Adolescent pediatric decision-making: A critical reconsideration in the light of the data*. HEC Forum. Published online: http://link.springer.com/article/10.1007/s10730-014-9250-8

Rawls, J. 1997. The idea of public reason revisited. In *John Rawls: Collected papers*, ed. S. Freeman, 573–615. London: Harvard University Press.

Raz, J. 1986. *The morality of freedom*. Oxford: Clarendon.

Ross, L.F. 2006. What is wrong with the physician charter on professionalism. *Hastings Center Report* 36(4): 17–19.

Scanlon, T.M. 2002. Reasons, responsibility, and reliance: Replies to Wallace, Dworkin, and Deigh. *Ethics* 112(3): 519–520.

Taylor, J.S. 2013. Introduction: Children and consent to treatment. *HEC Forum* 25(4): 285–287.

Veatch, R.M. 1995. Resolving conflicts among principles: Ranking, balancing, and specifying. *Kennedy Institute of Ethics Journal* 5(3): 199–218.

Vygotsky, L.S. 1978. *Mind in society: The development of higher psychological processes*. Boston: Harvard University Press.

Weithorn, L., and S. Campbell. 1982. The competency of children and adolescents to make informed treatment decisions. *Child Development* 53(6): 1589–1598.

Williams, B. 1965. Ethical consistency. *Proceedings of the Aristotelian Society* 39: 103–124.

Williams, B. 1978. Politics and moral character. In *Public and private morality*, ed. Stuart Hampshire, 23–53. Cambridge: Cambridge University Press.

Xiao, L., A. Bechara, P.H. Palmer, D.R. Trinidad, Y. Wei, Y. Jia, and C.A. Johnson. 2011. Parent-child engagement in decision making and the development of adolescent affective decision capacity and binge drinking. *Personality and Individual Differences* 51(3): 285–292.

Chapter 4
Capacity, Consistency and the Young

Nicholas John Munn

Abstract Young citizens in modern liberal democratic societies are subject to various limitations on their rights and responsibilities that other citizens are exempt from. In particular, their criminal liability is lessened comparative to other citizens, and their entitlement to make medical and political decisions is reduced. In each of these domains, the justification for the differential treatment of the young is their incapacity. However, the time and methods with which capacity is attributed to young people differ between the medical, criminal and political domains. I argue that modern liberal democratic states owe to young citizens a consistent recognition of their capacity for autonomous decision-making, and that this recognition requires the legal status of young citizens to be updated and standardized over the domains under consideration. This requirement is not commonly satisfied by democratic societies, as the way in which their capacities are judged is inconsistent between the three domains under consideration.

Keywords Youth • Capacity • Voting • Political participation • Consistency

Introduction

Modern liberal democratic societies place various limitations on young people that are not applied to other citizens. These limitations can, as in the case of criminal culpability, diminish the liability of the young citizen for their actions. In other cases, such as medical or political decision-making, these limitations restrict the ability of the young persons affected to make decisions for themselves. An example is that when making medical decisions the best interests of the child, as determined by the relevant medical professionals and, often, their parents or guardians can be used to override the wishes of the young person. Different standards of criminal

N.J. Munn (✉)
Department of Philosophy and Religious Studies, Philosophy & Religious
Studies Programme, University of Waikato,
Hamilton, New Zealand
e-mail: nickmunn@waikato.ac.nz

© Springer International Publishing Switzerland 2016
J. Drerup et al. (eds.), *Justice, Education and the Politics of Childhood,*
Philosophy and Politics – Critical Explorations 1,
DOI 10.1007/978-3-319-27389-1_4

49

responsibility are applicable to young offenders than to those over the age of majority. Young people (usually all under 18) are systematically excluded from formal political participation through voting. Here I argue that the motivation for differential treatment of the young in each of these domains shares a common justification; an attribution of incapacity. In each of the medical, criminal and political domains, certain young people are taken not to be sufficiently capable of making decisions for themselves, to be entitled to make them. Other young people are taken to have the capacity to make their own decisions. However, between these domains, the attribution of capacity differs significantly. I argue that the core of this capacity requirement is shared by all three of these domains. If this is so, then the differential attribution of capacity to young citizens across these domains raises important issues of justice and responsibility. I will argue that modern liberal democratic states owe to young citizens a consistent recognition of their capacity for autonomous decision-making, and that this recognition requires the legal status of young citizens to be updated and standardized over the domains under consideration.

In the section "Normative Framework" I provide a brief analysis of the normative framework in which my claims are embedded, and make the case that the presence or absence of capacity for autonomous decision-making is crucial to the justifiability of our differential treatment of children and young persons. In the section "Limitations placed on young people" I describe the limitations placed on young people in each of the domains outlined above. In the section "The capacity standard", I argue that a single standard of capacity applies in each of these domains. In the section "The composition of capacity" I examine how that standard has come to be applied differently to young people depending on the domain, and address the consistency issues arising from the fact that this standard is applied in this variety of ways. Finally, I suggest some possible explanations of this inconsistency and examine what these mean for the attribution of capacity in the political domain.

Normative Framework

Before turning to the substantial analysis of the three domains I will clarify the normative framework in which this chapter is operating. As I have argued at length in other places, I take capacity to be a trumping consideration (Munn 2012a, b, 2013). That is, the presence of capacity for decision-making is what makes it unacceptable to deny someone the right or ability to make decisions for themselves, and the absence of capacity for decision-making is what creates the conceptual space for other considerations, such as paternalism, to be entertained. One is justified in restricting the decision-making of another on paternalistic grounds, just when the person who is being restricted, is in fact incapable of making the kinds of decisions in question. While it used to be common to argue that age tracked capacity sufficiently well that a simple age limit would suffice to delineate between the capable and incapable, such a position has become increasingly untenable. Andrew Franklin-Hall notes the alleged correlation between (young) age and lack of capacity on what he calls the 'standard view' of when paternalism is justified, while noting that this view does not work for all young persons, and is particularly unconvincing for those aged 14 and above (2013). I have argued that age is a bad proxy for capacity, in that it both fails to include relevantly capable young persons in the moral community, and fails to exclude relevantly incapable adults from the moral community (Munn 2012a).

Inclusion and evaluation on the grounds of capacity is not limited to young people, but is present in considerations of citizenship generally. For example, the disenfranchisement of cognitively impaired individuals, where it is done at all, is done specifically on the grounds that those so disenfranchised are incapable of making the relevant decisions (casting votes in elections) for themselves, and that as such, no wrong is done to them by excluding them from the franchise. Where a disenfranchised individual believes they have the capacity for political participation, they can, as in the US case of Doe v Rowe, challenge their disenfranchisement by showing that they have the relevant capacities. If they successfully show this, the justification for restricting their access to this good, voting, disappears.

Similarly, when we consider the position of young persons and the ways in which we treat them, we must ask ourselves what it is about children and young people that justifies treating them differently from everyone else. I have claimed elsewhere that it is only a lack of capacity that could justify this differential treatment, as any of the other options available generates inconsistencies in application; that is, it is seen and used as a reason to deny children some rights, but not as a reason to deny any others those same rights, even if they have/lack the consideration in question to the same degree as the children being discussed (Munn 2012a, b, 2013). This kind of consideration is noted by Archard and Skivenes, who criticize a tendency to hold children to a standard beyond that to which we hold adults, saying that what they call a principle of equity applies, that "a child should not be judged against a standard of competence by which even most adults would fail." (2009, 10) They go on to note that in various cases following Gillick, the English courts have utilized too high a standard of competency: the courts should have recognized the competence and acted on the wishes of the young persons in question. (Archard and Skivenes 2009)

Throughout this chapter, I intend when discussing capacity to mean the following: A person with the capacity to act in particular ways is a person who is capable of autonomous decision-making in that domain. Further, I take it that the ability to exercise a capacity for autonomous decision-making is a good in its own right, and that denying someone with this ability the right to exercise it is a wrong that should, other things being equal, be avoided. Someone capable of making a decision is entitled to make that decision for themselves. As is widely noted, young people are commonly considered not to be relevantly capable, and thus not to be subject to this norm. Instead, various norms regarding the status and control of children exist, such as the presence of paternalistic protections of children in the law of many countries, and the requirement, in the Convention on the Rights of the Child, that the best interests of the child be taken into account in decision-making, that is, that their welfare be considered. But the application of these other norms to children is only legitimate if it is true that they are not subject to the general capacity/capability norm. The practical domains I consider provide some empirical evidence that children are subject to the capability norm, and that as such in these instances the continued application of paternalistic or welfare based restrictions on their autonomy ought to be rejected: we should recognize and act on the capability of the young people in question.

So, I am making an empirical claim regarding the presence, across the political, criminal and medical domains, of a capacity for autonomous action in young people. The existence of this capacity itself provides a reason to reject particular normative frameworks which are predicated on a lack of this capacity. There may be considerations other than capacity which can operate in conjunction with it to justify differential treatment of young persons, but these considerations would need to be introduced and defended against the claim that capacity is a trumping consideration, and I have argued previously that common suggestions such as paternalism work only in the absence of capacity in those who are the targets of it. An example of this arises in the context of medical decision-making. We have traditionally treated children very differently from adults when making medical decisions, but as recognition of the capacity amongst those under the age of majority for autonomous decision-making has risen, the age at which children are allowed to make these decisions themselves has lowered. So, we are gradually making it the case that we treat more and more children as we do adults, in the medical domain. The law here reflects the practice, which is an expansion of recognition of autonomy to larger numbers of young people. The recognition of capacity triggers a rejection of the practice of differential treatment. Where there is no capacity for autonomous decision-making, the differential treatment remains justified, but my focus is on the areas in which young people are being recognized as capable, and in which our responsibilities towards and for them are changing in light of this recognition.

Limitations Placed on Young People

The content of 'young person' differs between the three domains I have outlined. The medical and political domains largely share a notion of the age of majority, before reaching which limitations are applied to the people in question. However, within medical decision-making, there are exceptions made to the basic practice of denying the young rights to make medical decisions for themselves. The age at which these exceptions take hold varies depending on the jurisdiction and the decision in question. By contrast, the political exclusion of young citizens admits of no exceptions. Before the age of majority, there is no provision made to demonstrate capacity to participate, nor to be included earlier than you would otherwise be entitled to be. Criminal capacity is distinct again. Differential capacity is recognized, but the thresholds for having the capacity to culpably commit criminal acts are much lower than those in the political domain. As such, adult criminal penalties are imposed on young people who are simultaneously judged incapable of making either medical or political decisions.

Political

The political limitations placed on young persons are simple and clearly defined. Those under the specified age threshold, usually 18, are disenfranchised. They are not entitled to register on the electoral rolls or to participate in elections through voting. I have argued elsewhere that these limitations are most defensibly considered to be implemented in recognition of a lack of capacity amongst the excluded for the kinds of behavior and analysis required for political participation (Munn 2012a, 2013). I have also claimed that this defense is insufficient, and that we have reason to relax, quite dramatically, our standards for the exclusion of the young. To summarize the position in the political domain: Capacity for political participation through voting is tied solely to age. Below the age of majority, there is an irrefutable presumption of a lack of capacity. Above the age of majority, capacity for political participation is assumed universally. Except in some very particular marginal cases, such as when individuals suffering from cognitive disability have been denied the right to participate, and then challenge the state in an attempt to have the right returned to them (Doe v Rowe 2001), no testing for capacity is ever permitted. The age of majority is remarkably consistent across democratic states. It ranges from 16 to 22, with 18 being the dominant level, shared by 59 of the 63 democracies in Blais et al.'s wide ranging study of voting rights (2001). Since this study, there has been some progress in lowering the age of enfranchisement in European jurisdictions such as France, Austria and Germany, albeit primarily at the local rather than the National level.

Medical

Medical decision-making is complex. Different decisions are placed in the hands of young people at different stages of their development, and the point at which decision-making capacity is recognized varies between jurisdictions and between issues. A young person in one jurisdiction may be recognized as having the capacity to consent to (or refuse) lifesaving treatment such as a blood transfusion, whilst not being recognized as having the capacity to obtain contraceptive advice or treatment. In another jurisdiction, someone of the same age would be recognized as having both these capacities, and in another, as having neither.

Broadly speaking, young persons are initially taken to lack entirely the capacity to consent to particular forms of medical treatment, and consequently responsibility for making decisions regarding medical treatment is placed in the hands of parents, guardians, or medical practitioners. As the young people develop capacity, they gradually gain responsibility for making the relevant decisions themselves, either independently or in conjunction with others as they choose. This latter component is important; as Kuther notes, many medical decisions are such that if a young person required parental consent to have them treated, the conditions would be likely not to be treated at all (Kuther 2003). For example, in the USA, many states recognize capacity to consent amongst minors aged 13–18 for a range of medical care, including "contraception, sexually transmitted diseases, pregnancy, alcohol and drug abuse, and psychiatric problems" (Kohrman et al. 1995). Along similar lines to this, the root of attribution of medical decision-making capacity to minors in the English legal system arises from the decision in *Gillick v West Norfolk and Wisbech Area Health Authority and another*. In this decision, the House of Lords held that those under the age of majority should nevertheless be presumed capable of making some decisions on their own medical treatment, if they are capable of understanding the nature and consequences of that treatment. Gillick concerned the discretion of a doctor to "give contraceptive advice or treatment to a girl under 16 without her parents' knowledge or consent provided the girl had reached an age where she had a sufficient understanding and intelligence to enable her to understand fully what was proposed, that being a question of fact in each case" (Gillick 1985). This reasoning has been generalized from both in England and in other common law jurisdictions, such as Australia, New Zealand and Canada. For example, in Australia, the majority in *Department of Health and Community Services (NT) v JWB (Marion's case)* held that "[a] minor is capable of giving informed consent when he or she achieves a sufficient understanding and intelligence to enable him or her to understand fully what is proposed" (1992).

The point at which a minor achieves this intelligence and understanding, and correspondingly the limitations on medical decision-making are lifted, is unclear, but it can begin at a very young age. Children as young as eight have been shown to display sufficient rationality to understand the consequences of different possible decisions, weigh the costs and benefits thereof, and to apply this understanding to their personal situations, in studies asking them to make medical decisions of their own accord, without the assistance of adults (Ladd 2002). There is now widespread recognition of the capacity of many below the age of political majority to make decisions in a wide range of medical contexts, and a growing consensus that when a particular individual has this capacity, they ought to be involved in, and have power over, the decision-making process (McCabe 1996; Kuther 2003; Sheldon 2004). This consensus is approved of by the young people concerned, who prefer to make even difficult medical choices themselves (Ruggeri et al. 2014).

Criminal

Young people in the criminal domain primarily have limitations placed on their liability. A purported lack of capacity is used to protect young people from the consequences of their actions. Jurisdictions differ, but the following pattern is predominant: Until a certain age, young persons are held to be entirely incapable of acting with the requisite intent to be held criminally liable for their behavior. This can range from "seven in Sudan, Jordan, and Pakistan" to "eighteen in Belgium, Panama, and Peru" (UNICEF 1998). At least 125 countries set the threshold in the broad range of 7–15, at which point they "may be taken to court and risk imprisonment for criminal acts" (Melchiorre 2004). There may then follow a period of some years during which a rebuttable presumption of incapacity (the *doli incapax* standard) holds; they are presumed to lack capacity for criminal wrongdoing, but the state may attempt to rebut the presumption. If successful, they may continue with a criminal prosecution.[1]

Once capacity has been established, there is commonly a further period during which young people bear a differential culpability under the law; the range/severity of punishments available to the state against them is reduced. Finally, either at the age of political majority or at a point relatively close to it, the young person becomes liable in a manner equivalent to that of other (adult) citizens of the state. One potential source of international consensus on the relevant ages comes from the United Nations Standard Minimum Rules for the Administration of Juvenile Justice, which provide that:

> 4.1 In those legal systems recognizing the concept of the age of criminal responsibility for juveniles, the beginning of that age shall not be fixed at too low an age level, bearing in mind the facts of emotional, mental and intellectual maturity (The Beijing Rules 1985).

The commentary to this rule attempts to tie the age of criminal responsibility to other social rights and responsibilities by noting that "in general, there is a close relationship between the notion of responsibility for delinquent or criminal behavior and other social rights and responsibilities (such as marital status, civil majority, etc.)" (The Beijing Rules 1985). However, in practice, criminal responsibility and its accompanying liability is attributed much earlier than political responsibilities.

The Capacity Standard

I have previously argued that the actual standards applicable for criminal and political capacity are functionally identical (Munn 2012b). "Each requires knowledge of the nature of the action in question, each requires an understanding of the consequences of engaging in that action, and each requires the demonstration of an ability to make a meaningful choice regarding the taking of the action" (Munn 2012b). This tripartite division has been recognized in the political context in the Doe Voting Capacity Standard, in the USA (Appelbaum et al. 2005). As capacity for political participation is, per David Archard, a "minimal standard" rather than an ideal one,

---

[1] While England has abolished the *doli incapax* presumption through statute in the *Crime and Disorder Act 1998*, s. 34, it remains in commonwealth countries such as Australia and New Zealand.

a standard for capacity ought to be applied equitably to all (Archard 2004). So if this standard suffices to determine political capacity, any individual satisfying this standard has political capacity and is entitled to object if the state of which they are a citizen prevents them from voting. Where adult citizens are excluded from the franchise on grounds of incapacity, it is for identical reasons. Australia for example allows for the political exclusion of those adult citizens who "by reason of being of unsound mind, [are] incapable of understanding the nature and significance of enrolment and voting" (Commonwealth Electoral Act 1918). They may neither be enrolled nor cast a vote in an Australian election.

Claire McDiarmid utilizes the same understanding of capacity in her analysis of the attribution of criminal responsibility to young citizens (2007). She begins with Antony Duff's position that punishment is an appropriate response to crimes committed by those he terms 'juvenile', people who are "neither so immature that they can certainly not be held criminally responsible, nor so mature that they are certainly as fit as any other adult to be held criminally responsible" (Duff 2002). This characterization encompasses the majority of those within the broad group of ages considered in the section "Limitations placed on Young People". McDiarmid then argues that in order for a child to be able to be tried for a crime, they must understand the trial process by which they are charged; the impact of their actions on others and appreciate what it would be like to be a victim of those actions; and understand the meaning and consequences of criminal behavior (2007). So, the structure of the capacity standard here is the same as that in the political case.

In the medical context, the explication of the tripartite division of capacity depends on the medical decision in question. However, the general form is consistent. One must ask whether the patient has knowledge of the facts pertinent to the decision in question, and satisfy themselves that the patient has been informed of his or her condition, prognosis, proposed treatments and alternatives. For the patient to have understanding relevant to their competence, they must understand the risks and potential benefits of each alternative and the consequences of choosing a particular alternative. Finally, they must satisfy the ability to choose criterion, by demonstrating the ability to relate a choice to a stable set of values. For adult patients, the satisfaction of these requirements is inextricably linked to the notion of informed consent, which requires medical professionals to make patients aware of the range of considerations at stake in particular medical decisions, and offer the patient the opportunity to choose which of the available options to pursue.[2] Younger minors are taken not to be capable of informed consent, and their opinions are accordingly not sought. As minors age, their opinions begin to be sought, and eventually come to be taken as binding. Rather than having fixed thresholds, young people are included in decision-making gradually as they mature and develop. An example of the tripartite division in practice arises in Canada, with the *Health Care Consent Act 1996* in Ontario, s4(1) of which states that:

---

[2] Although, note that there are problems with the way in which we commonly determine consent amongst adults (Clarke 2013).

A person is capable with respect to a treatment, admission to a care facility or a personal assistance service if the person is able to understand the information that is relevant to making a decision about the treatment, admission or personal assistance service, as the case may be, and able to appreciate the reasonably foreseeable consequences of a decision or lack of decision (Healthcare Consent Act 1996).

Here again we see that the structure of the attribution of capacity is the same as for the political and the criminal domains, featuring considerations of knowledge, understanding, and the ability to make a choice.

In each domain, then, the determination of capacity requires those under consideration to show that they have the requisite knowledge, understanding of that knowledge, and the ability to make a choice between their options. Yet while, for example, this capacity is taken to be present from the age of ten in England with regard to serious criminal acts such as murder (most famously, perhaps, in the Bulger case), it is not attributed by default in the medical case until the age of 16, and then again in the political case not until 18. In the remainder of this piece I consider what could justify such a differential. I address possible differences in the extension of the notion of capacity beyond the basic tripartite structure, and examine whether this general form (attribution of criminal responsibility first, then medical, and finally political) is consistent with these considerations.

The Composition of Capacity

How we determine capacity is consistent across these domains. By this I mean that the criteria for competence are the same. To be capable of acting autonomously in each domain, one must have knowledge; understanding; and the ability to make a choice between options. The differential attribution of capacity in each of these domains can nevertheless be consistent, if the extension of each criterion is different. So if the knowledge criterion is more stringent in the political domain than in the criminal, such that more or more complex knowledge is required before capacity is acknowledged, this would help justify the common practice of holding young people criminally liable prior to holding them politically capable. Possible areas of distinction are multiple. For instance, regarding knowledge, one can ask what information is required in each of the relevant domains before capacity is attributed to an individual. Regarding understanding, what are the relevant concepts and are some more difficult to grasp than others? Similarly, frequency of opportunities to engage in relevant decision-making could make understanding the decisions easier. Here I simply examine some ways in which the domains under consideration may differ on these counts, and note that it is not clear that these provide a defense of our current apparent inconsistency in the treatment of the young between the domains.

Reasons unrelated to capacity may also lead to societies attributing capacity differentially. For example, political decision-making may be considered sufficiently important to justify an attribution of capacity that does not closely track actual capacity amongst the included, but rather, over-excludes. This holds whether we focus on real or perceived importance. However, suggestions of this kind are problematic insofar as, particularly in the political domain, capacity itself is the only justifiable ground for exclusion from participation (Shapiro 1999; Munn 2012a, 2013).

Knowledge: Expected Consequences

If capacity in each domain relies on the same factors, to similar degrees, than satisfying the requirement in one domain is evidence of ability to satisfy the same requirement in another domain. However, being recognized as capable has differing consequences, depending on the domain in which that recognition occurs. In conjunction with something like a paternalistic impulse, this could help explain the differing attribution of capacity. Being recognized as capable in both the medical and criminal domains carries with it substantial consequences. In the criminal domain, recognition of capacity enables legal punishment. One becomes liable for one's actions in a way that another deemed incapable (through age or cognitive impairment) is not. Medically, recognition of capacity requires respect for autonomy, including the autonomy to act against the recommendations of medical professionals. Refusal to accept lifesaving treatment is the right of an autonomous agent, but can be overruled when the refuser is deemed incompetent to make decisions of this kind. By contrast, expected consequences in the political domain are negligible. One ought to expect their vote not to matter, in the vast majority of situations (Gelman et al. 2012; Feddersen 2004). However, if expected consequences actually motivated the differential attribution of responsibility across these domains, we would expect to see a reversal of the common progression of responsibility. A state risks least in attributing political capacity to a young person, and yet they attribute this responsibility later than in either of the other domains.

Knowledge: Complexity of Information

Perhaps the content of the knowledge standard differs between domains, despite the apparent similarity in requirements. If so, it would follow that when more complex information is required, attribution of capacity should be deferred. It is simply more difficult to be capable in a domain where capability requires understanding of a more complex array of systems.

Medical requirements are highly variable, and often very complex. What a patient needs to know regarding their prognosis, treatment options and so on depends on the condition under consideration. Some decisions, such as choosing between generic and branded drugs, are trivial. Others, such as deciding between competing cancer treatments, are massively important. Criminal requirements involve complex and non-intuitive legal processes, but they are broadly consistent – most of the requisite knowledge doesn't depend on the act/crime in question. If one understands the legal framework, the details of how, for example, a criminal trial proceeds are not relevant to the capacity to act criminally. Politically, there is an important distinction between what one might want to know, and what one needs to know. The degree to which any actor needs to know details of the political system in order to be capable of participation is minimal, and there is widespread opposition both in theory and practice to any attempt to impose knowledge requirements on those currently enfranchised. Again, the knowledge requirements for the attribution of political rights seem incongruent with the late stage at which this capacity is attributed to young people.

Understanding

It is difficult to generate a consistent distinction based on requirements for understanding. One way to distinguish between two domains in their difficulty to be understood is by looking at whether the reasoning involved in either of them is significantly more abstract than in the other. Concrete data, requiring less introspection, is easier to grasp. However, attempts to cleanly delineate between the medical, criminal and political domains on these grounds are unlikely to prosper. Each contains a complex mix of abstract and concrete data relevant to decision-making. While it is clear that the immediacy of impact on the person in question is higher for medical and criminal decisions than political ones, this has no bearing on whether the decisions are any easier for those making them.

Another potential distinction arises from frequency of opportunity to act within the domain. More frequent opportunities to engage in decision-making within some particular domain increase the likelihood that one understands the relevant considerations. It is, however, unclear how to cash out the idea of opportunities for action here. If we restrict political action to voting, then young people have by law no opportunity to do so prior to turning 18, and thereafter they have the same few opportunities as the rest of society. By contrast, there is no general rule for the frequency of medical decision-making opportunities, as they depend on individual circumstances. Opportunities to make these decisions could be non-existent for some young persons and constant for others. In the criminal domain there is an obvious sense in which all people are being constantly presented with opportunities to engage in criminal acts, whether trivial or serious. Yet the relevant understanding is that of a general rule, to obey the law, rather than a series of discrete understandings of the countless opportunities to break particular laws in particular ways. As such, one could argue that there is a single point at which one has the understanding of what it is to obey the law. Thereafter, one is simply exercising a pre-existing capacity.

Importance: Personal

Medical & criminal competence are more immediately relevant to individuals than political competence, as in each of these cases, the individual concerned has a vested interest in the adjudication of capacity being favorable to them, where 'favourable' will be an adjudication of competence in the medical case, and of incompetence in the criminal case. In the medical context, a young person with well-formed intentions regarding their choice of treatment from amongst the available options requires the attribution of capacity in order to act autonomously. If their claim to capacity is rejected, their autonomy will be undermined and placed in the hands of others, who are under no obligation to act according to the young person's wishes. So, the medical context increases the interest an individual has in being adjudged capable. There is also risk in the opposite direction, as the incorrect attribution of capacity to a young person who goes on to refuse medical treatment they didn't properly understand can cause them profound, even fatal harms. In the criminal context, a young person deemed incapable avoids prosecution in the conventional justice system, and is instead subject to a different range of penalties, often significantly less severe. Recognition of capacity in the criminal context increases vulnerability post-judgment. These considerations provide some reason to engage in stricter determination of capacity in these domains than in the political domain, where the personal importance of the act of voting is comparatively weak. However, as we have seen, the opposite is commonplace.

Importance: Social

Medical decisions are private in a way that political and criminal decisions are not, and as such, a public interest defense of ignoring demonstrated capacity in order to protect some other value is less viable. Being adjudged capable of making a medical decision for oneself is highly important for the individual concerned, and for their friends and family, but seldom has broader public ramifications.

However, while this type of justification at least partially explains the widespread practice of, for example, preventing those under 18 from voting, it does not justify it. As I have argued elsewhere, other considerations such as this are, in the political context, utilized only to exclude the young, and they would only be acceptably utilized if their use was consistent, such that anyone to whom they applied was excluded by them. As that neither is nor is likely to become the case, young people cannot justifiably be excluded from political participation on these grounds (Munn 2012a, 2013). The attribution of political capacity reflects the nature of modern democracies and generates a social investment in the rejection of capacity for young people. Accepting the political capacity of the young would require admitting the wrong done to young people by their exclusion until this point, and would significantly alter the demographics of the political system by introducing a substantial body of new voters whose desires and preferences would need to be considered and weighed against existing groups.

In the criminal domain, the case is somewhat different as factors other than capacity are relevant to the exercise of authority over those liable, whether young or not. Accordingly, it seems possible to argue on public interest grounds either that a particular individual be imprisoned or controlled regardless of their capacity for knowing and understanding the legal status of the actions for which they are being charged, or to argue in favor of discretion, refusing to charge a particular, capable individual to the extent available under the law. These issues arose in the James Bulger case in England, where despite the young age of the culprits, their actions were widely held to show that they must have understood the wrong they were going. Moreover, the severity of this wrong was such that treating the culprits as capable was expected and even demanded by the general population. Such an approach is of course morally problematic, but it is both possible and actual.

Explaining the Inconsistencies

One important distinction lies in the application of considerations other than capacity. A paternalistic justification for refusing to treat the capacities of a young person in the medical or criminal domain as an overriding consideration in favor of acting according to the wishes of that young person is at least potentially justifiable, while paternalism is inadmissible as a reason for exclusion in the political domain. While one can acknowledge that a 14 year old has the requisite capacity to culpably commit a criminal act, having knowledge of the nature and significance of the act in question, that it is criminal rather than merely 'wrong', and has the ability to choose between committing this act and avoiding it, one can nevertheless claim that the 14 year old should not be prosecuted, or should be prosecuted to a differing/lesser standard than is possible under the law, on the grounds that a non-existent or reduced punishment is better for them.

Discretion also plays a valuable role in the criminal law. As what is at stake is the choice, by agents of the state, of whether to inflict a particular kind of punishment on the young offender, there is a relevant consideration other than capacity which drives the decision as to prosecution. Such discretion is not used solely when addressing the criminal status of young persons. Agents of the state have a broad discretion when investigating a range of criminal activity, as to whether they choose to charge any individual with offences. So for example, a police officer has discretion when determining whether to formally charge any person with minor offences relating to traffic violations and similar. Prosecutors in New Zealand, for example, have discretion, even when "there is sufficient evidence available to provide a reasonable prospect of conviction" (Crown Law 2013, 8) to determine whether to pursue a prosecution at all. When discretion is used by agents of the state in considering the case of young people, this is not differential treatment of them, but rather an extension of an existing and widely accepted component of law enforcement, which applies independently of the capacity of the person under consideration.

In the political domain there is no corresponding discretion on the part of the state regarding the inclusion of relevantly situated actors in the franchise. A state is compelled to include resident adult citizens in good standing in the franchise, and would similarly, under the capacity determination I have argued for be compelled to include any capable young people in the franchise. Capacity is sufficient for political inclusion of citizens in good standing, and trumps age.

Conclusion

I have argued that the requirements to satisfy capacity in each domain do not justify the differential attribution of capacity across them. In particular, the thresholds for attribution of capacity for political participation are high, comparative to the requirements for capacity involved in voting. If the capacity criterion were the only consideration relevant to the age at which thresholds were set in each of these domains, the thresholds would need to be realigned. However, it appears that in both the medical and criminal contexts, although not the political, there are other considerations, such as paternalism and discretion, which can be used to warrant rejecting or weakening a reliance on capacity.

These other considerations serve as at least partial justification for not treating particular individuals as capable when determining whether, in the criminal context, to hold them criminally accountable, or, in the medical context, to grant them autonomy in choosing medical treatment. Paternalism is the broadest of these, and is applicable in both the medical and criminal domains, although its application is restricted to various degrees depending on the jurisdiction.[3] In the criminal domain, discretion is available to various agents of the state throughout the legal process, and can be utilized to diminish culpability, without thereby implying a diminution of recognized capacity.[4] The political context is distinct in that the only ground on which political exclusion is justifiable is due to a lack of capacity.

With these considerations in mind, some tentative conclusions can be drawn. In both the criminal and the medical domains there is a gradual recognition of capacity as a young person ages and develops. The limitations placed by the state on their autonomy (in the medical context) and liability (in the criminal context) are gradually lifted in line with this increasing capacity. At some stage, prior in the majority of jurisdictions to the stage at which the person gains political majority, they are

---

[3] There are of course many issues with the concept of paternalism. These are beyond the scope of this paper, but suffice it to say that a justification grounded in paternalism is tenuous at best (Dworkin 2014).

[4] Again, the way in which discretion is utilized is problematic. It predominantly acts to the advantage of the dominant groups within society, and a failure to utilize it harms the most vulnerable in societies (Davis 1998).

treated as fully capable. In the medical context this is achieved through a determination of capacity to make particular decisions, performed in many cases by the medical professionals proposing treatment. In the criminal context the development of capacity may be presumed by statute, or determined pre-trial when agents of the state want to lay criminal charges against a young person in the specified age ranges for the application of *doli incapax*.

Both these gradual approaches can be starkly contrasted to the all or nothing threshold for political participation, both for the time at when they begin, and for the abruptness of the shift in the political domain. In neither case does the comparison show the political participatory standard in a good light. The gradual development of capacity amongst the young is ignored in political practice when participation is strictly delineated via a fixed voting age, as it is in all democratic states. Further, the voting age itself is indefensibly higher than the age at which the capacity for comparatively more complex, important and difficult decisions in the criminal and medical domain is attributed to young people.

References

Appelbaum, P.S., R.J. Bonnie, and J.H. Karlawish. 2005. The capacity to vote of persons with alzheimer's disease. *American Journal of Psychiatry* 162(11): 2094–2100.

Archard, D. 2004. *Children, rights and childhood*. London: Routledge.

Archard, D., and M. Skivenes. 2009. Balancing a child's best interests and a child's views. *International Journal of Children's Rights* 17: 1–21.

Blais, A., L. Massicotte, and A. Yoshinaka. 2001. Deciding who has the right to vote: A comparative analysis of election laws. *Electoral Studies* 20: 41–62.

Clarke, S. 2013. The neuroscience of decision making and our standards for assessing competence to consent. *Neuroethics* 6: 189–196.

Commonwealth Electoral Act (1918), s93(8).

Crown Law. 2013. *Crown law prosecution guidelines*. http://www.crownlaw.govt.nz/uploads/prosecution_guidelines_2013.pdf

Davis, A.J. 1998. Prosecution and race: The power and privilege of discretion. *67 Fordham L. Rev. 13*. Available at: http://ir.lawnet.fordham.edu/flr/vol67/iss1/2

Department of Health and Community Services (NT) v JWB (Marion's case) (1992) 175 CLR 218.

Doe v Rowe, 156 F. Supp. 2d 35 (D.C. Me. 2001).

Duff, A. 2002. Punishing the young. In *Punishing juveniles: Principle and critique*, ed. Antony Duff and Ido Weijers, 115–134. Oxford: Hart Publishing.

Dworkin, G. 2014. Paternalism. *The Stanford Encyclopedia of Philosophy*. http://plato.stanford.edu/archives/sum2014/entries/paternalism. Accessed 19 Nov 2014.

Feddersen, T.J. 2004. Rational choice theory and the paradox of not voting. *The Journal of Economic Perspectives* 18(1): 99–112.

Franklin-Hall, A. 2013. On becoming an adult: Autonomy and the moral relevance of life's stages. *The Philosophical Quarterly* 63(251): 223–247.

Gelman, A., N. Silver, and A. Edlin. 2012. What is the probability your vote will make a difference? *Economic Inquiry* 50: 321–326. doi:10.1111/j.1465-7295.2010.00272.x.

Gillick v West Norfolk and Wisbech Area Health Authority (1985) 3 All ER 402 (HL).

Health Care Consent Act (1996), s. 4(1). (Ontario, Canada.

Kohrman, A., et al. 1995. Informed consent, parental permission, and assent in pediatric practice. *Pediatrics* 95: 314–317.

Kuther, T.L. 2003. Medical decision-making and minors: Issues of consent and assent. *Adolescence* 38(150): 343–358.

Ladd, R.E. 2002. Rights of the child: A philosophical approach. In *Children as equals: Exploring the rights of the child*, ed. Kathleen Alaimo and Brian Klug, 89–105. Boston: Boston University Press.

McCabe, M.A. 1996. Involving children and adolescents in medical decision-making: Developmental and clinical considerations. *Journal of Pediatric Psychology* 21(4): 505–516.

McDiarmid, C. 2007. *Childhood and crime*. Dundee: University Press.

Melchiorre, A. 2004. *At what age? … Are school children employed, married and taken to court?* 2nd edn. Right to Education Project. http://www.right-to-education.org/resource/what-age-%E2%80%A6are-school-children-employed-married-and-taken-court-2nd-edition. Accessed 14 Nov 2014.

Munn, N.J. 2012a. Capacity testing the youth: A proposal for broader enfranchisement. *Journal of Youth Studies* 15(8): 1048–1062.

Munn, N.J. 2012b. Reconciling the criminal and participatory responsibilities of the youth. *Social Theory & Practice* 38(1): 139–159.

Munn, N.J. 2013. Capacity-testing as a means of increasing political inclusion. *Democratization* 21(6): 1134–1152.

Ruggeri, A., M. Gummerum, and Y. Hanoch. 2014. Braving difficult choices alone: Children's and adolescents' medical decision making. *PLoS ONE* 9(8): e103287. doi:10.1371/journal.pone.0103287.

Shapiro, Ian. 1999. *Democratic justice*. New Haven: Yale University Press.

Sheldon, M. 2004. Medical decision-making for children and the question of legitimate authority. *Theoretical Medicine* 25: 225–228.

UNICEF. 1998. *Innocenti digest, juvenile justice*. http://www.unicef-irc.org/publications/pdf/digest3e.pdf. Accessed 4 Feb 2015.

United Nations. 1985. *Standard minimum rules for the administration of juvenile justice ("The Beijing Rules")*. https://www.ncjrs.gov/pdffiles1/Digitization/145271NCJRS.pdf. Accessed 7 June 2014.

Chapter 5
Eating Disorders in Minors and the Role of the Media. An Ethical Investigation

Christoph Schickhardt

Abstract In his paper, Christoph Schickhardt proposes an ethical analysis of the role of the media for the development of eating disorders such as Anorexia Nervosa and Bulimia Nervosa and related issues such as unhealthy weight control behavior in children and adolescents. Eating disorders are highly severe mental diseases and relatively common among minors. Although their pathogenesis is complex, there is considerable evidence suggesting that the idealizing presentation of very slim bodies in the media, to which many children are exposed intensively for years since early childhood, might contribute to minors' risk of developing eating disorders. This raises ethical questions concerning the well-being and rights of children and adolescents as well as the rights and responsibility of the media. Applying a liberal-egalitarian point of view, Schickhardt argues that while using seductive presentations of thin bodies is no core element of the freedom of the media, it jeopardizes central elements of children's well-being. Putting susceptible and vulnerable young people at risk for eating disorders is ethically inacceptable. Measures to protect minors and foster their media literacy and resilience are due. In his conclusion, the author mentions some concrete measures which might be suitable.

Keywords Eating disorders • Anorexia nervosa • Bulimia nervosa • Media • Children • Ethics

Introduction

The central topic of this article is the role of the media for the onset and maintenance of Eating Disorders (EDs), particularly Anorexia Nervosa (AN) and Bulimia Nervosa (BN), in adolescents. However, I do not want to confine the article to fully manifest EDs. Ethics concerned with EDs such as AN and BN in minors should also

C. Schickhardt (✉)
National Center for Tumor Diseases (NCT), University Hospital Heidelberg, Heidelberg, Germany
e-mail: christophschickhardt@web.de

© Springer International Publishing Switzerland 2016
J. Drerup et al. (eds.), *Justice, Education and the Politics of Childhood*,
Philosophy and Politics – Critical Explorations 1,
DOI 10.1007/978-3-319-27389-1_5

look at related phenomena. Overall, the role of the media is worth scrutinizing, from an ethical perspective, with regard to the following phenomena:

(a) the internalization of the ideal and value of thinness;
(b) attitudes and concerns regarding one's own body such as body dissatisfaction;
(c) attitudes and behaviors concerning eating and caloric intake such as dieting, self-induced vomiting or abuse of laxatives;
(d) development of under-threshold forms of EDs;
(e) development of full ("over-threshold") EDs.

This is just a simplifying list of subcategories of the relevant phenomena. As I will explain in detail below, the phenomena (a-d) are usually all part of a person's development of full ED. However, they can also occur without resulting in full ED. In this article, I will mainly touch on the phenomena (a-d) with regard to the problem of full EDs. However, I also want to raise ethical awareness for the related phenomena (a-d): it is ethically problematic and appears to be a matter of injustice, socially induced wronging and harmful to children's well-being, when a child, as a result of thin body image exposure, deeply internalizes the ideal of thinness as primary value (a) or displays other phenomena of the kinds (b-d), even if these phenomena do not result in full ED.

Eating Disorders in the Ethical and Philosophical Literature

There are some existing works by medical ethicists dealing with concrete issues that sometimes arise during clinical therapy of patients with (severe and extreme degrees of) EDs. The major ethical issue concerns forced feeding (Giordano 2010; Matusek and Wright 2010). The question is whether and under which circumstances caretakers and health professionals are allowed or even required to ignore a patient's refusal of caloric intake and to intervene by force in order to save a patient's life. However, except for some contributions from the field of medical ethics dealing with that question, EDs have widely been ignored by scholars of philosophy, including political philosophy and social ethics. This is astonishing for several reasons. First, as will be mentioned in detail below, EDs and related symptoms are of social relevance since they are very dangerous and relatively common among young people. Second, unlike many other diseases such as cancer, they might be considered as a specifically "moral" illness (Giordano 2003, 2005, 2008): Persons with ED have a high ideal (of beauty and thinness) that they have deeply internalized and tenaciously try to live up to. Depending on the concrete ED, they act with extreme determination and self-discipline, displaying traits of perfectionism and striving for absolute control over their body and their physiological needs and impulses. When they do not meet their goals or fall short of their self-imposed rules, they have feelings of shame, guilt and moral failure. Third, despite the neglect of the topic in philosophical disciplines, *non*-philosophers have been critical of the ethicality of the media's impact on EDs.

The Complexity of Eating Disorders

EDs are a very difficult and complex matter. Nothing about EDs is completely clear or simple — from their nature and definition to the epidemiological numbers and statistics to their causes, not to mention their treatment. The scientific understanding of EDs is limited. For a philosophical or ethical investigation of EDs in general and an assessment of the role of the media with regard to EDs in particular, it is necessary to learn about the scientific literature and existing empirical knowledge of EDs. Among the theoretical and philosophical questions raised by EDs are issues concerning the nature of causation and predictive factors of human behavior as well as the nature of and the coping with risks and uncertainties. In what follows I will try to offer, on the basis of the scientific literature, an extensive introduction to the most important aspects of EDs in general and the role of the media for EDs in particular. The aim of this extensive introduction is (i) to allow readers without specific expertise in the field of EDs to become familiar with the complex nature of EDs in general; (ii) to give some details concerning the role of the media in the onset of EDs which will also imply information about the role of the media for the above mentioned phenomena (a–d), for instance the role of the media for the internalization of the ideal of thinness; (iii) to enable the reader to become aware of the epistemic and methodological challenges, difficulties and limitations of the scientific literature and the current understanding of EDs and the role of the media with regard to them. Dealing with the challenges and limitations surrounding scientific understanding of EDs is part of the *ethical* challenge of dealing with EDs.

Definition of Eating Disorders

There are two worldwide recognized authorities which answer the question what kinds of EDs exist and what they consist of: First, there is the *International Statistical Classification of Diseases and Related Health Problems* (ICD-10) (WHO), which is the diagnostic handbook sponsored and published by the United Nation's World Health Organization. Second, there is the *Diagnostic and Statistical Manual of Mental Disorders* (DSM-V), the handbook published by the American Psychiatric Association (APA 2013).[1]

> According to the DSM-V (APA 2013) a person suffers from **Anorexia Nervosa** if she displays the following criteria:
>
> A. Restriction of energy intake relative to requirement, leading to a significantly low body weight.

---

[1] Both, the ICD-10 and the DSM-V, share the view that AN and BN are psychosomatic disorders. Until the most recent revision of the DSM, published as the fifth edition (DSM-V), both manuals agreed that the only EDs which could be sufficiently specified by diagnostic criteria were AN and BN.

B. Intense fear of gaining weight or persistent behavior that interferes with weight gain, in spite of significantly low body weight.
C. Disturbance in the way in which one's body weight or shape is experienced, undue influence of body weight or shape on self-evaluation, or persistent lack of recognition of the seriousness of the current lowness of body weight.

To evaluate the severity of AN, the DSM-V provides the following criteria, using Body Mass Index (BMI) as an evaluative standard: mild: $BMI \geq 17$; moderate: BMI 16–17; severe: BMI 15–16; extreme: $BMI < 15$. It is rare that individuals with AN seek professional help for their disorder. They often lack insight or deny the problem and its severity (p. 340). As to the associated features of AN, the DSM-V adds: "The semi-starvation of AN, and the purging behaviors sometimes associated with it, can result in significant and potentially life–threatening medical conditions. The nutritional compromise associated with this disorder affects most major organ systems and can produce a variety of disturbances."

According to the DSM-V a person suffers from **Bulimia Nervosa** if she meets the following behavioral and psychological criteria:

A. Recurrent episodes of binge eating. An episode of binge eating is characterized by both of the following: (1) Eating within a discrete period of time an amount of food that is definitely larger than what most individuals would eat in a similar period of time and similar circumstances. (2) A sense of lack of control over eating during the episode.
B. Recurrent inappropriate compensatory behaviors in order to prevent weight gain, such as self-induced vomiting; misuse of laxatives, diuretics or other medications; fasting or excessive exercise.
C. The binge eating and inappropriate compensatory behaviors both occur, on average, at least once a week for 3 months.
D. Self-evaluation is unduly influenced by body shape and weight.

To evaluate the severity of BN, the DSM-V provides the following criteria: mild: average of 1–3 episodes of inappropriate behaviors (binging and purging) per week; moderate: 4–7 episodes per week; severe: 8–13 episodes per week; extreme: 14 or more episodes per week. Individuals with BN typically are within the normal weight or overweight range (BMI between 18.5 and 30).

In its last edition, the authors of the DSM have added Binge Eating Disorder (BED) to the specified mental EDs. BED is, roughly speaking, an analogue to BN with the important difference that there is no inappropriate compensatory behavior for binging. In this article I mainly focus on AN and BN for they are more severe and have been studied more intensively.[2]

---

[2] In order to include clinically severe conditions of individuals that do not fully meet the criteria of, among others, AN and BN, the DSM-V introduces new subcategories as forms of specified eating disorders: Atypical Anorexia Nervosa for persons who qualify for AN except the significant underweight, and Bulimia Nervosa of low frequency and/or limited duration for persons who meet all criteria of BN except that the binge eating occurs less than once a week and/or less than for three months. This is relevant for children. For various reasons, children did not "fit" – and to some extent do still not – "fit" into the categories and criteria of EDs (Nicholls et al. 2000).

The Epidemiology of Eating Disorders

As to the occurrence of EDs, some preliminary notes are necessary. There are no numbers that are highly reliable in terms of statistics and representativeness. There are no official numbers by national statistic or health offices or the WHO.[3] A study cited in many articles dealing with the epidemiology of AN is the one by Keski-Rahkonen and colleagues (2007). In a 1975–1979 birth cohort of 2545 finish female twins, they found a 2.2 % lifetime prevalence of full AN according to the DSM-IV criteria and of 4.2 % of broad AN. The incidence of full AN in young women between the age of 15 and 19 was calculated as 270 per 100,000 and the incidence of broad AN was calculated as 490 per 100,000. An American study examined the natural history of threshold, subthreshold, and partial EDs in a community sample of 496 adolescent girls over an 8-year period (Stice et al. 2009). Lifetime prevalence by age 20 years was 0.6 % and 0.6 % for threshold and subthreshold AN, 1.6 % and 6.1 % for threshold and subthreshold BN, and 1.0 % and 4.6 % for threshold and subthreshold BED. Overall, 12 % of adolescents experienced some form of ED. Studying a sample of about 8000 female and male adolescents among 13 and 18 in the US, researchers report the following life time prevalences (of these adolescents!): 0.3 % for AN, 0.9 % for BN, 1.6 % for Binge Eating, 0.8 % for subthreshold AN and 2.5 % for subthreshold Binge Eating (Swanson et al. 2011). The median ages at onset were the following: 12.3 years for AN, 12.4 years for BN, 12.6 years for BED, and 12.6 years for subthreshold BED. Although the validity of all epidemiological studies can be questioned for various reasons, there appears to be enough evidence to show that EDs, including subthreshold EDs, are relatively common in the population of young people (Huemer et al. 2011).[4]

Regarding the course and outcomes of EDs, psychologists commonly agree that EDs are severe, dangerous and difficult to treat. AN seems to be one of the most

---

[3] For epidemiological studies on EDs (i.e., studies concerning the occurrence of EDs) there are several difficulties and issues (Smink et al. 2012; Pinhas and Bondy 2011). For instance, available samples are too small to be representative, or persons conceal their disease or do not undergo clinical treatment and therefore cannot be found in registries. Further, we need to distinguish between incidence and prevalence. The *incidence* is the number of *new* cases in a defined population over a determined period. The incidence is usually formulated as a rate of new cases per 100,000 persons per year. The *prevalence* is the number of all persons in a certain population suffering from a disease. The prevalence tells us how many persons of a defined population are or were affected by a certain disease within a defined time. The life time prevalence is the proportion of persons affected by the disease at any point in their life time (Smink et al. 2012).

[4] Pediatric EDs are more common than diabetes 2 (Campbell and Peebles 2014), and AN is the third most frequent chronicle disease among young women between 10 and 19 (Kohn and Golden 2001) and "relatively common among young women" (Smink et al. 2012). The non-specified EDs, that is the EDs that do not fulfill all criteria of AN and BN according to DSM-IV are more common than AN and BN, but are severe as well (Campbell and Peebles 2014). A relevant number of patients with formerly defined non-specified EDs would now qualify for the specified EDs according to the new DSM-V criteria (Lock et al. 2015).

dangerous and devastating among all mental disorders.[5] Keski-Rahkonen and colleagues (2007) report a clinical recovery rate within 5 years after AN onset of 66.8 % for full AN and 69 % for broad AN. In other terms, more than 30 % had not fully recovered from AN even 5 years after onset. A German short term study of 57 inpatient adolescents with AN and a mean age of 15.8 years found that 1 year after being discharged from the treatment center only 28 % had fully recovered and that 59 % had a poor outcome (Salbach-Andrae et al. 2009). A relevant number of patients with onset of AN or BN during adolescence are affected for a duration of at least 3 years (Pinhas and Bondy 2011; Huemer et al. 2011). The medical severity of patients with EDs not otherwise specified (EDNOS) is not much lower than for those with complete criteria of AN and BN. The outcomes for EDNOS patients intermediate to that of patients with AN and BN in all primary outcomes (Peebles et al. 2010). AN is considered to have one of the highest, if not *the* highest mortality rate of psychiatric diseases (Huemer et al. 2011; Smink et al. 2012).[6]

The Etiology and Risk Factors of Eating Disorders

The pathogenesis of EDs is still not fully understood. Researchers commonly agree that the etiology of EDs is complex and plurifactorial and that the risk factors or determinants of EDs originate from various dimensions. In general, no single risk factor has been found to predict the onset of EDs and no single factor seems to be necessary for EDs. It is questionable to what extent one might refer to "causes" and causation regarding human behavior and human attitudes such as displayed in EDs. So it might be better to refer instead to "risk factors" for the onset and maintenance of EDs which would be in line with much of the psychological literature. Risk

---

[5] The (few) follow up studies of the outcomes are particularly problematic in terms of generalizability because they often rest on a small sample of 40–100 affected persons – usually persons who have been registered as patients in health care units. One problem of studies on recovery rates consists in the difficulties of differences between the studies with regard to the definition of full (or partial) recovery, for example in terms of weight recover or the number of months of being without any symptoms.

[6] As to mortality, the most significant number is the Standardized Mortality Ratio (SMR), which compares the mortality in a specific cohort, for instance a cohort of AN patients, with the mortality in a corresponding "normal" or "mean" population cohort of persons not affected by the disease. It is appropriate however to clarify that while the mortality rates report the *relation* of persons diagnosed with AN at a certain point in their life and cases of death, such relations are not necessarily *causal*. For example, when patients with AN die of suicide it is problematic to assert to which extent AN was the cause of death. Suicidality is relatively high among AN and BN patients (Campbell and Peebles 2014; Smink et al. 2012). A 2005 study of a sample of 954 AN patients reported a SMR of 10, which means that patients' risk to die was 10 times higher than expected in the corresponding population without AN (Birmingham et al. 2005). In a follow up study researchers investigated SMR in a total of 6009 females with at least one admission to hospitals for AN. The overall SMR of the AN cohort was 6.2 times higher than in a corresponding general population cohort and had a high rate of suicide (Papadopoulos et al. 2009).

factors can emerge and play a role in a developmental sequence (Huemer et al. 2011). Further, there are complex and dynamic interactions and interdependences between the various factors, which further complicates our understanding of the pathogenesis of EDs and the estimation of the impact of single factors. Persons with EDs are thought to have genetic or biological predispositions which are activated by socio-cultural or psycho-social factors (Bakalar et al. 2015).

The most important risk factors are (i) age, namely early adolescence for AN and mid- and late adolescence for BN (Kohn and Golden 2001), and (ii) gender, namely female. The relative risk for females in comparison with males is around 10 to 1 (Jacobi et al. 2004). There is some evidence that even younger people are increasingly affected by EDs or related symptoms. Further risk factors commonly mentioned in the literature are the following: (iii) genetic and biological predispositions, (iv) family discord and high demanding parents, (v) temperamental traits such as seeking control or perfectionism; (vi) general psychiatric morbidity: there is a correlation between anxiety disorders and EDs; (vi) previous stressful events, traumata, sexual abuse; (vii) exposure to media contents of idealized thin body figures; (viii) body dissatisfaction and weight concerns; (ix) dieting; (x) (perceived) social pressure to be thin, for example from media contents, comments of parents or peers on body shape, or expectations towards fashion models and ballet dancers; (xi) internalization of thinness as an ideal and standard for oneself.[7]

The Role of the Media on Eating Disorders and Related Phenomena

In light of the plurality of risk factors, our limits in understanding the importance of each factor and the complexity of their interactions, the question arises: why should we focus on the media as a specific risk factor for EDs? The reasons for focusing on the media consist first in the basic assumption that the role of the media is of considerable significance with regard to EDs, even though the impact of the media cannot be reliably quantified. Second, the media appear to be an important factor for phenomena like body dissatisfaction and dieting that contribute to the onset of EDs but which negatively affect the interests and well-being of children even independently from their promoting or triggering effect on the onset of EDs. Third, if it is true, as empirical evidence suggests, that commercial media contents from entertainment and advertisement contribute to the risk for EDs in adolescents and also promote phenomena in adolescents that might be negative even without triggering EDs, this raises questions in terms of ethics and social justice. Fourth, unlike risk factors like gender or adolescence, the media is a social factor that might be mitigated, abolished or counterbalanced if addressed by adequate policies.

---

[7] For an overview of risk factors see (Huemer et al. 2011; Jacobi et al. 2004; Campbell and Peebles 2014; Bakalar et al. 2015).

In what follows, I will first try to illustrate that the media play an important role for EDs and related phenomena such as body dissatisfaction and dieting; second, I will analyze and assess the role of the media in terms of ethics and justice. The relevance of the media consists in media contents which present extremely slender bodies or thinness in a positive way. I refer to thin body figures as shown in different kinds of media programs and in advertisements such as television programs (entertainment programs), televised commercials, magazine reports or ads, or ads in the streets. I mean all images that present or show thin body figures in a way suggesting that thinness or extreme slenderness is beautiful, an ideal to follow and a primary value or a means to reach important values such as happiness, success, life satisfaction, attractiveness, friends, social regard and recognition. Of course, the ways in which these messages surrounding thin bodies are communicated and understood by consumers and particularly by children are complicated and often highly sophisticated.

Like the etiology of EDs in general, the particular role of the media for the development, onset and maintenance of EDs is still debated and not fully understood. We cannot certainly say that specific thin body images *cause* EDs in adolescents. Many studies suggest that media contents are a risk factor for EDs and contribute to an environment that is prone to EDs. An important limitation of many studies consists in their cross-sectional design that permits only relational conclusions concerning media exposure and EDs, but no causal conclusions. Thompson and Heinberg (1999) note that it is unknown whether media exposure to thin body figures is an etiological factor in body image concerns and eating pathologies or whether women with body images concerns and eating pathologies chose to expose themselves to such media messages at a higher rate than less affected persons. A major challenge in understanding, estimating, or even quantifying the impact of the media is to capture how children, during years of childhood and adolescence, are exposed to thinness idealizing pictures as shown by all kinds of media, and to measure the long term exposure. This cannot be done, of course, in experimental (laboratory) study designs and is hard to investigate retrospectively.[8] A further difficulty is that the influence of the media may operate via several intermediate factors. In order to illustrate the different ways in which the media appear to increase the vulnerability and risk for the onset of EDs, I introduce a diagram (Fig. 5.1) following the models elaborated by Stice and colleagues (Stice 2001; Stice and Shaw 2002). The aim of the diagram is to shed light on the different ways in which thin body media contents may increase factors such as body dissatisfaction and dieting which in turn favor EDs.[9]

---

[8] Ideally, to understand the role of the media we would need studies with some hundreds of adolescents with common, every day, long term media exposure and a control group of persons who with regard to all important dimensions and factors correspond to the first group but have never been exposed to thin body media contents. Such study designs are impossible to realize, not to mention the impossibility to replicate such an ideal study design.

[9] The diagram illustrates the complexity of the media influence within the net of interrelated factors for EDs. At the same time the graph permits to focus on single factors and pathways of media influence. This is helpful since first it allows us to take into consideration evidence from the litera-

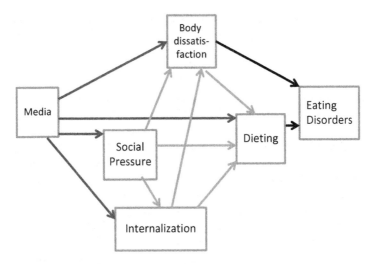

Fig. 5.1 Pathways from thin body media contents to eating disorders

(a) Dieting and eating disorders: Dieting is one of the most investigated risk factors for EDs. The basic idea is that EDs arise from dieting which gets out of control and becomes a psychosomatic dynamic on its own with self-strengthening feedback circles. Dieting is a salient risk factor for future development of EDs or related symptoms. However, it has not been proven that dieting *causes* EDs (Stice et al. 2007). In a prospective cohort study of a huge, though not representative sample of 6900 adolescent girls, aged between 9 and 15 years, Field and colleagues (2008) found that dieting was a significant and independent risk factor for starting to purge or to purge and binge eat at least once a week. The frequency of dieting among girls is astonishing. Among 8500 pupils aged 9–17 years in the Republic of Ireland in 2002, 12 % of the girls reported being on a diet in order to lose weight and 28 % of the girls said they should be on a diet (Gabhainn et al. 2002).

(b) Body dissatisfaction and eating disorders: Body dissatisfaction and body concerns are an important and well studied risk factor for EDs. According to an 8 year prospective study of adolescent females, body dissatisfaction emerged as the most potent predictor of EDs (Stice et al. 2011). In a synthesis of research studies on body dissatisfaction the authors suggest that there is "reasonably consistent prospective and experimental support for the assertion that body dissatisfaction is a risk factor for bulimic pathology" (Stice and Shaw 2002). On

---

ture concerning single pathways in which the media act on factors for EDs. Second, the diagram illustrates the single factors such as body dissatisfaction which appear to be increased by the media thin body contents and which negatively affect children even when not resulting in EDs. I will work backwards, beginning with dieting as a risk factor for EDs and ending by treating the role of the media for single ED factors. Of course, the graph's limitations need to be mentioned as well. It is a schematic and simplifying attempt to display the complicated and mediated role of thinness idealizing media contents for EDs by reconstructing the media's influence on interrelated factors.

the basis of longitudinal studies, weight concerns, negative body images and dieting can be considered variable risk factors for bulimic disorders (Jacobi et al. 2004).

(c) Body dissatisfaction and dieting: There is empirical support for the contention, which is also quite intuitive, that body dissatisfaction gives rise to dieting - which in turn is a risk factor for EDs (Stice and Shaw 2002; Stice 2001). In a 5-year longitudinal study (Neumark-Sztainer et al. 2006), researchers found statistically significant correlations, independently from BMI, between body dissatisfaction and dieting and unhealthy weight control behavior.

(d) Internalization, body dissatisfaction and dieting: The internalization of the media thin body ideal is of special interest from an ethical point of view. It raises, for instance, the question whether it is the internalization of a value or disvalue. Internalization means that a person accepts the thin ideal body shape as a value and adopts this ideal as a standard to follow for herself. Internalization of the thin body model ideal predicts increased body dissatisfaction (Carr and Peebles 2011). In a synthesis of empirical studies on the effect of internalization (Stice and Shaw 2002) the author reports that there is relatively strong support for the thesis that internalization is a risk factor for growing body dissatisfaction. In a meta-analysis (Cafri et al. 2005) the authors found that in women internalization of the thin model has a significant relationship with the subjective body image. A Suisse study of 819 boys and 791 girls, aged 14–16, showed that girls scored much higher on the internalization than boys and suggested that internalization was the most important predictor of body dissatisfaction (Knauss et al. 2007). According to a systematic review of socio-environmental factors, thin body ideal internalization is positively associated with disordered weight control behavior (Wang 2013).

(e) The media and the perceived pressure to be thin: Perceived pressure to be thin is a central factor of body dissatisfaction with the media playing a key role (Carr and Peebles 2011). It is interesting that adolescents are in some way aware of being negatively affected by media appearance images and feel under pressure. In a study of 3000 adolescents in Ireland (average age 14,7), 70 % felt adversely affected by media images of body figure and 25 % believed the body shapes portrayed by the media were far too thin (McNicholas et al. 2009). In a study of 548 female adolescents in the USA, 69 % answered that magazine pictures influenced their idea of their perfect body and 47 % that they wanted to lose weight because of magazine pictures (Field et al. 1999).[10] A meta-analysis of 25

---

[10] With regard to the role of media thin images on weight concerns and body dissatisfaction, there is a great amount of studies available. These studies are usually either experimental and made in a laboratory or correlational. The experimental studies, which take place in labs, have the advantage of yielding evidence for causal relations. They are however somehow artificial, and in the laboratory they cannot reproduce the kind of every day exposure to media contents for months and years that is typical of many children and adolescents in western countries. The second sort of research design is just about correlations between measures of body dissatisfaction and the media consume as self-reported at one single moment by the research subjects. These correlational studies cannot illustrate causal relationships but might say more about long term patterns. A quite typical

experimental studies concluded that "body satisfaction for women is significantly lower after viewing thin media images than after viewing images of average size women, of cars or houses" (Groesz et al. 2002). Studies suggest that the perceived pressure to be thin predicts body dissatisfaction (Stice and Shaw 2002). In a meta-analysis the authors found in women that perceived pressure to be thin has a significant relationship with the subjective body image (Cafri et al. 2005). Internalization during adolescence of the media's ideal of thinness is an important channel of the media's influence on body dissatisfaction (Dittmar and Howard 2004; Carr and Peebles 2011) (Dittmar and Howard 2004; Carr p. 60). In a meta-analysis of experimental and correlational studies on the role of the media in body image concerns among women, Grabe and colleagues (2008) found that media exposure is linked to women's body dissatisfaction, increased investment in appearance and increased endorsement of disordered eating behaviors. It should be added that media thin images seem to have stronger effects on the body dissatisfaction of *vulnerable* girls or women who already have thin body concerns (Stice and Shaw 2002). From a meta-analysis of 33 experimental laboratory studies, Hausenblas and colleagues (2013) conclude that "idealized images in the media may have the most harmful and substantial impact on those individuals already at risk for developing an ED. Individuals in the high risk group showed a moderate and significant increase in depression and body dissatisfaction."

A study with an almost unique study design aimed to evaluate the impact of the introduction of western TV on EDs among Fijian girls. In the local region of Nadroga, two cohorts were surveyed, one of 63 girls just 1 month after the introduction of western TV in 1995, and another cohort of 65 girls of the same place and age in 1998 3 years after the introduction of TV. Among the girls with access to television for 3 years, the number of girls reporting self-induced vomiting to control weight increased from zero to seven and the number of girls who scored high on ED related attitudes had doubled and were significantly associated with dieting and self-induced vomiting (Becker et al. 2002). This study has some limitations such as the small number of recruited girls, the focus on ED related attitudes and behaviors instead of EDs, and the lacking differentiation between western television in general and idealizing thin images in television or

---

experimental study was conducted on a sample of 160 female and 197 male adolescents of an Australian high school, aged between 13 and 15. The sample was divided in one experimental group and one control group. The participants of the first group were shown 20 televised commercials containing idealized images of slim women, the participants of the control group were shown commercials without that kind of contents. The participants were asked three times - before watching the commercials, immediately after watching and 15 min afterwards – how they were feeling "right now" with regard to weight dissatisfaction and overall appearance dissatisfaction. Results showed significant effects of commercials on the girls, just the girls: the girls exposed to the thin model commercials showed significantly increased body and weight dissatisfaction immediately after and 15 min after watching the thin image commercials, whereas before watching the commercials their dissatisfaction was equal to that of the control group (Hargreaves and Tiggemann 2003).

other media. However, backed by qualitative interviews with girls of the second cohort, the authors emphasize the linkage of exposure to western television to changes in the girls' attitudes towards weight loss, dieting and slim figure ideal. 83 % of the girls who were interviewed 3 years after television introduction responded that they felt television had specifically changed their peers' attitudes towards weight and body shape. 77 % of all interviewed girls (and 85 % of the girls who scored high on EDs attitudes or reported self-induced vomiting) responded that television had influenced their own body image. This study backs the thesis of the cultural context in the epidemiology of EDs and particularly of westernized modern mass media culture.[11]

A very recent German study (Götz et al. 2015) among 241 young persons, almost exclusively girls and young women, undergoing therapy for acute EDs aroused great debate in the German public. Interestingly, the study draw attention to one single TV format, the casting show "Germany's Next Top Model" (GNTM), which is the German adaption of a format licensed for US media company CBS, instead of the media in general. 71 % responded that there was one single TV show which particularly influenced their history. Without having any predefined list of TV shows and without any similar support or indications, 39 % of the girls indicated GNTM as the format which particularly influenced them. Most reported experiencing the TV format as strengthening their own drive for developing an ED. However, some experienced the TV format as triggering the ED. 85 % agreed with the statement that GNTM may favor the onset of EDs like AN and BN.

What conclusions can we draw from these findings of the literature with regard to the role of the media? There are much too many factors beyond the media for stating that the media are the cause of EDs. Also, the vast majority of girls and people in general is exposed to idealizing thin body messages by the media *without* developing EDs. Reviewing the literature Levine and Murnen (2009) conclude that there is still not enough empirical evidence to conclude with certainty that the media is a causal risk factor of EDs. However, they write that there are many hints and studies suggesting that the media play a role in EDs, even though the media's role must be understood as interrelated with and depending on other factors, particularly internalization. I think that in addition to all the different kinds of studies and (self-)reports suggesting that the media's thin body idealization do increase the risk in adolescents of developing EDs, there are two further reasons for considering the media a causal risk factor. First, common sense suggests that children and adolescents, who are highly susceptible to all kinds of influences and who have a very strong inclination of comparing themselves to others, are deeply influenced by highly sophisticated and manipulative images of very thin happy women to which they are often massively exposed since the earliest years of childhood by hours of televisions per day (!) and thousands of ads per year in the streets. It is hard to imagine that all these suggestive positive images may not affect and influence children and adolescents, be it direct influence on the child herself or indirect influence on the child via shaping

---

[11] For the cultural history and cultural context of EDs cf. Bemporad (1997).

the views and values of the peers. Second, many professionals, based upon their everyday experiences from working with patients suffering from EDs, claim that the media often do play an important role in the onset and maintenance of EDs and accordingly criticize such media contents with great determination (Dittmar). The media therefore seem to contribute to a social context within which EDs flourish (Spettigue and Henderson 2004). In other terms, as suggested by Kelly Brownell, a US expert in EDs, and adopted by the UK National Center for Eating Disorders, the media contribute to a "toxic environment" within which EDs are more likely to occur (Jade 2009). The question of how to deal with the strong but yet limited evidence concerning the role of the media is itself an ethical question.

An Ethical Perspective on the Different Interests at Stake

I will treat the role of the media as a matter of social justice. The normative framework of the following ethical analysis and evaluation of the role of the media is a liberal-egalitarian one. It is liberal as it attributes great value to the capacities and rights to freely determine one's own life. The liberal orientation includes two key elements of great relevance for our topic. First, the value of personal autonomy as well as of competencies and opportunities, which foster personal autonomy: It is good and desirable that children and young people develop personal autonomy. Personal autonomy is – in very abstract and simplifying terms - a net of intellectual, emotional and personal capacities and resources that enables a person to chose and live her own life, to develop and pursue her own plan and conception of good life and happiness, to be herself, to emancipate herself, to develop her personality, to determine her own system of values and beliefs with a substantial degree of emotional and intellectual independency.[12] Second, everybody's liberties should be protected and may be restricted only for good reasons, particularly for the reason of preventing harm to others. The egalitarian aspect of my approach translates into the claim that, in relation to adults, all children and adolescents are to be considered as equals and as enjoying equal moral status (Schickhardt 2012, Chap. 5). We owe them equal recognition. This does not mean always treating children and adults in an identical manner. It means attributing equal value to the interests of children and adults.[13]

I will first point out the values and interests at stake with regard to the children. The backdrop for defining their interests consists in a liberal conception of children's well-being. Children and adolescents who still lack intellectual capacities and personal maturity cannot (fully) determine their fundamental interests on their own. So even liberals who are usually reluctant to determine what is good for others need to do this when it comes to young children. From a liberal viewpoint, I will propose two goods as important elements of children's general well-being or best interest. The first is happiness. A child should be happy, feel safe and be free of pain, anxieties, burdens and discomfort. Furthermore, a child should have her

---

[12] For an overview on the concept of personal autonomy cf. Buss (2013).

[13] For this kind of understanding equality cf. Ronald Dworkin (2013).

chances and opportunities for future happiness protected and fostered. The second important element of a children's general best interest consists in personal auton- omy. It is in the child's best interest to develop personal autonomy and to develop into an autonomous person (Schickhardt 2012).

Given the significantly increased mortality, the most valuable good or interest jeopardized by EDs is the very life of the affected children or young persons. Mental and somatic health, which is always seriously harmed through EDs, is essential for children in maintaining and developing their personal sense of happiness and auton- omy. The 'goodness' or beneficent qualities of life and health are of such outstand- ing importance and fundamentality that there is no need for further explanation. EDs also impair children's right to an open future (Feinberg 1980). For they inter- nalize the ideal of thinness and are fixed on the value dimension of thin body appear- ance (having begun the process in early childhood or adolescence) to such an extent that they fail to recognize the presence of alternative values and ways of living. EDs and the fixation on one single (dis)value lead to an extreme impoverishment of life during childhood and adolescence with immense opportunity costs. Young persons who have deeply internalized the ideal of thinness and/or suffer from EDs miss innumerous possibilities to enjoy life, be happy, learn about themselves and the world, make experiences and to develop and foster competencies and capacities. Young people have an objective interest in learning about a plurality of values, conceptions of good life and ideals. In other terms, they have an interest in not undergoing value and virtue indoctrination. If, by exposure to the media, they con- ceive thin body appearance as the "normal" or only way to pursue happiness and to find social recognition and self-esteem, children's interest in learning about the plu- rality of values and various ways of living is harmed. In line with this, and given their strong drive to social comparison, children have an interest in truthfulness and in not being deeply manipulated or mislead about the aspects of human and social reality, which are of critical importance for their identity. This interest is harmed if children, particularly girls, consciously or unconsciously conclude from the media that many other girls or women are as thin and slim as the ones presented there, and that almost every girl could be such if she just worked with discipline and determi- nation on her physical appearance. Children also have an interest in body satisfac- tion and "happy eating", that is in eating without thinking of dieting, without excessive and misled body concerns and without being affected by senses of shame, guilt or regret. Children might have many reasons to be unsatisfied with their body or to keep caloric intake under a certain control. However, aspiring with cruel deter- mination and obsession to unrealistic, unachievable, and unhealthy body ideals is no good way of being concerned about one's body and eating. The above-mentioned elements of children's well-being that are jeopardized by EDs are not all of equal importance, but none of them is negligible. They are all relevant elements of chil- dren's well-being. We might consider them as constitutive of children's rights or as crucial elements of children's well-being. From an ethical point of view, they require care, protection, and respect by others. They are necessary elements of respecting children as persons.[14]

After concentrating on the children's interests at stake, we need to take a look at the legitimate rights and interests of the media, i.e. of all professionals and stakeholders involved in media and advertisement activities. In general, the media – or more precisely, the individuals working with the media – may refer to rights that are widely and traditionally recognized and emphasized by liberal thinkers: first of all, the freedom of the media and the press. Advocates of the media might also rely on the right of free speech, the right of economic freedom including rights of free marketing and advertising and the freedom of artistic activities. From a liberal approach, there is no doubt that, at least at a prima facie level, all of these rights should be recognized and warranted in a democratic society. However, it is not indifferent that by using thin body pictures the media also pursue the interest of maximizing profits.

Last, it is worth remembering that in addition to the media and the children who possibly might be affected by media thin pictures, there is a numerous number of media consumers, including minors and adults, who are not at risk but whose interests and rights are at stake as well. Restrictions or other interventions on the media with regard to thin body depicturing would concern many consumers' right to freedom of the media, including the right to free access to all sorts of media contents. However, since the possibility of having free and unrestricted access to idealizing media pictures of very slim body figures is no core element of consumers' media rights, I will not take it into further consideration.

Responsibilities and Justice

To this point, one should have a basic overview of EDs, the role of the media with respect to EDs, as well as the interests and rights of both the adolescents and the media that are at stake. We now need to ethically assess and evaluate the conflict between the children's and the medias' rights and interests in terms of justice. In

---

[14] The following text (Lintott 2003) might give us a very vague and approximate idea of how EDs may affect the thoughts and feelings of adolescents. "Imagine this: You wake up at 5 a.m., dizzy, with an empty feeling in the pit of your gut. Your first thoughts are of food, but not in any simple sense. Instead of thinking about some delicious meal that might satisfy your hunger, you think quite the opposite. You think that today you will not eat until 5 p.m., or 6 p.m., or, best of all possibilities, not at all. You deliberate, figuring when you will *have* to eat, and how you will be able to avoid eating until then, without detection. Today, you affirm, as you do every day, that you will eat less than yesterday. Before falling asleep last night, while doing your sit-ups in bed, you already made a plan to run five *extra* miles this morning to make up for the potato you ate yesterday. You are guiltily aware that you were not *supposed* to eat that potato; you know you *should* have eaten only some celery. You know that if you eat, you may lose control and devour more food than most people eat in a week. But you find comfort in your confidence that if this happens, you can deal with it; you can vomit it up. You know the tricks—how to make yourself vomit, silently and quickly if need be."

what follows, I will propose some arguments that the media might use in objection to anyone who holds them responsible and blames them for their influence on the development of EDs and related phenomena in children.

(a) The media might argue that they do not *intend* to put at risk or harm children. We can concede that intention is relevant in ethics as well as in criminal law. However, the criticism does not state that the media intentionally cause risk or harm for children. Blameworthiness is not confined to the goals or primary intentions of human actions. From the moment that the media know or can know that thin body pictures are a risk factor for EDs in children, they are to be held responsible for these consequences of their actions, even if they are not intended.

(b) The media might also refer to scientific uncertainty and claim that the influence of thin body images on the development of EDs in children is not fully proven and ascertained beyond any doubts. Here, a lot depends on the degree of certainty and scientific evidence we require with regard to the role of the media for EDs. A further important question is where to place the burden of proof and what must be proved: the harmfulness or the harmlessness of media images. Were it a case of criminal accusation or a case of compensation for experienced harms, it would be just to require a degree of certainty concerning the concrete *harmful* causality of media images beyond reasonable doubts. In contrast, I will focus on the prospective dimension of potential future risks for children, analogous to the general approach of child protection policies as assumed and implemented, for example, with regard to the advertising or selling of alcohol or tobacco to children. When it comes to risks and potential harms, the lack of complete certainty cannot justify continuing to act in a way that is very likely to harm children. The right to inflict risks on fundamental interests of persons without their consent is very limited, even if we have no complete certainty of the amount and likelihood of the risk. Besides the role of the media for the onset of full or subthreshold EDs, we certainly know of other negative impacts on adolescents, for instance on body satisfaction, internalization and attitudes towards eating.

(c) The media might also claim that the number of the adolescents affected by thin media contents is very small compared to the majority of media consumers who are not affected. The media could add that mass media cannot realistically be required to take into consideration the special needs and vulnerabilities of every single person. It is true of course that the majority of children with regular exposure to thin body pictures do not develop EDs or related phenomena. However, first, the number of children that are or might be negatively affected and pushed further to develop EDs or related issues is not extremely small, neither in relative terms, nor in absolute terms. Second, we have no right to harm anybody, even if the majority of people concerned by our action is not harmed. Third, even if many adolescents are resilient to the negative influence of the media, this does not justify that the media put them at risk and challenge their resilience resources.

(d) The media might say that it is not their fault if vulnerable children are exposed to and affected by certain thin body pictures. The media might claim that it is the duty of the parents or the public (e.g. the public school system) to provide children with media literacy, and add that the parents or the caretakers of every child have the duty to protect their child from individually harmful media exposure. There are two major flaws in this kind of arguing, however. As to the educational system, the media's claim would overestimate the potential of educational systems to resolve all kinds of socially induced problems. The hint to the educational system is a popular fig leaf for the non-taking of one's responsibilities. It appears unacceptable that the media or in general the industry, in order to search for and maximize private profits, create new seductive risks for children, and attribute the responsibility of protecting children from the consequences of these risks to the parents or the public. Furthermore, as a well known matter of fact, many children do not grow up in ideal circumstances, do not enjoy perfect care or protection and might have negligent caretakers or parents. The fact that these children are already not getting what they deserve or what would be ideal for their well-being cannot justify the bad consequences of the media's own contribution to their difficulties and risks. Such a justification is like scorn for these children.

(e) The media might also argue that by idealizing body thinness they do not add anything to the social environment and the social risk factors for EDs. According to this reasoning, they are just the "medium" which reflects the (dis)values, demands and widespread pathologies of society and cannot succeed in opposition to society. I concede that the emphasis on thinness and body shape is a widespread social phenomenon. However, this does not eliminate any responsibility. For instance, even though the consumption and abuse of alcohol is a widespread phenomenon in western societies, which was not created by the media, it appears perfectly reasonable that the media must not encourage or seduce children to consume alcohol. Furthermore, doing what the majority does or seems to expect is a weak justification of one's actions. The media have a certain scope and responsibility for their products on their own.

(f) The media could also argue that they do not force anybody to watch thinness idealizing media contents and that children deliberately and freely expose themselves to such contents. However, there are some objections to this argument. First, whereas it is true that children are not obliged to (regularly) watch a body shape TV entertainment show, they are constantly confronted with thin body pictures in advertisements during TV programs and in the public space (streets, stations etc.).[15] Second, we cannot treat children and adolescents as fully autonomous and competent adults. Children's consent and will are flawed and have little legitimating power when it comes to matters, which imply potential harm and danger for them. We may concede that restricting the broadcasting

---

[15] In its campaign for women's body confidence ("real beauty") the Dove company has produced a public accessible video entitled "beauty pressure", which attempts to illustrate the exposure of children to thin body images in everyday life.

of thin body idealizing pictures and messages would be a potential inference in children's will and media liberties. Since it is motivated to protect children from harm, it can be considered as a paternalistic intervention. Yet, this kind of paternalism towards children is perfectly in line with many other interventions and restrictions we place on children's will and liberties in order to protect or promote their interests and well-being. It is justified and even required since childhood, including puberty, is a specific period of very complex human and personal development, including lacking competencies and specific developmental vulnerabilities.

(g) Last, the media could argue that they are just exercising their legitimate rights and that potential negative effects on children are just side effects of doing what they have a right to do and thus legitimate and not blameworthy. As to the freedom of the media in a liberal society we need to remind that the sacred core and function warranted by the basic right of media freedom consist in freely informing about and criticizing the government and all persons and structures endowed with power. It is a civil right against the state. In contrast, in this article we are concerned with the relation between two civil parties, the media and the adolescents, and not between the media and the state. Furthermore, the thin body idealizing contents of media are mostly used for entertainment and advertising and therefore do not belong to the most valuable and most protected media activities such as informing about political and social questions and expressing political opinions. When it comes to a conflict of interests between two civil parties who are both entitled by certain rights, no party is entitled to maximally use and exercise her right without regard for the legitimate interests and rights of others.

Conclusion and Policy Measures

The question of idealizing thin body media contents and their role for the development of EDs in children concerns core elements of children's interests and well-being. In contrast, the interests of the media in advertising and broadcasting very thin body images is of minor importance for the media and represents only a marginal element of the freedom rights of the media. It is highly plausible that the media, in various ways, contribute to a toxic social environment where children are more likely to develop full or subthreshold EDs as well as related phenomena such as high body dissatisfaction, internalization of the thin body ideal and unhealthy weight control behaviors. There is no ethical justification for the media in inflicting such risks, harms and burdens on children. The media have responsibility for those effects, which might incline children towards EDs or related phenomena. Determined measures and restrictions to be placed upon the media in order to address the risks for children's well-being, which are associated with media thin body images, are not only legitimate and reasonable; these are measures we owe to children on behalf of the respect we give them as persons of equal moral rights and status. The state has the duty to protect the children if the media do not change.

There are various measures that might be suitable to protect children and which, if suitable, should be introduced:

- a duty not to show body figures with a BMI under 19[16];
- a duty not to encourage the development of EDs[17];
- a duty to declare if thin body pictures have been digitally modified[18];
- warnings: TV programs and fashion magazines which concentrate on thin body contents should offer room to warning and educational messages to be elaborated by youth protection agencies to offer children alternative and realistic messages;
- tax: there should be an extra direct or indirect tax on thin body contents that should be used with regard to EDs in adolescents, for instance for education campaigns, clinical support programs and scientific research.

References

APA, American Psychiatric Association. 2013. *Diagnostic and statistical manual of mental disorders: DSM-5*. Washington, DC [u.a.]: American Psychiatric Association.

Bakalar, Jennifer L., Lisa M. Shank, Anna Vannucci, Rachel M. Radin, and Marian Tanofsky-Kraff. 2015. Recent advances in developmental and risk factor research on eating disorders. *Current Psychiatry Reports* 17(6): 1–10.

Becker, Anne E., Rebecca A. Burwell, David B. Herzog, Paul Hamburg, and Stephen E. Gilman. 2002. Eating behaviours and attitudes following prolonged exposure to television among ethnic Fijian adolescent girls. *The British Journal of Psychiatry* 180(6): 509–514.

Bemporad, Jules R. 1997. Cultural and historical aspects of eating disorders. *Theoretical Medicine* 18(4): 401–420.

Birmingham, C. Laird, Su. Jenny, Julia A. Hlynsky, Elliot M. Goldner, and Min Gao. 2005. The mortality rate from anorexia nervosa. *International Journal of Eating Disorders* 38(2): 143–146.

Buss, Sarah. 2013. Personal autonomy. In *The Stanford encyclopedia of philosophy*, ed. E. N. Zalta. http://plato.stanford.edu/entries/personal-autonomy/. Accessed on 7 Sept 2015.

Cafri, Guy, Yuko Yamamiya, Michael Brannick, and J. Kevin Thompson. 2005. The influence of sociocultural factors on body image: A meta-analysis. *Clinical Psychology: Science and Practice* 12(4): 421–433.

Campbell, K., and R. Peebles. 2014. Eating disorders in children and adolescents: State of the art review. *Pediatrics* 134(3): 582–592. doi:10.1542/peds.2014-0194.

Carr, R., and R. Peebles. 2011. Developmental considerations of media exposure risk for eating disorders. In *The Oxford handbook of child and adolescent eating disorders: Developmental perspectives*, ed. James Locke. Oxford/New York: Oxford University Press.

Dittmar, Helga. https://campaignforbodyconfidence.files.wordpress.com/2010/11/execsummary-annex1.pdf. Accessed on 7 Sept 2015.

---

[16] Accordingly, Israel and France issued a law determining an obligatory minimal threshold for fashion models.

[17] France introduced a law against the encouragement of eating disorders.

[18] In its campaign for women's body confidence ("real beauty") the Dove company has produced a public accessible video entitled "evolution", which illustrates the massive potential impact of digital modifications on "pictures" of fashion models.

Dittmar, Helga, and Sarah Howard. 2004. Thin-ideal internalization and social comparison tendency as moderators of media models' impact on women's body-focused anxiety. *Journal of Social and Clinical Psychology* 23(6): 768–791.

Dworkin, Ronald. 2013. *Taking rights seriously*. Paperback ed. Aufl. Bloomsbury revelations. London [u.a.]: Bloomsbury.

Feinberg, Joel. 1980. The child's right to an open future. In *Whose child? Children's rights, parental authority, and state power*, ed. W. Aiken and H. LaFollette. Totowa: Rowman and Littlefield.

Field, A.E., L. Cheung, A.M. Wolf, D.B. Herzog, S.L. Gortmaker, and G.A. Colditz. 1999. Exposure to the mass media and weight concerns among girls. *Pediatrics* 103(3): E36.

Field, Alison E., Kristin M. Javaras, Parul Aneja, Nicole Kitos, Carlos A. Camargo, C. Barr Taylor, and Nan M. Laird. 2008. Family, peer, and media predictors of becoming eating disordered. *Archives of Pediatrics & Adolescent Medicine* 162(6): 574–579.

Gabhainn, Saoirse Nic, Geraldine Nolan, Cecily Kelleher, and Sharon Friel. 2002. Dieting patterns and related lifestyles of school-aged children in the republic of Ireland. *Public Health Nutrition* 5(03): 457–462.

Giordano, Simona. 2003. Persecutors or victims? The moral logic at the heart of eating disorders. *Health Care Analysis* 11(3): 219–228.

Giordano, Simona. 2005. Anorexia nervosa and its moral foundations. *The International Journal of Children's Rights* 13: 149.

Giordano, Simona. 2008. *Understanding eating disorders: Conceptual and ethical issues in the treatment of anorexia and bulimia nervosa*. Oxford: Clarendon.

Giordano, Simona. 2010. Anorexia and refusal of life-saving treatment: The moral place of competence, suffering, and the family. *Philosophy, Psychiatry, & Psychology* 17(2): 143–154.

Götz, Maya, Caroline Mendel, and Sarah Malewski. 2015. Dafür muss ich nur noch abnehmen – Die Rolle von Germany's next Topmodel und anderen Fernsehsendungen bei psychosomatischen Essstörungen. *Televizion* 28(1): 61–67.

Grabe, Shelly, L. Monique Ward, and Janet Shibley Hyde. 2008. The role of the media in body image concerns among women: A meta-analysis of experimental and correlational studies. *Psychological Bulletin* 134(3): 460.

Groesz, Lisa M., Michael P. Levine, and Sarah K. Murnen. 2002. The effect of experimental presentation of thin media images on body satisfaction: A meta-analytic review. *International Journal of Eating Disorders* 31(1): 1–16.

Hargreaves, Duane, and Marika Tiggemann. 2003. The effect of "thin ideal" television commercials on body dissatisfaction and schema activation during early adolescence. *Journal of Youth and Adolescence* 32(5): 367–373.

Hausenblas, Heather A., Anna Campbell, Jessie E. Menzel, Jessica Doughty, Michael Levine, and J. Kevin Thompson. 2013. Media effects of experimental presentation of the ideal physique on eating disorder symptoms: A meta-analysis of laboratory studies. *Clinical Psychology Review* 33(1): 168–181.

Huemer, J., R.E. Hall, and H. Steiner. 2011. Developmental approaches to the diagnosis and treatment of eating disorders. In *The Oxford handbook of child and adolescent eating disorders: Developmental perspectives*, ed. James Lock, 39–55.

Jacobi, C., L. Morris, and M. de Zwaan. 2004. An overview of risk factors for anorexia nervosa, bulimia nervosa, and binge eating disorder. In *Clinical handbook of eating disorders: An integrated approach*, ed. T.D. Brewerton, 117–164.

Jade, Deanne. 2009. *The media and eating disorders*. http://eating-disorders.org.uk/information/the-media-eating-disorders/. Accessed on 7 Sept 2015.

Keski-Rahkonen, Anna, Hans W. Hoek, Ezra S. Susser, Milla S. Linna, Elina Sihvola, Anu Raevuori, Cynthia M Bulik, Jaakko Kaprio, and Aila Rissanen. 2007. *Epidemiology and course of anorexia nervosa in the community*.

Knauss, Christine, Susan J. Paxton, and Françoise D. Alsaker. 2007. Relationships amongst body dissatisfaction, internalisation of the media body ideal and perceived pressure from media in adolescent girls and boys. *Body Image* 4(4): 353–360.

Kohn, Michael, and Neville H. Golden. 2001. Eating disorders in children and adolescents. *Paediatric Drugs* 3(2): 91–99. doi:10.2165/00128072-200103020-00002.

Levine, Michael P., and Sarah K. Murnen. 2009. "Everybody knows that mass media are/are not [pick one] a cause of eating disorders": A critical review of evidence for a causal link between media, negative body image, and disordered eating in females. *Journal of Social and Clinical Psychology* 28(1): 9–42.

Lintott, Sheila. 2003. Sublime hunger: A consideration of eating disorders beyond beauty. *Hypatia* 18(4): 65–86.

Lock, James, Maria C. La Via, and American Academy of Child. 2015. Practice parameter for the assessment and treatment of children and adolescents with eating disorders. *Journal of the American Academy of Child and Adolescent Psychiatry* 54(5): 412–425.

Matusek, Jill Anne, and Margarets O'Dougherty Wright. 2010. Ethical dilemmas in treating clients with eating disorders: A review and application of an integrative ethical decision-making model. *European Eating Disorders Review* 18(6): 434–452.

McNicholas, Fiona, Alma Lydon, Ruth Lennon, and Barbara Dooley. 2009. Eating concerns and media influences in an Irish adolescent context. *European Eating Disorders Review* 17(3): 208–213.

Neumark-Sztainer, Dianne, Susan J. Paxton, Peter J. Hannan, Jess Haines, and Mary Story. 2006. Does body satisfaction matter? Five-year longitudinal associations between body satisfaction and health behaviors in adolescent females and males. *Journal of Adolescent Health* 39(2): 244–251.

Nicholls, Dasha, Rachel Chater, and Bryan Lask. 2000. Children into DSM don't go: A comparison of classification systems for eating disorders in childhood and early adolescence. *International Journal of Eating Disorders* 28(3): 317–324.

Papadopoulos, Fotios C., Anders Ekbom, Lena Brandt, and Lisa Ekselius. 2009. Excess mortality, causes of death and prognostic factors in anorexia nervosa. *The British Journal of Psychiatry* 194(1): 10–17.

Peebles, Rebecka, Kristina K. Hardy, Jenny L. Wilson, and James D. Lock. 2010. Are diagnostic criteria for eating disorders markers of medical severity? *Pediatrics* 125(5): e1193–e1201.

Pinhas, L. and S.J. Bondy. 2011. Epidemiology of eating disorders in children and adolescents. In *The Oxford handbook of child and adolescent eating disorders: Developmental perspectives*, ed. James Lock, 15–38. Oxford/New York: Oxford University Press.

Salbach-Andrae, Harriet, Nora Schneider, Katja Seifert, Ernst Pfeiffer, Klaus Lenz, Ulrike Lehmkuhl, and Alexander Korte. 2009. Short-term outcome of anorexia nervosa in adolescents after inpatient treatment: A prospective study. *European Child & Adolescent Psychiatry* 18(11): 701–704.

Schickhardt, Christoph. 2012. *Kinderethik. Der moralische Status und die Rechte der Kinder.* Münster: Mentis.

Smink, Frédérique R.E., Daphne van Hoeken, and Hans W. Hoek. 2012. Epidemiology of eating disorders: Incidence, prevalence and mortality rates. *Current Psychiatry Reports* 14(4): 406–414.

Spettigue, Wendy, and Katherine A. Henderson. 2004. Eating disorders and the role of the media. *The Canadian Child and Adolescent Psychiatry Review* 13(1): 16.

Stice, Eric. 2001. A prospective test of the dual-pathway model of bulimic pathology: Mediating effects of dieting and negative affect. *Journal of Abnormal Psychology* 110(1): 124.

Stice, Eric, and Heather E. Shaw. 2002. Role of body dissatisfaction in the onset and maintenance of eating pathology: A synthesis of research findings. *Journal of Psychosomatic Research* 53(5): 985–993.

Stice, Eric, Emily Burton, Michael Lowe, and Meghan Butryn. 2007. Relation of dieting to eating pathology. In *Eating disorders in children and adolescents*, ed. T. Jaffa and B. McDermott, 45–56. Cambridge/New York: Cambridge University Press.

Stice, Eric, C. Nathan Marti, Heather Shaw, and Maryanne Jaconis. 2009. An 8-year longitudinal study of the natural history of threshold, subthreshold, and partial eating disorders from a community sample of adolescents. *Journal of Abnormal Psychology* 118(3): 587.

Stice, Eric, C. Nathan Marti, and Shelley Durant. 2011. Risk factors for onset of eating disorders: Evidence of multiple risk pathways from an 8-year prospective study. *Behaviour Research and Therapy* 49(10): 622–627.

Swanson, Sonja A., Scott J. Crow, Daniel Le Grange, Joel Swendsen, and Kathleen R. Merikangas. 2011. Prevalence and correlates of eating disorders in adolescents: Results from the national comorbidity survey replication adolescent supplement. *Archives of General Psychiatry* 68(7): 714–723.

Thompson, J. Kevin, and Leslie J. Heinberg. 1999. The media's influence on body image disturbance and eating disorders: We've reviled them, now can we rehabilitate them? *Journal of Social Issues* 55(2): 339–353.

Wang, M.L., K.E. Peterson, M.C. McCormick, and S.B. Austin. 2014 Jul. Environmental factors associated with disordered weight-control behaviours among youth: A systematic review. *Public Health Nutrition* 17(7): 1654–1667. doi:10.1017/S1368980013001407. Epub 2013 Jun 19.

WHO, World Health Organization. *International statistical classification of diseases and related health problems: ICD-10*. 10. rev. Aufl. Geneva.

Part II
Justice for Children

Chapter 6
Equality of What for Children

Lars Lindblom

Abstract This paper revisits the equality of what-debate and asks whether previous conclusions hold if we analyze the arguments from the perspective of children. It makes three claims. First, that even if welfare cannot be justified as an equalisandum for adults, it remains a reasonable position for the case of children. This claim is argued for by showing that Dworkin's rejection of equality of welfare relies on an idea of responsible agency that is inappropriate for the case of children. Equality of welfare cannot, by this route, be rejected with regards to children. Second, we owe children welfare rather than opportunity for welfare. Here it is argued that Richard Arneson's move from equality of welfare to equality of opportunity for relies on the same kind of problematic assumption about responsible agency as Dworkin's argument for resources. However, the assumption about responsible agency still holds for adults, and for them we need an equalisandum that takes responsibility into account. Moreover, since children will grow up to be adults, they will need preparation for this stage in life. Therefore, both welfare and the appropriate responsibility-sensitive equalisandum will be relevant for children. The third claim is that a general theory of the equalisandum of justice should have a structure like Cohen's (99:906–944, 1989) equality of access to advantage. Advantage is understood as consisting of both welfare and resources, and access is comprised of both actually having something that is an advantage and having the opportunity to achieve a good.

Keywords Equality of what • Justice • Children • Equalisandum • Advantage

Introduction

At the very beginning of Ronald Dworkin's *Sovereign Virtue* (2000, pp. 12–13), there is an example where a father draws up a will and must decide how to distribute his resources between his children. Among his children are a playboy with

L. Lindblom (✉)
Department of Historical, Philosophical and Religious Studies,
Umeå University, Umeå, Sweden
e-mail: lars.lindblom@umu.se

© Springer International Publishing Switzerland 2016
J. Drerup et al. (eds.), *Justice, Education and the Politics of Childhood*,
Philosophy and Politics – Critical Explorations 1,
DOI 10.1007/978-3-319-27389-1_6

expensive tastes, a prospective politician, a poet with modest needs and a sculptor who works with expensive materials. The example is presented to show the difference between thinking about equality in terms of welfare and in terms of resources.[1] Equality of welfare is the view that holds that resources should be distributed to achieve as high a degree of equal welfare as possible, and equality of resources is the view that distribution should aim at equality of total resources. As is well known, Dworkin argues in favor of the latter, and the example is developed to indicate why this is an attractive theory. If the man's children have chosen different paths in life, it seems reasonable that they bear the responsibility for these choices. As we shall see, if welfare were the equalisandum of justice, then it would not be possible to take account of this responsibility.

Dworkin wants us to think of the man's children as adults. It is easy to assume that they are, because it is easy to guess that the man is old if he is drawing up his will. If we do so, many of us will also find it natural to disregard the welfare of the children and focus on their life choices, their responsibility. I propose that if we had assumed that the children were, say, around 5 years old, then we would see the implications of the example differently.

This paper revisits the equality of what-debate and asks whether previous conclusions hold if we analyze the arguments from the perspective of children.[2] It aims to show that we have reason to re-think several things that we thought we knew about the equalisandum of justice. It takes the debate on the appropriate equalisandum of justice as its starting point and is structured so that it covers all the main candidates in that debate: welfarism, Dworkin's resourcism, Arneson's idea of opportunity of welfare, Rawls's primary goods, the capability approach and Cohen's equal access to advantage. The analysis of these theories leads up to the conclusion that a general account of the equalisandum – general in the sense that it incorporates considerations regarding both children and adults – will have interesting structural similarities to Cohen's account of the equalisandum.

This paper does not provide the final word on what is good for children; it aims to investigate what the above arguments concerning the correct metric of justice imply when we take account of children. This means that the important debate on the intrinsic goods of childhood, *i.e.*, what is good for children qua children, falls outside the scope of the paper.[3] The theories I investigate, moreover, are theories of ideal theory, which means that I will not discuss issues that arise in non-ideal theory. I will discuss the concept of welfare, especially in its hedonistic form, but I will not

---

[1] The man has one further child who is blind. Arguably, it would be unfair if the blind child was not in any way compensated for his or her blindness. This complicates the formulation of equality of resources, but in the course of developing his theory, Dworkin shows how his theory can handle such issues and give compensation. This is an important aspect of equality of resources, but, arguably, not essential to discuss for the purposes of this paper.

[2] The term children could refer to descendants or to persons in childhood, it is children in the latter sense of the word that is the focus of this paper.

[3] For an overview of the issues raised in that debate, and a perspective on justice from those starting points, see Gheaus 2015.

have much to say on the different interpretations of this concept.[4] My focus, with regards to this value, will be, for reasons of space and focus, to show that there is some surprising arguments for welfare as a part of an equalisandum that takes, not only adults, but also children into account.

I shall make three claims. *First*, even if welfare cannot be justified as an equal-isandum for adults, this remains a reasonable position for the case of children. I argue for this claim by showing that Dworkin's (2000) rejection of equality of wel-fare relies on an idea of responsible agency that is inappropriate for the case of children, and that therefore equality of welfare cannot be rejected with regards to children. *Second*, we owe children welfare rather than opportunity for welfare. Richard Arneson's (1989) move from equality of welfare to equality of opportunity for welfare cannot be made for the case of children. His argument for this position relies on the same kind of problematic assumption about responsible agency as Dworkin's argument for resources. However, the assumption about responsible agency still holds for adults, and for them we need an equalisandum that takes responsibility into account. Moreover, since children will grow up to be adults, they will need preparation for this stage in life. Therefore, both welfare and the appropri-ate responsibility-sensitive equalisandum will be relevant for them. This also leads up to the *third* claim: a general theory of the equalisandum of justice should have a structure like Cohen's (1989) equality of access to advantage. This theory has two characteristics that are especially useful for a general theory in this area. Advantage is understood as consisting of both welfare and resources, and access is comprised of both actually having something that is an advantage and having the opportunity to achieve a good. This point will be developed by a discussion of Colin Macleod's (2010) analyses of Rawls's theory of justice and of the capability approach. The problem that he finds with Rawls's primary goods can be understood as showing the need for an equalisandum with the characteristics of Cohen's advantage, and his discussion of the capability approach indicates the need for a conception along the lines of Cohen's access.

Equality of Resources

In order to provide support for equality of resources, Dworkin (2000) argues against what was once the default position concerning the equalisandum of justice: equality of welfare. Dworkin's claim is that equality of welfare cannot handle personal responsibility, and that it, for this reason, mandates unfairness. Dworkin argues with the help of examples, and in the following I will attempt to show that for the case of children, these examples fail to provide us with reason to reject equality of welfare. Obviously, the concept of childhood is contested. There are questions about what characterizes a child, what childhood is and where to draw the limit between child-hood and adulthood. (Cf. Schapiro 1999) All these issues are important, but I set

---

[4] Cf. Bagattini and Macleod (2015).

them aside here. In order to fix ideas, I will present my arguments with five-year old children in mind.[5]

Welfare can be understood in several ways, and Dworkin starts by making the distinction between preferentialism and hedonism. Preferentialism is the view that welfare consist of preference satisfaction, and hedonism is the idea that welfare is the experience of pleasurable mental states. I will focus on Dworkin's arguments against the hedonistic version of welfare. One reason for this is that it is not clear, I would argue, that small children have preferences, or at least not enough preferences for this approach to be useful. As research on the concept of preference has shown, it is quite a cognitive feat to achieve a coherent preference ordering.[6] (Cf. Hausman 2012) A second reason for this is that I have the intuition that children should have a happy childhood,[7] and hedonism seems to capture much more closely the meaning of happiness one has in mind when saying this, than preferentialism.[8]

Dworkin's first argument against the hedonistic version of equality of welfare aims to show that even though this conception of equality aims to treat people equally with regards to value, it fails. To see why, compare two scholars, one of which who forgoes happiness in order to make progress in her research and one who focuses less single-mindedly on his work in order to also enjoy himself. Now, if happiness were what counts, justice would demand that we redistributed so that the first scholar reached the same level of welfare as the second. However, the difference between the two scholars comes from them having different ideas about what is important in life. Why should we say that this is an unfair inequality?

Dworkin's argument turns on the idea of responsibility for one's ambitions. Redistribution between the scholars seem uncalled for because they have *chosen* different paths in life and in such choices we are responsible for ourselves. Welfare is, hence, the wrong equalisandum for grown-ups, since it does not register

---

[5] I have chosen five-year olds as the example case, because they are not still toddlers in that they have some capacity for choice, but still too young to be held responsible for how they choose.

[6] Indeed, given the very demanding criteria for having preferences, it could be claimed that the same argument goes for adults, which would make the reasons to focus on hedonism even stronger. Since I do not need this stronger claim, I will not investigate this alternative argument here.

[7] There is, of course, much more that could be said about the concept of welfare, but for reasons of scope and space, I must set that a side for another time. For a good overview of the question of children and welfare, with an interesting argument for thinking about welfare in terms of the objective list conception, see Skelton 2015.

[8] None of the philosophers in the equality of what-debate makes use of Nozick's pleasure machine-argument (Nozick 1974, pp. 42–45), but it may have occurred to the reader that this problem presents itself here. Let me, therefore, say a few words about this problem with regards to the argument for hedonism that is being advanced. The problem is the following. If pleasurable experience is a good, would it not be better to load children into machines that stimulates their brains to experience happiness? Can this implication be avoided? The position that I argue for in this paper does not consist of only welfare, but combines welfare and preparation for adulthood for children, as well as resourcism for adults. Being put into a pleasure machine seems in conflict with preparation and is inconsistent with resourisism. This means that as a practical matter, putting children in the pleasure machine is inconsistent with the theory in its entirety. There is, of course, much more to say about the theoretical issue, but that will have to wait for another time.

responsibility. Even if Dworkin's argument goes through for the case of adults, it does not work to show that equality for children should not concern welfare. Adults are responsible agents. They have developed their understanding, foresight and responsibility. Children are not adults, in that they have yet to develop those capacities.[9] Since children are not responsible for their ambitions, the argument cannot be used to argue for equality of resources for children. One conclusion one could draw from this is that neither welfare, nor resources can play the role of the equalisandum. My approach will instead be to look for a more general account of the equalisandum that can incorporate both approaches.

Dworkin imagines that one counterargument to his rejection of hedonism would be to grant that people have different ambitions in life, but to say that those who do not value welfare are making a mistake. The point would be that since welfare is a uniquely rational goal, it should be the equalisandum of justice. Dworkin gives two replies. The first is that this kind of hedonist is wrong, welfare is not a uniquely rational goal. There are many things to value. And clearly, some of us, myself included, value other things higher than personal happiness. However, the situation is far from as clear-cut when we consider children. Why wouldn't it be correct to say that a happy childhood is a very important goal? It seems to be the common sense view that children should have happy childhoods. The question here, moreover, is not what an adult person should choose as a goal in life, but what we owe to children. Responsible agents should be free to choose their goals and ambitions, but children do not satisfy the criteria of responsible agenthood, therefore Dworkin's reply is beside the point for the question of what we owe children.

Dworkin's second reply concerns political neutrality. For reasons of legitimacy, political philosophy must take account of pluralism, in order to make it acceptable for each citizen to both govern and be governed. Therefore, a theory of justice must be neutral between conceptions of the good. The idea that people should value welfare is not neutral, whereas resourcism makes room for neutrality, since it leaves the question of the good life up to each person to figure out on the basis of a just share of resources. Now, the idea that we owe children a happy childhood differs from the idea that citizens should care about welfare in three important and related ways that make the argument from political neutrality irrelevant for the case of children. First, by saying that children should be happy, one does not say that children should go through life, including adulthood, with the ambition of becoming happy. Second, arguably, at least two things are important in childhood, preparation for adulthood and happiness. It is not incoherent to say that we owe children happiness in distributive quandaries, and that neutrality is important when we raise children into politically free and equal agents. Only for the latter is a political neutrality argument relevant. Those views can be held simultaneously. Third, it might well be the case that a happy childhood is a precondition for developing into a free and equal citizen.

---

[9] It might, as in the case with preferences above, be the case that not all adults have developed these characteristics either. In that case, Dworkin's theory might also fail for adults. Since my focus is on children, I will not investigate that question here, but rather rely on the notion that there is a difference generally between children and adults.

Therefore, the neutrality argument fails to rebut the idea that we owe children happiness.

We have now come to what is probably the most discussed part of Dworkin's argument against hedonism, the argument concerning expensive tastes.[10] An expensive taste is a taste that it costs more than average tastes to satisfy. If one needs champagne to achieve the level of welfare that other people get through drinking beer, then one has an expensive taste. Now, says Dworkin, imagine a society that has achieved equality and a person, Louis, which finds that he is missing something in his life. Louis sets out to develop a taste for pre-phylloxera claret and plovers' eggs. Since these goods are so expensive, Louis' equal share of resources will not provide him with very much of them and his welfare will be lower than that of other people. The implication of equality of welfare seems to be that we ought to redistribute resources to Louis. However, this seems wrong. Why should others subsidize Louis' new expensive hobby? The reason why they should not have to do this is, of course, that Louis is responsible for his ambitions. The expensive taste argument is, hence, not an argument about cost, but rather it makes a point about responsibility. On a resourcist theory Louis would carry the cost for his new expensive taste. He still has the same level of resources as everybody else. Now, as we have said, children are not responsible for their ambitions. Their ambitions are not the result of their own autonomous choice. This is importantly different from the case of Louis. The argument that adults can be responsible for their expensive taste does not give us a reason to discard welfare as the equalisandum for children.

However, there is more to be said about the problem of expensive tastes. Dworkin's most fundamental counterargument is that we need a conception of equality of resources to even make sense of equality of welfare. More specifically, we need a conception of *fair shares* in order to handle problems like that of Louis. He should be free to choose how to live his life, but not free to trespass on the fair share of others. To explain what the justice demands with regards to expensive tastes, hedonism would need to appeal to a conception of a just share of resources. But this is just to appeal to a conception of equality of resources. The idea, then, is that we have to start from a conception of fair shares, and then we can let people take responsibility for the ambitions they develop on this basis. If we believe that people are responsible for their ambitions, we should, therefore, prefer equality of resources to equality of welfare. Do we need an account of fair shares for children's welfare as well? No, if children are not responsible for what ambitions they develop this strategy won't get off the ground. The necessary connection between a fair share and ambitions, i.e., responsibility, is not there to do the work. The reason that we needed the idea of a fair share in the first place, was to account for the case of Louis, an adult who decides to develop an expensive taste. If children cannot decide to develop ambitions or tastes in such a way that it makes them responsible for their

---

[10] Arneson has a very similar argument for his position, equality of opportunity for welfare. For the same reasons that are presented above concerning Dworkin's expensive tastes argument that argument does not succeed for the case of children. For reasons of space, and in the interest of avoiding repetition, I shall not discuss Arneson's version of the argument individually.

choices, then we have no need for a notion of fair shares. Children's happiness is important, regardless of how their tastes and ambitions have come about.[11] Even if Dworkin's argument go through for the case of adults, welfarism is still a reasonable position for the case of children.

Equality of Opportunity for Welfare

Richard Arneson (1989) has famously pointed out that Dworkin overlooked a salient position when he argued for the wholesale rejection of welfare as the equalisandum of justice. What Dworkin's argument shows is just that responsibility is important, but this does not in itself necessitate the move to resources. Instead, Arneson argues, we could opt for the theory of equal opportunity for welfare. This is the view that justice is achieved when each person faces equally valuable decision trees, so that their sets of alternatives have equal value in terms of welfare. In the previous section, I tried to show that welfare is still a live option as an aspect of a general theory of the equalisandum of justice that takes both adults and children into consideration. In this section, I will investigate Richard Arneson's suggestion that correct metric of justice is not welfare, but opportunity for welfare.

Arneson sums up the problem he sees with equality of welfare in the following manner: "Individuals can arrive at different welfare levels due to choices they make for which they alone should be held responsible" (Arneson 1989, p. 83) He invites us to consider a case where two autonomous people gamble. The gamblers have equal opportunity for welfare and use these opportunities voluntarily to gamble. One of them gets rich while the other ends up poor, and they, therefore, end up with different levels of welfare. It would seem intuitive to hold the gamblers responsible and find this inequality just. However, if we return to the 5 year olds, this seems wrong. Firstly, a child at the age of five lacks important responsibility characters, such as developed foresight, which makes it inappropriate to hold him or her responsible. Secondly, our intuitions for the case of children are, at least sometimes, in direct conflict with those of the adult case. Arguably, a parent of a five-year old would return the stakes to something like the original distribution, while, possibly,

---

[11] It might be asked if this does not mean that the theory becomes very costly. What about children who are very difficult to make happy, perhaps from being used to an unjustly high standard of living? First, notice the structure of the argument here. What I try to do is to show why Dworkin's argument does not go through for children. My counterargument at this specific point can be correct, even if this implies a costly theory. Secondly, Dworkin's expensive taste argument is an argument about responsibility, it is not about cost. Moreover, Dworkin denies that equality can be too costly. He is in favor of strict equality of resources unconditionally. Thirdly, this is an argument in ideal theory. It takes place under the assumption that the parents of the children have just allocations of resources. The problem of unjustly high standards of living is a problem for non-ideal theory. Related to this point is also that other aspects of the account of the equalisandum developed in this paper will also be relevant to the question of what we owe children, which means that the implications of welfarism will be counteracted by the resourcist parts of the theory.

making allowance for this being a learning opportunity about the dangers of gambling. In other words, a parent would not hold the children responsible, but instead focus on their welfare and their future prospects in life. This case gives us no reason to abandon equality of welfare for children.

A second case concerns two persons who chose to devote themselves to different kinds of goals in life. One concentrates on his own welfare and the other focuses on what Arneson calls an aspirational preference, namely to save the whales. The latter will achieve less self-interested welfare than the first. For adults, we would not redistribute to the less well-off person, since we hold that adults are responsible for their ambitions. But clearly, we do not hold small children responsible for their ambitions in that way. Arguably, a parent would redistribute back to equality and, perhaps, even reward the child that focused on other-regarding interests. This would be reasonable in the light of children having interests in both welfare and in how they develop as persons.[12] Again, we find no reason to give up welfare as the equalisandum for children.

But what is the appropriate equalisandum for adults? How should we chose between Arneson's and Dworkin's accounts? The arguments I have made have all concerned children, but I have said nothing that would indicate that these arguments show that equality of resources or equality of opportunity is mistaken for the case of adults. Here we should return to argument concerning equal shares that we discussed at the end of the previous section. I take this argument from Dworkin to show that resources is the appropriate equalisandum for adults. Since adults should be held responsible for their preferences, it is important that these preferences are formed on the basis of a fair share of resources. Arneson's theory of welfare cannot stand on its own; for adults we need a theory of fair shares. But children's happiness is important regardless of the causal paths the led up to it. In other words, Dworkin's argument against welfare is correct for adults, but misses its goal for the case of children. We, therefore, end up with a rather complex account of the equalisandum of justice, since the argument thus far has implied that we need a general theory, where welfare is the equalisandum for children and resources for adults.

Equal Access to Advantage

What we have now is an account of the equalisandum that says that both welfare and resources are important. This is also the position of G.A Cohen, who is well-known for proposing that what justice should be concerned with is equal access to advantage (1989). In this section, I will investigate the similarities between the position we have developed thus far and Cohen's theory. In the next section, I will then attempt to illustrate the usefulness of this kind of account of the equalisandum.

---

[12]As I say below, this is an area in which there are trade-offs. I am not claiming that all parents would make the same decisions in this situation, and if the inequality is very small it might not even be worthwhile to rectify it, all I claim is that there is a tendency in the indicated direction.

Now, the reason for advantage being the correct equalisandum, says Cohen, is that both welfare deficiencies and resource deficiencies are distinct forms of unjust disadvantage. *Advantage*, then, for Cohen consists of both welfare and resources. Moreover, as Cohen notes, both Dworkin and Arneson can be understood as proposing conceptions of equality of opportunity, and Cohen's theory has a similar structure, even though he prefers a different terminology. By *access* he means to include both the standard meaning of opportunity, but he also treats "anything which a person actually has as something to which he has access." (Cohen 1989, p. 917) This stipulation is needed because one may be unable to make use of an opportunity, and this inability can also be a kind of injustice.

We can now see how we can structure our results with the help of Cohen's theory.[13] The argument has lead up to two conclusions. First, a general theory of the equalisandum should comprise of both welfare and resources. Second, children should *have* welfare, whereas the theory of justice for adults should include the notion of opportunity in the general sense that Cohen uses the term. The concept of advantage includes both welfare and resources, and the idea of access consists of both direct having and of opportunity. *Advantage*, on the theory we have developed, comprises of welfare for children and resources for adults. *Access*, on our theory, makes room for both having welfare and for the kind of opportunity that resources give. In other words, what we have developed is a theory that is structurally similar to equal access to advantage.

Our results have a structure. However, there is one more important aspect to discuss that relates to the form of the theory. Children will become adults, and an important part of their upbringing is to prepare them for this. Clearly, only focusing on the child's happiness during the years of childhood would not be a feasible method of preparation. There is a trade-off to be made between childhood happiness and preparation for adulthood, even though some level of happiness in childhood is probably a precondition for successful preparation. This trade-off is not the kind that could be avoided by finding that one value or one period of life is more important than the other. Childhood, including adolescence, takes up about 20 % of human life lived to old age, which is much too much to be declared unimportant. That adulthood would always be less important than childhood seem a very counterintuitive position. Both childhood and adulthood are important; both welfare and resources must play a role in our account of justice for children. An important difference between these values is that welfare is tied to childhood, whereas the concern for resources is forward-looking. This means that there will be times where the demands of welfare and those of resourcism comes into conflict. This position seems intuitive in the sense that it would explain the trade-offs one faces as a parent between one's children's present happiness and future prospects.

---

[13] There are, perhaps, further complications that need to be discussed; it might be the case that Cohen's Tiny Tim argument shows that welfare is important for adults as well, but for reasons of focus and space, I will leaves this matter to another time.

The Agency Assumption, Primary Goods and Capabilities

Some readers will recognize the structure of the arguments that I have presented. Colin Macleod (2010) has developed similar analyses of Rawls's idea of primary goods and of Sen's and Nussbaum's capability approach. His claim is that there is an unjustified assumption in the justifications of these theories. He calls this the Agency Assumption and describes it as follows:

> First, in thinking about what constitutes justice-salient advantages we assume that persons have and can exercise the two moral powers. Second, in virtue of their possession of the moral powers agents must assume responsibility for their ends. Third, persons are able and expected to interact with others in ways that respect the agency of fellow participants in social cooperation. (Macleod 2010, p. 179)

This is phrased in terms of Rawls's theory (2001), but the general gist generalizes. The agency assumption in a more general form, then, says that persons have the ability to exercise responsibility, that they must assume this responsibility and that they must act responsibly towards others. In this section, I present Macleod's discussion of primary goods and capabilities, and try to show both that Macleod is right about these two theories of the equalisandum being problematic when we consider children, and that these problems can be resolved if we think of the equalisandum in terms of the equal access to advantage account suggested in this paper.

Macleod argues that primary goods are irrelevant for the case of children, since children do not yet possess the characteristics for which the theory was developed. Primary goods matter to those who have the ability to use these resources for autonomous agency, but are irrelevant for children who lack this ability. They are not yet autonomous agents in possession of the two Rawlsian moral powers. The equalisandum for children must therefore be something else than primary goods. Moreover, even if we would attempt to derive a conception of the equalisandum from the adult version of primary goods for use for the case of children, we would run into the problem of incomplete derivation. This is the problem that not all that is important about childhood can be cashed out in terms of primary goods. Childhood is not "a mere preparatory phase of life" (Macleod 2010, p. 182). To see how this is a problem, compare two schools. One has a great program for extra—curricular activities and the other does not. But both are equally successful in providing the pupils with primary goods. In other words, compare a good and fun school with a school that is just good. Is this difference unfair? Intuitively, we would say that children of the second school have a valid compliant. However, this complaint cannot be cashed out in terms of primary goods. Macleod goes on to say: "Yet surely the difference is one that is salient from the point of view of justice since it is unreasonable to hold the children responsible for the significant differences in the quality of their childhoods." (Macleod 2010, p. 182–183) If this is correct, then we need an account of the equalisandum for children that do not rest on the agency assumption. Macleod suggests that in order to make sense of his results we should investigate whether there are intrinsic goods of childhood, but notice that if the important difference between the two schools is that one is more fun than the other, then hedonistic welfare seems to do the trick nicely. What is needed is a conception of the equalisandum along the lines of Cohen's advantage. In that way we can say both that resources, e.g., primary goods, are important for adults and that welfare is important for children.

Let us now turn to Macleod's analysis of the capability approach of Nussbaum (2000) and Sen (1999). This is the view that justice should be concerned with capabilities. To explain this concept, it is helpful to start with the distinction between functionings and capabilities. A functioning is something one can be or do, like being nourished or to read. A capability is an ability to achieve a functioning. The capability approach, then, says that the equalisandum should not be thought of as functionings, but as capabilities. The reason for this choice of dimension has to do with the agency assumption. People are responsible for their own ends, and, hence, should be free to choose them. This seems reasonable for the case of adults, claims Macleod, but if children have not yet developed to the stage when they can be responsible for their choices, then the capability approach will be inappropriate as the equalisandum of justice. One way to get around this problem would be to say that for children the equalisandum should be functionings. However, another way to go, that would also solve the problem that Macleod identifies, is to turn to equal access to advantage. Since access includes both having and having the opportunity to achieve a good of justice, we get a general account of the equalisandum, which makes room for both the considerations relevant for children and for adults. Children should have happiness, whereas adults being responsible for their choices, should have opportunity to achieve the goods of justice. What we have found, then, is that Macleod's playground argument against Rawlsian primary goods points us in the direction of an equalisandum that consists both of resources and welfare, i.e., advantage, and that his argument against the capability approach show the usefulness of a theory that includes Cohen's notion of access.

The aim of this paper has been to investigate what conclusions follow if we look at the equality of what-debate from the perspective of children. What we have found is that the arguments then point in the following direction. We owe children both happiness and preparation for adulthood. Justice for adults should be understood as equality of resources. Both these point can be subsumed under the umbrella of equality of access to advantage. As was noted in the beginning of this chapter, there are other arguments that are important for this issue, such as those presented with regards to the debate on intrinsic goods of childhood. However, we can conclude that by doing something important – thinking about justice from the perspective of children – we end up with something surprising, namely the conclusion that a theory much like Cohen's equal access of advantage has much that speaks in favor of it when both adults and children are considered.

Acknowledgements I am indebted to the participants of the MANCEPT workshop on Children and Political Philosophy and the audience at a presentation of this paper at Umeå University. Special thanks to Sara Belfrage, Anca Gheaus, Kalle Grill and Niklas Möller. This work was supported by a grant from the Swedish Research Council.

References

Arneson, R. 1989. Equality and equal opportunity for welfare. *Philosophical Studies* 56: 77–93.
Bagattini, A., and C. Macleod (eds.). 2015. *The well-being of children in theory and practice*. Dordrecht: Springer.
Cohen, G.A. 1989. On the currency of egalitarian justice. *Ethics* 99: 906–944.
Dworkin, R. 2000. *Sovereign virtue*. Cambridge: Harvard University Press.
Gheaus, A. 2015. The intrinsic goods of childhood' and the just society. In *The well-being of children in theory and practice*, ed. Alexander Bagattini and Colin Macleod, 35–52. Dordrecht: Springer.
Hausman, D.M. 2012. *Preference, value, choice, and welfare*. Cambridge: Cambridge University Press.
Macleod, C. 2010. Primary goods, capabilities, and children. In *Measuring justice. Primary goods and capabilities*, ed. Ingrid Robeyns and Harry Brighouse, 174–192. Cambridge: Cambridge University Press.
Nozick, R. 1974. *Anarchy, state, and utopia*. New York: Basic Books.
Nussbaum, M. 2000. *Women and human development: The capabilities approach*. Cambridge: Cambridge University Press.
Rawls, J. 2001. *Justice as fairness: A restatement*. Cambridge: Harvard University Press.
Schapiro, T. 1999. What is a child? *Ethics* 109: 715–738.
Sen, A. 1999. *Development as freedom*. New York: Knopf.
Skelton, A. 2015. Utilitarianism, welfare, children. In *The well-being of children in theory and practice*, ed. Alexander Bagattini and Colin Macleod, 85–103. Dordrecht: Springer.

Chapter 7
Social Policy and Justice for Children

Gottfried Schweiger and Gunter Graf

Abstract Empirical evidence clearly shows that child poverty is a growing concern in the industrialized world and that the well-being of children is deeply affected by growing up in poverty in at least two ways. On the one hand, a low socioeconomic status jeopardizes the access to goods and services that are necessary for the current well-being of children. On the other hand, growing up in poverty also, in various ways, negatively affects the well-being in later life. On the basis of the capability approach, we will show that the systematic protection and advancement of the well-being of children, and hence the reduction of child poverty, is a key task of social justice, which should therefore guide policy design and implementation. However, we will also discuss the special composition of the well-being of children and point out how it poses difficulties for state action in this regard. In particular, we will argue that the importance of love and affection for a child's well-being limits considerably the possible political measures to provide fair life chances to all children. This again reflects the insight that poverty should not be reduced to economic inequality.

Introduction[1]

The extent and depth of child poverty is one of today's most serious problems. Despite the absence of consensus on how it should be conceptualized and measured, all existing studies are clear in stating that the figures are alarmingly high. This is both the case for an absolute understanding of poverty as it is generally used for the global scale and poorer countries, as for a relative concept of child poverty, which

---

[1] This Research was funded by the Austrian Science Fund (FWF): P26480.

G. Schweiger (✉)
Centre for Ethics and Poverty Research, University of Salzburg, Salzburg, Austria
e-mail: Gottfried.Schweiger@sbg.ac.at

G. Graf
Centre for Ethics and Poverty Research, University of Salzburg, Salzburg, Austria

International Research Centre for Social and Ethical Questions, Salzburg, Austria
e-mail: ggraf@ifz-salzburg.at

© Springer International Publishing Switzerland 2016   101
J. Drerup et al. (eds.), *Justice, Education and the Politics of Childhood*,
Philosophy and Politics – Critical Explorations 1,
DOI 10.1007/978-3-319-27389-1_7

is used to capture and assess child poverty in richer countries (UNICEF IRC 2013). For example, according to the National Center for Children in Poverty in the United States, more than 16 million (22 %) children under the age of 18 lived in poor families in 2011 (Addy et al. 2013). On a global scale the World Bank recently reported that more than 400 million children live in severe poverty (Olinto et al. 2013). These figures, as disturbing as they are, can only provide the starting point to examine the normative dimension and injustice of child poverty from a philosophical perspective. In this article we want defend basically two claims that seem crucial in this respect: first, that child poverty is a serious violation of social justice for children, in that living and growing up in poverty affects the well-being of children negatively in at least two ways – on the one hand, it jeopardizes the access to goods and services which are necessary for the current well-being of children; on the other hand, growing up poor also negatively affects, in a variety of ways, the well-being in later life. Our second claim is that although the state has a duty of creating social justice to provide for those children and alleviate their poverty, it is confronted with certain obstacles in the composition of children's well-being, development and well-becoming. We will limit our discussion in this article to child poverty in developed countries that do provide a system of social protection for children. There are significant differences between and within such welfare states and we have to keep our discussion on an abstract level that ignores them but we are confident that our general treatment of the topic of child poverty still provides insights that are applicable to different contexts and states.

Our considerations point towards a more inclusive social policy for children in poverty, which should be guided by the goal of social justice for all children and of giving them the opportunity to live a life in well-being and well-becoming. By concentrating explicitly on the normative aspect of child poverty and connecting it to its influence on the well-being and well-becoming of children, we also put forward the view that empirical and explanatory knowledge alone, as produced by the social sciences, is neither enough to fully understand child poverty nor can it alone guide practice and politics. In fact, such empirical research is often interspersed by normative assumptions and goals seldom made explicit, which is, or so we will argue, a serious omission for any theory of poverty.

Social Policy, Justice and the Well-Being of Children

The claim that social policy should be generally concerned with the well-being of people and with questions on how it can be secured and promoted is uncontroversial. Social policy asks for the conditions that shape the existence of every human being and analyses the economic, social and political systems which affect the lives people are effectively able to lead. In doing so, it focuses particularly on those members of society who are, for different reasons, in a rather weak social position. Or, to put it differently, it concentrates its efforts around the most vulnerable persons, and the securing and promoting of their well-being are at the heart of social policy considerations (Dean 2012). A look at the empirical evidence shows that one of those groups which deserve special attention is the one of children, and this is the case for at least two reasons: firstly, childhood is a phase of high vulnerability and dependency. Due to their cognitive, emotional and physical immaturity, children are inherently dependent on other persons for their well-being for a considerable time. They need to be cared for and suffer serious harm if experiences of love and belonging are missing in their lives or if they are neglected and abused. Furthermore, in many circumstances they need guidance of a more experienced care giver in order to achieve and sustain even a minimum level of well-being and to make the right choices that shape their well-becoming. The second reason, which is related to the previous one, is that childhood plays a fundamental and formative role in the development of any human being – problems and difficulties in childhood very often translate into disadvantages in adulthood. Experiences of suffering and misrecognition during the childhood are not only problematic for the current state of being a child, but also for life chances in the future. Justice for children and its implementation in social policy is hence concerned both with the actual well-being and the well-becoming of children, and these two dimensions come together in the idea of equality of opportunity that we want to give all members of society.

One influential theory that can inform normative reasoning within social policy is the capability approach, which states that the evaluations of societal arrangements, quality-of-life assessments and judgments about social justice or development should primarily focus on people's capabilities and functionings, which enable the conceptualization of their opportunities (Sen 1999; Nussbaum 2011; Robeyns 2005). Functionings are the activities and states that make up a person's life; they are the different "beings" and "doings" living consists in. And since human existence consists of many different doings and beings, the category of functionings is a broad one. Being healthy and educated, having a shelter, taking part in the life of the community are examples of them that are just as good as being undernourished, killing animals or feeling emotional distress. In any case, it is very important to note two things. First, they have to be distinguished clearly from the resources employed to achieve these functionings, even if most of them depend heavily on some input from them. Second, a mental metric as used by utilitarians can be seen as a relevant subcategory of functionings (e.g. being happy) but does not – by far – include all the necessary information about an individual's circumstances. Rather for the capability approach it is not enough to only look at the functionings realised by a person in order to compare his situation to those of others but especially at the capabilities one person has. Capabilities are defined as the functionings a person actually has access to and reflect the person's freedom to realize different achievements. To give an example, eating is a functioning while the real opportunity to eat is the respective capability.

A person's capabilities depend on many different so-called conversion factors, which means that capabilities are a product of a person's abilities and skills as well as the political, social and economic context she finds herself in. And of course they usually depend on resources. Without the necessary goods it is just not possible to live a self-determined life according to one's own conception of the good. What matters in the end is, in the perspective of the capability approach, what each and every person is effectively able to do and to be, not what he or she possesses. According to the approach, a minimal condition for social justice is that a certain threshold of functionings and capabilities is guaranteed for every member of society, and that human flourishing is not the privilege of a small elite but a real option for everyone. The human potential for self-realization and for unfolding particular powers, which waste away if not fostered and stimulated, ground basic claims of justice which clearly influence the way a society should be arranged. Every person should be seen as an end, not simply as the agent or supporter of the ends of others. Where this threshold has to be set is a question that cannot be determined independently of context and deliberation processes. However, the guiding idea used in the capability approach is that it denotes a level, "beneath which it is held that truly human functioning is not available to citizens" (Nussbaum 2006, 71).

Despite some recent discussions on the topic of social justice for children, it is still not sufficiently developed in the capability approach and most considerations are concerned with fully mature and reasonable adults (Dixon and Nussbaum 2012). We want to try to give a first brief sketch of what justice for children from a capability perspective could mean.[2] We see the well-being and well-becoming of children as the normative benchmark and goal of social justice, which means that every child has a claim to growing up in well-being and to have those opportunities necessary for well-becoming and to develop into an autonomous member of society. Such a focus on well-being and well-becoming does justice to the claims of *children qua children* and to the phase of childhood as one of crucial development (Graf and Schweiger 2015b). But well-being and well-becoming are not to be understood as states of mere subjective satisfaction. They are multi-dimensional and encompass a whole range of different capabilities and functionings. A fully developed theory of social justice for children would have to clarify those capabilities and functionings in detail and also discuss their distribution. Our aims are more modest here. We do not think that for a critique of child poverty as unjust and harmful such a fully elaborated theory is necessary – rather we need to engage with those dimensions of injustice against the background of a first and incomplete idea of justice that can guide our examination of the reality of child poverty and the knowledge we have about it.

We do not wish to explore here the deep and sophisticated debate on the currency of justice but rather sketch why capabilities and functionings appear to be the right choice if one is concerned with justice for children (Anderson 2010). Capabilities and functionings have the advantage of being sensitive to differences in the usage of goods and resources and they are sensitive to discrimination and other injustices that affect the conversion of resources into capabilities and functionings. A theory of justice for children should be concerned with what they are actually able to do and be. Capabilities and functionings are ends, whereas resources or goods are means and, therefore, a focus on capabilities and functionings is able to directly compare differences in what ultimately matters: the well-being and well-becoming of children. For children, resources are also very often only of indirect importance

---

[2] We give a much more comprehensive account in Graf and Schweiger (2015a).

and mediated through their care-givers and other institutions. Income, wealth and voting rights for example are of no direct use for small children but do heavily affect their well-being and well-becoming. A capability approach seems more suited to capture these dependencies. But what selection of capabilities and functionings are qualified to serve for comparisons in well-being and well-becoming and should be specified as the currency of justice? Before we will explore this question, we want to begin by asking whether the currency of justice for children should be capabilities or functionings or both.

Most capability theorists prefer capabilities over functionings because of the high value of autonomy and choice. Within the broader setting of political liberalism most authors within the capability approach argue that people should have central capabilities but it should be left to their own choice whether or not they want to realize them into functionings (Nussbaum 2011). An example that is often used is that of the capability to be well nourished, which certainly is a central one, but that people should still have the option to fasten and if one chooses to do so and therefore does not realize the functioning of being well nourished this does not poses a problem of justice. This argument has a lot of force but it also has its limitations that are well acknowledged by capability theorists: first, the problem of adaptive preferences, which can not only lead people to adapt to unjust circumstances and the deprivation of even central capabilities but also has an effect on people wanting to realize certain capabilities into functionings. Think of a society in which women have the right to vote and all necessary access to do so safely but most decline because of their ideological conviction that women are not capable of political decision-making. Most would agree that justice should also be concerned with such an issue and one should not be satisfied with simply providing the capability to vote but to make the participation of women actually happen. It is also the functioning that counts. In the case of children a focus on functionings is further supported by the already mentioned limited capacity to act autonomously and rationally. Children do not just need the capability to have education but they should realize it and acquire the functioning of being educated because this is relevant for their actual and their future well-being. The same goes for other important capabilities like being healthy, being socially included or having shelter, nourishment and clothing. Another practical reason why functionings are of importance is that they are measurable – at least a lot more easily than capabilities – and comparable (Alkire 2002).

There is also a fluent passage between capabilities and functionings and they both have a certain plasticity. There are many stages between having the capability to be well nourished to the realization of the functioning to be well nourished and both can be satisfied in various ways. Having this capability can mean to have immediate access to food that is in the refrigerator, it can mean to have access to a supermarket and to have the funds to buy food there, to be well nourished can mean to have just eaten one's favorite sandwich or it can refer to a person that is actually hungry because she has not eaten for a few hours but is healthy and has in general enough and good meals. At a closer look the boundary between capabilities and functionings becomes less clear. These arguments support our view that they are both of importance for well-being and well-becoming and that a theory of justice for children does not need to make a general decision on which one is more important overall. Rather, if a set or list of capabilities and functionings is chosen it has to be made explicit if and for whom the benchmark is a capability or a functioning. For example, for a 8 year old child education should be interpreted in terms of a clearly defined functioning – the 8 year old should actually go to school – while for a 16 year old it could be interpreted in terms of a capability – a 16 year old should have the opportunity to go to school but is also free to choose "training on the job" to be become a plumber.

Now, there are many functionings and capabilities which are relevant for the well-being and well-becoming of children. For the purpose of this article, though, we want to focus on four of them, which are of particular relevance for social justice for children and to which all children in any given society are entitled to up to a level that their well-being and well-becoming is protected: health, education, self-respect and inclusion. To put it in the terminology of the capability approach: we are concerned here with the capabilities of children to be healthy, to be educated, to experience self-respect and to be included. All these are capabilities or, if realized, functionings that children can have to a varying degree based on internal and external conversion factors such as their biological make-up, their social and natural environment and their interactions with others or the resources they command. There is a long and unresolved discussion within the capability approach about how a set or list of central capabilities and functionings can be chosen and justified, and we do not claim to have a new solution to this problem. Rather, we argue that there are good reasons to think of these four capabilities and functionings as central and as important in any such a list or set. Surely, there are other important capabilities and functionings for the well-being and well-becoming of children as well (Biggeri and Mehrotra 2011), but our claim that child poverty is unjust and harmful for those children can already be supported comprehensively by focusing on those four. Therefore, our arguments in this article can be understood as part of a bigger project to examine the injustice of child poverty and they are not exhaustive. They provide a first and limited approach to a philosophical evaluation of child poverty.

The reason to select health, education, self-respect and inclusion is twofold: firstly, all of them represent particularly fundamental aspects of human existence, and there is vast agreement in the capability approach that they are *intrinsically valuable* elements of a good human life (Nussbaum 2000; Sen 1999; Alkire 2002); secondly, they are also *instrumentally valuable,* which means that they have a key function in relation to many other dimensions of life, starting in childhood and lasting until old age. They tend to promote the evolvement of other capabilities if adequately cultivated, but may have an extremely corrosive effect if endangered (Biggeri et al. 2011; Wolff and De-Shalit 2007). These interactions and possible synergies deserve particular attention when justice for children is at stake.

The Injustice of Child Poverty

In this section we will argue that child poverty is unjust and a moral wrong because it violates children's legitimate claims to justice, severely harming their well-being and well-becoming. Children in poverty are denied adequate access to important capabilities and functionings which constitute justice and which must be available to live a life in well-being. Rather, child poverty is a source of ill-being and ill-development. Therefore, the injustice of child poverty is related to two different areas of concern: the actual well-being of the child and the well-becoming of the child, that is, the effects of child poverty later in life. Both are important in any consideration of the evaluation of child poverty. We will now examine child poverty and its relation to those four basic capabilities of health, education, inclusion and self-respect, and we will particularly look at the life-course effects of child poverty on them. We do not want to apply concrete thresholds of each of these four capabilities in order to determine the injustice of child poverty. Instead we view it as sufficient to show that poverty has a certain negative affect on these capabilities, which is connected to harm and to suffering. Furthermore, we suggest that these negative effects cannot be traced back to choices that these children made for which they could be made responsible. In addition we claim that the injustice is constituted by the fact that children in poverty as a group are negatively affected in these four capabilities in comparison to their non-poor peers. Here we follow a line of argument that was developed by Ingrid Robeyns in her criticism of gender injustice (Robeyns 2003). She writes that for some inequalities in capabilities it is unreasonable to assume that they exist because of different preferences, so for example that a certain social group like migrants or women would choose to be unhealthy. For children we believe that this argument is even stronger. Inequalities between children cannot attributed to preferences and also, if they show a social gradient, to natural characteristics. If the group of children that live in poverty shows lower results in health, education, self-respect and inclusion it is reasonable to attribute this inequality to factors that they cannot control and that are socially produced. They fare worse without a good justification and that is unjust, because all children have equal claims to these important capabilities and functionings.

Health is most definitely a basic capability and a fundamental prerequisite to realize many, if not most other capabilities and functionings in life (Venkatapuram 2011). The literature on the relation of health and poverty has grown over the last years and is now conclusive on the negative effects of poverty and socio-economic inequalities on both children and adults (Braveman et al. 2011). In developing countries, causes related to poverty such as under- and malnutrition, poor hygiene, lack of access to health care and clean water lead to the early death of millions of children each year (Liu et al. 2012). But also in rich countries, children growing up in poverty are not only more likely to have health problems during childhood, but also suffer significantly more often from ill-health in their later lives and die younger than their non-poor peers (Conroy et al. 2010). The pathways are multifactorial and influenced by environmental elements, housing conditions, behavioral patterns, inadequate nutrition, restricted access to health care and to information. Poverty seems to be influential even before birth, as some evidence of negative health outcomes for children resulting from chronic stress due to poverty and financial strains during pregnancy suggests (Dunkel Schetter and Glynn 2010). Ill health also translates into other problems which affect well-being and has a significant impact on education, inclusion and self-respect, as well.

The second capability we have defined as important regarding justice for children is education, which is, again, also a prerequisite for many other capabilities and functionings and for the realization of real freedoms in life (Leßmann 2009; Walker and Unterhalter 2010). Education is the basis for reasonable decision-making processes and the ability to choose and to participate in a whole range of social, cultural, political and economic activities. It is not unreasonable to speak of knowledge as power – education being the first step to both acquire that power and critically reflect the choices and actions of oneself and those of others. The influence of poverty on education and on later outcomes in life is well studied: children growing up in poverty have lower academic achievements, face more problems in acquiring skills and knowledge in reading, writing and mathematics; they have more behavioral problems in schools and are more likely to drop out of school and training (Duncan and Murnane 2011). They are given lower grades than their non-poor peers, and still only a few children from lower socio-economic backgrounds pursue tertiary education (Condron 2011). Such problems in area of education weigh heavily and are closely connected to unemployment and to the persistence of a poor economic status over the life course. Although most of the literature focuses on the relation between poverty and schooling and academic achievement, a concept of education that does not go beyond these terms would be too narrow, leaving out broader and yet also important aspects of education, in the sense of the ideals of enlightenment and humanism. Further research shows that there is a clear connection between education and health, and that early childhood education does promote better health outcomes in later life (Albert and Davia 2010).

Inclusion or belonging is the third capability at which we want to take a closer look. We understand inclusion as the ability to engage in activities understood as standard in a certain community. Likewise, exclusion would mean the involuntary inability to engage in such activities (Millar 2007). In a broad sense, the concepts of inclusion and exclusion can be understood as covering many aspects of health, education and self-respect as we discuss them here, too, but we would rather employ a more narrow understanding. Inclusion and belonging refer more to activities like being able to go on a holiday trip, to have adequate and not stigmatizing clothing, toys and school materials, to be able to go to the cinema, to engage in shared activities or clubs or to be able to invite other children over (Ridge 2002; Main and Bradshaw 2012). Inclusion is about "fitting in" without shame and, as children grow older, also being heard and included in decisions about their lives. Children's well-being and their well-becoming is to a great extent dependent on the possibility of being part of the community in which they live and grow up and to engage in activities that are viewed as the norm by themselves and by others; the ability to engage in such activities is crucial to friendships. The danger of exclusion, as well as isolation and loneliness is closely connected to poverty, not only due to the limitation in the financial funding parents are able to provide, but also because of the general environment in which most poor children grow up, not child-friendly settings, insecurity and frustration, as a result of the lack of time caregivers and parents have for them or because an engagement would have high personal and psychological costs (Russell et al. 2008). Child poverty comes with many different experiences of exclusion, can permanently disrupt the sense of belonging and community, and is influential to anti-social and criminal behavior, which often demolishes future prospects.

The fourth basic capability we will examine here is that of self-respect, that is the ability to have a positive self-relation. This capability describes especially the subjective dimension of well-being and how children view themselves, their experiences and their relationship to others and their environment. As we laid out before, we define well-being as the composition of highly interrelated, dynamic subjective and objective dimensions, which is also supported by many other works (Camfield et al. 2009; McAuley and Rose 2010). Many children do, in fact, experience their poverty and the poverty of their families and parents negatively, and most do not have adequate coping resources to deal with them. Poor children are often the targets of bullying; they feel humiliated, ashamed, excluded and sometimes even responsible for their own poverty. This knowledge about the subjective dimensions of poverty and the inclusion of the voices and narrations of children is growing and insightful (Ridge 2002, 2009; Crowley and Vulliamy 2007). It clearly shows that poverty lowers the subjective self-perception of those children, and that such experiences, too, may have long lasting effects. Poor children have lower expectations for their lives and experience issues in self-confidence. The incidence of depression, drug abuse, self-aggression and suicide is higher in poor adolescents and adults who grew up in socio-economic disadvantaged conditions (Yoshikawa et al. 2012). This does not mean that every poor child will be certainly traumatized and that happiness, joy and positive self-relations and self-respect will remain unattainable for them, but research simply shows that poverty is, on a collective level, a significant negative influence.

We argued that poverty has a negative and severe influence on children's well-being and well-becoming, and that it is therefore unjust, as those children fare much worse in those important capabilities and functionings compared to their non-poor peers. We have concentrated our argument on four of such basic capabilities – health, education, inclusion and self-respect – and examined the theoretical and empirical evidence supporting our claims. We are aware that this is just a partial examination, but one that is further supported by the growing literature on children's well-being in its relation to poverty. Child poverty is a severe injustice from which those children – in the EU, they make up for 20 % of all infant population – neither necessarily nor naturally suffer, but rather the result of systemic failure of the respective societies in providing adequately for all of their children. Especially the publicly acclaimed and politically supported ideology of market-based desert and merit cannot claim any legitimacy, as long as children remain victims of such unequal starting chances and opportunities in their lives. Child poverty is therefore one of the main obstacles to stand in the way of a socially just access to many central capabilities and functionings. Unfortunately, the trajectories of the economic crisis and the welfare reforms triggered by it point towards an even more unequal distribution of life chances due to child poverty, which, if not tackled, translates into further injustices over their course of life.

Social Policy and the Limits of Justice

In this section we will now turn our attention to the associated duties of justice towards children in poverty and the limits of social policy in providing justice for children who are suffering from poverty or social inequality. So far, we have argued that all children are entitled to an adequate threshold of basic capabilities and functionings, and that this can provide meaningful guidance to design social policy. The concepts of well-being and well-becoming can be understood as such a set of capabilities and functionings, and serve as the point of reference to evaluate children's lives and the impact of poverty on them.

At this stage of the argument the question arises who should be held responsible for securing justice for children who suffer from poverty and social inequality. We cannot offer a full account of responsibilities here, but we think that a social connection model of responsibilities as it was outlined by Iris Young in regard to structural injustices is helpful in this regard (Young 2011). It goes beyond the classic view called the "liability model" that the knowing and voluntary causation of harm despite other options is the central reason for attributing responsibilities to an agent. Rather, it deduces grounds of responsibilities from the fact that people participate – knowingly or unknowingly, voluntarily or involuntarily – in structural processes bringing about harm to certain social groups. The causal relationships of these processes and the exact role of an individual's action in them, however, are often blurry and it is unclear how to judge them within a liability model. But in a social connection model, features such as an agent's power, interests, and privileges matter for her moral responsibility to combat existing injustices. In addition, especially when it comes to the injustice of child poverty, the closeness of a person to the child seems to confer certain responsibilities for justice as it is e.g. the case in child-parent relationships. Nevertheless, an account of moral responsibilities drawing on a social connection model must give moral weight to circumstances where it is possible to identify agents causing and upholding an injustice. But this should be seen as one reason among others and not as the only one that counts.

From such a perspective, it becomes clear that there are many agents in the child's environment who have different degrees of moral responsibilities to alleviate child poverty even if they are not or only indirectly involved in its causation. For instance, the state, the civil society, the local community, the family and parents, the peers and, at least to some extent and from a certain age and maturity, the children themselves have to be mentioned in this context. We cannot discuss all of them and their respective responsibilities to secure the capabilities of health, education, inclusion and self-respect we outlined above. We will rather focus on the role of social policy and some of its limits in regard to every child's need to close relationships, which are typically considered to be realized in the family. This insight is crucial since it connects to a major obstacle limiting certain ideals of equality and justice.

Social policy is closely connected to the social and political institutions of the state. They decide for which social policies they opt and implement the relevant measures. And since the state with its institutions is generally very powerful, at least in the welfare states we have in mind, it should be seen as one of the main agents in alleviating child poverty and its social policy is one of the main measures in doing so. The state also clearly has strong interests in there being fewer children growing up in poverty, because this will decrease the social benefits it has to pay to these children and their families during the whole course of their lives. Furthermore, it plays an important role in upholding the structures generating child poverty which strengthens its responsibilities for the alleviation of child poverty even more. When it comes to the described capabilities of health, education, inclusion and self-respect, the social policies of a state can make a huge difference in how the children under its control are doing and this takes place in at least two ways. On the one hand they can make sure that the negative consequences of child poverty in these domains become alleviated. There are ways to allow its children, for example, to have access to quality health care and education despite of the low socioeconomic position their parents might be in which will increase their chances to live a life in well-being and well-becoming even if their poverty remains a fact. On the other hand, social policies might tackle structural issues causing child and family poverty in the first place and not only its consequences. Then, a more fair and equal society is the aim and the problem is addressed at its root.

There are many obstacles social policies have to face if they want to work for these aims. There are financial constraints, entrenched political structures as well as motivational problems. But there is also a challenge arising from the particular needs of children. One crucial element for both their well-being and well-becoming is their receiving, from a very early age, a satisfying amount of nurture, care, love and emotional support, which are certainly primary essential conditions for well-being and well-becoming (Liao 2006). Indeed, a right to an upbringing embracing these elements has even been found its way into a number of international declarations and bills on the rights of children.[3] Many theoreticians, researchers and policy makers are convinced that the family – understood in a broad sense – provides the best environment for interpersonal relationships to give children what they need (Nussbaum 2000; Archard 2004). There, its different members are bound together by mutual affection, concern and loyalty, and it creates for each and every member, but especially for children, a place for identity formation and a "context of choice from which individuals can deliberate about the merits of different conceptions of

---

[3] Examples for this are the Declaration of the Psychological Rights of the Child (1979), the Declaration of the Rights of the Child in Israel (1989), the Declaration of the Rights of Mozambican Children (1979), and The Bill of Rights of Children in Divorce Actions, USA (1966).

the good" (Macleod 2002, 215). We also know, however, that not every family lives up to this ideal. Many children suffer from maltreatment and neglect, not to mention the absence of a systematic support system for their well-being and well-becoming. And while such cases may occur in families of all social layers, there is clear evidence that poverty is a major risk factor for child maltreatment and child neglect (Slack et al. 2011; Cawson 2002) and that the mere maintenance of positive and supporting relationships is difficult in situations of poverty, where the emotional and social environment that is so important for children is in so many ways distorted and disrupted. This does not mean, of course, that poor people are, in general, not able to provide an adequate care environment. Poverty does make it, nevertheless, more difficult in many circumstances.

From these considerations, at least two crucial insights for social policy measures towards the alleviation of child poverty follow: first, child poverty can only be dealt with systematically in an ecological perspective. All the different social agents and social institutions influencing the child and his or her capabilities matter, but of particular importance are the core family and close caregivers. Only if they live in circumstances free from poverty and social exclusion there is a real chance of reducing child poverty effectively. However, and this is the second insight, the special composition of the well-being of children and their need for loving and caring relationships limits considerably the possible political measures to provide fair life chances to all children. The range of the state's influence in substituting the values present in functioning families for those children who do not experience love and care from the early life stages is restricted. The provision of child care services is, indeed, a way to even up certain disadvantages, but a full compensation is hardly ever possible. Love and care cannot, by principle, be (re)distributed like most material resources, and as a consequence, serious social inequalities are very likely to persist. This becomes particularly clear for those children who have experienced serious harm and neglect in the first years of their lives and who will, even with the best compensational measures, remain disadvantaged.

In summary, social justice for children in poverty requires a detailed look at the special composition of the well-being of children. Social policy measures to alleviate child poverty cannot be reduced to a (re)distribution of economic goods and services, but they must embrace aspects of love, care and the quality of interpersonal relationships. To which extent this is possible and what measures the state is allowed to take in the private realm of the family is subject of open debate. Without approaching these questions, however, a crucial element of social justice for children – and therefore of social justice in general – will be overlooked.

References

Addy, S., W. Engelhardt, and C. Skinner. 2013. *Basic facts about low-income children: Children under 18 years, 2011*. New York: National Center for Children in Poverty. http://www.nccp. org/publications/pdf/text_1074.pdf.

Albert, C., and M.A. Davia. 2010. Education is a key determinant of health in Europe: A comparative analysis of 11 countries. *Health Promotion International* 26(2) (October 8): 163–170. doi:10.1093/heapro/daq059.

Alkire, S. 2002. *Valuing freedoms: Sen's capability approach and poverty reduction.* Oxford/New York: Oxford University Press.

Anderson, E. 2010. Justifying the capability approach to justice. In *Measuring justice: Primary goods and capabilities*, 1st ed, ed. Harry Brighouse and Ingrid Robeyns, 81–100. Cambridge/New York: Cambridge University Press.

Archard, D. 2004. *Children: Rights and childhood*, 2nd ed. London/New York: Routledge.

Biggeri, M., and S. Mehrotra. 2011. Child poverty as capability deprivation: How to choose domains of child well-being and poverty. In *Children and the capability approach*, 1st ed, ed. Mario Biggeri, Jérôme Ballet, and Flavio Comim, 46–75. Basingstoke/New York: Palgrave Macmillan.

Biggeri, M., J. Ballet, and F. Comim. 2011. Children's agency and the capability approach: A conceptual framework. In *Children and the capability approach*, ed. Mario Biggeri, Jérôme Ballet and Flavio Comim, 22–45. Basingstoke/New York: Palgrave Macmillan.

Braveman, P., S. Egerter, and D.R. Williams. 2011. The social determinants of health: Coming of age. *Annual Review of Public Health* 32(April 21): 381–398. doi:10.1146/annurev-publhealth-031210-101218.

Camfield, L., M. Woodhead, and N. Streuli. 2009. What's the use of ‚well-being' in contexts of child poverty? Approaches to research, monitoring and children's participation. *The International Journal of Children's Rights* 17(1) (January 1): 65–109. doi:10.1163/1571818 08X357330.

Cawson, P. 2002. *Child maltreatment in the family: The experience of a national sample of young people.* London: NSPCC.

Condron, D.J. 2011. Egalitarianism and educational excellence: Compatible goals for affluent societies? *Educational Researcher* 40(2) (March 29): 47–55. doi:10.3102/0013189X11401021.

Conroy, K., M. Sandel, and B.,Zuckerman. 2010. Poverty grown up: How childhood socioeconomic status impacts adult health. *Journal of Developmental & Behavioral Pediatrics* 31 (2) (February): 154–160. doi:10.1097/DBP.0b013e3181c21a1b.

Crowley, A., and C. Vulliamy. 2007. *Listen up! Children and young people talk: About poverty.* Wales: Save the Children. http://www.savethechildren.org.uk/sites/default/files/docs/wales_lu_pov_1.pdf.

Dean, H. 2012. *Social policy*, 2nd ed. Cambridge: Polity.

Dixon, R., and M. Nussbaum. 2012. *Children's rights and a capabilities approach: The question of special priority.* (Chicago Public Law & Legal Theory Working Paper, no. 384). http://papers.ssrn.com/sol3/papers.cfm?abstract_id=2060614.

Duncan, G.J., and R.J. Murnane (eds.). 2011. *Whither opportunity? Rising inequality, schools, and children's life chances.* New York/Chicago: Russell Sage Foundation/Spencer Foundation.

Dunkel Schetter, C., and L.M. Glynn. 2010. Stress in pregnancy: Empirical evidence and theoretical issues to guide interdisciplinary researchers. In *The handbook of stress science: Biology, psychology, and health*, ed. Richard J. Contrada and Andrew Baum, 321–343. New York: Springer.

Graf, G., and G. Schweiger. 2015a. *A philosophical examination of social justice and child poverty*, 1st ed. Basingstoke: Palgrave Macmillan.

Graf, G., and G. Schweiger (eds.). 2015b. *The well-being of children: Philosophical and social scientific approaches*, 1st ed. Berlin: DeGruyter.

Leßmann, O. 2009. Capability and learning to choose. *Studies in Philosophy and Education* 28(5) (January 31): 449–460. doi:10.1007/s11217-009-9123-9.

Liao, S.M. 2006. The right of children to be loved. *Journal of Political Philosophy* 14(4): 420–440.

Liu, L., H.L. Johnson, S. Cousens, J. Perin, S. Scott, J.E. Lawn, I. Rudan, et al. 2012. Global, regional, and national causes of child mortality: An updated systematic analysis for 2010 with time trends since 2000. *Lancet* 379(9832) (June 9): 2151–2161. doi:10.1016/S0140-6736(12)60560-1.

Macleod, C.M. 2002. Liberal equality and the affective family. In *The moral and political status of children*, 1st ed, ed. David Archard and Colin M. Macleod, Oxford/New York: Oxford University Press.

Main, G., and J. Bradshaw. 2012. A child material deprivation index. *Child Indicators Research* 5(3) (June 9): 503–521. doi:10.1007/s12187-012-9145-7.

McAuley, C., and W. Rose (eds.). 2010. *Child well-being: Understanding children's lives*. London/Philadelphia: Jessica Kingsley Publishers.

Millar, J. 2007. Social exclusion and social policy research: Defining exclusion. In *Multidisciplinary handbook of social exclusion research*, ed. Dominic Abrams, Julie Christian, and David Gordon, 1–16. Chichester: Wiley.

Nussbaum, M.C. 2000. *Women and human development—The capabilities approach,* 1st ed. Cambridge/New York: Cambridge University Press.

Nussbaum, M.C. 2006. *Frontiers of justice. Disability, nationality, and species membership.* Cambridge, MA/London: The Belknap Press of Harvard University Press.

Nussbaum, M.C. 2011. *Creating capabilities: The human development approach*, 1st ed. Cambridge, MA/London: Belknap Press of Harvard University Press.

Olinto, P., K. Beegle, C. Sobrado, and H. Uematsu. 2013. *The state of the poor: Where are the poor, where is extreme poverty harder to end, and what is the current profile of the world's poor?* Washington, DC: World Bank. http://siteresources.worldbank.org/EXTPREMNET/Resources/EP125.pdf.

Ridge, T. 2002. *Childhood poverty and social exclusion: From a child's perspective.* Bristol: Policy Press.

Ridge, T. 2009. *Living with poverty: A review of the literature on children's and families' experiences of poverty.* Research Report No 594. London: Department for Work and Pensions. http://research.dwp.gov.uk/asd/asd5/rports2009-2010/rrep594.pdf.

Robeyns, I. 2003. Sen's capability approach and gender inequality: Selecting relevant capabilities. *Feminist Economics* 9(2–3): 61–92.

Robeyns, I. 2005. The capability approach: A theoretical survey. *Journal of Human Development* 6(1): 93–114.

Russell, M., B. Harris, and A., Gockel. 2008. Parenting in poverty: Perspectives of high-risk parents. *Journal of Children and Poverty* 14 (1) (March): 83–98. doi:10.1080/10796120701871322.

Sen, A. 1999. *Development as freedom.* New York: Anchor Books.

Slack, K.S. et al. 2011. Understanding the risks of child neglect. In *Child maltreatment: A collection of readings*, 182–201. Thousand Oaks: SAGE

UNICEF IRC. 2013. *Child well-being in rich countries: A comparative overview.* Innocenti Report Card 11. Florence: UNICEF Innocenti Research Centre. http://www.unicef.org/media/files/RC11-ENG-embargo.pdf.

Venkatapuram, S. 2011. *Health justice.* Cambridge/Malden: Polity Press.

Walker, M., and E. Unterhalter (eds.). 2010. *Amartya Sen's capability approach and social justice in education.* Basingstoke: Palgrave Macmillan.

Wolff, J., and A. De-Shalit. 2007. *Disadvantage.* Oxford: Oxford University Press.

Yoshikawa, H., J.L. Aber, and W.R. Beardslee. 2012. The effects of poverty on the mental, emotional, and behavioral health of children and youth: Implications for prevention. *American Psychologist* 67(4): 272–284. doi:10.1037/a0028015.

Young, I.M. 2011. *Responsibility for justice,* Oxford political philosophy. Oxford/New York: Oxford University Press.

Chapter 8
The Politics of the Level Playing Field. Equality of Opportunity and Educational Justice

Johannes Drerup

Abstract This chapter provides an analysis of some of the most important criticisms of equality of opportunity as a principle of educational justice. In a critique of the critique the author shows that the apparent plausibility of recent non-egalitarian criticisms can be traced back to tensions between particular interpretations of autonomy as an aim of education and equality of opportunity as a principle of educational justice. The author argues that in contrast to adequacy conceptions, conceptions of equality of opportunity are better able to take into account the *educational* dimension of educational justice, both in terms of the justification of autonomy as an educational aim and in terms of the specific structure of educational practices and constellations. Finally, he shows that based on the theoretical and normative framework of liberal perfectionist accounts of the politics and ethics of education a 'responsibility-sensitive egalitarianism' can reconcile and resolve some of the tensions between equality of opportunity and autonomy as an educational aim.

Keywords Equality of opportunity • Equality • Education • Responsibility • Autonomy

Introduction

Ideals of equality of opportunity command broad support in public and academic debates on educational justice. The widespread usage of the concept goes along with its notorious lack of clarity. It is of course rather common that complex philosophical concepts are essentially contested (Gallie 1955). In the case of equality of opportunity, however, some critics even take into question whether it can be regarded

J. Drerup (✉)
Institute of Educational Science, WWU Münster,
Georgskommende 33, 48143 Münster, Germany
e-mail: johannes.drerup@uni-muenster.de

© Springer International Publishing Switzerland 2016   115
J. Drerup et al. (eds.), *Justice, Education and the Politics of Childhood*,
Philosophy and Politics – Critical Explorations 1,
DOI 10.1007/978-3-319-27389-1_8

as a coherent concept at all (e.g. Wilson 1991; cf. Jencks 1988, p. 533). Due to this lack of conceptual clarity and in light of a variety of older (Bourdieu and Passeron 1971) and more recent criticisms (Satz 2007; Anderson 2007; Giesinger 2007b) the "classical idea" (Giesinger 2011, p. 43) of educational justice has lost a lot of its initial appeal.

Some of the most prominent criticisms of equality of opportunity were put forward by defenders of adequacy-based conceptions of educational justice. Therefore, in what follows I will begin with some short remarks on current debates between defenders of egalitarian and non-egalitarian conceptions of justice in education (section "Educational equality and/or educational adequacy"). In the next section I will reconstruct basic conceptual elements that are constitutive of conceptions of equality of educational opportunity and discuss some of the major theoretical criticisms these conceptions attracted in recent times (e.g. the problem of stunted ambition) (section "Equality of opportunity: standard criticisms"). In the final section I develop a critique of these critiques. I will argue that the apparent plausibility of recent non-egalitarian criticisms can be traced back to tensions between particular interpretations of autonomy as an aim of education and equality of opportunity as a principle of educational justice. In line with this, I will show that in contrast to adequacy approaches conceptions of equality of opportunity are better able to take into account the *educational* dimension of educational justice, both in terms of the justification of autonomy as an educational aim and in terms of the specific structure of educational practices and constellations. Furthermore, I will argue that based on the theoretical and normative framework of liberal perfectionist accounts of the politics and ethics of education a modified version of a 'responsibility-sensitive egalitarianism' (Mason 2006) can reconcile and resolve at least some of the tensions between equality of opportunity and autonomy as an educational aim (section "Responsibility-sensitive egalitarianism, perfectionist autonomy and the justification of education"). Thus, it should be noted that my argumentative aim is rather limited in scope. Most importantly, I will not discuss many of the conflicts between equality of opportunity and other relevant principles traditionally discussed in the literature (e.g. parental autonomy, concern for the worst off). Nevertheless, I think that a reconstruction of the intricate difficulties associated with the concept of equality of educational opportunity is necessary for the further clarification of the general place of conceptions of equality of opportunity in an egalitarian theory of educational justice.

Educational Equality and/or Educational Adequacy

The appropriate role and function of principles of equality in theories of educational justice are highly contested. Contemporary sufficitarian approaches to educational justice typically combine adequacy standards (threshold conceptions) with democratic-egalitarian ideals (e.g. equal citizenship; democratic equality; equal respect and dignity) as normative criteria for criticizing unacceptable inequalities above the threshold (e.g. Satz 2007; Anderson 2007; Liu 2006; Giesinger 2012). These hybrid, pluralist theories of educational justice seem to have the advantage of providing a democratic justification of educational aims, that is compatible with established liberal principles (e.g. state neutrality) and avoids some of the major problems associated with egalitarian conceptions of educational justice (e.g. levelling down objection; incompatibility with parental autonomy). This tendency towards different forms of value pluralism, shared among theoreticians with a rather egalitarian and rather non-egalitarian orientation is at least partly due to the complexity of the normative problems involved in debates about educational justice. Since these problems cannot be adequately dealt with by relying on a monistic evaluative framework Brighouse and Swift, referring to their sufficitarian critics, conclude:

> If sufficitarians can be pluralist about values, and invoke non-sufficitarian principles to avoid unpalatable consequences, they should allow egalitarians to do the same (2009, p. 126).

Similarly, also defenders of an adequacy based approach incorporate relational-comparative elements into the definition of what is to count as enough:

> For in defining educational adequacy, it is impossible to avoid the question 'adequate *for what*?' The answer necessarily vests adequacy with a relational quality. (...) Adequacy is thus a function of the range and the contours of the overall distribution. It is a principle of bounded inequality (Liu 2006, p. 347).

Along these lines, Debra Satz not only departed from the original 'doctrine of sufficiency' (Frankfurt 1987) by conceding that comparative-relational elements should be embodied in adequacy standards (Satz 2007), but recently even tried to transform Rawls principle of 'fair equality of opportunity' into an adequacy based approach (Satz 2014). Thus, adequacy and equality based approaches do not necessarily have to be regarded as mutually exclusive. This does not imply, however, that they do not differ in important normative respects (for instance with regard to questions concerning the evaluation of inequalities above the threshold).[1] The increasing

---

[1] Especially the interpretation, application and weighting of different principles (e.g. parental freedom; regard for the worst off, sufficiency, equality of opportunity) with regard to different societal contexts and different educational systems remains essentially contested in adequacy and egalitarian conceptions of educational justice. This is also due to the fact that theories of educational justice heavily rely on empirical assumptions (while respective data are often not available) and conflicting intuitions (whose status is disputed within different methodologies). Many of the conceptual, normative and pragmatic issues a theory of educational justice has to clarify cannot be dealt with conclusively without recourse to empirical data (Brighouse 2002, p. 14 f.). This especially holds for assumptions concerning the feasibility of the implementation and application of certain principles. In general, it is rather implausible to assume that principles of educational justice could be attributed in a 1-to-1 fashion to particular policies and practices (Calvert 2014, p. 81). What follows from a particular principle is certainly not arbitrary, but nevertheless open to different conflicting interpretations. Likewise, assumptions concerning the feasibility of the implementation of certain principles *do not suffice to show that these principles do not ground legitimate normative claims*. This is one of the reasons why my primary focus in this paper is not on issues such as the "imprecision objection" against equality of opportunity (cf. Jacobs 2010).

popularity of sufficiency standards (usually in combination with other principle, like democratic equality) in contemporary theories of educational justice, which is accompanied by a shift in the political rhetoric from equality of opportunity to adequacy (Koski and Reich 2006), is to a large extent motivated by the apparent incoherence of conceptions of equality of opportunity. It remains questionable though, whether non-egalitarian attempts succeeded in developing an appropriate substitute position for the normative void left by the principle of equality of opportunity. On the contrary, it seems that non-egalitarians, apart from putting immense normative weight on the "mysterious line" (Casal 2007, p. 316), replace a rather vague concept and principle (equality of opportunity) by a variety of equally (or even more) vague concepts and principles (dignity, equal citizenship etc.), whose internal coherence as reciprocally supportive principles of educational justice is in many cases rather unclear and open to interpretation.[2] Although I cannot develop a detailed criticism of these positions here (cf. a critical discussion: Drerup 2015; see also: Jacobs 2010; Macleod 2013), in light of the widespread agreement among non-egalitarians to abandon equality of opportunity as a principle of educational justice, it seems worthwhile to take a closer look at the specific arguments put forward against it.

Equality of Opportunity: Standard Criticisms

Every conception of equality of opportunity relies on normative criteria that define under what kind of conditions what kind of inequalities are to be regarded as legitimate or illegitimate. Thus, criticisms which state that conceptions of equality of opportunity are ideological instruments to justify educational inequalities are, at least in this generalized form, somewhat misguided, because the very idea of equality of opportunity implies a justification of (potential) inequalities.[3] Equality of opportunity is meant to ensure fairness of a certain kind, a *level playing field*, which often entails an unequal distribution of goods, but is not to be conflated with equality of outcomes.[4] Different conceptions of equality of opportunity can be placed alongside a continuum between extremely formal and extremely substantive conceptions, depending, for instance, on how much normative weight is ascribed to

---

[2] By criticizing the non-egalitarian critique I do not want to defend the rather implausible claim that threshold conceptions have *no* role to play in a theory of educational justice.

[3] It is certainly true that equality of opportunity *can* be used as a means to legitimize illegitimate states of affairs, for instance, when the normative criteria a conception presupposes are themselves the product of illegitimate societal power-relations. Nevertheless, this is not necessarily the case for every conception of equality of opportunity, since alternative conceptions may be used to criticize questionable societal power-relations and to delegitimize the corresponding justificatory orders.

[4] Nevertheless, from the perspective of concern of educational equality highly unequal outcomes *can* count as a reason against a particular conception of equality of opportunity. For a recent defense of equality of outcome as a principle of educational justice: Ben-Shahar (2015).

individuals' or groups' actual ability to realize a particular set of opportunities and in how far differential outcomes are interpreted as evidence of the effective realization of the conception. The more "outcomes-sensitive" (Burbules 1990, p. 223) a conception, the higher will be the probability that choices that do not conform to the goal, set by the conception (opportunity for X), will be qualified as problematic or even wrong and not as an expression of genuine choice (cf. for this problem: Schramme 2014). In these cases inequality of outcomes is often interpreted as evidence of a lack of equality of opportunity, which is, however, a non-sequitur (Nash 2004).[5] The more formalist a conception of equality of opportunity, the more probable it is that the notion of 'choice' utilized in the conception does not take into account relevant internal or external conditions that may have thwarted the realization of an opportunity. Thus, the question, whether established criticisms of equality of opportunity as being a myth or illusion are warranted, depends not just on the societal context in which these criticisms are applied, but first and foremost on the conception of equality of opportunity one presupposes in the evaluation of a particular institutional arrangement.

Conceptions of formal equality of opportunity usually require that positions that confer some societal advantage should be open to all applicants and distributed by criteria relevant for the successful exercise of an occupation or office, such as qualification, and not by criteria where this is (usually) not the case, such as race, gender etc. More substantive conceptions of equality of educational opportunity vary with regard to the *class* of individuals who should have relevant opportunities (e.g. groups with specific needs, all individuals in a particular society or even all individuals around the world) (Jencks 1988), with regard to the *level* of the education system, where the conception should be applied (Gosepath 2014), with regard to the *sources* of legitimate inequality, which can be subdivided between *obstacles* (e.g. talent) and *criteria of access* ((Burbules 1990, p. 221; preconditions of choice (e.g. autonomy-competencies, basic literacy) necessary to overcome these obstacles (in case, this is possible)), and with regard to the *scope* or *metric* of goods and worthy practices that should be regulated by equality of opportunity, that is, the goals towards which opportunities are directed (Westen 1985, p. 842).[6] These central conceptual elements of the *concept* of equality of opportunity (e.g. sources, scope) can be interpreted in different ways in competing *conceptions* which differ with regard to their demandingness. An extreme interpretation of legitimate sources of inequality would aim at a neutralization of *all* different circumstances that have some effect on individuals' relative access to advantage (cf. for a critique of the 'neutralization approach': Mason 2006). Similarly, a very demanding interpretation of the scope of equality of opportunity may require "that equality of opportunity prevails in a

---

[5] Thus, equality of opportunity not only implies the possibility of failure, but also the possibility that the agent makes a second order choice and chooses a different option or choice environment (cf. for an analysis of 2nd order choices to choose or not to choose: Sunstein 2014). Nevertheless, from the perspective of concern of educational equality highly unequal outcomes *can* count as a reason against a particular conception of equality of opportunity.

[6] Cf. different conceptions: Westen (1985), Roemer (1995), Arneson (2002) and Mason (2006).

society only when all worthy human capacities are encouraged, developed, and rewarded" (Arneson 2002, p. 15). Principles of equality of opportunity alone, however, do not provide justificatory reasons for why these goods, goals or worthy practices should be regarded as valuable in the first place. They only specify how to evaluate unequal access to these goods. Thus, equality of opportunity as such is neither desirable nor undesirable (Westen 1985, p. 850) and remains a (rather) empty ideal, if it is not specified and justified with regard to the value of the goods that are to be regulated by the ideal. As Satz puts it:

> We cannot avoid grappling with the question of *which opportunities matter* – which institutions, lives and social practices do we have reason to value (2014, p. 42)?

Debates about the place and the function of the principle of equality of opportunity in a theory of educational justice therefore never just deal only with the value of equality, but with the value of equality in relation to some other values (Hirose 2009). With regard to the case of educational equality of opportunity this implies that informed judgments about educational justice need to rely on some notion of the concept of education and the value of educational aims. Thus, equality of opportunity can only be justified with reference to an account of the evaluative and political justification of education (cf. Giesinger 2014). Even though there are some attempts to base equality of opportunity on strictly sufficitarian principles, the structure of substantive conceptions of equality of opportunity furthermore always involves a *relational-comparative* element that specifies legitimate limits of unequal access to particular goods.

The meritocratic conception of educational equality, which was introduced into the debate by Brighouse and Swift, is a close relative of Rawls conception of 'fair equality of opportunity' and is one of the most widely discussed conceptions of equality of opportunity.[7]

> The Meritocratic conception: An individual's prospect for educational achievement may be a function of that individual's talent and effort, but it should not be influenced by her social class background (Brighouse 2010, p. 28).

One of the guiding ideas behind the meritocratic conception is fairness and the postulate that inequalities should be the result of fair procedures. In modern societies education and educational achievement, while certainly also intrinsically valuable, have a strong positional element in the sense that the life prospects of individuals are influenced to a high degree by the education they receive and by the relative advantages a comparatively good education implies in the competition for social positions.[8]

---

[7] It remains disputed, whether Rawls conception of 'fair equality of opportunity' is to be interpreted as a principle that should be applied to the field of education or whether some form of educational justice (e.g. an adequacy approach) is one of the social presuppositions that have to be in place before the principle can legitimately be applied in the context of a well-ordered society (Stroop 2014, p. 117).

[8] Singling out the social class background as an illegitimate source of inequality is a common choice, as a strong correlation between family background and school achievement is regularly

One rather obvious objection raised by the meritocratic conception is that it seems arbitrary from a moral point of view to treat inequalities that are due to social class background differently from inequalities due to natural talents. As neither of them is freely chosen, it seems illegitimate to evaluate them differently. Thus, Brighouse introduces a more radical conception, without, however, deciding which of the two conceptions he endorses.

> The Radical Conception: An individual's prospects for educational achievement should be a function neither of that individual's level of natural talent or social class background but only of the effort she applies to education (ibid. p. 29).

But also the radical conception that aims to neutralize both the influence of talent and of social class is confronted with objections that refer to the close relation between ambition, effort and social class background. Thus, conceptions of equality of opportunity lead to illegitimate ascriptions of lack of effort and ambition that hold individuals responsible in cases where this cannot be regarded as legitimate (cf. Satz 2014, p. 38). Especially in the context of education where agents are not yet fully and globally autonomous the illegitimate ascription of choice and responsibility ('It's your own fault and you deserve to suffer the consequences') can be highly unfair and have severe stigmatizing effects (Anderson 1999). This *problem of stunted ambition* in turn may lead one to extend criteria of illegitimate sources of inequality to also cover ambition and effort. Even though such an "*extreme* conception" (Brighouse and Swift 2014a, p. 18) seems not to be defended by anyone in the discussion, it's neutralizing tendency still points to an important problem for egalitarian conceptions of educational justice: The more sources of inequalities count as illegitimate, the less place seems to be left for choice and responsibility, which are established and important aims of education themselves. If, however, no one is to be regarded as responsible for anything, this does not speak in favor of the ideal of equality (Giesinger 2007b, p. 372).

Closely related to the problem of stunted ambition is the *problem of the naturalization of talent*. As Satz put it:

> There's no pre-given level of inborn, native talent that can form the baseline for applying the principle of fair equality of opportunity; at best, we can try to appeal to the idea of a child's 'potential', but even here we face hard problems in determining what this is, independent of social and environmental factors (Satz 2014, p. 39).

It seems epistemically impossible to differentiate between "the natural and the social side of a talent" (Meyer 2014, p. 147), because 'talent' is nothing given, but itself essentially dependent on the education an individual receives in a given

---

shown to be the case by PISA and other large scale assessment studies. Talent and effort in turn correspond to institutionalized and socially established meritocratic principles and intuitions and thus are often regarded as legitimate sources of inequality. Even if one is critical concerning particular reward structures that are constitutive of capitalistic economies, it remains a fact that the race metaphor highlights aspects of our society that cannot be changed overnight (if they can be changed at all). Or, as Brighouse puts it: "Of course, society is not a race. But our society is relevantly like a race" (Brighouse 2010, p. 30).

educational system (Stojanov 2007, p. 34).[9] We do not typically assume that potentials merit reward, but actual accomplishments (Anderson 2004, p. 101 f.).[10] Strict non-egalitarians, by contrast, usually deal with these problems (stunted ambition/naturalization of talents) by just setting a specific threshold that is to be reached by everyone, without placing normative weight on the specific sources that cause different forms of inequality.

Another criticism of conceptions of equality of opportunity concerns *application and transfer problems* between general conceptions of equality of opportunity and domain-specific features of the field of education and educational justice. Principles of equality of opportunity presuppose that it is legitimate, given appropriate circumstances, to hold individuals responsible for the consequences of their choices. Since "the value of free choice presupposes certain capacities on part of the choosing person that we usually do not ascribe to children" (Stroop 2014, p. 129; cf. also Stojanov 2013), it seems to make little sense to apply equality of opportunity to educational constellations. According to Stroop, "the crucial point is that the pedagogically-motivated and the justice-orientated talk of educational opportunities are not equivalent" (Stroop 2014, p. 128). The pedagogically-motivated aspect of the usage of equality of opportunity, however, is to be reserved for something like "active learning" that does not present the defense of a "justifying claim" (ibid.). Non-egalitarians solve this problem by operating with threshold conceptions that determine which basic abilities and competences have to be in place for an education system to count as just and for agents to be legitimately regarded responsible for their own decisions. Thus, Giesinger concludes that as "soon as we think of educational justice in terms of educational aims, it is natural to introduce the notion of a threshold that is set by these aims. You can reach a certain aim or fail to reach it" (2014, p. 70).

All three criticisms present important problems for an educational conception of equality of opportunity. The unabated popularity of equality of opportunity as a slogan or buzzword is probably also due to the fact that it seems to combine two values which are both regarded as central for modern liberal democracies: autonomy and/or liberty ('choice' and 'opportunity') and equality. Interestingly enough, all three criticisms of equality of opportunity in one way or another rely on the value of autonomous choice. While traditional rejections of equality as an ideal of social justice often rest on the assumption that in the name of equality individual responsibility and autonomy are nullified, in the case of equality of opportunity as a principle of educational justice it is the other way round. *Because* personal responsibility (and thus some form of personal autonomy) is regarded as the "core of the

---

[9] Apart from these epistemological difficulties, ascriptions of different levels of native talent are especially problematic in pedagogical constellations. The recognition of individuals as potentially autonomous agents with an open future, who are principally able to transcend (and thus are not fixed by) their social or cultural background or their allegedly native talents, is often regarded as an important criterion for the evaluation of educational arrangements (Stojanov 2008).

[10] It is important to note that the meritocratic conception remains agnostic concerning the question how *different* groups of similar talent should be treated.

'opportunity' idea" (Roemer 1995, p. 1; p. 4) it seems unreasonable to apply principles of equality of opportunity to the educational field without further reflection. The ascription of autonomy and responsibility in situations where social and individual conditions of autonomy are not met (e.g. questionable forms of socialization and corresponding internalized self-conceptions; lack of competencies), can be regarded as disrespectful and as an illegitimate ideology (problem 1 and 3). The same holds for reductionist identifications of individuals prospects for educational achievement with their socially inherited or 'native' talent, which also conflict with the value of (respect for) autonomy (problem 2). Even though these critiques offer some important insights, I will argue in the next section that in the case of educational justice autonomy and equality of opportunity are to be regarded as inseparable ideals.

Responsibility-Sensitive Egalitarianism, Perfectionist Autonomy and the Justification of Education

In the following I will defend three claims. Firstly, I will show that tensions that non-egalitarians typically associate with principles of equality of opportunity are not contingent upon a particular conception of educational justice, but are built into the structure of educational constellations themselves (section "Equality of educational opportunity and the justification of education"). Secondly, I will argue that autonomy as an educational aim and equality of educational opportunity are not necessarily mutually exclusive, but to a certain extent mutually supportive principles (section "Autonomy and responsibility in educational interaction orders"). Thirdly, I will argue that based on a substantive conception of equality of opportunity and a perfectionistically structured conception of autonomy, at least some of the tensions between autonomy and equality of opportunity can be resolved (section "Responsibility-sensitive egalitarianism and perfectionist liberalism").

Equality of Educational Opportunity and the Justification of Education

A central problem shared by many contemporary theories of educational justice is that they usually tend to apply assumptions of general 'ideal' (Rawls 2003) or, to use the term coined by Sen, 'transcendental' (Sen 2010) theories of justice to the field of education without giving an adequate theoretical analysis of education and educational practices. This widespread neglect of the specific structure of educational practices and the necessarily different presuppositions of a general and a domain specific theory of justice has been a major obstacle for the development of an *educational* theory of justice in education. To clarify the place of principles like equality of opportunity in a theory of educational justice, one has to specify the place of educational justice *in* educational practices, institutions and constellations (cf. Levinson 2015). As Meira Levinson puts it:

> I am struck, however, by the fact that no contemporary theorist has proposed a comprehensive theory of educational justice itself. These forays into specific questions about the intersection between justice and educational aims, policies, or practices almost always refer out to more general theories of justice, or to a more general value that is understood to adhere to justice: justice as fairness, luck egalitarianism, capability theory, antiracism, care theory, liberalism, autonomy, or the like (Levinson 2015, p. 1).

Instead of applying general theories of justice to the field of education an educational theory of justice has to ask "educational questions about education" (Biesta 2011a, p. 190). Thus, one should be reminiscent of the fact that educational practices and constellations are *asymmetrical* interaction orders that are usually justified by taking recourse to paternalistic rationales (Drerup 2013). In the case of the evaluation of educational practices from the perspective of concern of educational justice, paternalistic orders of justification, that aim at the good of the agent (e.g. well-being or autonomy), are deeply intertwined with non-paternalistic rationales that aim at some other-regarding good (e.g. some conception of the public good).

Because educational interventions are not to be identified with "causes", but with "opportunities" (Biesta 2011b, p. 130) and individual educational achievement does always to a certain extent depend on the active participation or "uptake" (Wilson 1991, p. 30) of these opportunities, also non-egalitarians cannot *guarantee* that all children reach the threshold (however one may define it). Consequently, in the attempt to bring all children above the threshold also non-egalitarians regard educational paternalism legitimate (Giesinger 2007b, p. 378).[11] Thus, questions of educational justice are not just intertwined with questions concerning the *value* of education (and educational opportunities), but also with questions concerning the (paternalistic) justification of educational arrangements and interaction orders. Both justificatory questions cannot be dealt with separately, without neglecting important dimensions of the normative issues at stake.

While non-egalitarians stay agnostic with regard to different sources of inequality and their relative normative relevance, when it comes to the (paternalistic) justification of educational arrangements, however, the processes and background conditions that result in certain actions or (un-)equal educational achievement are of central importance. With regard to the justification of educational paternalism, it is not enough to just assume that paternalism is legitimate per se until a certain threshold is reached. To evaluate and justify paternalistically motivated educational arrangements one, among others, has to differentiate between such choices that should be interpreted as a result of (potentially unjust) circumstances and opportunity

---

[11]This does not imply that non-egalitarians *have to* guarantee that all agents reach a certain threshold (which is impossible). It only implies that they have to take into account the *educational dimension* inherent to attempts to ensure a threshold. Due to the impossibility of guaranteeing a certain threshold (e.g. via educational technologies), non-egalitarians often tend to measure adequacy not in terms of results, but opportunities (Jacobs 2010, p. 252).

structures and such choices, where this is not the case. In *both* justificatory domains (educational paternalism and educational justice) one therefore has to distinguish "*culmination outcome*", which measures certain results, from "*comprehensive outcome*", which also takes the fairness of different procedures into account that lead to certain results (Sen 2010, p. 51). As it is a matter of fairness not to ascribe responsibility to agents who completely (or gradually) lack autonomy (e.g. due to the problem of stunted ambition), it is also a matter of fairness to differentiate between different sources of inequality that brought about a certain result. Likewise, it depends on the evaluation and relative weighting of these factors, whether particular forms of educational paternalism are warranted or not. If one stays agnostic concerning the relative weighting of these factors in either of *both* justificatory domains one reproduces exactly those kinds of problems one is so eager to criticize with regard to the ideal of equality of opportunity. The tensions that non-egalitarians typically associate with principles of equality of opportunity, therefore are not contingent upon a particular conception of educational justice, but are built into the structure of educational constellations itself.

Autonomy and Responsibility in Educational Interaction Orders

Arguably the most important criticism against equality of opportunity rests on the assumption that ascriptions of autonomy and responsibility are illegitimate in educational constellations. Instead it is argued that the educational aspect of educating for autonomy should be understood as some kind of "active learning" which can be interpreted as a precondition of autonomy. This assumption displays a misconception of the structure of educational practices. To understand the specific relation between different conceptions of autonomy and different conceptions of educational justice it is necessary to clarify the role of autonomy in a theory of educational justice more generally as well as the role of ascriptions of autonomy in educational practices in particular. Even though it is obvious, that children do not possess all agential capacities necessary for holding them fully responsible and autonomous (Macleod 2010), it is nonetheless implausible to treat them as mere products of their environment. Similarly, it is highly problematic to ascribe responsibility to children (or to adults) with regard to actions and behaviors, which are beyond their control. *Never* to ascribe responsibility to them, however, is incompatible with respecting them as potentially autonomous persons and with the aim of educating them for autonomy more generally. As Calvert puts it:

> Choice also provides a justification for a widely supported aim of education, that of developing agency. It suggests that children be taught in such a way that their agency and sense of responsibility for their own life is developed. (…) Suitable conditions for holding young children responsible for their choices will be quite constrained and may legitimate only very minor and temporary inequalities. But it is not unreasonable to expect that even very young children must sometimes bear the costs of their choices (Calvert 2014, p. 79).

Since small children can already be regarded as locally and gradually autonomous in many ways (Bou-Habib and Olsaretti 2015), they consequently can also be properly held (at least gradually[12]) responsible for their actions within *very* limited constraints (Calvert 2014, p. 76).[13] Consequently, it is a pedagogical truism that children have to take responsibilities within appropriate constraints to become able to learn to understand themselves as autonomous agents who are responsible for their own actions.[14] These constraints, as fair background conditions of choice, in turn can be specified, among others, by principles of equality of educational opportunity. Even though it is obviously often very difficult to discern between a genuine choice and the circumstances that cause or shape choices,[15] it is certainly not impossible and not pedagogically illegitimate to make judgments about favorable conditions of choice and such conditions where ascriptions of choice are rather questionable. Thus, contrary to non-egalitarian approaches a reflected and meaningful educational perspective forbids to regard children as totally non-autonomous and non-responsible under some threshold and to do the opposite when the threshold is reached. This neglect of the developmental and transitional aspect of education in general and of educating for autonomy and responsibility in particular is one reason why approaches that base equality of opportunity *solely* on sufficiency principles in the form of threshold conceptions of autonomy cannot be applied to educational constellations without neglecting the structure of educational interaction orders (cf. the approaches defended by Satz 2014 and Mason 2006).

Moreover, it is correct that in the case of equality of educational opportunities we principally have to speak of "mandatory opportunities" (Howe 1989, p. 319 f.). Nevertheless paternalistically structured opportunities are still educational *opportunities* which are certainly not incompatible with autonomy as an educational aim:

> Overriding choices, even children's choices, is an unacceptable approach to expanding opportunities. It is a much better approach to argue that because children need to be developmentally prepared to recognize, judge, and exercise opportunities, restrictions on their

---

[12] Aas Hirose puts it: "I think that responsibility is not a matter of all/nothing, yes/no, one/zero, or black/white. Responsibility comes in degrees" (Hirose 2015, p. 184).

[13] "Because it is rarely right to hold children responsible for their choices, very little inequality will be permissible and the costs of bad choices need to be severely curtailed – particularly any long-term costs. It is disproportionally harsh to require individuals to bear heavy ongoing costs for poor childhood choices" (Calvert 2014, p. 80). Thus, "even when we give appropriate weight to personal responsibility, we have a reason of justice not to require people to bear the costs of their choices when that would leave them destitute" (Mason 2006, p. 218).

[14] This is one reason why the so called 'learning argument' can be defended on anti-paternalistic grounds (Giesinger 2007a) and paternalistic grounds (Sunstein 2014). In the first case one should not interfere with the irrational choices of agents, because otherwise they won't be able to learn from their mistakes. In the second case, agents should be forced to choose (even if they do not have this preference), because otherwise they will not learn to make autonomous decisions, which is regarded as detrimental for their well-being.

[15] How to draw the relevant line between circumstances and choices depends on the social ethos of a given society (cf. Mason 2006, p. 220; Roemer 1995, p. 9).

choice might be justified in specific cases; but such interventions, if they are to remain *educational*, must still retain some elements of personal choice and active involvement. (Burbules 1990, p. 226).

Since autonomy is a central educational aim, autonomy-facilitating or promoting educational practices have to be structured in a way that is conducive to the process of becoming an autonomous and responsible agent. If, however, ascriptions of autonomy and responsibility are central (or even constitutive) for educational practices that facilitate autonomy, and if these ascriptions can only be legitimate when fair and equal opportunity structures and background conditions of choice are in place, then the analytical distinction between equality of opportunity "through" education and education "for" equality of opportunity should not be interpreted as referring to two entirely separate domains that are governed by completely different educational principles. Equality of opportunity relies on educational preconditions that are specified along different interpretations of different sources of inequality, scope etc. *and* can be applied to educational constellations.[16]

One of the major rationales behind conceptions of equality of opportunity is to make it *easier* for *comparatively* disadvantaged children to achieve valuable goods. This also holds with regard to the provision of a "substantive opportunity to become an autonomous person" (Brighouse 2002, p. 9). Thus, there is an essentially *socio-relational and gradual* element[17] built into the notion of autonomy as an educational aim and into the principle of equality of educational opportunity. The critique of a conflation between the justice-oriented and the pedagogically-oriented talk of equal opportunities (Stroop 2014) rests on the assumption that in educational constellations autonomy is to be interpreted as a 'range-property' (Rawls), an all-or-nothing affair. From the standpoint of the justification of educational practices and in light of principles of equality of educational opportunity, however, it does not appear "natural" (Giesinger 2014, p. 70) that an autonomy based conception of educational justice has to rely on a threshold conception of autonomy.

Based on a gradual conception, autonomy and responsibility come in degrees. Depending on the competencies, the context of choice, the biography etc., an ascription of autonomy and responsibility may be more or less legitimate. The legitimacy

---

[16] This does obviously *not* imply that it would not be worthwhile for all children to reach the thresholds set by adequacy approaches (which is not the case in contemporary Western societies). I take into question, however, that threshold approaches (or hybrid non-egalitarian approaches) are sufficiently demanding when it comes to the evaluation of legitimate inequalities. It first and foremost depends on the value of the opportunities and the conditions provided to reach these opportunities whether an educational system can count as just from the perspective of concern of an egalitarian conception of educational justice.

[17] Thus, I don't think that distributive and relational interpretations of equality are mutually exclusive (cf. the criticism of distributive conceptions of equality by: Anderson (1999) and Stojanov (2013). "The distributions themselves can *express* inegalitarian relationships" (Brighouse and Swift 2014b, p. 27), also because they lead to unequal conditions of autonomy. Unequal conditions for autonomy, in turn, can lead to unequal social relationships.

of ascriptions of autonomy, furthermore, also depends on whether the relevant social contexts of choice and opportunity structures are *fair* from the standpoint of justice. It is not only implausible and unfair, for instance, to ascribe autonomy irrespective of the value of the options an agent faces, it is also unjust to ascribe *equal degrees* of autonomy[18] irrespective of the relative value of options in different opportunity structures.[19] Without drawing normatively relevant distinctions between different contexts of choice, thus, we can neither make sense of the educational relevance of different degrees of autonomy within particular opportunity structures nor of the injustices that accompany unequal background conditions of choice. As different competencies to deal with particular obstacles – *above and below some threshold* – are not irrelevant for the justification of educational arrangements, the same holds also for the evaluation of these arrangements from the standpoint of a substantive conception of equality of opportunity.[20] Or, as Wallimann-Helmer puts it: "(…) equal opportunity must be conceived as an egalitarian conceptualization of claims of liberty" (Wallimann-Helmer 2012, p. 539).

Thus, with regard to the question of the legitimacy of ascriptions of autonomy and responsibility within particular opportunity structures, problems of the justification of education intersect with problems of the justification of educational inequalities. Because the legitimacy of ascriptions of (gradual) autonomy and (gradual) responsibility to children depend on considerations of equality of opportunity (and *vice versa*), autonomy as an educational aim and equality of educational opportunity are not necessarily incompatible, but intertwined and in important respects, mutually supportive principles.[21]

---

[18] Due to reasons of space I do not discuss the problem of interpersonal comparability with regard to the specification of preconditions of autonomy relative to different opportunity structures.

[19] Equalizing opportunities may imply a leveling down of the opportunities of other agents. This, however, is neither necessarily the case nor necessarily illegitimate (cf. Brighouse and Swift 2014b, p. 42 f.). One problem typically associated with conceptions of equality of opportunity is that in contrast to threshold conceptions, they do not operate with a fixed goal or end-state. This, however, can also be regarded as an advantage of equality of opportunity. The critical potential of principles of equality of opportunity lies, among others, in their ability to adapt to changing social and distributive relations of inequality, by constantly questioning the moral status quo within a given society. The social dynamics inherent to changing societal inequalities, however, cannot be covered by solely relying on threshold conceptions.

[20] While the critique of equality of educational opportunity states that it allows for illegitimate ascriptions of autonomy, a substantive conception of equality of educational opportunity can provide criteria and normative resources to differentiate illegitimate from legitimate ascriptions of autonomy.

[21] Cf. also the analysis of: Wallimann-Helmer (2012). Even though autonomy as an educational aim and principles of fair equality of opportunity can be interpreted as mutually supportive principles, this obviously does not imply that both values are not in conflict with a variety of other values and principles.

Responsibility-Sensitive Egalitarianism and Perfectionist Liberalism

To rethink the politics of the level playing field means to rethink the specific relation between educational conceptions of equality of opportunity and different conceptions of autonomy and responsibility. To substantiate the claim that autonomy and equality of educational opportunity are not mutually exclusive but naturally allied ideals, it is necessary to give a more detailed analysis of how these principles should be specified and applied to the specific problems posed by educational constellations (the problem of stunted ambition and the problem of the naturalization of talents). I will argue that the theoretical and ethical framework of liberal perfectionism in combination with a responsibility-sensitive egalitarianism offers some promising theoretical options to deal with the problems at stake.

Debra Satz recently offered a defense of Rawls' conception of fair equality of opportunity that explicitly focuses on the problem of stunted ambition. She notes that a conception of fair equality of opportunity which simply brackets influences of culture and socialization seems a far too weak principle. Conversely, a conception that would aim at a neutralization of all influences of socialization on educational achievement would be far too strong (Satz 2014, p. 39), as it tends to conflate equality of opportunity with equality of outcome. Thus, Satz presents some criteria to delineate legitimate and illegitimate socialization influences:

> (…) socialization influences are problematic: when (a) they are predicated on, or support, ideas of the unequal worth of persons; or (b) they confine people to choices within less than decent sets of options; or (c) they fail to equip people with the ability to 'cope with the preferences (our) upbringing leaves us with' (ibid., p. 41 referring to Rawls).

The rationale behind these criteria is that – given different forms of socialization - each person should have a "reasonable chance at a decent life in which they can relate to others on terms of equality" (ibid.). Satz' proposal shows that conceptions of equality of opportunity do not necessarily have to abstract from environmental and cultural factors that inevitably prefigure what autonomy and responsibility can and should mean in educational contexts. Thus, she provides theoretical resources to deal with the problem of stunted ambition, resources that have to include and to rely on some *substantive* notion of autonomy or hypothetical consent – especially when applied to not yet *fully* autonomous agents. We do not in fact know what the authentic preferences of developing agents will be (or would be, given a particular form of socialization), but we assume that equality of some kind is a necessary condition for a decent and autonomous life ((cf. "less than decent sets of options"; "the ability to 'cope with the preferences (our) upbringing leaves us with'")). Thus, we assume that X would (or should) choose Y, if X were to have enjoyed the 'right' form of socialization. The choices that agents actually make, thus, are not interpreted as their "true choices" (cf. the criticism of Nash 2004, p. 364). As Yuracko puts it:

Since there is no neutral, or nonsocializing, social context within which individuals can make their choices, claims that social contexts distort authentic choices while others protect or encourage authentic choices rest initially on a substantive conception of authentic choices. Since no one, of course, knows what individuals' authentic choices would be, or if such choices could ever exist, the concept of authenticity is simply a proxy for the kinds of choices the theorist thinks people should make (Yuracko 2003, p. 84 f.).

This implicit conflation of seemingly formal principles with substantive notions of the good has often been criticized in a variety of contexts (cf. the criticism of Oshanas conception of autonomy by: Christman 2004 or Laborde 2006 criticism of the French hijab debate), because it allows for the interpretation of practices, self-conceptions and choices as non-autonomous, if they do not conform to a liberal-perfectionist standard of autonomy.[22]

But this criticism does not discharge us from unavoidable judgments and decisions with regard to the preferences, ambitions (problem of stunted ambition) and corresponding opportunities in the domain of education. When we make judgments about the value of different forms of socialization we cannot rely on children's subjective preferences and desires, because "children have limited ability to shape their own socialization" (Satz 2014, p. 40). If we want to criticize illegitimate forms of socialization and unjust opportunity structures at all we have to rely on perfectionist judgments that clarify *what* we regard as *objectively* worthwhile forms of socialization, fair opportunity structures and valuable choices.[23] Thus, the concern for

---

[22] There are many different conceptions of (liberal) perfectionism (cf. Henning 2009, 2010, 2012; Düber 2014) in the debate between political liberals and liberal perfectionists. Some of them primarily focus on promoting the capacities that constitute personal autonomy; others primarily intend to favor valuable options over base ones. Both approaches are not necessarily incompatible (Wall 1998, p. 6). I cannot go into detail here with regard to the debate between political liberals and liberal perfectionists. In general, I am rather skeptical concerning the possibility of justifying education and access to educational goods without making judgments about the worth of particular practices and the ways of life they constitute. Furthermore, as the focus of relational egalitarians on oppressive social relations is too restricted in scope because it does not capture other forms of inequality that matter, political liberal approaches fail in demonstrating how the equal access to central educational goods that cannot count as *necessary* conditions for equal citizenship, mutual respect etc. can be justified within a theoretical framework that claims to be free of perfectionist premises. Likewise, it is questionable, whether the focus on the necessary conditions of political participation etc., does not present a contested perfectionist standard itself by suggesting that everyone should have an interest in being able to participate (irrespective of what the actual preferences of agents might be). Moreover, the fact that there is widespread disagreement concerning the most adequate interpretation of concepts like equality of opportunity, education or autonomy, does not imply that all conceptions are equally plausible (cf. Mason 2006, p. 221).

[23] Strict equality of outcomes is certainly incompatible with choice and responsibility. A strictly procedural conception of equality of opportunity, however, is compatible with too many kinds of choices, because it remains agnostic with regard to the relative value of different choices. If we want to make judgments about the conduciveness of different opportunity structures for the development of autonomy, we have to rely both on an outcome sensitive conception of equality of opportunity and on an *outcome sensitive conception of autonomy*. We neither want children to exercise their developing autonomy in any kind of way, nor do we want to provide as many options as possible for them (irrespective of their value), but we want to offer them valuable opportunities for the realization of valuable forms of autonomy. Accordingly, an opportunity structure that sys-

equality and the concern for the promotion of opportunity structures and social relations which are conducive to the development of valuable forms of autonomy as a precondition of a flourishing life cannot reasonably be *separated* in the domain of education. As Sypnowich puts it:

> Much liberal anxiety about the potential for anti-individualism in perfectionist theories stems from a failure to appreciate perfectionism's potential to serve individualistic purposes, once it is properly construed as a precondition for the improvement of human flourishing and the fair allocation of opportunities for flourishing. (...) Certainly before Rawls there was a longstanding egalitarian tradition, derived from Marx, which sought to enable equal human flourishing, in which perfectionism and egalitarianism were one (Synopwich 2012, p. 585).

Conflicts between different values and principles are unavoidable in attempts to theorize educational justice and not *all* tensions that result from the problem of stunted ambition can be resolved on the basis of a perfectionist conception of autonomy and a substantive conception of equality of opportunity. Nevertheless, without these conceptions we will neither be able to differentiate between legitimate and illegitimate, fair and unfair ascriptions of responsibility and autonomy in different contexts of choice, nor will we be able to criticize unjust and autonomy-undermining practices, forms of socialization and opportunity structures.

This focus on the background conditions of choice neither implies that all socialization influences are to be regarded as equally illegitimate nor does it imply that all socialization influences should be *neutralized*. Within the framework of a *responsibility-sensitive egalitarianism* it suffices to *mitigate* these influences (Mason 2006, p. 94 ff.) and to leave room for the development and realization of autonomy where the ascription of responsible agency is reasonable, given the value and structure of particular opportunities. Metaphorically speaking this means that we cannot and should not clear the playing field from *all* unchosen obstacles, but we can and should try to get rid of those, that hamper the realization of valuable practices and choices. A mitigation approach that is constrained by a perfectionist principle of valuable autonomy (among others),[24] will not be limited to counteracting the effects of different *social* circumstances (ibid.). Giesinger is right when he states, that "it is not clear why inequalities of motivation and natural endowment should be seen as morally acceptable, while a complete neutralization of inequalities

---

tematically leads to disadvantages for some groups or systematically produces questionable choices cannot be legitimate from a liberal-perfectionist standpoint. This does not imply that children do not need to learn to take responsibility for their own choices. It only implies that not all choices in all domains of choice should be regarded as equally important and equally conducive to the development of *valuable* autonomy. This distinguishes a liberal perfectionist conception of autonomy and a substantive conception of equality of opportunity from a libertarian conception of autonomous choice and a formal conception of equality of educational opportunity.

[24] A mitigating approach can and has to rely on a variety of other principles (e.g. egalitarian, sufficitarian or prioritarian) that specify the limits of its scope of application (Mason 2006, chapter 6). Due to reasons discussed above (section "Autonomy and responsibility in educational interaction orders"), however, I am skeptical concerning attempts to base equality of educational opportunity on sufficiency principles.

of ability due to family background is required" (Giesinger 2011, p. 12). Individuals can neither be regarded responsible for their social background nor for their genetic makeup. Thus, from the perspective of a responsibility-sensitive egalitarianism, we should not make a difference in attempting to counteract both kinds of obstacles.

The widespread skepticism concerning the assumption of 'native abilities' as normatively relevant criteria of justice (problem of the naturalization of talents) is certainly justified, when one takes into account, that arguments of this kind have often been misused as ideological constructions (Stojanov 2013) to legitimize allegedly natural inequalities. Most of this skepticism, however, rests not on genuine theoretical reasons and empirical evidence, but rather on *political* reasons (Pinker 2002). Thus, it would be premature to believe that a theory of educational justice could do entirely without anthropological assumptions and empirical evidence about human nature (as if human beings could live *outside* nature). Likewise, it does not seem a very convincing argument to criticize *all* anthropological assumptions as "essentialism" (in the sense of a pejorative term). There are different kinds of essentialism (e.g. Quante 2014) – not all ideological or metaphysical – and there is a powerful egalitarian and perfectionist tradition that is based on the assumption that the political equality of human beings is based on their equal nature (Henning 2010, p. 764), a nature that does not fundamentally differ (e.g. Rousseau, Condorcet, Mill).

> In fact, a development of individualistic traits depends on material conditions. (…) If someone says: *We are equal because we are human, therefore we deserve equal conditions*, this does not imply that all persons are the same (Henning 2012, p. 570).

It is certainly correct, that judgments about natural inequalities among individuals also depend on culturally established assumptions concerning capacities which should be regarded as worthwhile. Thus, not *all* developmental obstacles for the realization of *all* capacities can count as problematic, but only those obstacles that hamper the development of worthwhile talents. If we do not want to base a theory of justice on the assumption that individuals create themselves out of nothing just on the bases of choice plus culture (which would be the rather odd subjectivist result of a radically anti-essentialist framework), we have to assume that there must be *something*, a potentiality, that develops (or does not develop) given appropriate circumstances and choices (Henning 2012, p. 569).

> It is not a 'given', but neither it is nothing: it is a limited range of potentialities that may or may not become actual, depending on choice and circumstances. Wise choices and enabling circumstances are so important because we *want* these potentialities to develop in a good way. And there are empirical ways to investigate the value of choices and circumstances (ibid.).

According to this line of thought, questionable normative assumptions (e.g. about human nature) can only be criticized on the basis of empirical knowledge (e.g. about human nature), that allows us to identify obstacles for the development of a flourishing life (Henning 2013, p. 225). The assumption that different (native) potentialities and abilities are not irrelevant for educational decisions, because they provide reasons to offer more and better opportunities and resources to some

(Calvert 2014, p. 75) in order to provide the material preconditions for equal developmental opportunities (Henning 2009, p. 849). There is no contradiction in assuming that children have certain native abilities at a certain time (in the sense of an egalitarian and open anthropology) and to identify certain developmental obstacles. There are myriads of ways to develop and realize 'experiments in living' (Mill), based on our common nature *and* there are objectively better or worse social and material conditions that either facilitate or do not facilitate this realization for all human beings: Human beings, for instance, must eat and sleep. If human beings lack food and sleep, this is objectively bad for them. Without assumptions about our common nature we lack criteria to criticize questionable social arrangements (Henning 2009 p. 853). Moreover, individuals, to a certain extent have to realize their potentialities themselves, thus the assumption that knowledge about the good based on evidence about human nature is incompatible with liberty is unfounded (Henning 2012, p. 571). There are no good liberal reasons to be (or to remain) an anti-essentialist (Henning 2009, p. 854). Thus, principles that spell out what it means to level the playing field should not ignore knowledge about human nature and the problem of the naturalization of talents does not present insurmountable problems for an egalitarian and perfectionist theory of justice.

Last but not least, it is important to note, that equality of educational opportunity is just one aspect of educational justice. Since the "principles we use to distribute things vary with the nature of things we are distributing" (Jencks 1988, p. 532), every plausible egalitarian conception of educational justice has to limit the scope of principles of equality of opportunity. Because there "are dimensions of the lives of children that matter from the point of view of justice but which are not integral to the successful development of the moral powers of autonomy" (Macleod 2010, p. 182), it is necessary to support dimensions of children's lives that can be regarded as constitutive of a good childhood and therefore should be secured independently of any considerations that involve autonomy and equal opportunities. To avoid implausible implications a substantive conception of equality of opportunity therefore has to be embedded in a (perfectionist) theory of a good childhood (cf. ibid. p. 188).

Conclusion

Since any "effort to theorize educational justice in a comprehensive fashion needs to rest on its own foundations, rather than applying a more general theory to specifically educational questions" (Levinson 2015, p. 11), principles of educational justice cannot be adequately justified without a theoretical account of the specific structure of educational practices and constellations. Along this line of thought, I argued that contrary to established standard criticisms autonomy as an *educational* aim and equality of *educational* opportunities are not incompatible, but mutually supportive principles. Furthermore, based on a substantive conception of equality of opportunity and a perfectionistically structured conception of autonomy, at least some of the tensions between autonomy and equality of opportunity can be resolved. Thus, we need not and should not abandon equality of educational opportunity as *one* aspect of an egalitarian theory of educational justice.

References

Anderson, E. 1999. What is the point of equality? *Ethics* 109: 287–337.

Anderson, E. 2004. Rethinking equality of opportunity: Comment on Adam Swift's How not to be a hypocrite. *Theory and Research in Education* 2: 99–110.

Anderson, E. 2007. Fair opportunity in education: A democratic equality perspective. *Ethics* 117: 595–622.

Arneson, R. 2002. *Equality of opportunity.* http://plato.stanford.edu/entries/equal-opportunity/. Accessed 9 Feb 2014.

Ben-Shahar, T. 2015. Equality in Education – Why we must go all the way. *Ethical Theory and Moral Practice*. doi:10.1007/s10677-015-9587-3.

Biesta, Gert. 2011a. Disciplines and theory in the academic study of education: A comparative analysis of the Anglo-American and Continental construction of the field. *Pedagogy, Culture and Society* 19: 175–192.

Biesta, G. 2011b. Warum "What works" nicht funktioniert: Evidenzbasierte pädagogische Praxis und das Demokratiedefizit der Bildungsforschung. In *Wissen, was wirkt. Kritik evidenzbasierter Pädagogik*, ed. Johannes Bellmann and Thomas Müller, 95–122. Wiesbaden: Springer VS.

Bou-Habib, P., and S. Olsaretti. 2015. Autonomy and children's well-being. In *The nature of children's well-being. Theory and practice*, ed. Alexander Bagattini and Colin Macleod, 15–33. Dordrecht et al.: Springer.

Bourdieu, P., and J.-C. Passeron. 1971. *Die Illusion der Chancengleichheit. Untersuchungen zur Soziologie des Bildungswesens am Beispiel Frankreichs*. Stuttgart: Klett.

Brighouse, H. 2002. *Egalitarian liberalism and justice in education*. London: Institute of Education.

Brighouse, H. 2010. Educational equality and school reform. In *Educational equality*, ed. H. Brighouse, J. Tooley, and K. Howe, 15–70. London/New York: Continuum.

Brighouse, H., and A. Swift. 2009. Educational equality versus educational adequacy: A critique of Anderson and Satz. *Journal of Applied Philosophy* 26(2): S. 117–128.

Brighouse, H., and A. Swift. 2014a. The place of educational equality in educational justice. In *Education, justice and the human good. Fairness and equality in the education system*, ed. Kirsten Meyer, 14–33. Oxon/New York: Routledge.

Brighouse, H., and A. Swift. 2014b. *Family values. The ethics of parent-child relationships*. Princeton/Oxford: Princeton University Press.

Burbules, N. 1990. Equal opportunity or equal education? *Educational Theory* 40: 221–226.

Calvert, J. 2014. Educational equality: Luck egalitarian, pluralist and complex. *Journal of Philosophy of Education* 48: 70–85.

Casal, P. 2007. Why sufficiency is not enough. *Ethics* 117: 296–326.

Christman, J. 2004. Relational autonomy, liberal individualism, and the social constitution of selves. *Philosophical Studies* 117: 143–164.

Drerup, J. 2013. *Paternalismus, Perfektionismus und die Grenzen der Freiheit*. Schöningh: Paderborn et al.

Drerup, J. 2015. Genug ist genug? Zur Kritik non-egalitaristischer Konzeptionen der Bildungsgerechtigkeit. *Zeitschrift für praktische Philosophie* 2: 89–128.

Düber, D. 2014. Paternalismus, Perfektionismus und Public Health – neuere Literatur zu den Grenzen liberaler Neutralität. *Zeitschrift für Philosophische Forschung* 68: 527–544.

Frankfurt, H. 1987. Equality as a moral ideal. *Ethics* 98: 21–42.
Gallie, W.B. 1955. Essentially contested concepts. *Proceedings of the Aristotelian Society* 56: 160–180.
Giesinger, J. 2007a. *Autonomie und Verletzlichkeit. Der moralische Status von Kindern und die Rechtfertigung von Erziehung*. Bielefeld: Transkript.
Giesinger, J. 2007b. Was heißt Bildungsgerechtigkeit? *Zeitschrift für Pädagogik* 53: 362–381.
Giesinger, J. 2011. Education, fair competition, and concern for the worst off. *Educational Theory* 61: 41–54.
Giesinger, J. 2012. Bildung als öffentliches Gut und das Problem der Gerechtigkeit. *Zeitschrift für Pädagogik* 57: 421–437.
Giesinger, J. 2014. Educational justice and the justification of education. In *Education, justice and the human good. Fairness and equality in the education system*, ed. Kirsten Meyer, 65–79. Oxon/New York: Routledge.
Gosepath, S. 2014. What does equality in education mean? In *Education, justice and the human good. Fairness and equality in the education system*, ed. Kirsten Meyer, 100–112. Oxon/New York: Routledge.
Henning, C. 2009. Perfektionismus und liberaler Egalitarismus. Ein Versuch ihrer Vermittlung. *Deutsche Zeitschrift für Philosophie* 57: 845–860.
Henning, C. 2010. Natur und Freiheit im Perfektionismus. Zum Verständnis der Natur der Menschen in progressiven Traditionen. *Deutsche Zeitschrift für Philosophie* 58: 759–775.
Henning, C. 2012. Human nature, liberty and equality: Sher's perfectionism as anthropology. *Ethical Perspectives* 19: 565–575.
Henning, C. 2013. Vom Essentialismus zum Overlapping Consensus – und zurück? Anthropologie und Ethik bei Martha C. Nussbaum und Alasdair MacIntyre. In *Die anthropoligische Wende*, ed. Hügli Anton, 241–256. Basel: Schwabe.
Hirose, I. 2009. Reconsidering the value of equality. *Australasian Journal of Philosophy* 87: 301–312.
Hirose, I. 2015. *Egalitarianism*. London/New York: Routledge.
Howe, K. 1989. In defense of outcome-based conceptions of equal educational opportunity. *Educational Theory* 39: 317–336.
Jacobs, L. 2010. Equality, adequacy, and stakes fairness: Retrieving the equal opportunities in education approach. *Theory and Research in Education* 8: 249–268.
Jencks, C. 1988. Whom must we treat equally for educational opportunity to be equal? *Ethics* 98: 518–533.
Koski, W., and R. Reich. 2006. *The state's obligation to provide education: Adequate education or equal education?* https://www.law.berkeley.edu/files/reich-koski_paper.pdf. Accessed 8 Nov 2014 (cited with permission of the authors).
Laborde, C. 2006. Female autonomy, education and the Hijab. *Critical Review of International Social and Political Philosophy* 9: 351–377.
Levinson, M. 2015. *Theorizing educational justice: Some reflections on methods and substance*. Unpublished manuscript (cited with permission of the author).
Liu, G. 2006. *Education, equality, and national citizenship*. http://www.yalelawjournal.org/article/education-equality-and-national-citizenship. Accessed 8 Nov 2014.
Macleod, C. 2010. Primary goods, capabilities, and children. In *Measuring justice. Primary goods and capabilities*, ed. Harry Brighouse and Ingrid Robeyns, 174–192. Cambridge et al.: Cambridge University Press.
Macleod, C. 2013. Justice, educational equality, and sufficiency. *Canadian Journal of Philosophy* 40: 151–175.
Mason, A. 2006. *Levelling the playing field. The idea of equal opportunity and its place in Egalitarian thought*. Oxford/New York: Oxford University Press.
Meyer, K. 2014. Educational justice and talent advancement. In *Education, justice and the human good. Fairness and equality in the education system*, ed. Kirsten Meyer, 133–150. Oxon/New York: Routledge.

Nash, R. 2004. Equality of educational opportunity. In defence of a traditional concept. *Educational Philosophy and Theory* 36: 361–377.

Pinker, S. 2002. *The blank slate. The modern denial of human nature.* New York: Penguin.

Quante, M. 2014. *Pragmatistische Anthropologie und Ethik in Anwendung: Eine philosophische Skizze.* https://www.uni-muenster.de/imperia/md/content/kfg-normenbegruen dung/intern/ publikationen/quante/63_quante__pragmatische_anthropologie.pdf. Accessed 9 Feb 2015.

Rawls, J. 2003. *Politischer Liberalismus.* Frankfurt am Main: Suhrkamp.

Roemer, J. 1995. *Equality and responsibility.* http://new.bostonreview.net/BR20.2/roemer.html. Accessed 9 Feb 2015.

Satz, D. 2007. Equality, adequacy, and education for citizenship. *Ethics* 117: 623–648.

Satz, D. 2014. Unequal chances: Race, class and schooling. In *Education, justice and the human good. Fairness and equality in the education system,* ed. Kirsten Meyer, 34–50. Oxon/New York: Routledge.

Schramme, T. 2014. Non-comparative justice in education. In *Education, justice and the human good. Fairness and equality in the education system,* ed. Kirsten Meyer, 51–64. Oxon/New York: Routledge.

Sen, A. 2010. *Die Idee der Gerechtigkeit.* München: Beck.

Stojanov, K. 2007. Bildungsgerechtigkeit im Spannungsfeld zwischen Verteilungs-, Teilhabe- und Anerkennungsgerechtigkeit. In *Gerechtigkeit und Bildung,* ed. Michael Wimmer, Roland Reichenbach, and Ludwig Pongratz, 29–48. Paderborn et al.: Ferdinand Schöningh.

Stojanov, K. 2008. Bildungsgerechtigkeit als Freiheitseinschränkung? Kritische Anmerkungen zum Gebrauch der Gerechtigkeitskategorie in der empirischen Bildungsforschung. *Zeitschrift für Pädagogik* 54: 516–531.

Stojanov, K. 2013. Bildungsgerechtigkeit als Anerkennungsgerechtigkeit. In *Bildungsgerechtigkeit jenseits von Chancengleichheit,* ed. Fabian Dietrich, Martin Heinrich, and Nina Thieme, 57–70. Wiesbaden: Springer VS.

Stroop, C. 2014. Fair equality of opportunity and educational justice. In *Education, justice and the human good. Fairness and equality in the education system,* ed. Kirsten Meyer, 113–132. Oxon/New York: Routledge.

Sunstein, C. 2014. *Choosing not to choose.* Online:http://papers.ssrn.com/sol3/papers.cfm?abstract_id=2377364. Zugriff am 08.03.2014

Synopwich, C. 2012. Perfectionists, Egalitarians and old Fogeys: Sher and equality. *Ethical Perspectives* 19: 575–589.

Wallimann-Helmer, I. 2012. *Die Abhängigkeit zwischen Chancengleichheit und Freiheit.* http://www.ethik.uzh.ch/ufsp/ma/ivowallimannhelmer/WallimannHelmer_Abhaengigkeit_zw_CHGundFPUBL.pdf. Accessed 1 Apr 2015.

Wall, S. 1998. *Liberalism, Perfectionism and Restraint.* Cambridge: Cambridge University Press.

Westen, P. 1985. The concept of equal of opportunity. *Ethics* 95: 837–850.

Wilson, J. 1991. Does equality (of opportunity) make sense in education? *Journal of Philosophy of Education* 25: 27–31.

Yuracko, K. 2003. *Perfectionism & contemporary feminist values.* Bloomington: Indiana University Press.

Chapter 9
Child Psychological Abuse, Public Health and Social Justice: The *Cinderella Law* Debate

Mar Cabezas

Abstract This chapter aims to answer two questions: first, whether intra-family psychological – or emotional – abuse of children fulfils the criteria to be considered a question of social justice, and second, if it entails an issue of public (mental) health *per se* in light of the recent debate on the British Cinderella Law project. In order to answer these questions, I will firstly focus on the current debate, pointing out how psychological abuse has generally only been tackled if it co-occurs with other types of maltreatment or if it is the consequence of those other types. Secondly, I will try to shed light on the different attitudes towards mental and physical health and, in turn, towards physical and emotional abuse, also in relation to parental duties. Thirdly, I will explore the open questions on the nature of emotional abuse that could help to understand the disagreements and to analyze whether it is a corrosive disadvantage to children in terms of health and justice. In my conclusion I will finally advocate for the need of specific legal recognition of emotional abuse as a threat to children's health and well-being and, as such, as a question of public health and social justice that should receive much more attention.

Keywords Child psychological abuse • Public health • Social justice • Negligence • Mental health

The Visibility of Child Emotional Abuse: The Cinderella Law Project[1]

Whilst a basic agreement on the relevance of physical health for children's well-being and well-becoming has been achieved, the debate on children's mental health does not find the same recognition. A recent British law project against intra-family emotional

---

[1] This Research was funded by the Austrian Science Fund (FWF): P26480.

M. Cabezas (✉)
Centre for Ethics and Poverty Research, University of Salzburg, Salzburg, Austria
e-mail: mmarcabezas@gmail.com

© Springer International Publishing Switzerland 2016
J. Drerup et al. (eds.), *Justice, Education and the Politics of Childhood*,
Philosophy and Politics – Critical Explorations 1,
DOI 10.1007/978-3-319-27389-1_9

137

maltreatment,[2] popularly known as the "Cinderella Law", is a current example that reveals the main points of disagreement and assumptions about children's mental well-being as well as its role as a question of social justice and public health.

The aim of this law proposal is to change criminal law, in order to bring it in line with the civil code, where emotional neglect is recognized. The Cinderella Law project tries thusly to recognize also in criminal law the cases of emotional abuse[3] that does not necessarily need to co-occur with other types of already penalized abuses, such as exploitation, physical maltreatment, (physical and material) neglect and sexual abuse, so that social workers, police and the rest of agents involved in protecting children can work with the support of a unified legal background. Criminal law does recognize neglect, but only in the material and physical sense. In this sense, the new proposal tries to surpass the limits concerning emotional neglect (Action for Children 2013).

British criminal law, more precisely the "Children and Young Persons Act 1933" (Chapter 12 23 and 24 Geo 5),[4] which is more than 18 years old, recognizes neglect of children. However, emotional or psychological child abuse, when it does not co-occur with other kinds of maltreatment, is not legally regulated *per se*. Likewise, the reference to mental injury in the US "first appeared in national legislation against child abuse and neglect in 1974" (Thompson and Kaplan 1996, 144), but is still not recognized apart from neglect. Something similar happens in other European criminal codes, such as the Spanish one. The Spanish penal code protects children specifically from emotional abuse only when it occurs with physical and material neglect, sexual and physical abuse, or if it is a tool to obtain another kind of illegal result. Thus, emotional abuse is only mentioned in the penal code in relation to inducement of minors, corruption, prostitution, induction to suicide, and exploitation. It therefore ignores the fact that children can be (seriously) emotionally abused, while they are neither necessarily neglected in terms of material needs, nor physically or sexually abused.[5]

The aim is not to criminalize caregivers, institutionalize children or oblige parents to kiss and embrace their children. It is eye-catching however how the debate in the media, as a reflection of socially shared values, appeals to an exaggeration of correctness (Furedi 2014) and connects the prohibition of emotional abuse with the obligation to love, when it actually only deals with the legal recognition of child psychological abuse and emotional neglect.

The debates in the media show the difficulty of penalizing a set of conducts that are still socially seen as not so severe. It also ranges from those who regard it as a

---

[2] I will use "emotional abuse", "emotional maltreatment", "psychological abuse" and "psychological maltreatment" as synonyms, since authors refer to this phenomenon with all these concepts indistinctively.

[3] The cases of psychological abuse suffered by children where the aggressor is another minor would surpass the scope of this chapter.

[4] See http://www.legislation.gov.uk/ukpga/Geo5/23-24/12

[5] See Title II, articles 180–189 and art.223, 233; 148, 153 and 155 from the Spanish Penal Code (2015).

necessary step to guarantee children's well-being and well-becoming (Action for Children 2013) to those who understand it as a way of criminalizing the caregiver who is also a victim of domestic violence (Nicolas 2014), or an intromission into the family life and the private sphere, fearing that such proposals could cause more damage than benefits for children criminalizing any improper behavior (Hope 2014). In this sense, this current debate points to the debate on "the legitimate scope of public health, the balance between public health and civil liberties, and the appropriate roles of the federal government and the states" (Gostin and Powers 2006, 1053–1054).

A law against an induction to suicide, like article 143.1 from the Spanish Penal Code,[6] does not generate a debate on whether that law might be a slippery slope to obliging caregivers or relatives to ensure children's happiness. A law project against emotional abuse, on the other hand, does generate a debate on whether such a law would constrain parental autonomy, would be a way of criminalizing many unskilled caregivers and would oblige parents to love their children. Still, there is a vast gap between not emotionally abusing your children and loving them, in the same way as there is a huge gap between inducing children in certain ways to suicide and taking care of their happiness. Defending a law against psychological abuse is not the same as defending or obliging caregivers to love their children, as there is no *continuum* between not abusing someone and doing a positive extra action in order to benefit them. In this sense, it is noteworthy how some of the criticisms against the Cinderella Law project – and measures against specific emotional abuse beyond associations with sexual abuse or physical abuse and neglect more generally – are directed at the problems that a right to be loved would imply, suggesting that not being cruel to someone would directly imply being kind, caring and loving.

In fact, it is not a banal remark – in order to show the social invisibility of emotional abuse – to point out that even the fictional character chosen to exemplify the debate in the mass media is not only a case of emotional neglect, which is what is needed to be stressed. Cinderella was not only emotionally abused, but also exploited and neglected in terms of shelter, clothing, nutrition and presumably also education. How can a law project, whose aim is to deal with the recognition of emotional abuse, publicly succeed, when even the choice of its name refers to a condition that is not under question, as it is already protected and does not exactly correspond to the actual discussion? In other words, the problem is rather if and how a state should protect children who suffer from emotional abuse, but are resilient enough not to present psychosomatic syndromes, who do not suffer from a PTSS,[7] and whose parents are verbally cruel and/or terrorize them, but despite that provide them with the right shelter, education, food and basic material needs. So far, it seemed as though children had to suffer a double victimization in order to make emotional abuse visible. In fact, social workers only intervene when there is a case of sexual or physical abuse and neglect, or a very severe case of emotional neglect with "vis-

---

[6] Book II, Title I, Art. 143.1: "Any person inducing to suicide will be punished with 4 – 8 years in prison".

[7] Posttraumatic stress syndrome.

ible effects", but not when it is 'only' emotional or psychological abuse (Trickett et al. 2009, 31). This practice shows how emotional abuse is not taken as seriously as other types of abuses, despite the devastating consequences for the children, and also ignores the fact that there are two subtypes of neglect: physical and emotional.

A reversal of the logics of the current practice demonstrates its absurdity: it would be like saying that we do not heal a broken leg unless we see that this physical injury has an effect on your mental health and causes you extreme fear of falling again. Therefore, the question to be raised is why children's mental distress and emotional injuries cannot be healed and taken seriously as a question of public health *per se,* as is common practice with physical health. If this is not seen as such, it would be very difficult to socially accept that it should be punished *qua* emotional abuse, even if it does not co-occurs with other types of abuses. For this reason, I could not agree more with the need for a specific legislation against emotional abuse and the idea that "emotional abuse should be a focus of the interventions designed to help maltreating parents with more effective parenting strategies and should also be a focus of the interventions designed to help the child recover from the consequences of maltreatment" (Trickett et al. 2009, 28).

To provide an example: if a child has an accident at home and cuts herself, her parents are obliged to do something about it. Parents who leave their child bleeding alone there for hours will probably be considered negligent. If the injury is not the consequence of an accident, but the result of the parents' action, the state will intervene against the parents, even if the injury did not mean a risk to the child's life. When the injury is not physical but emotional, the attitude is fundamentally different: if a child carries emotional or psychological injuries, parents feel no immediate obligation to do something to that effect – probably because they do not even know what to do. Besides that, and as a result of a lack in public emotional education, those who decide to take action are likely to react in different ways, trying a variety of solutions, while everybody knows how to heal a cut on your arm. In other words, no one would feel attacked if the state or the public health system recommended not putting tabasco on your child's open wound. However, people tend to react defensively to any direction or regulation in the field of mental health, as the debate on the Cinderella Law project shows.

Another example could be the case of children with little signs of cigarette burns on their arms as a result of their parents' actions: even though such injuries will most likely not kill a child, anyone who notices such bad parental behavior will surely report it and the state will take action. In this example, emotional injuries are the consequences of the parents' behavior. However, if emotional injuries result from utterances, if parents talk habitually in an insulting, cruel and pejorative way to their children and someone witnesses it, there are probably not many people who would bring it to the authorities, believing that such behavior is perhaps pitiful and an inadequate way of speaking to a child, but none of their business. Needless to say, most people will find it ridiculous to call the police, reporting on parents who are treating their children with verbal contempt, while most people would at the same time surely take action against physical violence.

Although analogies always miss out on little differences, the point I want to make here is that physical health and care, like hygienic, nutrition etc., are a mandatory responsibility for caregivers and the state, while mental or psychological health seems to be 'optional', both in terms of parental, school or political obligations, and of legal protection.[8] Schools, caregivers and the state have the obligation to take measures to project children's physical health and to educate them in a way that enables them to take care of themselves in the future.

Nevertheless, the debates on projects like the Cinderella Law highlight a normative question about shared values, namely, that it is neither widely accepted that parents have an ethical obligation to take care and protect their children's mental health to the same extent,[9] nor that they need to educate them to have healthy habits on that behalf, and at the same level, that this is accepted as opposed to physical issues – because in contrast to the former, the latter seems to be a private subjective sphere where consensus is harder to achieve.

As I will try to examine in the following section, the reasons why it can be perceived as a too demanding or unrealistic law project are related to both, conceptual open questions on the nature of emotional abuse and justice, and, above all, normative positions about what we want to tolerate as a society and what we perceive as relevant.

Some Open Questions on Child Psychological Abuse

The answers to the questions generated by the Cinderella Law debate are closely connected to other open questions and ambiguities still affecting approaches to conceptualize psychological or emotional abuse. In what follows, I will therefore try to shed light on the core questions in relation to the nature of psychological abuse. These include chronicity, severity, interactions with other forms of abuses and the nature of the correlation between maltreatment and violence.

In general terms, psychological or emotional abuse and maltreatment is defined as a repeated pattern of caregiver behavior or extreme incident(s) of conveying to children that they are worthless, flawed, unloved, unwanted, endangered or only valuable when they meet another's needs (APSAC 1995, 2). From another point of view, it "refers to acts or omissions, other than physical abuse or sexual abuse, that

---

[8] Emotional education is simply not an integral part of the school curricula and preventive mental health care is not provided at the same level as preventive measures against physical health's problems. As M. Seligman explains, "psychological immunization" (2007, 5) should also be a priority in terms of health, the same way children are vaccinated to better overcome or avoid potential physical diseases.

[9] Although at a common sense level, we may all recognize the importance of mental well-being, the fact that emotional education, parental skills training etc., are not mandatory shows how in fact the social attitudes towards mental health are different from the attitudes towards physical health. Briefly said: whilst parents regularly visit their pediatrician with their children since they are born, the same responsibility in relation to mental health is neither officially demanded, nor assumed.

caused, or could have caused, conduct, cognitive, affective, or other mental disorders. Psychological or emotional maltreatment frequently occurs as verbal abuse or excessive demands on a child's performance" (Trickett et al. 2011, 4) and normally includes "the restriction of movement; patterns of belittling, blaming, threatening, frightening, discriminating against, or ridiculing; and other non-physical forms of rejection or hostile treatment" (Norman et al. 2012, 2).

Emotional abuse consists not only of actions, but also of omissions. In this sense, it also includes emotional abandonment, referring to the absence of positive attention from their parents or the persistent lack of response to their emotional and interpersonal needs. In other words, the caregivers are "emotionally distant and unresponsive to the child's bids for comfort and help" (Shaffer et al. 2009, 38).

The vagueness of such definitions entails problems when it comes to creating policies as the Cinderella Law project in the UK has recently shown: if the limits of the problem are not well settled, it is harder to agree upon measures against it. Likewise, it is hard to asses a value to the prevalence rates, not only because many cases may not be reported, but also "because they capture a wide range of parenting behaviors, and there is little to no consensus across studies as to what phenomena should be included" (Shaffer et al. 2009, 37). In fact, it implies a wide range of dysfunctional, irresponsible and hostile nonphysical parental behaviors (Hart et al. 1997).

However, these definitions still imply some open questions that make it hard to agree upon the kind of measures a state should adopt or upon the concrete responsibilities.

One of the causes of disagreement is the chronicity condition. From the social perspective, child abuse is defined as any parental behavior that interferes negatively with children's development and health. In this sense, some authors (Sanmartín 2008; Cantón Duarte and Cortés Arboleda 1997) argue that chronicity is not needed in order to constitute a case of psychological abuse and state instead that such a criterion becomes perverse. In comparison to sexual abuse, no one would say that a child has to be raped more than once in order to consider the action itself abusive; nor would anyone doubt that it is a case of sexual abuse. Thus, one open question on the definition of psychological abuse (also open in relation to physical one) is whether it is an issue of how severe the action/omission is, or of how often it happens. Depending on the answers to this question, some experts (Martínez and de Paúl Ochotorena 1993) would define sporadic actions and omissions as incorrect or dysfunctional, but not abusive. Some others, like the above cited, would consider one instance to be enough to say that a child has *once* been a victim of psychological abuse. As it has been pointed out earlier, "there is a weaker societal consensus about how to distinguish emotional abuse from suboptimal parenting than there is for other forms of abuse, especially physical and sexual abuse which are also perceived as more dangerous and more prevalent and thus requiring more attention from the child protection agencies" (Trickett et al. 2009, 28).

Nevertheless, one aspect seems to be forgotten. Beyond the discussion on whether a child is emotionally abused if it is regularly insulted, seldom insulted, or just once or sporadically insulted, how children interpret such aggression, and how they deal with it are central criteria as well. Omitting the way children process this would not only objectify children – as such a view implies that they are passive and all the same –, but it also forgets other variables, such as children's resilience, and their mental ways of coping with such incidents. This should also be taken into account, especially if the burden of emotional maltreatment lies not only on the caregiver's actions, but also on the effects on the child. Children that are constantly insulted may develop a way of relativizing what is happening in her environment – surely as a self-protecting strategy – while children that are seldom insulted may give higher significance to such experiences, so that they could have more severely negative effects on their well-being.

Secondly, in relation to the previous criterion, another open question is how to measure the different occurrences of emotional abuse, not only in terms of chronicity, but also in terms of severity. If something very sever occurs only once, it would probably have more negative effects on the child than if something very subtle happens chronically. Potentially, the first case may lead to a post-traumatic stress syndrome, while the effects of the second case may spread shyly through different fields of the child's life.

Needless to say, "it is probable that most of us have some experience of emotional maltreatment in childhood. However this usually occurs under conditions which lack sufficient intensity, frequency and duration to have lasting negative effect" (Thompson and Kaplan 1996, 143). In any case, this does not imply that it loses its abusive nature. In this sense, the question is how the state should deal with the cases of chronic non-severe abusive behaviors and rare cases of severe adverse parental behaviors.

Another key question is, thirdly, whether or not psychological abuse should include the set of cognitive, emotional and behavioral consequences of physical and sexual abuse, or should, on the contrary, be treated separately. Psychological maltreatment is "the core component in child abuse and neglect," and it entails a destructive power given the "broader nature of its effects" (Hart et al. 1997, 31). Evidently, not every kind of emotional abuse implies sexual and/or physical abuse or material neglect, but neglect, sexual and physical abuse imply emotional abuse.

With respect to this criterion, some authors (O'Hagan 1993; Grusec and Walters 1991) defend that psychological abuse is a form of maltreatment with its own behavioral patterns and that the concrete emotional, cognitive and behavioral consequences from other forms of abuse should not be taken into account as part of its definition. In doing so, they defend that emotional maltreatment should be considered a form of maltreatment *per se*. This lack of social recognition *qua* emotional abuse could certainly explain why emotional maltreatment stays in the shadows in legal terms when it does not co-occur with one of the other types of maltreatment. In other words, it seems harder to punish only psychological abuse when the caregivers are not negligent in another area,[10] which could explain the adverse reactions to the Cinderella Law project by some sectors.

---

[10] Compared to physical abuse, the effects of psychological abuse are less visible and more time and checks are required to detect it. Sometimes the effects arise in time as an accumulation of little abusive acts.

Obviously, physical and sexual abuses as well as neglect imply emotional abuse and negative cognitive, emotional and behavioral outcomes for affected children.[11] Likewise, it may be easier to check if children's caregivers fail to provide age-appropriate food, shelter, medical care, clothes, etc., than to check, for instance, whether they are regularly insulted and treated with contempt at home. But psychological abuse cannot be reduced to a consequence of these cases, nor can it be ignored if it occurs alone. Although it is likely to be accompanied by other forms of maltreatment, especially physical abuse and/or neglect (Trickett et al. 2009, 27), this is not a necessary connection. Neglect co-occurred with emotional abuse in 61 % of the surveyed cases (Mennen et al. 2010). Likewise, neglect can be emotional or material, while the two forms of neglect do not always have to coincide. Children may have all their material needs covered and still be persistently abused in psychological terms.

Thus, the conceptual disjunctive would be whether children who suffer sexual abuse, for instance, actually suffer a double victimization in the form of sexual and emotional abuse, or if they suffer only a kind of child abuse that entails emotional negative consequences. Because in fact, "the vast majority of the negative consequences of maltreatment are psychological in nature" (Hart et al. 1997, 48).

Furthermore, forms of emotional abandonment performed due to excess can also be included (Doyle 2014) as forms of psychological abuse as long as they also entail negative consequences for children's well-being and well-becoming, such as severe overprotection, over emotional dependency or inadequate behavior in relation to the age of the child,[12] which promotes immaturity and encroaches on children's normal development and autonomy if it is continued over time.

In relation to the fourth and last open question, emotional maltreatment deals with the sometimes fuzzy boundaries between abuse, violence and conflict. Conflictivity can be related to violence, as Gelles and Straus (1979) argue, but it does not have to be directly connected to abuse. Likewise, violence might be understood in relation to severe physical aggression. However, it is more often and more widely accepted that whatever intentional action/omission or aggression, verbal or physical, that causes harm is an act of violence. In this sense, violence would not only refer to extremely harmful forms of aggression (Baron et al. 1994, 7).

In conclusion, it should not be forgotten at this point that the main concern here is not only the caregivers' actions, but the children's health and well-being, so that a formal definition could also be useful, focusing on the negative effects on children's well-being and mental and physical health. Given the vagueness and conflicts of some definitions and in line with some other experts, I support the use of an operative definition (McGee and Wolfe 1991; Cantón Duarte and Cortés Arboleda

---

[11] Especially if emotional abuse is defined by virtue of its consequences, the co-occurrence is clear. In addition, emotional abuse is very often a means to perpetrate other types of abuses: verbal threats and terrorizing are often found in cases of sexual and physical abuse.

[12] For example, treating an adolescent as a baby can entail some feeling of humiliation and lack of recognition.

1997): according to this understanding, psychological abuse is any continuous action or omission[13] that tends to emotionally or cognitively attack a minor. Thus, the working criteria these experts use to consider a case as psychological abuse are mainly the measurable effects on children's development. I will adopt these criteria since they help avoid ambiguities in terms of conceptual or too abstract definitions. The measurable effects here refer to (1) the level of the child's adaptation, (2) the child's health. In addition, they also focus on (3) the caregivers' behavior – not their intentions. For these authors, one of the main traits is the persistent verbal hostility towards children, including insults, contempt, constant criticism, threats and blockage of their initiatives.

Among these actions and omissions, psychological or emotional abuse includes to reject, ignore, terrorize, isolate children, as well as to expose children to conjugal or domestic violence, and to deprive them of feelings of love, affection and security. Four subtypes of emotional abuse can be distinguished, namely: spurning, terrorizing, isolating, exploiting/corrupting (Feerick 2006). Being terrorized means that parents threaten to commit suicide or exposing their children to violence, etc., while spurning, which is the most common one, usually includes insulting, rejecting, blaming and ridiculing the child (Trickett et al. 2009, 27). Thus, with Zuravin (1991), I assume that the occurrences of observable and/or quantifiable or evaluable effects, as well as their adaptation to the age variable, are key criteria in order to discern whether one faces a real case of abuse.

The State's Responsibilities: Social Justice and Public Health

Mental well-being and health are clearly essential for a person's development. In fact, both, physical and mental health, are widely considered fundamental dimensions of human well-being. Emotional abuse can entail devastating effects for children's health. In addition, the distribution of emotional health among children is unfair, for it depends on caregivers' skills and resources that are not fairly distributed, although the unfair situation is avoidable and changeable through education and positive parenthood programs. Due to the fact that part of the debate on the Cinderella Law project arises from the petition to charge the state with a public responsibility in relation to parenthood and children's well-being, I will now shift the focus towards the normative criteria needed to distinguish a negative event from a problem of public health and social justice.

Both concepts, social justice and public health, are closely connected: a problem considered a question of public health will entail a problem of social justice (Benatar et al. 2011, 647). Likewise, "justice is viewed as so central to the mission of public health that it has been described as the field's core value" (Gostin and Powers 2006, 1053). In a way, affirming that something is a problem of public health is already

---

[13] This would be a way of recognizing emotional abuse as a form of maltreatment *per se* without denying the overlap with – and the psychological effects of – the other types of abuses.

making a normative statement, as it implies the defense of some core idea of justice and the will to minimize the impacts of hazards on human life that generate disadvantages (Beauchamp and Steinbock 1999, 105–108).

As Gostin and Powers clearly highlight:

> A commitment to social justice lies at the heart of public health. This commitment is to the advancement of human well-being. It aims to lift up the systematically disadvantaged and in so doing further advance the common good by showing equal respect to all individuals and groups who make up the community. Justice in public health is purposeful, positivistic, and humanistic (Gostin and Powers 2006, 1060).

However, not every question of social justice has to deal with public health, while all the questions of public health are related to social justice. Thus, child emotional abuse would be a question of social justice if its occurrence and effects are objectively determinable and if they can socially be influenced (Anderson 2010).

The first criterion is crucial to avoid subjective preference and it allows for the emergence of criticism and sharable standards. The second condition is a way of avoiding the problem of damages or disadvantages caused by the action of non-moral agents, like non-human animals. These include accidents, such as natural catastrophes, that are not linked to human action as well as tragic events that are not controllable. Both would remain outside of the scope of social justice (Cabezas et al. 2014). In other words, and in relation to the old ought/can debate: if it is out of human's hands, then it is not a question of social justice.

Likewise, social justice goes beyond the cases of health emergencies, but deals with the best way of distributing goods and resources in order to minimize hazards and guarantee equal respect to the citizens' interest in their well-being. Child emotional abuse is clearly a threat to those citizens' well-being. Hence, the question is whether this kind of threat can be objectively measured and whether it is alterable and somehow controllable through human policies. If the answer to both questions is positive, child emotional abuse would be a problem of social justice. However, it still needs to be explored whether it is also a question of public health. To make clear that child emotional abuse is not only a misfortune, but also a problem of social justice and a question of public health would provide a different perspective on the debate on projects defending a penalization of this type of maltreatment. It would turn this debate from being perceived as an excessive demanding law project dealing with private and non-negotiable parental habits into a basic and urgent question in terms of children's health.

Thus, the criteria to consider this problem as a question of public health are the following:

(1) Firstly, the issue "must place a large burden on society" (Schoolwerth et al. 2006, 1). This means that the disease or the problem – for it does not have to be a disease *per se* in order to be a question of public health; just think of the case of adolescent pregnancies, for instance – distressing the health of citizens should directly or indirectly affect a considerable amount of the respective society's population. Furthermore, data proving that the figures are increasing should be available, as they imply that this is a real risk for that society's well-

being. As these authors point out, "this burden is experienced in terms of mortality and morbidity, quality of life, and cost and is perceived as a threat by the public; that is, there is a sense of fear that the disease is out of control" (*ibidem*).

(2) Secondly, there should be an unequal distribution of this problem. In order to be considered a question of public health, the issue should affect "minorities and disadvantaged individuals to a greater extent" (*ibidem*), that is, normally those who lack the necessary resources to properly deal with it.

In relation to the first two criteria, the connection to social justice is evident: "The level of government best situated for dealing with public health threats depends on the evidence identifying the nature and origin of the specific threat, the resources available to each unit for addressing the problem, and the probability of strategic success" (Gostin and Powers 2006, 1056). The issue needs to affect a great number of people, its impact should be increasing and it should be possible to gather empirical data about the question itself. In turn, to be categorized like that, it needs to be objectively measurable.

(3) "There must be evidence that *upstream* preventive strategies could substantially reduce the burden of the condition" (*ibidem*). In relation to social justice, this means that the problem should be socially changeable. If the social, economic and political factors that contribute to it can neither be changed nor impact the occurrence of the problem, then one would be dealing with a question of arbitrariness outside the human scope of action.

(4) The final point relates to the first and third criterion: even though there could have been attempts to control the problem or disease, not all possible preventive strategies have been developed yet. This means that there is still room for policies and strategies that could make a difference and have not been accomplished yet.

In conclusion, the inner connection to justice is evident: public health policies assume principles of justice (Ruger 2010, 42), dealing with fair treatment and health improvement. Now the question is whether child emotional abuse could also meet the criteria of both, social justice and public health.

Child Psychological Abuse and Justice: A Question of Public Health?

Emotional abuse damages children's health by definition: it prevents them from achieving central capabilities and functioning (Cabezas et al. 2014), while health, at the same time, is a good that may be fairly distributed through some means and measures. Now, the question is whether granting that children may not be emotionally abused is publicly demandable and, whether such abuses do not need to co-occur with other kinds of abuses. In other words: Does child psychological abuse constitute a problem of social justice? And is it therefore also an issue of public health that could justify the need for specific laws and public measures against it?

In order to answer these questions, it is crucial to examine whether or not the negative effects of emotional abuse are objectively measurable and socially changeable, primarily in relation to social justice. Nevertheless, as the second section demonstrates, one of the main problems concerning the policies on emotional abuse is the definition of the problem itself. It seems to be difficult to establish whether or not the issue meets the above-mentioned criteria when there is still a lack of general consensus on the clear-cut limits of emotional abuse.

In any case, I will not take into consideration studies on the emotional, cognitive and behavioral negative consequences of physical and sexual abuse at this point, but will rather focus only on the data revealing the effects psychological abuse has on children's health. Likewise, I will assume the criteria of the operative definition of emotional abuse. I accept that instances of such abuse need to be repeated in time; but they do not necessarily need to be chronical or severe. It is true that such a definition would be self-affirmative for this section, because it implies that something constitutes a form of child emotional abuse if it entails measurable effects referred to the level of children's adaptation, children's health, and the caregivers' behavior – and that is what I aim to prove here. However, this section focuses on how emotional abuse in fact implies negative objective measurable effects on children's well-being as well as their mental and physical health. This is an important step to avoid the problem of being vague when we distinguish factors that entail a significant harm, and therefore justify legal intervention, from factors that do not (Thompson and Kaplan 1996, 147).

Emotional abuse, both its occurrences and its negative effects, is objectively measurable, as the work done by psychologists and psychiatrist has shown. One can examine whether a child is being/has been humiliated at home, insulted, terrorized, spurred, etc., and how often this happens by self-evaluative tests and other common diagnostic tools in psychological practice (i.e. drawings, story-telling, role-playing, or by using teddy bears and dolls to reflect what happens to them, etc.). Likewise, one can recognize and measure the negative effects on children's performances at school, as well as their self-esteem or behavior. Similarly, emotional abuse is socially changeable. If this were not the case, psychological and educational interventions would be pointless. Preventive measures such as psychological and emotional education, for both parents and children (in order to better detect the problem and stop the negative consequences, or at least reduce them) are proven to be efficient if they are consistently offered (VVAA 2009; Mayer and Salovey 1997).

Similarly, and not only in relation to the conditions that need to be fulfilled to be considered a problem of social justice, the issue also meets the criteria of public health: criterion 3 and 4 are satisfied, because it is clear that not everything that can be/could have been done in this field of mental health and prevention has yet been done. There is still a lack of consistent programs dealing with mental health, positive parenthood and emotional education in healthcare and public education systems. To phrase it differently: if psychological abuse were to be considered a crime against children's health, as is physical abuse and neglect, and if there were measures and more monetary investment on that, the problem would surely be reduced and its social perception would be modified. Ultimately, such measures have the potential to change our knowledge about these problems and may result in a less tolerant attitude towards them.

The problem is not that it is not measurable, but that many cases remain unreported due to the social stigma of mental health issues and the definition of the problem: even though many children are not considered abused have in fact experienced some kind of emotional abuse in their life (Norman et al. 2012, 2, 22).

Specifically in relation to the first condition necessary to be considered a question of public health, it is important to highlight how emotional abuse implies a highly negative effect on a society's quality of life. Therefore, it should be perceived as a threat to society's well-being. "Emotional maltreatment is primarily damaging to the self and to the self's view of the world" (Hart et al. 1997). And as such, it entails costs for that society, meaning that it is a threat to public health, not only something negative that affects our private sphere. It will affect your performance at school and work, your life's expectations, your life plans, etc. (Finkelhor et al. 2007).

The Adverse Childhood Experiences (ACEs) test is another example that demonstrates why child emotional abuse constitutes a burden to a society (first condition).[14] This test of ten questions explores traumatic experiences during childhood to show how seeing or experiencing one and often several traumatic situations during childhood is more common that one might think: 64 % of the surveyed people reported such experiences. From the ten questions, one is directly related to emotional abuse, but five others are concerned with witnessing some kind of violence, or experiencing negative situations in others such as whether a family member went to prison or you lived with someone mentally ill. All of these questions point to children's mental well-being. The point here is not that these traumatic experiences are *per se* a question of injustice, but that children go through traumatic experiences more commonly than it is generally perceived.

In relation to the high costs on the society's quality of life, emotional abuse "has an adverse influence on early psychological development with potentially profound effects on childhood development and adult functioning" (Thompson und Kaplan 1996, 147). As any overexposure to stressful situations, emotional abuse may imply severe damage to children's neurological, behavioral and physical development (Hart et al. 1997, 45; Grisolía 2008, 113–130; Bowlby 1988). In general terms, "both prospective and retrospective studies consistently showed an association between exposure to child physical abuse, emotional abuse, and neglect and adverse health outcomes" (Norman et al. 2012, 22). As this authors' research shows, emotional abuse increases the risk of suicidal behaviors, drug abuse, and obesity, depressive and eating disorders compared to non-abused children (Norman et al. 2012, 3, 16–21).

Regarded in the relation to its effects on the quality of life and implications of high costs to public health, it is true that being the victim of a trauma does not determine long-term effects or reactions. These also depend on other personal skills, age,

---

[14] More information about the ACEs test and findings can be consulted in: http://acestoohigh.com/aces-101/

social networks, resilience, etc. However, while personal traits are flexible and diverse, it does not mean that there is a lack of relevant conclusive data about the connection between emotional abuse in childhood and mental and physical health problems, such as depression, cardiopathies, anxiety disorders, etc.: "longitudinal studies show the destructive power in long terms of emotional maltreatment" (Hart et al. 1997). These include anxious attachments, behavioral problems, hyperactivity and distractibility, difficulties in the ability to learn and to solve problems, a lack of enthusiasm, low self-esteem, high dependence, self-abusive behavior and serious psychopathology (36–46).

Fairness and distribution are at the core of the second criterion, and emotional abuse meets it in two senses: firstly, it is unfairly distributed, because non-abusive behavior depends on parental skills, and these depend on how considerate or sensitive parents are in treating their children, how they deal with stress, their coping styles, etc. These, in turn, depend on current hazards and how lucky a child is to be born into one family instead of another one. This is particularly relevant because no official emotional or psychological training is systematically offered and no positive parental skills education is provided. In consequence, this means that it depends on how well-prepared your parents are whether or not you are going to suffer psychological abuse. Secondly, it is also unfairly distributed in the sense that parents living in economically challenging situations, with poor social networks, stress managing problems, drug abuse problems, etc. are more likely to emotionally abuse children and neglect their needs. However, it is not only a problem of socially excluded families, but a transversal and educational one. And thus, it becomes a problem of public mental health.

Conclusion

I have presented how the recognition and regulation of measures on emotional abuse against children is problematic, not because it does not meet the required criteria, but especially because of the social perception of the importance of mental health and the suspiciousness with respect to any normative regulation on what happens in the private sphere. Aside from very severe cases, these kinds of regulations are perceived as a threat to autonomy and parental rights. However, the attitude is different when the normative question on how children should be treated is focused on material goods or physical health.

I have also shown how the core of the problem lies in two main questions. The first one is the normative disagreement on the minimum values we share as a society with respect to how parents should treat children concerning emotional health and well-being. Although solving this puzzle surpasses the scope of this chapter and much more work needs to be done in this respect, I have tried to shed light on the fact that the hidden values and assumptions on every position should be openly discussed in order to overcome these still unanswered questions. The second question, central to this chapter, would be the biased attitude to the – in a sense artificially constructed – dichotomy between mind and body (Lane et al. 2000), mental health and physical health, as if they were not connected, and as if one were completely independent from the other one. In this sense, I would like to conclude that mental health is not only equally important as, but in some sense also indivisible from physical health and that many injustices will go unnoticed until it is too late, unless the perception of this issue undergoes a change.

For these reasons, it is important to highlight that it will be very difficult to tackle the problem, unless the legal changes are not accompanied by social changes with respect to the values, the mentality and what is accepted – that such changes are possible is shown by the example of couple relations and domestic violence. If the social network does not perceive problems of emotional abuse as severe problems, and if there is no social pressure against it, it will be difficult to reveal a dysfunctional event in the private sphere until it becomes severe or co-occurs with other abuses that are much more socially unaccepted, such as sexual abuse or physical abuse. For this reason it is crucial to change the perception of emotional abuse and to start seeing emotional education and psychological well-being as an issue of social justice, but also as a problem of public health that affects not only the abused children, but also their future relations and parental styles. Beyond the objective data, the question whether emotional abuse need be included in legal policies without co-occurring with other abuses is a normative question. Whether or not caregivers insult a child, use contemptuous vocabulary, or terrorize their children can be objectively measured. However, the normative problem lies in the question whether the state should control and regulate such behavior, regardless of the caregivers' collaboration, or whether every caregiver should go through the same evaluative system as adoptive parents do, for instance.

To conclude the argument: emotional abuse should not be translated into a problem of physical public health in order to be understood as a question of mental public health. At the same time, it does not have to be translated into a psychiatric health issue: psychological health issues are also relevant *per se* and not seeing them as such is precisely what leads to the normative problem: because mental health is usually neither valued nor taken as seriously as physical health – and this needs to be changed.

References

Action for Children. 2013. *The criminal law and child neglect: And independent analysis and proposal for reform*. London. http://www.actionforchildren.org.uk/media/3331/criminal_law_and_child_neglect.pdf. Accessed 8 May 2015.

Anderson, E. 2010. Justifying the capability approach to justice. In *Measuring justice: Primary goods and capabilities*, ed. herausgegeben von Harry Brighouse und Ingrid Robeyns, 1. Aufl., 81–100. Cambridge/New York: Cambridge University Press.

APSAC. 1995. *Guidelines for psychosocial evaluation of suspected psychological maltreatment in children and adolescents*. Chicago: American Professional Society on the Abuse of Children.

Baron, R., A. Richardson, and R. Deborah. 1994. *Human aggression*. New York: Plenum Press.

Beauchamp, D.E., and B. Steinbock (eds.). 1999. *New ethics for the public's health*. New York: Oxford University Press.

Benatar, S.R., S. Gill, and I. Bakker. 2011. Global health and the global economic crisis. *American Journal of Public Health* 101(4): 646–653. doi:10.2105/AJPH.2009.188458.

Bowlby, J. 1988. *A secure base: Clinical applications of attachment theory*. London: Routledge.

Cabezas, M., G. Graf, and G. Schweiger. 2014. Health, justice, and happiness during childhood. *South African Journal of Philosophy* 33(4): 501–511. doi:10.1080/02580136.2014.967593.

Cantón Duarte, J., and Ma. Rosario Cortés Arboleda. 1997. *Malos tratos y abuso sexual infantil: causas, consecuencias e intervención*. Madrid: Siglo XXI.

Children and Young Persons Act. 1933. http://www.legislation.gov.uk/ukpga/Geo5/23-24/12. Accessed 8 May 2015.

Doyle, C. 2014. *Child neglect & emotional abuse: Understanding, assessment & response*. Los Angeles: Sage.

Feerick, M. (ed.). 2006. *Child abuse and neglect: Definitions, classifications, and a framework for research*. Baltimore: Paul H. Brookes Publishing Co.

Finkelhor, D., R. Ormrod, and H. Turner. 2007. Re-victimization patterns in a national longitudinal sample of children and youth. *Child Abuse & Neglect* 31(5): 479–502. doi:10.1016/j.chiabu.2006.03.012.

Furedi, F. 2014. The Cinderella Law: Emotional correctness gone mad. *The Independent*. http://www.independent.co.uk/life-style/health-and-families/features/the-cinderella-law-emotional-correctness-gone-mad-9231233.html. Accessed 8 May 2015.

Gelles, R., and M. Straus. 1979. Determinants of the violence in the family: Toward a theorical integration. In *Contemporary theories about the family*, vol. 1, ed. Wesley R. Burr, Reuben Hill, F. Ivan Nye, and Ira L. Reiss, 549–581. New York: The Free Press.

Gostin, L., and M. Powers. 2006. What does social justice require for the public's health? Public health ethics and policy imperatives. *Health Affairs* 25(Juli): 1053–1060. doi:10.1377/hlthaff.25.4.1053.

Grisolía, J. 2008. Efectos neurológicos. In *Violencia contra niños*, ed. José Sanmartín, 113–126. Barcelona: Ariel.

Grusec, J., and G. Walters. 1991. Psychological abuse and childrearing belief systems. In *The effects of child abuse and neglect. Issues and research*, ed. Raymond H. Starr Jr., and David A. Wolfe, 186–202. New York: The Guildford Press.

Hart, S., N. Binggeli, and M. Brassard. 1997. Evidence for the effects of psychological maltreatment. *Journal of Emotional Abuse* 1(1): 27–58. doi:10.1300/J135v01n01_03.

Hope, C. 2014. Parents who deliberately starve children of love face jail under new Cinderella Law. *The Telegraph*. http://www.telegraph.co.uk/news/health/children/10732982/Parents-who-starve-children-of-love-face-jail.html. Accessed 8 May 2015.

Lane, R., L. Nadel, and G. Ahern. 2000. *Cognitive neuroscience of emotion*. New York: Oxford University Press. http://site.ebrary.com/id/10317735.

Martínez, R., and J. de Paúl Ochotorena. 1993. *Maltrato y abandono en la infancia*. Barcelona: Martínez Roca.

Mayer, J., and P. Salovey. 1997. What is emotional intelligence? In *Emotional development and emotional intelligence*, ed. P. Salovey and D.J. Sluyter, 3–31. New York: Basic Books.

McGee, R., and D. Wolfe. 1991. Psychological maltreatment: Toward an operational definition. *Development and Psychopathology* 3(01): 3. doi:10.1017/S0954579400005034.

Mennen, F., K. Kim, J. Sang, and P. Trickett. 2010. Child neglect: Definition and identification of Youth's experiences in official reports of maltreatment. *Child Abuse & Neglect* 34(9): 647–658. doi:10.1016/j.chiabu.2010.02.007.

Nicolas, J. 2014. Is new 'Cinderella's Law' on emotional neglect 'draconian and unhelpful'? *Community Care*. http://www.communitycare.co.uk/2014/04/10/new-cinderellas-law-emotional-neglect-draconian-unhelpful/. Accessed 8 May 2015.

Norman, R., M. Byambaa, R. De, A. Butchart, J. Scott, and T. Vos. 2012. The long-term health consequences of child physical abuse, emotional abuse, and neglect: A systematic review and meta-analysis. *PLoS Medicine* 9(11): e1001349. doi:10.1371/journal.pmed.1001349.

O'Hagan, K. 1993. *Emotional and psychological abuse of children.* Toronto/Buffalo: University of Toronto Press.

Ruger, J. 2010. Health capability: Conceptualization and operationalization. *American Journal of Public Health* 100(1): 41–49. doi:10.2105/AJPH.2008.143651.

Sanmartín, J. 2008. *Violencia contra niños.* Barcelona: Ariel.

Schoolwerth, Anton C., M.M. Engelgau, T.H. Hostetter, K.H. Rufo, D. Chianchiano, W.M. McClellan et al. 2006. Chronic kidney disease: A public health problem that needs a public health action plan. *Preventing Chronic Disease [serial online]* 3(2). http://www.cdc.gov/pcd/issues/2006/apr/pdf/05_0105.pdf.

Seligman, M. [1995] 2007. *The optimistic child: A proven program to safeguard children against depression and build lifelong resilience.* New York: Houghton Mifflin Harcourt.

Shaffer, A., M. Yates Tuppett, and B. Egeland. 2009. The relation of emotional maltreatment to early adolescent competence: Developmental processes in a prospective study. *Child Abuse & Neglect* 33(1): 36–44. doi:10.1016/j.chiabu.2008.12.005.

Spanish Penal Code. 2015. *Agencia Estatal Boletín Oficial del Estado.* www.boe.es/legislacion/codigos. Accessed 8 May 2015.

Thompson, A.E., and C. Kaplan. 1996. Childhood emotional abuse. *The British Journal of Psychiatry* 168(2): 143–148. doi:10.1192/bjp.168.2.143.

Trickett, P., F. Mennen, F. Kim, and J. Sang. 2009. Emotional abuse in a sample of multiply maltreated, urban young adolescents: Issues of definition and identification. *Child Abuse & Neglect* 33(1): 27–35. doi:10.1016/j.chiabu.2008.12.003.

Trickett, P., S. Negriff, J. Ji, and M. Peckins. 2011. Child maltreatment and adolescent development. *Journal of Research on Adolescence* 21(1): 3–20. doi:10.1111/j.1532-7795.2010.00711.x.

VVAA. 2009. *Avances en el estudio de la Inteligencia Emocional.* Fundación Botín: Santander.

Zuravin, S. 1991. Research definitions of child physical abuse and neglect: Current problems. In *The effects of child abuse and neglect: Issues and research,* xiv, ed. Raymond H. Starr Jr., and David A. Wolfe, 100–128. New York: Guilford Press.

Chapter 10
Epistemic Injustice and Children's Well-Being

Christina Schües

Abstract Children have a fine sense of injustice. But can they report their experiences? Are their voices heard? This essay criticizes conceptions of justice that focus merely on the offender, and, thus, dismiss the experiences of the affected. In order to discuss children's life, it is necessary to include their experiences and perspectives, and to give them their own voice. By addressing ethical and epistemic injustice, this approach enfolds the sense of injustice itself, it poses the question of how to describe injustice as a phenomenon on its own, and depicts prejudices caused by ageism, racism, or sexism that may exclude the testimony of particular persons, for instance children. Children belong to the group that is particularly vulnerable to being affected by ethical and epistemic injustice because their testimony is dismissed quite easily. They are born into and live in relations, they did not choose. Based on these relations children experience the surrounding world, they feel trust or mistrust, and they face injustice or justice towards themselves or others. Ethical and epistemic injustices violate the children's well-being.

Keywords Justice • Children • Trust • Relations • Ethics • Shklar • Fricker • Society

Introduction

The *3. World Vision report on children* is guided by the notion of justice.[1] The authors and editors, Sabine Andresen and Klaus Hurrelmann, focus on the question "How just is our world?" In order to answer this question they interviewed children as part of an investigation into their lives. The authors of this empirical study argue that children must be and can be given their *own voice* because they are "experts of

---

[1] The *3. World Vision* children's report by Andresen and Hurrelmann (2013) focuses on Germany. However, for the purposes of this essay I take this empirical study as evidence of children's interests and views around the world.

C. Schües (✉)
Institute for the History of Medicine and Science Studies, University of Lübeck,
Lübeck, Germany
e-mail: schuees@imgwf.uni-luebeck.de

© Springer International Publishing Switzerland 2016
J. Drerup et al. (eds.), *Justice, Education and the Politics of Childhood*,
Philosophy and Politics – Critical Explorations 1,
DOI 10.1007/978-3-319-27389-1_10

155

their life world, their feelings, opinions and experiences".[2] They can be informants and a source of knowledge about their lives and their well-being. Even very early in life they have a strong sense of injustice. When asked what they think about a good life or well-being, they bring up topics that are central to philosophical and social debates about justice and injustice. Their sense of injustice is strongly linked to inequality, and they can very clearly *describe* their situation of life, for example concerning poverty and experienced exclusion.[3]

Contrary to the theories of, for instance, Sigmund Freud or Lawrence Kohlberg, more recent studies in moral psychology by researchers such as Gertrud Nunner-Winkler show that children are not egocentrically driven when they are very young.[4] Very early on in life they have a fine sense of what others need. When we speak of children, it is of course impossible to give an all-encompassing generalization. Children's age, gender, circumstances or contexts – all of these are characteristics that make them a diverse group. They have different interests, they live in different social contexts and legal systems. Children are not simply non-adults; they have their specific competences, a moral status, and world-views. However, it is interesting that children themselves speak from their perspective about the "world of adults".[5]

Just as in the World Vision study on children, I will focus on children aged between 6 and 11 years. In this age group, children are usually in primary school and mostly develop their concern for others in a more conceptual and reflective way. In this paper, I enfold the thesis that children have to be heard in questions of justice and injustice. If they are not listened to when they report on an injustice concerning him or herself or someone else, then this dismissal can be called an *ethical* and *epistemic* injustice.

Intuitively we might agree that children must be heard when they talk about what they have seen or heard; however, often adults do not speak *with* children but *about* them. The empirical study by Andresen and Hurrelmann shows that children themselves are very competent in providing information about and interpretations of their own childhood, their being, and their well-being. This might not mean that a child's perspective is sufficient for them to know enough about injustice in the world, and the injustice within their own lives in particular. The basic conviction that children should be listened to is linked to the strong belief that their lives and the just or unjust relationships and structures they live in stand for the condition of the world. The well-being of children is a mirror of the state of justice in the world. The idea of taking injustice as a personal phenomenon and the belief that children can and should be asked about their experiences of injustice are not self-evident.

Justice can be described from the perspective of an offender or from the perspective of a victim, and it can be described with a focus on social structures or

[2] Andresen and Hurrelmann (2013: 26).
[3] Andresen and Hurrelmann (2013: 46).
[4] Gertrud Nunner-Winkler (1998, 2009).
[5] Andresen and Hurrelmann (2013: 48).

cultural norms and values.[6] However, most philosophical expositions of justice from Plato to John Rawls, from Aristotle to Michael Walzer, focus instead on the perspective of the offender who is held responsible for his action or on institutions which are more or less just. I will begin my discussion by showing at first how a conception of justice excludes the perspective of those who are affected by injustice. My reason for introducing Plato's cognitive notion of justice is that we can learn from it that this type of concept essentially *excludes* the experiences and reports by those who are affected by injustice. Very briefly, I will show, the exclusion of children from communication and discourse is not just a question of the will of adults but also of a concept itself. As a consequence, I will argue that speaking about injustice must also include all those who are affected by injustice, in particular children with their own experiences, perspectives and voices.[7] Linking the issue of injustice to the theme of trust will prepare the fundamental thesis presented in the final part of the paper. If a child's testimony of injustice is not heard – even though it is factually true – then an ethical as well as an epistemic injustice is being committed against her.

What is considered as just or unjust, as promoting happiness or harm depends upon the ethical perspectives held by the individual and by society, but also on the personal interests or on the question of who has the power to define justice or injustice. Most people easily utter the judgment "This is unjust!" Observations about injustice have inspired many authors from antiquity to the present. But Paul Ricœur remarks: "The sense of injustice is not simply more poignant but more perspicacious than the sense of justice, for justice more often is lacking and injustice prevails. And people have a clearer vision of what is missing in human relations than of the right way to organize them. This is why, even for philosophers, it is injustice that first sets thought in motion."[8] With this quote, a general intention of this paper is nicely introduced. There is a double meaning of "the sense of injustice": The sense of injustice means being affected by an unjust action or structure and it means to be sensible to incidents or situations of injustice. In this second meaning, the sense of injustice is taken as an epistemic notion and as a means to detect injustice.

---

[6] In this paper, I will not discuss questions of justice and agency in general. In addition, I will not be concerned with the question who or which institutions are responsible for injustice or justice. These questions are very interesting. However, my focus will be on the question of how to detect and report injustice. This question includes the concern that a child's testimony should not be dismissed *because* it is given by a child.

[7] The argument of this paper will not include the question of whether or not children should be heard on their interests and wishes. Thus, here I do not discuss how children may participate in decision making processes. For the discussion how children should be heard in regard to choices that concern them, see Brighouse (2003). Distinct from children's participation in decision-making is listening to children concerning reports about situations or incidents in reality. Here a concern is rather whether a report is true or correct and whether it corresponds with what 'really' happened.

[8] Ricœur (1992: 198).

From a Justice of the Offender to a Sense of Injustice

The historical path of the philosophical framework of injustice began with Plato who addressed injustice as the other side of justice.[9] Plato understands injustice as a misdirected psychic energy, which disorders the soul of the offender. Given this, he hold an epistemological and ethical notion of justice and injustice. Such concepts of justice cannot address the perspectives of those who are affected by just or unjust actions because only the mind of the offending person is in focus. In Plato's understanding, the one who knows the just way will act in a just way. Therefore, the concept of justice is only useful for the evaluation of the offender's soul and for the education of how to act in a just way.[10]

I will discuss Plato's notion of justice because his approach shows a perspective and a limitation that make the introduction of children's concern *conceptually* impossible. I will then turn to alternative concepts of injustice that include an awareness of the experiences and perspectives of the persons affected by injustice.

Contrasting Socrates' concept of the virtuous soul with Judith Shklar's practice of virtue shows a difference between the focus on the offender and the focus on the person affected by persons who have acted unjustly. Socrates, the philosopher of the Agora, and Judith Shklar, a political philosopher at Harvard University, were both deeply interested in justice, and even outraged about the unreflected use of the notion. Plato's Socrates observed that although no one really knows what justice means everyone still speaks as if they did. In his dialogues, he reveals the ignorance of rhetorically talented citizens while searching for a viable concept of justice. For Plato acting unjustly destroys the right order of the soul, and doing so also destroys virtue, the excellence of a person. This understanding of injustice as the disorder of the individual soul is transferred to the polis, which when it is unjust falls apart into inconsistent elements.

In many Socratic dialogues, also in the first book of the *Politeia*, Plato's investigations revolve around the question of "How should one live?" This is particularly important in light of the fact that "justice is the excellence of the soul, and injustice is a defect of the soul".[11] Injustice does not only undermine the virtue of an actor; injustice – if it prevails – ruins and destroys human and social relationships by bringing about discord, hatred and infighting. "Then the just soul and the just man will live well, and the unjust man will live ill."[12] Socrates' opponent Thrasymachus takes the position that the unjust action is useful to the strong because he thereby gains an advantage over the weaker person. Only the fool, as the strategist Thrasymachus puts it, does not act for his own benefit. Both positions – the one of Socrates and that of Thrasymachus – have primarily the happiness or human flourishing (*eudaimonia*) of the *offender* in mind. Both positions focus on the cognition

---

[9] Here I agree with Judith Shklar (1990: 29).

[10] In addition: Plato's conception of the states is found in analogy to the soul.

[11] Plato (book I).

[12] Plato (book I).

and on the consequences of an action *for* the offender, but neglect the suffering an action inflicts on others. Under this cognitivist model, injustice is a problem *only* for the offender. This focus on the offender has significantly influenced present discourses on justice, including the criminal justice system.

In order to address those who are affected and injured by injustice, it is essential to construe a concept of injustice as a phenomenon with its own qualities. This is done by the approach by Judith Shklar in her book *The Faces of Injustice*.[13] She clearly criticizes the concept of Plato that focuses on the knowing and virtuous soul because it is blind to injustice, to its real problems, to the situation and the *concrete* experiences of the affected person. *Conceptually* it cannot give a voice to those who suffer an injustice. Regardless of whether they are adults or children, the perspective must be shifted from the "soul" of the offender to those who are affected and who are suffering from unjust persons or from unjust structures. When considering injustice I will not discuss the whole realm of structural or institutional injustice.[14] Rather I focus on the perspective of the experience and the suffering of an injustice and the question who can report about it. Certainly, injustice is more than a lack of justice, and vice versa justice is more than the absence of injustice.

Judith Shklar argues that injustice is a phenomenon that deserves its own exposition and requires a particular kind of sense if it is to be detected in daily life. Therefore, she argues for a cognitive program which means that we need to view the *sense of injustice* as a *practice of virtue*. The *sense* of injustice is twofold. Firstly, it has a *normative* sense of judging a relationship or structure as somehow not right or undesirable for the person affected. Second, it has an *epistemological* meaning in which a *sense* of injustice means seeing the suffering and injuries of others, and distinguishing between injustice and misfortune. From the perspective of an affected person misfortune can be perceived as an injustice or, conversely, a perceived injustice may also prove to be a misfortune. In the context of attentiveness and in distinction to authors of distributive justice such as John Rawls and Michael Walzer, Shklar wants to establish a sense of injustice as a normative political force, as the practice of virtue. The sense of injustice inheres a sensibility to perceive injustices as a negative experience that should not be. Mostly injustice expresses itself in suffering and suppressive hurt, such as the imposition of unemployment, violence or structural exclusion. Thus, people need a particular *sense* of detecting injustice for themselves or for other people.

Against abstract conceptions of justice, she calls for sensitivity to the experience of injustice as an important prerequisite to formulating and implementing justice. Thus, the starting point of her theoretical work is attentiveness to the negative experience of injustice. A consequence is that those who are affected by injustice and

---

[13] Shklar (1990).

[14] Different normative theories have also addressed the issue of injustice. Examples are theories of recognition, such as for instance by Axel Honneth (1995) and the capability approach of Amartya Sen (2009) and Martha Nussbaum (2013). They are all very important approaches. However, I limit this paper to a line of thinking that can be used in discussing the credibility of reports about injustice.

those who see injustice for other people are given a voice because the philosophical framework itself allows for it. Detecting a suffering or harm because of injustice does not necessarily mean having knowledge about society's structures, cultural norms, human behavior or actions, or other sources of injustice.

At first conclusion, we can see that the difference between the Platonic approach that *conceptually* excludes injustice as it affects the victim and one that focuses on it is *epistemologically* and *ethically* substantial. The latter clearly moves the discussion from the offender's disposition to a relational concept which addresses the experience of the affected. Secondly, the divergence between disregarding a person's suffering and making it a concern is perceptually and morally significant. Moreover, thirdly, there is an asymmetrical distinction between listening to adults but not to children. That is, some people are not willing to listen to children but only to adults expressing their experiences of injustice. All three aspects are questions of epistemic and ethical injustice. In the following section, I continue the discussion about the account of Judith Shklar and her focus on the *experience* of injustice and its manifestations. Then, I will discuss the question of who may report about injustice.

Sensing Injustice

In order to pin point negative experiences more precisely, Shklar focuses on negative phenomena such as injustice and misfortune. Her turn to negative experiences initiates a negative social philosophy that emanates from the negativity of violence, injury or other unacceptable experiences. She insists that we first speak about cruelty, the experience of fear, and the fear of having fear.[15] Her motive in this approach is the avoidance of the worst case scenario. In her view, philosophy has to begin with the negativity of experiences of injustice and not with positive norms of justice. Therefore, she addresses the negative *experience* of injustice. However, these experiences of injustice may in fact turn out to have been caused by misfortune. There is thus a problem in distinguishing injustice from mere misfortune.

The question of *what* is described as misfortune and what is described as injustice depends on the particular discursive power of defining the merits of a case, on the perspective of interest, and on the point of view of the affected person. As Shklar has observed, the willingness to call an event unjust often correlates with the willingness and ability to help those who are affected.[16] The distinction between injustice and misfortune is used to sharpen the sense of injustice and to clarify how to respond to the injury of another person. The sense of injustice includes sensitivity,

---

[15] Shklar writes: "The fear we fear is of pain inflicted by others to kill and maim us, not the natural and healthy fear that merely warns us of avoidable pain. And, when we think politically, we are afraid not only for ourselves but for our fellow citizens as well. We fear a society of fearful people." (1989: 29).

[16] Shklar (1990, 1f.).

empathy, and a talent for interpretation, but also a cognitive interest in searching for the cause of an event and developing a moral understanding of the needs of others. Thus, it is a question of perceiving properly the causes and circumstances of an incident in order to decide whether it should be seen as an injustice or a misfortune. A misfortune has a cause that was not in human hands even though it may have taken place in an interpersonal context. People see or hear of earthquakes, rockfalls, or avalanches; they find the victims or learn what has happened to them. Then it is decided (by whom?) *how* to deal with such misfortunes. Hence, the search for the cause of a perceived injustice is an opportunity to find criteria for distinguishing between a misfortune and an injustice.

There are two possible ways to consider an injustice. The first is that someone feels she has been treated unjustly and feels entitled that we, as observers, regard and understand what has happened to her. In her "version of the victim" she relates a particular incident to the perceived injustice. Others may regard this same incident as a simple misfortune. The primary concern is to accept and understand the perspective of the person who is affected. The second possibility is that someone who is affected by something negative does not realize that this incident is in fact an injustice. This can be particularly the case when people are affected by structural injustices, such as inequality of opportunities, or by undetected prejudices, such as having the "wrong" name, gender, age, or ethnic belonging. They do not experience an incident *as* injustice.[17] Shklar understands the difficulty of identifying persons who are affected by injustice, and her argument is meant to strengthen the position of the affected person and make people sensitive to the injustices of others. This idea can also be used to strengthen the position of children, their sense, i.e. sensibility, of injustice, and their perspectives on injustices.

Injustice for children can occur in many different realms of life. They can be confronted with poverty, inequality, lack of health care, and so on. Discussing injustice according to a particular theme, such as poverty, is one possibility of discourse. The other possibility is to discuss a particular group, such as children. Injustice in regard to children is done by addressing different methodological approaches and perspectives: First, statistics, reports, and figures can be used to detect where and how children have fewer life chances, are less wealthy, have less access to societal goods, less education etc. Such records represent an objective view. Second, in empirical studies children can be asked about their views in interviews or conversations. In this subjective perspective, children can report what they take to be injustice or misfortune. This view presupposes that talking about an experience can provide access to that experience or even to just or unjust actions or structures in society. Third, the voice of someone talking about the experience of injustice or

---

[17] Schweiger and Graf (2014) discuss the relation between an objective and subjective experience of injustice. There are specific problems of evaluating the experience of injustice in the case which does not involve injustice and the case of injustice which does not accord with an experience by the affected person. There is also some literature on "adaptive preferences" and the question whether it is to be regarded as a deficiency in rationality (Khader 2009). To follow up this line of argument would expand this paper into discussions about capability approaches and further aspects of how to take injustice as being "normal".

misfortune is heard and then a third person investigates and questions the conditions of the narrated experience. Fourth, an injustice occurs but the persons who are affected do not experience something unjust happening. Here, a third person interprets this particular relationship or structure as unjust or as misfortunate. However, it seems all these different aspects are relevant to all human beings. Hence, the question arises which approach is *particularly* relevant to children. Overall, children have a very fine sense of when to "blame" a "stupid stone" which caused an injury or when to reproach someone.

Children's Well-Being, Injustice and Trust

What is particular to children and their experience of injustice? In order to answer this question it is useful to ask about the context in which children experience justice or injustice.

An important and primary context in which children may be confronted with unjust situations is the family.[18] It is here that children first become conscious of justice and injustice.[19] The experience of injustice in the family might be preceded by negative interpersonal experiences such as being harmed and/or suffering pain. Sometimes an unjust family situation is considered by children as normal; in that case the issue of injustice might not even come up for the child. Children are always born into a certain context that is preexistent to them. They find themselves in a relational context which existed before them and which they did not choose. This relational context in the family also provides their first introduction to trust, care, and love. The beginning of a person is in a relation because a child is born by a woman and from that moment on lives within that relational context. Thus, regardless of whether a child is caringly welcomed or brutally dismissed, the formation and development of this relationship is essential for the child. This relationship is most often characterized by trust. Trust is a basis to understanding and a source of further trust. Thus, trust is essential to relationships. But trust also precedes mistrust and is fundamental to the perception of justice or injustice. Sometimes however this relationship is disrupted or neglected, and the child experiences abandonment and a first break down of a relationship of trust.[20]

Trust and justice play out in different dimensions, yet they are intertwined. Trust means a claim on the one who is trusted, whether this be the parents, relatives,

---

[18] The notion of family is used here in a very broad sense. It refers to the persons with whom a child spends most time and who cares for him or her. In his chapter "The morality of authority", John Rawls describes that family is important for the child's development of a sense of right and justice (Rawls 1971: 462–479).

[19] Munoz-Dardé (2002): 255, also fn.).

[20] For further reading about the emotional dimensions of minimally decent parents see the capability approach by Mullin (2012). Further aspects of trust I discuss in regard to the question whether trust needs transparency (Schües 2013).

friends, or others who are close to the child. The relation of the child to her parents is a dependency relationship; the relation of the parents to the child is a relationship of responsibility. The child's trust does not have to be gained as it is already there. But the child's trust can be broken or disappointed. Hence, parents can destroy this trust, and then perhaps regain it if it has been lost. Thus, during a child's development her trust is shaped, disappointed or supported in interaction with different persons. The disappointment of trust will not take place without hurting her feelings. Yet an adult with limitless trust would be naive. What is the meaning of the *claim* that is implied by trust? The claim contains an expectation that is at the same time an imposition. If we trust someone, then we make ourselves vulnerable to that person, expect her to be trustworthy and to refrain from misusing or abusing our trust.[21] This expectation, or imposition, of trust has to do with being vulnerable to the other person and with the relationship itself. The relationship of trust is responsive and somehow fair, and it is a basis for a responsible interaction with each other, an assumed guarantee for normality and for a supportive relation. Furthermore, the older a child gets, the more she will participate in societal institutions, such as kindergarten or school. Similar to the family, here as well trust and confidence depend on good relationships that are just and fair. Justice can shape feelings of trust in a more general sense. Not to get something might be hurtful, but it can be just. Even though trust is elementary and can be disappointed, it becomes more stable by relationships of justice which are – in the end – more reliable.

Experienced injustice, however, tends to create mistrust, and thus does not further good relationships among people. On a social dimension, inequality, poverty, or enduring injustice over generations concerns everyone. But children are especially vulnerable to situations of injustice because they are strongly dependent on stable supportive relationships. Clearly young children are not able to change the life circumstances they are born into or that are shaped by adult actions. Thus, being vulnerable to injustice is not so much a question of age but also a question of context and of the parents on whose status and well-being they depend. The UN Declaration of the Rights of the Child gives priority to the interests of children, but a child nevertheless lives as part of a family and accordingly lives within its particular system of wealth, support, and values. Thus, children are more or less vulnerable according to their life contexts. Even though most children's lives are positively influenced by their family context, this does not mean that their well-being and best interests will always be of primary importance. The point of the UN Declaration of the Rights of the Child is that giving priority to the best interests of the child means supporting them as individuals and not simply as members of a particular group. This can make a difference, for instance, when supporting unaccompanied refugee minors.

The ethical concern about injustice towards children and their well-being is important in many respects. In this essay, I am not focusing on particular unjust situations, such as violence against children, social concerns about education and the flourishing of the next generation, economic pressure, poverty, malnutrition, or war and conflict situations. Instead I would like to bring into focus the aspect of

---

[21] Schües (2015).

neglecting children's voices *because* they are children, that is, because of particular prejudices against this age group. The prejudices against children's testimony can be even stronger if they seem to be in the "wrong" family or ethnic group. Here I am not saying that children are always mistrusted when they talk about what they have experienced. Rather, I am addressing the phenomenon that if children's credibility is doubted or dismissed, then this can happen because of *ageism*. For instance, a criminal act, like sexual harassment, against a child might not be an act of injustice; even though it wrongs the child. But not believing the child when she reports about her experience *because* she is a child that I take to be a sign of mistrust and, as I will discuss in the next section, as a case of epistemic injustice.

I use the concept of the child's well-being in a normative sense since it has a guiding function when rights or duties conflict.[22] Recognizing the *normative* perspective means to claim that, children are persons and have a status as a subject, and so they have rights, just as parents and other close persons, as well as society, have obligations towards them. Children have a normative status regardless of their age and competence. Therefore, the concept of well-being includes the idea and practice that the child's will and decisions deserve to be respected,[23] but also that their experiences and perceptions are considered to be insightful and true. Thus, even though children are immature persons and even though children might live in asymmetrical relationships because of their different needs, dependencies, and situatedness as members of a family, a child's *voice of testimony* must be heard and considered. The question of "Whose voice is heard?" is not ethically indifferent; it is a question of justice and a question of interpretation, as I would like to enfold in the next section.[24]

Above I showed the importance of perceiving injustice very specifically from the perspective of the person who is affected. This thought plays an important role in Judith Shklar's thinking. Her argument that there should be a change of focus from an abstract concept of justice to a sense of injustice, which is charged with the moral virtues of sensitivity and empathy, is shared by Miranda Fricker as well. She also investigates epistemic justice, however, the question of who may give testimony of injustice.

---

[22] See more arguments about the normative content of well-being and its relational structure in Schües and C. Rehmann-Sutter (2013: 32).

[23] Giesinger (2013: 1–15).

[24] It might be argued that is not only the question whether children should be heard but more importantly *how* they can be heard. The article by Brighouse, discusses this question: How should children be heard?, (2003). However, in this interesting article, Brighouse focuses merely on how children can be heard concerning their interests and wishes. He discusses the rights of children and their dependency on adults to negotiate their interests, wishes, and activities in life. The criteria of decision-making by the adult focus on the question: "What is good for the child?" Hearing a child's testimony is different: Certainly the child's voice has to be interpreted, but the criteria for judgments are found in the facts and merits of a reported case of injustice. To believe a witness means to have a description of a case and, perhaps, to investigate into further details about the case. Such further investigation might or might not involve further testimonies.

Epistemic Injustice

Both Fricker and Shklar argue that we should develop a sense of and sensitivity for injustice. Hence, both emphasize the importance of epistemology – yet they do so in different ways. The distinction between misfortune and injustice is of primary interest for Shklar, leading her to focus on the question: "What counts as injustice?". Fricker on the other hand focuses on the ethically negative consequences of prejudices resulting in a *testimonial epistemic injustice*. She develops the thesis that injustice is not simply an ethical problem but also, and very poignantly so, an epistemic one. This epistemic question opens up another ethical dimension that is also important for the issue of trust.

Fricker shows how in order to detect injustice we need testimonies. But who can be considered a witness of injustice? Whom do we believe? Do we believe the words of children? She describes two forms of epistemic injustice in the following way: "Testimonial injustice occurs when prejudice causes a hearer to give a deflated level of credibility to a speaker's word; hermeneutical injustice occurs at a prior stage, when a gap in collective interpretive resources puts someone at an unfair disadvantage when it comes to making sense of their social experience."[25] Both forms of *epistemic injustice* lead to the problems that, firstly, the experience, situation or structure of injustice is not understood properly because the narrative is not taken to be true or understandable. Second, the person who experiences injustice is either not believed because she does not have credibility with the hearer, or she cannot formulate the injustice because that particular concept is socially missing. Third, a person is affected by an injustice but cannot conceptualize it *as* an experience because she individually is not able to reflect upon and talk about it. For instance, she might have emotional problems or is deeply ashamed because of an incident of injustice. Again, she cannot give testimony. In all of these mentioned examples, the child is taken as someone who does not know, is not credible, is lying or is someone who cannot be believed for other "reasons". And these other "reasons" might be based on such characteristics as race, gender, age, class or ethnic group. All of these forms of discrimination have in common that they reduce a person to a single characteristic so that they do not merit any credibility. Typically one would say: "She's just a child! She must have gotten it wrong! Too much imagination!" and then dismiss her testimony.

Fricker herself does not talk specifically about children, but her account of injustice can also be read with a concern for the respect that should be accorded to children.[26] The importance lies in the idea that we should not talk about children as if they were objects, were insignificant or without a moral status of their own. Children, regardless of how old they are, live in relationships that can be better or worse, more or less just, trustful or mistrustful. Children are part of relations and of family in a

---

[25] Fricker (2007: 1).

[26] Carel and Györffy (2014) wrote a rather short follow-up of Fricker's paper concerning children within the health care system.

way that is co-constitutive of the relations themselves. Younger and older children express their feelings and they tell of what has happened to them, what they have seen. Their experiences are bound up with the relations they live in. Children need flourishing, stable, trustful, and respectful relations for their well-being and development.

Not to believe a child's testimony – even though she has first-hand insight of what has actually happened – amounts to an epistemic injustice that disregards her as a knowing subject. If this is done systematically and is considered "normal" then the child's well-being is affected. "Persistent testimonial injustice can indeed inhibit the very formation of self."[27] Epistemic injustice hinders a child's formation of a stable self and her development of self-respect, leaving her incapable of trustful relations. If good relations are essential to the well-being of children, then mistrust will essentially ruin these relations. This also has consequences for society. If familial or societal relations are violated by an act, or worse by repeated acts, of epistemic injustice, then the well-being of the upcoming generation is endangered. Thus, not to believe a child for the wrong reasons will destabilize her future development but also the future development of societal relations. Since a child's well-being must not only be ensured in the present but also in the future, there are grave consequences to how a society chooses to treat its children. Children's well-being depends on ethical and epistemic justice.

Testimonial injustice excludes human beings from trustful conversations. Children need trustful relations and this concern involves not only fair and just relationships in the family and in society, but also a general attitude of *moral sensitivity* and *thoughtfulness* by their parents, teachers, and other close adults. If children are confronted with epistemic injustice, then they are faced with a double injustice. They are affected because even though they may be able to trustfully report about their experiences and observations, they are not believed and not taken as trustworthy. This ignorance and dismissal by the hearer is directed against the person who reports but also denies any trustful relation with that person. Hence, this exclusion from testimony can be judged as an ethical injustice.

Having a moral sensitivity for injustice might not be simply a question of age. Surely babies or toddlers do not yet have a perception of what is just or unjust but as soon as children think in terms of relations between people, and as soon as they are able to make comparisons they develop a sense of injustice.[28] It might even be the case that children do not have the same prejudices adults sometimes have. However, sometimes children's intuitive judgments need to be complemented by further thinking about questions relating to causes, prerequisites or preconditions of their experiences. In this context the question arises whether a witness might not have credibility *just* because of their young age or for other reasons.

Overall three general aspects are important for giving testimony: Reliability, holding on to the said, and the search for pre-requisites and preconditions of an incident. These three aspects are not just aspects of competency but rather aspects,

[27] Fricker (2007: 55).

[28] Nunner-Winkler (1998, 2009).

which could guide further investigation once a testimony is heard. The *reliability* of the person who gives testimony is indeed a very important aspect of credibility. But does this importance inhere in the assumption that every individual is epistemically reliable in all matters? It is certainly not the case that testimonial injustice automatically takes place as soon as someone is not treated seriously as a possible source of knowledge. Thus, the reliability of a person giving testimony is an issue. And this issue can only be properly addressed if the criteria for considering someone as reliable are not founded on the principles of age, gender, race or other characteristics, which are irrelevant to credibility per se.

The capacity of *holding on to the said* is an aspect that Paul Ricœur describes as one of the relevant elements of testimony. He emphasizes that besides the elements of formal judicial testimonies there are also moral and normative aspects to the act of testimony, such as the demand that the speaker holds onto the correctness of the said.[29] I am sure that many children can do that but it is not sure whether they will preview how long they might have to stick to their report and how strongly it could be criticized by those who have doubts.

The third important aspect about judging whether someone can be given credibility has to do with their capacities for reporting in (a) a *hermeneutical reasonable framework* and for considering (b) the *prerequisites* and *preconditions* of an action or situation of injustice.

(a) Mentioning the hermeneutical reasonable framework concerns the problem that, as Carel and Győrffy argue, especially young children "will always be at a hermeneutical disadvantage" within an adult system (2014: 1256). However, they are discussing Fricker's approach for children's experience within the healthcare system. Moreover, they are discussing only problems and decisions for a child herself and her well-being. They observe that the "interpretative frameworks [of a child] are foreign to such an adult system" (Carel and Győrffy 2014: 1257). As already mentioned at the beginning of this paper, children speak from their perspective about the "world of adults". From the perspective of adults, it is not always clear whether children's reports or expressions should be judged by 'adult's criteria'. Yet, it is not always clear *what* these 'adult criteria' are. For instance, the realms of family or school are not contexts that are only constituted by 'adults'. I would argue when looking closely at most social contexts, we would reveal that very different people heterogeneously construe them. If only a certain set of 'adult criteria' was heard then not only *children* as persons are dismissed but also their *report* as contribution for the description of the case is lacking. Hence, it is not only a question of respect but also of truth finding and reality description to include children as witnesses in cases of injustice. It is the challenge to interpret and understand the language and perspective of a child from within before denying her credibility simply because she is "childish".

---

[29] Ricœur (2008: 10ff.).

(b) The point about the *prerequisites* and *preconditions* of an action or situation of injustice refers to the aspect that someone who gives testimony has to know the conditions and contexts but also the relevant facts of a case. Hence, the child's report in regard to justice and injustice must be addressed in its epistemic and ethical aspects, but often further considerations and reflective thinking need to complement it. The sensitivity for those who experience injustice must also take into account not only the voices of children but also the familial, social and cultural norms by which a situation is considered. The reflective thinking about some relevant norms is illustrated in an example given by Amartya Sen (2009: 14, 201). He tells a story about a flute that is to be given to somebody. There are three children who would like to have this one musical instrument. Who should get it? What is the principle of justice that we should use to decide this question? Should we give the flute to the one who knows how to play it? The one who built it? The child who has the greatest need for it? Actually, should distributive justice be based merely on the criteria of use, effort or need? Should a society, a group, or a family normatively orient its judgments about justice using hedonistic utilitarian, libertarian, or economic egalitarian principles? Thus, in order to see through the question of injustice, not only sensitivity but also reflective thinking and theoretical knowledge are needed. However, sensitivity remains primary because the question about the principle of justice is only asked once the question of injustice has been raised. One might oppose that we also need criteria for judging. Indeed we need criteria. Any report, regardless whether it comes from an adult or a child, will be considered based on its facts and judged for its truth. The criteria of judging are important but they are not in the focus of this essay; in order to even think about whether a report should be considered and whether or not it is true, it must have been heard. However, if someone is not listened to because she is a child then criteria of judgment or truth are not really applied. Thus, the three criteria mentioned above are important after a report or a testimony is heard. Then, as it would be done with any testimony, for instance reliability should also be granted to a child but if, for instance, a child had only heard the rumor about an unjust incident but has no first hand knowledge then her reliability might not be sufficient. But this would also hold for an adult. The criteria mentioned shall not be used to simply dismiss a child's, particularly a young child's, report but rather to ask the right question and think about further interpretations of the words (Carel and Györffy 2014). A reasoning, that bases its criteria on the idea that children do not meet these criteria anyway, is a version of ageism. Hence, epistemic injustice of children is just like epistemic injustice due to racism or sexism.

Children's experiences or perceptions of injustice usually take place in an existential environment such as the family or institutions like kindergartens or schools. If people do not believe them, then usually they cannot go to someone else. This does not seem to be a particular characteristic applying only to children as the impossibility of being able to simply go to someone else is shared with those who are affected by racism, sexism, or other forms of elementary forms of social discrimination. If someone is not believed because she is a person of color or female, disabled or old, then she has also a problem that is based on particular social prejudices and discriminatory attitudes. When someone is unjustly not believed (even though that person tells the truth) and if this happens routinely, then this fact shows that the person is not considered to be part of society. Not to be allowed to take part in communication means to be excluded from social relations, and not to be given credibility for wrong reasons undermines trustful relationships. This does neither further the relations within society nor a child's well-being in the present or future. It is in the best interest of children to live in an epistemically and ethically just society.[30]

References

Andresen, S., and K. Hurrelmann. 2013. *Kinder in Deutschland 2013. 3. World Vision Kinderstudie.* Weinheim/Basel.

Brighouse, H. 2003. How should children be heard? *Arizona Law Review* 45: 691–711.

Carel, H., and G. Györffy. 2014, October 4. Seen but not heard: Children and epistemic injustice. *The Lancet* 384: 1256–1257.

Fricker, M. 2007. *Epistemic injustice: Power and ethics of knowing.* Oxford: Oxford University Press.

Giesinger, J. 2013. Kindeswohl und Respekt. *EthikJournal* 1. Jg/2. Ausg.: 1–15.

Honneth, A. 1995. *The Struggle for Recognition: The Moral Grammar of Social Conflicts.* Trans. Joel Anderson. Cambridge: Polity.

Khader, S.J. 2009. Adaptive preferences and procedural autonomy. *Journal of Human Development and Capabilities: A Multi-Disciplinary Journal for People-Centered Development* 10(2): 169–187.

Mullin, A. 2012. The ethical and social significance of parenting: A philosophical approach. *Parenting* 12(2–3): 134–143.

Munoz-Dardé, V. 2002. Children, families, and justice. In *The moral and political status of children,* ed. D. Archard and C.M. Macleod, 253–272. Oxford: Springer.

Nunner-Winkler, G. 1998. The development of moral understanding and moral motivation. *International Journal of Educational Research* 27: 587–603.

Nunner-Winkler, G. 2009. Prozesse moralischen Lernens und Entlernens. *Zeitschrift für Pädagogik* 55(4): 528–548.

Nussbaum, Martha C. 2013. *Creating capabilities: The human development approach.* Boston: Harvard University Press.

Plato. *Politeia.* Trans. Benjamin Jowett. http://classics.mit.edu//Plato/republic.html.

Rawls, J. 1971. *A theory of justice.* Cambridge, MA: Harvard.

Ricœur, P. 1992. *Oneself as Another.* Trans. K. Blamey. Chicago: The University of Chicago Press.

Ricœur, P. 2008. *An den Grenzen der Hermeneutik. Philosophische Reflexion über die Religion.* Freiburg: Alber.

Schües, C. 2013. Wagnis Zukunft: Braucht Vertrauen Transparenz? In *Vertrauen und Transparenz – Für ein neues Europa,* ed. A. Hirsch, P. Bojanić, and Ž. Radinković, 56–80. Belgrad: Institute for Philosophy and Social Theory.

Schües, C. 2015. Vertrauen oder Misstrauen vertrauen? In *Friedensgesellschaften. Zwischen Verantwortung und Vertauen,* ed. A. Hirsch and P. Delhom, 151–176. Freiburg: Alber.

---

[30] I like to thank Paul Lauer, and the editors of this volume for their very helpful comments.

Schües, C., and C. Rehmann-Sutter. 2013. The well- and unwell-being of a child. *Topoi* 32(2013): 197–205. Open Access: http://link.springer.com/article/10.1007/s11245-013-9157-z.

Schweiger, G., and G. Graf. 2014. The subjective experience of poverty. *Northern European Journal of Philosophy* 15(2): 148–167.

Sen, A. 2009. *The idea of justice*. Cambridge, MA: Belknap.

Shklar, J. 1989. The liberalism of fear. In *Political thought and political thinkers*, ed. S. Hoffman, 21–38. Chicago: University of Chicago Press.

Shklar, J. 1990. *The faces of injustice*. New Haven/London: Yale University.

Part III
The Politics of Childhood

Chapter 11
Keeping Their Kids: Cultural Minorities and the Lives of Children

Josephine Nielsen

Abstract In this chapter Josephine Nielsen argues that liberal multiculturalists should recognize a minority right to raise and keep children within particular cultural communities. She begins by expounding why children should be acknowledged within theories of multiculturalism, and political philosophy more generally. She argues that, if minority members value their culture, then they consequently have an interest in the continued existence of their cultural communities. Along these lines, she defends the position that in order for cultural communities to exist in the future, children, as potential community members should be brought up in the cultural and normative context of these communities. This is her argument for the secondary interest held by members of minority communities. She is convinced that if her arguments hold for the primary and secondary interests of minority members, a defeasible right to children being raised and kept within cultural communities can be justified. Nielsen concludes by considering three possible objections to her proposal.

Keywords Liberal multiculturalism • Group-differentiated rights • Minority members • Cultural value

Introduction

The stolen generations in Australia, residential schools in Canada, and high percentage of black children being removed from their parents by white social workers in the United States – there are numerous examples of children being removed from their cultural communities for "their benefit" that have devolved into the visible harm to both them and their communities. For this reason a discussion of the interests of children and cultural communities is sorely needed.

J. Nielsen (✉)
Department of Philosophy, Queen's University, Kingston, Canada
e-mail: 11jn15@queensu.ca

© Springer International Publishing Switzerland 2016
J. Drerup et al. (eds.), *Justice, Education and the Politics of Childhood*,
Philosophy and Politics – Critical Explorations 1,
DOI 10.1007/978-3-319-27389-1_11

There already exists an expansive literature discussing the rights and responsibilities of parents and children *qua* parents and children. Theorists ask whether
parents of a particular child can have rights with regard to their child that go beyond
protecting their child's best interests.[1] Concerning children, some topics that have
been considered are whether the age of consent is justified, and whether there should
be a children's liberation movement.[2] While these investigations are of great importance, little attention has been paid to how cultural membership *of children* can
shape the lives and interests of both adults (parents and non-parents) and children.
In this chapter I will consider what interests adults and children might have, *qua*
members of cultural minorities, and what sort of right may arise from those interests. I will argue that members of cultural minorities have a primary interest in their
cultures continuing, so long as they value their culture. This primary interest
depends on all community members having a secondary interest – that of children
being raised and kept within their cultural communities. I conclude that, if some
interests can lead to rights, then the primary and secondary interests I argue for lead
to the defeasible right to children being raised and kept within their cultural
communities.

I begin by expounding why children should be acknowledged within theories of
multiculturalism, and political philosophy more generally. I will then argue that, if
minority members value their culture, then they have an interest in the continued
existence of their cultural communities. I approach this argument from three different directions – two forward-looking, one backward-looking. I then go on to argue
that in order for cultural communities to exist in the future, children should be
brought up from within. This is my argument for the secondary interest held by
members of minority communities. If my arguments hold for the primary and secondary interests of minority members, then there is a defeasible right to children
being raised and kept within cultural communities. I will conclude by considering
three possible objections to my proposal.

Children and Multiculturalism

I am working within a multicultural framework and so, rather than justifying multiculturalism generally, I will limit my comments to how I understand minority rights
within such a theory, and why I take children to be central to the practicability of
such rights. While the minority rights that are proposed in theories of multiculturalism have taken various forms, I roughly follow Will Kymlicka's understanding of
these rights as being *group-differentiated*; rights that are held by individuals by
virtue of their membership in particular minorities and the disadvantage they face in
comparison to the majority (Kymlicka 1995). While not all multicultural theorists

---

[1] Cf: (Brennan and Noggle 1997; Brighouse and Swift 2014; Clayton 2006; Noggle 2002; Reshef 2013).

[2] Cf: (Purdy 1988; Munn 2012; Firestone 1970).

agree with Kymlicka's specifics with respect to minority rights,[3] I nevertheless think something general can be said that will be acceptable to most; namely that minority rights, however construed, are meant to ameliorate the disadvantages experienced by minorities within larger societies. Theorists disagree most deeply on the specifics of how minority rights are distributed between different types of minorities – for example, how minority rights might vary between national minorities, indigenous peoples, ethnic/immigrant groups, religious minorities, etc. In order to avoid this tumultuous debate, I propose that what I have to say about the interest in, and the right to, raising and keeping children within a particular cultural community holds for all ethnocultural minorities.[4]

One reason for thinking that members of cultural minorities should be accorded certain special rights is that such rights allow them to live their lives according to their own conception of the good within a larger society that favors different conceptions, thereby disadvantaging minority members. For example, a Québécois may greatly value being able to live her life in French. Prior to Bill 101 being enacted in Quebec, English was the dominant language in commerce and this meant that Francophones often did not have the option to work in French. In some cases the requirement to work in English harmed the self-understanding and dignity of Francophones. The solution was to proclaim French as the official language of public life in Quebec. There is still a debate about whether, in practice, the right to receive services in French should be viewed as an individual right or as a group right.[5] However, within theories of multiculturalism, language rights can be understood as being group-differentiated, a right accorded to individuals who belong to minorities in virtue of limiting the disadvantage those individuals would otherwise experience.

But as multicultural theories are presently defined, children are largely ignored. These theories are concerned with ensuring the rights and freedoms of political actors – adults. By being concerned with the rights of adults, multicultural theorists limit their concern for rights to the present, even if that present is one that is constantly rolling forward. This means that, if we take a time slice in order to evaluate the minority rights that are currently in place, it appears that they only apply to adults because it is only adults who are viewed as the relevant subjects of political theories. This also means that it looks as though the rights of current political actors (adults) may have adverse effects on future political actors (again adults) as there appears to be no connection (or at least no clear connection) between current and

---

[3] Cf: (Carens 2000; Spinner 1994; Tamir 1993).

[4] It is standard in this literature to distinguish inter-generational ethnocultural groups from lifestyle associations, such as surfers or chess players. I will follow that convention in this paper, and focus on intergenerational ethnocultural groups.

[5] In this context a *group right* should be understood as distinct from a *group differentiated right*. Whereas a group differentiated right is held by individuals based on their membership in minority cultures, a group right is held by the group itself.

future individuals.[6] Such an understanding, however, is inadequate in that it ignores that children are members of political communities, and so also have political interests. Once children are recognized as members with interests, it becomes easier to see the connection between the current political community and the future political community; the interest of the future political community is currently accounted for by recognizing that these are the interests of the present children. In this way we can account for how present minority rights are forward looking and how these rights, or at least some of them, do not have expiration dates. Without recognizing children as members of political communities it is difficult to justify how current minority rights continue to exist in the future. For this reason a multicultural theory that recognizes children as members – political individuals, though not political actors – will be more comprehensive than one that does not.

The Primary Interest in Continued Existence

In this section I argue that members of cultural communities, if they value their community, have an interest in its continued existence even after their deaths. Relying on Samuel Scheffler, I outline three ways to come to this conclusion, two forward-looking and one backward-looking. However two points must be emphasized before going further. First, when I refer to parents, other non-parenting adults, and children as having an interest in children being raised and kept within a particular cultural community, I am not referring to them *qua* parents, non-parenting adults, or children. Instead, I maintain that they all have these interests *qua* members of the community. Such a distinction means that, for example, Ginny may have a parent-specific interest that conflicts with her member-specific interest.[7] Second, when I refer to such interests translating into rights, I view these rights as placing duties upon the state, not on individual members. Therefore such a right will require the state to give special support to minority communities, but will not require parents or children to remain members against their wishes. I explore the substantive

---

[6] For example, in Quebec anyone who has not received an English education in Canada must send their children to French primary and secondary schooling. This is a policy meant to bolster the language rights of current political agents, which critics view as infringing the freedom of future generations of political agents. In order to evaluate the policy, however, I argue we should not think about two disconnected generations of adults, but rather need to explicitly consider the interests of children, including their interests as members of cultural and political communities. Cf: (Taylor 1994).

[7] Male circumcision may be a possible example of such a conflict for some parents. A Jewish parent, who is deeply committed to her religion and culture, may wish her son to be circumcised when thinking about the matter *as a member of her community*. On the other hand, when considering the matter *as a parent* she may be worried about the side effects of circumcision or the possibility of something going wrong. These worries may lead her, *as a parent*, to be disinclined towards having her son circumcised. This is case where an individual's interests *qua* community member comes into conflict with her interests *qua* parent.

implications of this right in my dissertation, but let me just state here that I think it is particularly relevant for establishing policies regarding adoption (Nielsen Forthcoming).

Individual Permanence and Self-Understanding

Multiculturalism requires some account of the value of culture and of cultural membership. Because "culture" is so expansive, and does not play the same role in the lives of all individuals, it seems to me that it makes more sense to speak of aspects of culture – or cultural artifacts – when discussing how and why individuals experience their cultures as valuable. With respect to tradition, Scheffler has argued that individuals find value in the knowledge that their traditions will continue to be practiced in the future. While "traditions" cover practices of a wide range of associations, I limit myself to the practices that can be thought of as cultural traditions, attached specifically to cultural communities. If Scheffler is correct that we attach value to the future practices of our traditions, we can ask: how can we explain why certain cultural traditions, and our connection to their future practitioners, are valuable to us? The future practitioners are our current children and so if we can establish why future practitioners are important to us, then we can begin to understand why children are important to us *qua members of cultural communities.*

One plausible explanation for personal routine is that it helps us develop a sense of personal identity and persistence over time. Personal routine allows us to establish stability in our lives, but also in the external world, thereby giving us a sense that we are the same person we were the day before, and that we will be tomorrow. Our personal routines also allow others to reinforce that we are the same individual that we believe ourselves to be through their interactions with us and their knowledge of who we are. (Consider the barista who knows your coffee order every morning before you ask for it.) Scheffler argues that something similar can be said about traditions in general, and on my reading cultural traditions, only on a larger scale. He explains that "traditions are by their nature collective enterprises, which are sustained not only by the allegiance of many adherents over long periods of time, but also by the adherents' mutual recognition of one another as collaborators in a shared enterprise" (Scheffler 2010). These shared experiences (e.g., public rituals, ceremonies, observances, etc.) are a way of showing ourselves, and others, that we are a particular kind of people; "[t]he continuing presences of others who participate in the same routines as we do, and who recognize us as fellow participants, provides us with regular confirmation that the reality of our participation seeks to enact" (Scheffler 2010). In this way we can think of specifically *cultural* traditions as a way for individuals to (a) confirm their persistence in general, (b) confirm that they are a member of a particular group, and (c) confirm that there is such a group within which they believe themselves to be a member. It seems that, at least for some individuals, such group membership, and the participation in particular traditions, helps to orient their lives, and gives them meaning, in such a way that significantly affects their self-understanding.

However the identification of oneself as a particular kind of person (i.e., as member of a particular cultural group) can only take place if (i) that particular cultural group actually exists, and (ii) there are others (both members and non-members) who recognize us as members over time.[8] Just as children are needed if minority rights are to have long-term relevance and existence, as argued in section "Children and multiculturalism", children are also needed if individuals are to be able to continue understanding themselves as member of a particular group. Group membership plays a significant role in the lives of many individuals and so should be a major concern for theorists, whether liberal or not (though particularly for liberals and liberal multiculturalists). While we may not be able to say that particular cultural traditions contribute to every individual's conception of themselves and their good life, we can say that participating in cultural traditions in general often plays a part in an individual's self-understanding and conception of the good. If, in particular, liberal multiculturalists are concerned with individuals being able to live according to their own wishes, then this involves being able to participate in cultural traditions generally, and if further, cultural traditions rely on the existence of cultural communities, then it seems that liberal multiculturalists should be committed to helping these communities persist.[9] This persistence, as I understand it, requires children and, as such, liberal multiculturalists should be concerned with the interests that community members have in children being raised and kept within their cultural frameworks.

Into the Future

In addition to contributing to an individual's self-understanding, participating in cultural traditions allows some individuals to feel a part of something larger than themselves. However, it's unclear that the "something larger" can be any old group (Scheffler 2010). For example, Scheffler argues that, while we're all members of the group *homo sapiens*, many of us do not place the significance and value in this fact that some of us strive for (Scheffler 2010). In attempting to identify the characteristic of groups and associations and their respective traditions that we tend to find value in, Scheffler argues that one of our reasons for wanting to identify with groups is that we think that caring and valuing things other than ourselves contributes to our

---

[8] Cf: (Appiah 2005).

[9] I follow Kymlicka's distinction between claims of internal restrictions and external protections such that liberal states will help to preserve groups through rights concerning external protections that accord with liberal values. That is to say, not all groups will be given special rights, nor will all groups be protected by the state. See my reply to objections in section "Objections" below for a further elaboration on this point.

flourishing (Scheffler 2010). It is from the valuing of things other than ourselves that we come to wish that those particular things continue on after we cease to exist.

> [The] logic of valuing implies that, if we do value things other than ourselves, then things other than ourselves come to matter to us, and if they are the kinds of things whose survival can be in question, then their survival normally comes to matter to us as well...So insofar as we wish to care about, and to value, things other than ourselves, the position in which we wish to put ourselves is one in which there are things other than ourselves whose survival matters to us...So if we value the survival and flourishing of things other than ourselves, then it matters to us that those things should survive and flourish even if we are dead (Scheffler 2010).

Many of us, I take it, think that traditions hold some sort of value in our lives. Otherwise why would we partake in them? And so, on Scheffler's logic, we have reason to care about whether our traditions survive after our deaths.

Scheffler's argument concerning the value we place on traditions provides significant insight into the discussion of culture and future generations. It seems that individuals who participate in cultural traditions often find value in them and believe that it would be a good thing if those traditions continued on after their deaths. However I don't think it's sufficient for the value of the traditions to continue on if they are practiced by individuals in the far future who have no connection with current practitioners. Some concrete connection with current practitioners is necessary for our ability to say that a cultural tradition has in fact continued to exist, but also for our ability to understand the value as continuing.[10]

Imagine that Ginny and Harry both attended (wizarding) Hogwarts and were both members of Gryffindor house, as were their parents and grandparents before them. They take great pride in this fact and place considerable value in their (wizarding) Hogwarts and Gryffindor traditions. Because of this they both hope that their children, their grandchildren, and their great-grandchildren will also attend (wizarding) Hogwarts, belong to Gryffindor house, and partake in the traditions that they did as children. Ginny and Harry see this as a way of the value of (wizarding) Hogwarts, the four houses, and the accompanying traditions to continue on into the future. Unbeknownst to them, after their deaths (wizarding) Hogwarts is forced to close and the wizarding community dies off. But after 500 years muggles[11] decide to open a school that is coincidentally also called Hogwarts (let it be known as (muggle) Hogwarts) that also has four houses – Gryffindor, Hufflepuff, Ravenclaw, and Slytherin. Despite Gryffindor once again being a house at a school named Hogwarts, and miraculously developing traditions that appear to be those Ginny and Harry partook in, it is unlikely that they would think that the value they placed in their Gryffindor house and its traditions would once again appear just because there was now a Gryffindor house at (muggle) Hogwarts. On the other hand, if the future

---

[10] Alan Patten argues that we can identify a culture as continuing to exist based on if its members were taught within institutions that were run predominantly by other community members. This is the sort of argument I have in mind for identifying cultural communities over several generations. Cf: (Patten 2011).

[11] Muggles are normal, non-wizarding people such as ourselves who generally have no knowledge of the wizarding community.

Hogwarts was related to (wizarding) Hogwarts, having been continued by wizards, Ginny and Harry would be more likely to think that the value that they place in their school, their house, and the school's traditions had continued on 500 years in the future. This goes to suggest that it isn't just the case that individuals want seemingly similar or identical traditions to be practiced in the future by anyone, but rather that they have an interest in *their* traditions being practiced by individuals with whom they have a specific type of connection. This interest can also be understood as an interest in passing their cultural traditions down to the next generation – the children – in their cultural community.

Into the Past

The foregoing two discussions were concerned with how the future of cultural traditions play an important role in the lives of many individuals. In this section I contend that cultural traditions can also ground who it is we are in virtue of linking us to the past. But how does looking to the past justify an interest in the continued existence of cultural communities? After all, there are many cultures that have gone out of existence long ago, but despite our inability to participate in them currently, we can still learn from them and find value in them. It is precisely the inability to participate in them, however, that removes the type of value with which I am concerned. We might be able to study the Beothuk of Newfoundland[12] and appreciate their practices and traditions in the abstract, but we are not able to ground ourselves *in* their practices and traditions, viewing them as part of who we are and what contributes to the value we find in our lives. In order to be able to experience the more fundamental value of a culture, similar to what I discussed in the previous section, the culture must continue to exist.

I return once again to Scheffler, for not only does he have insightful things to say about traditions and the future, but also about traditions and the past. He writes:

> one sees oneself as inheriting values that have been preserved by others. One is heir to, and custodian of, values that have been handed down by those who went before. These values themselves enrich one's life, and one's status as heir and custodian gives one's life an additional significance and importance that it would not otherwise have had (Scheffler 2010).

This seems correct to me: by continuing on traditions (and other cultural artifacts) that have been passed down to us by our parents, grandparents, other family members, and our community at large, we have a way of grounding ourselves in the past, a way of understanding ourselves as coming from a long and rich history. This, of course, does not imply neither that all individuals find value in the traditions that others attempt to pass down (some may find no value in any of the traditions that they are offered), nor that individuals find value in all of the traditions that are offered to them. Nonetheless, it seems safe to say that at least some individuals find

---

[12] The Beothuk were an aboriginal tribe from Newfoundland who were went extinct in 1829.

value in some of the traditions that are passed down to them, in part because traditions give them a way of better understanding where they have come from, and also in part because traditions link them to a community that not only currently exists, but one that existed in the past, and will hopefully continue to exist in the future.

Cultural membership is not the *only* thing that can give us a sense of who we are, but it does seem to play a significant explanatory role in our lives. When children in Western, historically Christian, cultures go on Easter egg hunts Easter morning, we can look to the past to explain why they do so. A story can be told about how the tradition originally started, how it has developed over the years and why a particular family tends to celebrate in a particular way. Even if the origin story of a particular practice is not known by a family, they can still feel a deep connection with the practice and others who also partake in it. Such a connectedness can help explain why an individual continues to act in a certain way, and may feel distress at the thought of giving up a particular cultural practice.

It need not be the case that I value *all* of my culture and its traditions, nor that all of the traditions matter to me in the same way. Nor do they have to influence how I understand myself and the relationships I have with other people. Being a member of a culture is one way in which we develop our identities, for identities do not pop into existence from nowhere. They are crafted against the backdrop of other individuals and our experiences with them. And even in the cases when cultural membership is rejected, an individual's rejected culture still informs how she now sees herself (e.g., I may once have been a practicing Christian, but now I am not). In this way we can begin to appreciate why it is that cultural communities and traditions are important to children as well as adults.

Having highlighted the importance of membership to children for grounding who they are, it is also necessary to acknowledge that cultural membership is important to children in different ways depending on their development. It would be strange to say that an infant has the same interest in membership as a 15 year old does. Instead, it seems most appropriate to say that the infant has a general interest in membership that develops into an interest in a specific membership as she grows up. Otherwise it would be akin to saying that an infant has an interest in becoming a neuroscientist rather than having an interest in developing the skills needed to pursue some job in the future. Regarding the ability to one day acquire a job, parents, and presumably those around her including the state, are under an obligation to ensure that she develops the skills and capacities necessary for gaining employment as an adult. But those obligations will change over time as she develops. At the age of two the obligation will perhaps be to ensure that she can learn at least one language proficiently. At the age of five the obligation will be to help her learn to read, write, and do basic math. As she grows older the obligation that others have towards her will change depending on her abilities and on what she enjoys and has an affinity for. While we may say that well-rounded children are at least exposed to music, it would be strange to say that parents have an obligation to force a teenager to take piano lessons if either she hates the piano or if she clearly has no affinity for it.[13] Her parents, on the other hand, may have an obligation to support her love of, and abilities in, the sciences. Again, it is clear that she doesn't have a specific interest in becoming a neuroscientist as an infant, but as a teenager she may well have developed precisely that interest.

The development of job interests in children can be seen as analogous to children's interest in culture and community. When an infant is born she does not have an interest in growing up within a particular cultural community. Because she has only limited connections with individuals, she can't be said to have sufficiently strong ties to one particular cultural community. But as she grows, and develops deeper ties with individuals and cultural practices, she develops an interest in belonging to that particular community. So alongside the development of children from infants to adults comes the development of interests in general membership in *a* cultural community to a specific interest in membership in a *particular* cultural community. This is not to suggest that children cannot be removed from their cultural communities, nor that they cannot develop relationships outside of them. But children do develop relationships as they grow older and interact more with certain individuals and practices. It would be strange to say that these developments can't lead to some sort of interest in maintaining these relationships and practices. Because children develop interest in particular cultural communities, they thereby have an interest in the survival of those communities.[14]

I have outlined three different ways of understanding why it is that individuals have an interest in their cultural communities continuing to exist. First, the continued existence of our cultures allow for the acknowledgement of permanence both by individuals themselves, and by others. Second, it allows us to see the value we find in our cultural traditions as continuing on in the future. Third, it allows us to ground ourselves in a culture that has existed in the past and will ideally continue to exist in the future. For these reasons I contend that individuals have a primary interest in their cultures continuing to exist in the future.

The Secondary Interest in Child-Members

I contend that the primary interest in cultural communities continuing to exist relies on a secondary interest – an interest in there being child-members in cultural communities. While it's conceivable to imagine a science fiction scenario where a cultural community continues to exist, and even flourishes, with only an influx of adult

---

[13] There are of course parents who do exactly this. I have doubts about this being in the best interest of the teenager. At the same time children (teenagers) should be encouraged to stick with things that they don't particularly like at first, but this does not mean that they should be forced to continue on with things even after they have shown over a long period of time that either they do not enjoy the activity or that they have no affinity for it.

[14] Here again I am concerned with broadly liberal minority communities. Children are unlikely to have interests in remaining in cultural communities that actively abuse them, but they do have an interest in remaining in communities that nurture them.

converts, this seems unlikely to be realistic. It would seem that children are integral to cultural communities existing and flourishing. Think of the numerous examples where children have been taken away from their cultures with the intent of assimilation into the dominant society (e.g., the stolen generation in Australia, residential schools in Canada, etc.) and the impact it has had on the cultural communities. Traditions have been lost, substance abuse has skyrocketed, and communities have been pulled apart. So, I contend, if it is the case that individuals have an interest in their communities continuing to exist in the future, then they also have an interest in there being child-members in those communities. I further contend that, if it is the case that certain types of interests can lead to, at least defeasible rights, then these two interests lead to the group-differentiated right to raise and keep children within cultural communities.

Objections

While I hope that what I have said is intuitive upon reflection, it is a novel way of looking at the relationship between parents, non-parenting adults, children, and cultural communities. As such there will inevitably be pushback. I respond here to three possible objections.

First, it might be said that what I've proposed places too many obligations on parents and children to remain in, and faithful to, cultural communities and traditions that they wish to leave. As such it seems to limit the freedom that liberalism is so committed to. This sort of objection, however, dismisses what I iterated at the beginning of the chapter – the group-differentiated right to raise and keep children within cultural communities should be understood as being held against the state, not against individuals. Therefore such a right requires funding, recognition, and aid from states, but does not limit the freedoms of individual members by forcing them to maintain their cultural membership. In the terminology of Kymlicka, it is a right concerned with *external protections*, not *internal restrictions* (Kymlicka 1995).[15]

Second, it might be pointed out that individuals rarely belong to only one cultural community. In this way it appears that conflicts between cultural communities will arise concerning their right to raise and keep children. My response is similar to the one I have given above. The right to raise and keep children is a right held against the state, not against individuals. As such multiple communities can, for example, claim funding from the state while not having conflicts with regard to who is a community member. The right to raise and keep children will ensure that children and adults have access to resources from many cultural communities rather than requiring them to pick one community over all others.

---

[15] For helpful discussions of the complexities of regulating internal restrictions and of enabling exit rights in the context of potentially illiberal groups, see the essays in Eisenberg and Spinner-Halev, *Minorities within Minorities* (Eisenberg and Spinner-Halev 2004), and in relation to children in particular, see David Archard, "Children, Multiculturalism, and Education" (Archard 2002).

Third, it may be pointed out that parents and teenagers can have conflicting interests in their cultural communities and traditions. Parents may wish to leave the group while their teenager may wish to stay, or vice versa. There are likely many cases of this however what I have proposed here does not, and cannot, address these situations. Instead, these conflicts should be addressed in a theory that looks at parents *qua* parents and children *qua* children rather than parents and children *qua* members of cultural communities. I therefore leave this for a different discussion.

Conclusion

I have argued that liberal multiculturalists should recognize a minority right to raise and keep children within particular cultural communities. Such a right recognizes the importance of culture in the lives of individuals and the need to ensure their continued access to it. While many cultural minorities may not be actively persecuted (though of course many others are), it's insufficient to think that benign neglect will allow these communities to flourish. Liberal multiculturalism already recognizes this, though not with respect to the importance of children. What I have argued here is that children are vital to cultural communities and their members and, therefore, we should recognize a (defeasible) minority right to raise and keep children within cultural communities.

References

Appiah, A. 2005. *The ethics of identity*. Princeton: Princeton University Press.
Archard, D. 2002. Children, multiculturalism, and education. In *The moral and political status of children*, ed. David Archard, and Colin Macleod, 142–159. Oxford: Oxford University Press.
Brennan, S., and R. Noggle. 1997. The moral status of children: Children's rights, parents' rights, and family justice. *Social Theory and Practice* 23: 1–26.
Brighouse, H., and A. Swift. 2014. *Family values: The ethics of parent-child relationships*. Princeton: Princeton University Press.
Carens, J.H. 2000. *Culture, citizenship, and community: A contextual exploration of justice as evenhandedness*. Oxford: Oxford University Press.
Clayton, M. 2006. *Justice and legitimacy in upbringing*. Oxford: Oxford University Press.
Eisenberg, A., and J. Spinner-Halev. 2004. *Minorities within minorities: Equality, rights and diversity*. Cambridge: Cambridge University Press.
Firestone, S. 1970. *The dialectic of sex: The case for feminist revolution*. New York: Morrow.
Kymlicka, W. 1995. *Multicultural citizenship: A liberal theory of minority rights*. Oxford: Clarendon.
Munn, N. 2012. Reconciling the criminal and participatory responsibilities of the youth. *Social Theory and Practice* 38: 139–159.
Nielsen, J. Forthcoming. *Interests and rights: Minority communities, parents, and children*. PhD diss., Queen's University.

Noggle, R. 2002. Special agents: Children's autonomy and parental authority. In *The moral and political status of children*, ed. David Archard and Colin Macleod, 97–116. Oxford: Oxford University Press.

Patten, A. 2011. Rethinking culture: The social lineage account. *American Political Science Review* 105: 735–749.

Purdy, L.M. 1988. Does women's liberation imply children's liberation? *Hypatia* 4: 104–124.

Reshef, Y. 2013. Rethinking the value of families. *Critical Review of International Social and Political Philosophy* 16: 130–150.

Scheffler, S. 2010. The normativity of tradition. In *Equality and tradition: Questions of value in moral and political theory*, 287–311. Oxford: Oxford University Press.

Spinner, J. 1994. *The boundaries of citizenship: Race, ethnicity and nationality in liberal states.* Baltimore: John Hopkins University Press.

Tamir, Y. 1993. *Liberal nationalism*. Princeton: Princeton University Press.

Taylor, C. 1994. The politics of recognition. In *Multiculturalism: Examining the politics of recognition*, ed. Amy Gutmann, 25–73. Princeton: Princeton University Press.

Chapter 12
Civic Education: Political or Comprehensive?

Elizabeth Edenberg

Abstract In this chapter Elizabeth Edenberg considers the problem children, conceived of as future citizens, pose to understanding the scope and limits of Rawls's Political Liberalism by focusing on the civic education of children. Can a politically liberal state provide all children the opportunity to become reasonable citizens? Or does the cultivation of reasonableness require comprehensive liberalism? In considering these questions, the author shows that educating children to become reasonable in the way Rawls outlines imposes a demanding requirement that conflicts with Rawls's aim of including a wide constituency in the scope of political liberalism. Rawls's aim of making reasonableness broadly inclusive for political purposes is in tension with his goal of using reasonableness as the standard that delineates the scope of liberal legitimacy. Edenberg argues that political liberalism can and should try to cultivate the reasonableness of its future citizens through the civic education of children. However, a defensible version of political liberal civic education requires introducing a bifurcation within Rawls's conception of reasonableness. A political liberal form of civic education should aim towards the inclusive scope of reasonableness by cultivating reasonableness in only two of what appear to be three senses that Rawls emphasizes. Teaching children that legitimacy requires embracing public reason demands more than may be justifiably required by a state that seeks to be broadly inclusive.

Keywords Rawls • Political liberalism • Education • Children • Civic education • Reasonable • Legitimacy

Introduction

In determining the proper scope of political liberalism and how it differs from comprehensive liberalism, one of the central test cases has been the civic education of children as future citizens. Rawls argues that political liberalism's approach to education "has a different aim and requires far less" than comprehensive liberalism

E. Edenberg (✉)
Department of Philosophy, Fordham University, USA
e-mail: eedenberg@fordham.edu

© Springer International Publishing Switzerland 2016
J. Drerup et al. (eds.), *Justice, Education and the Politics of Childhood*,
Philosophy and Politics – Critical Explorations 1,
DOI 10.1007/978-3-319-27389-1_12

(Rawls 2005a, 199).[1] The politically liberal state would only require the kind of education needed so that children as future citizens can understand the political conception of justice and cultivate important political virtues (*ibid*). To do so, civic education aims at cultivating the reasonableness of children as future citizens.

However, in order for political liberalism to remain distinctively *political*, rather than collapsing into a version of comprehensive liberalism, Rawls must show that cultivating reasonableness should not require all children to learn comprehensive liberal values. The challenge Rawls raises to his conception of a political liberal civic education is whether "requiring children to understand the political conception [of justice] in these ways is in effect, though not in intention, to educate them to a comprehensive liberal conception" (*ibid*).

In this chapter, I consider the problem that children pose to understanding the scope and limits of Rawls's *Political Liberalism* by focusing on the civic education of children. Can a politically liberal state provide all children the opportunity to become reasonable citizens? Or does the cultivation of reasonableness require comprehensive liberalism?

In considering these questions, I show that educating children to become reasonable in the way Rawls outlines imposes a demanding requirement that conflicts with Rawls's aim of including a wide constituency in the scope of political liberalism. Rawls's aim of making reasonableness broadly inclusive for political purposes is in tension with his goal of using reasonableness as the standard that delineates the scope of liberal legitimacy. I argue that political liberalism can and should try to cultivate the reasonableness of its future citizens through the civic education of children. However, a defensible version of political liberal civic education requires introducing a bifurcation within Rawls's conception of reasonableness. Political liberal civic education should aim towards the inclusive scope of reasonableness by cultivating reasonableness in only two of what appear to be three senses that Rawls emphasizes. Teaching children that legitimacy requires embracing public reason demands more than may be justifiably required by a state that seeks to be broadly inclusive.

The argument proceeds in three parts. First, I survey the debate over political versus comprehensive liberal approaches to civic education. Second, since one important goal of civic education is cultivating the reasonableness of future citizens, I outline the different criteria of reasonableness. Third, consider which aims of political liberalism are embodied in each criterion for reasonableness and whether these are appropriate targets of civic education. I argue that political liberal civic education should aim to cultivate reasonableness as a moral notion that is tied to respecting one's fellow citizens. This requires teaching children respect for the freedom and equality of one's fellow citizens as equal moral persons and respect for the fact of reasonable pluralism, but need not include teaching children that legitimacy requires public reason. Teaching these two criteria sets the minimum threshold for qualifying as reasonable and, I argue, ensuring that children meet this threshold is the most important goal of a political liberal civic education.

---

[1] Hereafter I will cite Rawls's *Political Liberalism*, expanded edition (2005a) as *PL*.

Political Versus Comprehensive Approaches to Civic Education

An education aimed towards having citizens embrace the political conception of justice must first ensure that citizens are reasonable.[2] The challenge concerning the civic education of children of unreasonable citizens is whether "requiring children to understand the political conception … is in effect, though not in intention, to educate them to a comprehensive liberal conception" (*PL*, 199).

In order to defend the distinctiveness of a political liberal civic education (PLCE) from a comprehensive liberal civic education (CLCE), Rawls argues that political liberalism's approach to education "has a different aim and requires far less" than comprehensive liberalism (*ibid*). Unlike the comprehensive liberalisms of Kant, Mill, and Raz that would condone educational requirements promoting comprehensive conceptions of autonomy or individuality "as ideals to govern much if not all of life," the politically liberal state would only require the kind of education needed so that children as future citizens can understand the political conception of justice and cultivate important political virtues (*ibid*). Rawls points to the "great differences in both scope and generality between political and comprehensive liberalism" and "hope[s] the exposition of political liberalism … provides a sufficient reply to the objection" (*PL*, 200). However, a number of philosophers and political theorists remain unconvinced that *Political Liberalism* contains a sufficient reply.

Common responses fall into three broad categories. First, some argue that when we examine civic education, the distinction between political and comprehensive liberalism *collapses*—Rawls fails to sufficiently distinguish the political liberal approach to civic education from comprehensive liberalism (Gutmann 1995; Callan 1996, 1997). Gutmann and Callan both argue that the educational implications of political liberalism converge with the educational implications of comprehensive liberalism insofar as civic education is intended to cultivate the reasonableness of future citizens.[3] Because the effects of PLCE are no different from CLCE, Rawls's political liberalism "is really a disguised instance of comprehensive liberalism"

---

[2] Rawls argues that the publicity condition of the political conception of justice will itself play an educative role. The narrow role of the political conception of justice will ensure the "minimum condition of effective social cooperation," for which the reasonableness of citizens is important. The wider role of the political conception includes the publicity condition, which is part of a citizen's education. Publicity ensures that citizens are aware of the principles of justice embodied in political and social institutions and are also aware of how "citizens' rights, liberties, and opportunities" are derived from "a conception of citizens as free and equal" (*PL*, 71). In this paper, I focus on the cultivation of reasonableness because this is a crucial first step for political liberal civic education and, thus, will be important in a child's civic education.

[3] Gutmann (1995) argues that in requiring civic education to encourage mutual respect between citizens, Rawlsian political liberalism converges with comprehensive liberalisms in the effect it has on children. Callan argues that the fault lies in teaching children the burdens of judgment, which serves as a "a powerful constraint on the background culture of liberal politics" (1997, 36) such that the distinction between political and comprehensive liberalism collapses.

(Callan 1997, 13, 40).[4] According to this line of response, not only did Rawls fail to distinguish PLCE from CLCE in his larger exposition of *Political Liberalism*—the very aim of cultivating reasonableness is precisely why the distinction between PLCE and CLCE collapses. Despite other differences between the systems' methodological aims, there is no difference between comprehensive liberalism and political liberalism when it comes to the education of children.

Second, some defend the distinctiveness of a political liberal approach to education, arguing that PLCE is both *distinctive* and *defensible*. Political liberals who defend the distinctiveness of PLCE follow Rawls in emphasizing the difference in scope by defending the freestanding nature of political justification or the basic structure restriction that teaches only those virtues required for political participation. The aim of these theorists is to expand on Rawls's own, insufficient, remarks and offer a direct reply to the charge that the distinction between PLCE and CLCE collapses. Macedo and Costa focus on political liberalism's freestanding requirement by defending the justificatory neutrality of PLCE.[5] This line of response defends the distinction in justification between political and comprehensive liberal approaches to education, even while admitting the practical effects of these differences may not be significant. Davis and Neufeld argue that the freestanding component, on its own, is not a persuasive defense of political liberalism's distinctive approach to civic education. Instead, they argue against the "convergence thesis" of Gutmann and Callan by emphasizing "both the basic structure restriction and the freestanding condition" (Davis and Neufeld 2007, 50, original italics removed). There are significant practical differences between teaching children to respect the burdens of judgment and teaching children to embrace comprehensive liberal autonomy because political liberalism restricts its discussions to the basic structure of society and the public political realm (Davis and Neufeld 2007, 62–67).[6]

---

[4] Mulhall (1998) also thinks the cultivation of reasonableness involves a comprehensive liberal conception of the person.

[5] Macedo emphasizes the freestanding component by showing that despite teaching civic virtues, politically liberal civic education remains neutral between reasonable comprehensive doctrines because they can be "publically justified independently of religious and comprehensive claims" (Macedo 1995, 477; See also Macedo 2000). Furthermore, this is the only form of neutrality we should expect. Claims to more "substantive" neutrality or fairness are "more apparent than real" (Macedo 1995, 484). However, the reasonableness component places important restrictions on the kinds of diversity permitted and hence Macedo defends "political liberalism with spine" (Macedo 1995, 470). Costa follows Macedo in defending the justificatory neutrality of politically liberal civic education. She can agree with Callan that the cultivation of political virtues "will necessarily have a deep effect on citizens' character" insofar as it requires the cultivation of reasonableness and in this sense a politically liberal civic education is not minimal. However, it is still distinctly political because a politically liberal civic education is publicly justifiable (Costa 2004, 7–9). See also Costa's extended discussion of the educational implications of Rawls's theory of justice in Costa 2011.

[6] Costa also emphasizes the importance of teaching children the burdens of judgment in order to cultivate reasonableness (2009, 2011).

Third, some argue that PLCE is indeed *distinctive—but not defensible* because the reasonableness requirement is too permissive of different comprehensive conceptions of the good. Some feminists have objected that by tolerating a wide variety of comprehensive doctrines as reasonable, political liberalism erodes tools for securing equality between the sexes (Okin 1994, 2004; Exdell 1994; Baehr 1996; Yuracko 1995, 2003).[7] A central concern of these feminists is the basic structure restriction. As long as citizens are reasonable when engaged in public political debate, their nonpublic views are of no concern to political liberals. As Okin, Exdell, Baehr, and Yurako argue, many traditional religious practices in the private sphere undermine women's equality, and thus including such religions as reasonable shows that political liberalism is indefensible without significant revision (Okin 1994, 2004; Exdell 1994; Baehr 1996).[8] Following a similar argument, that reasonableness is too permissive of different comprehensive doctrines to be defensible, Fowler has argued that because reasonableness is a lax criterion, political liberalism cannot protect children from certain damaging forms of upbringing (Fowler 2010, 368). These are important objections to the adequacy of political liberalism; however, adequately responding to these objections will go beyond the scope of this chapter. In this chapter, I try to show that PLCE is distinctive and more defensible than CLCE as a form of civic education, but do so by arguing for a bifurcation within Rawls's conception of reasonableness.[9]

All three lines of response agree that a political liberal civic education requires the cultivation of reasonableness. However, the differences lie in the implications of this requirement and whether, in light of this, political liberalism can be sufficiently distinguished from comprehensive liberalism. In the remainder of the chapter, I suggest a new way to draw the distinction. This departs from Rawls in significant ways, since I think much of the confusion lies in the divergent implications of embracing the different components of reasonableness. I will show that political liberalism has a distinctive approach to civic education; however, I argue that a defensible version of PLCE requires introducing a bifurcation within Rawls's conception of reasonableness.

[7] Hartley and Watson (2010) have defended Rawls from this charge, arguing that the reciprocity condition of reasonableness is restrictive enough to prohibit views that subordinate women to men. Okin has also argued that a robust form of civic education could counteract the problematic effects of comprehensive doctrines learned outside of the political realm (1994, 32); but note that the more robust the civic education is, the harder it will be to distinguish from comprehensive liberalism.

[8] Yuracko argues that due to the lax understanding of reasonableness, political liberalism should be rejected in favor of feminist perfectionism (Yuracko 1995, 2003). Lloyd (1995), De Wijze (2000) and Nussbaum (2003) defend political liberalism from feminist critiques on the basis of this split between what should be accepted for political justice and what can be permitted in nonpolitical realms. However, the response has not been satisfying to many feminists who continue to doubt the acceptability of the split between one's public and nonpublic practices (see, e.g., Okin's 2004 response to Lloyd and Nussbaum).

[9] I defend the conception of political liberal civic education that I propose from feminist objections in my dissertation, *Political Liberalism and Its Feminist Potential*.

The Criteria for Reasonableness

A political liberal civic education should be designed to cultivate the reasonableness of children as future citizens. However, Rawls uses the qualification of reasonableness for at least two different aims: (1) setting a broadly inclusive scope for the type of pluralism that should be respected by the political conception for justice and (2) determining whether citizens' arguments about political justice have appropriately used public reason in order to meet the standards of political liberal legitimacy. I will argue that Rawls's aim of making reasonableness broadly inclusive for political purposes requires a conception of reasonableness that serves as a minimum moral threshold of respect for one's fellow citizens.[10] This is distinct from Rawls's use of reasonableness as the standard that delineates the scope of liberal legitimacy. Educating children to become reasonable in all of the ways Rawls outlines requires more than would be justifiable for a broadly inclusive PLCE.

Recall that according to Rawls, reasonableness as a virtue of persons has several components.[11] First is a moral requirement of respecting our fellow citizens as free and equal moral persons.[12] Let's call this the *respect criterion* of reasonableness. To be reasonable, one must recognize oneself and one's fellow citizens as free and equal citizens who deserve fair terms of cooperation in society.[13] The second basic aspect of reasonableness that Rawls identifies can be understood as a moral requirement of respect for our fellow citizens as free and equal reasoners. What is respected here is not our fellow citizens' moral personhood, but their equal capacity

---

[10] I defend the minimal moral threshold conception of reasonableness in my dissertation *Political Liberalism and Its Feminist Potential.*

[11] In Lecture II, Rawls specifies two basic aspects of reasonableness considered as virtues of persons rather than directly defining the concept (*PL*, 48). Herein, I discuss these as three components because I will argue that what Rawls identifies as the second basic aspect has two distinct components that should be bifurcated. Leif Wenar has detailed 5 different aspects of reasonableness for both persons and comprehensive doctrines and argues that only some of these can be met without violating the restrictions Rawls elsewhere places on a political conception of justice (Wenar 1995). For the purposes of this paper, I am interested in the basic requirements for being a reasonable person, as this is of interest to the question of civic education designed to cultivate the reasonableness of children as future citizens.

[12] There will likely be a plurality of ways to interpret free and equal moral respect; however, examining these various approaches goes beyond the scope of this paper.

[13] Rawls discusses the first basic aspect of reasonableness in *PL*, 49–54. Rawls explains, "persons are reasonable in one basic aspect when, among equals, they are ready to propose principles and standards as fair terms of cooperation and to abide by them willingly, given the assurance that others will likewise do so" (*PL*, 49). Reasonable persons "desire for its own sake a social world in which they, *as free and equal*, can cooperate with others" on fair terms (*PL*, 50, emphasis added).

to reason freely about one's conception of the good. This aspect has two parts, which I will number separately for ease of exposition.[14] One must:

(2) recognize the burdens of judgment, which leads to recognizing the fact of reasonable pluralism and
(3) accept the consequences of this recognition by using public reason when "directing the legitimate exercise of political power" on matters of constitutional essentials and basic justice (*PL*, 54).

The burdens of judgment teach us that conscientious citizens may weigh evidence differently and come to differing, but equally reasonable, conclusions even after a full and free discussion has taken place (*PL*, 58).[15] Thus, recognizing the burdens of judgment leads to recognizing the fact of reasonable pluralism. Let's call (2) the *burdens of judgment criterion* of reasonableness. Rawls also argues that reasonable persons must accept the "consequences" of this recognition by using public reason when debating matters of basic justice or constitutional essentials. Let's call (3) the *legitimacy criterion* of reasonableness. Accepting that one must use public reason in matters of basic justice in order for political power to be legitimate is a way of demonstrating respect for persons, conceived of as free and equal reasoners, in light of the fact of reasonable pluralism. However, this criterion links the liberal principle of legitimacy to the basic qualification of reasonableness. Rawls's liberal principle of legitimacy holds that, "our exercise of political power is proper and hence justifiable only when it is exercised in accordance with a constitution the essentials of which all citizens may reasonably be expected to endorse in the light of principles and ideals acceptable to them as reasonable and rational" (*PL*, 217). I discuss the tight connection between reasonableness and liberal legitimacy below.

When a political liberal civic education aims to cultivate the reasonableness of children as future citizens, we need to ask which aspects of reasonableness are the appropriate targets of civic education. Which criteria of reasonableness are compatible with the inclusive scope of political liberalism? Which make PLCE too restrictive to remain distinct from CLCE?

---

[14] Rawls states, "the second basic aspect" of reasonableness "is the willingness to recognize the burdens of judgment and to accept their consequences for the use of public reason in directing the legitimate exercise of political power in a constitutional regime" (*PL*, 54).

[15] *PL*, 54–58 describes the burdens of judgment in detail.

Cultivating Reasonableness in Political Liberal Civic Education

Inclusive Reasonableness in Civic Education: Cultivating the Respect Criterion

One aim of the qualification of reasonableness is to include as many people as appropriate within the scope of political liberalism. This is tied to the general motivation that moved Rawls away from the comprehensive liberalism of *A Theory of Justice* towards the more inclusive and pluralistic approach to liberal justice in *Political Liberalism*. Rawls's key insight in *Political Liberalism* was to recognize that "a plurality of reasonable yet incompatible comprehensive doctrines is the normal result of the exercise of human reason within the framework of the free institutions of a constitutional democratic regime" (*PL*, xvi). This inevitable pluralism about morality creates difficulties in establishing a normative basis for a theory of justice. The solution Rawls proposed in *Political Liberalism* is to move away from comprehensive conceptions of justice, which are rooted in the truth of some moral theory, and towards a narrower political conception of justice, which is based on the overlapping consensus of reasonable comprehensive doctrines.

Rawls introduces reasonableness as a qualification intended to define the scope of plurality that political liberalism must address (*PL*, 36). Rawls distinguishes between *reasonable pluralism* and *pluralism as such*, arguing that political liberalism need only accommodate reasonable pluralism (*PL*, 36–37). Reasonableness should be seen as providing "minimal conditions appropriate for the aims of political liberalism" (*PL*, 60n.13). Rawls intends the qualification of reasonableness, in this vein, to be broadly inclusive of a diversity of comprehensive doctrines including "both religious and nonreligious, liberal and nonliberal" (*PL*, xxxviii). Rawls conjectures that most current moral doctrines and religions, except for certain varieties of fundamentalism, could qualify as reasonable (*PL*, 170).

The respect criterion of reasonableness seems to be best suited for Rawls's inclusive understanding of reasonableness. In distinguishing reasonable pluralism from pluralism as such, Rawls emphasizes that reasonable comprehensive doctrines still respect all people as moral equals. As Rawls explains, "all reasonable doctrines affirm … equal basic rights and liberties for all citizens" and doctrines that fail to do so are unreasonable (Rawls 2005b, 482–83). In addition, people are unreasonable if they are unwilling to propose or honor fair terms of cooperation (*PL*, 50).

Teaching children to be reasonable in the inclusive sense tied to the respect criterion is an important goal of a political liberal civic education. Respect for the equal basic rights and liberties of all citizens is a necessary component of being reasonable. Without this basic respect, a conception of justice is morally dubious because it would permit the subordination of certain classes of people to others. Doctrines that subordinate certain races, classes, or genders to others would not qualify as reasonable insofar as they deny that everyone is entitled to equal basic respect simply in virtue of being moral agents. We need not tolerate Nazis or Ku Klux Klan members who deny the equality of their fellow citizens.[16]

Political principles should attempt to be fair and treat everyone as free and equal moral persons. A civic education designed to cultivate the respect criterion will emphasize moral respect for all citizens as free, equal, and deserving of fair terms of cooperation. Since reasonableness sets the boundaries for who should be included within the scope of political liberalism, it should be broadly inclusive of many different comprehensive doctrines. A civic education that emphasizes the respect criterion is well suited for this goal because, despite their differences, many comprehensive moral doctrines include an account of respect for people as free and equal. Those that do not value respect are rightfully excluded from political liberalism as unreasonable. Of course, unreasonable citizens will not suddenly loose their rights and be expelled from society.[17] However, unreasonable objections do not threaten the adequacy of the political conception of justice. Since political liberalism sets its scope as respecting *reasonable* pluralism, the political conception of justice should be able to be endorsed by all reasonable citizens. Political liberalism need not bend justice to accommodate the unreasonable because justice should not be held hostage to views that undermine equal moral respect for persons.

If civic education is designed to cultivate respect-reasonableness, PLCE could remain distinct from CLCE. If all that is required for PLCE is teaching children to respect their fellow citizens as free and equal with oneself, one need not even be a liberal to accept this educational goal—this is the most widely inclusive scope of reasonableness that should be tolerated.[18] A comprehensive liberal education requires far more than teaching that one should respect one's fellow citizens' moral status.[19]

In addition, if the state only requires that civic education meet the respect criterion of reasonableness, there may be more latitude for differential parental choice in education. Ebels-Duggan has recently argued that political liberals should allow reasonable citizens latitude in choosing the worldview in which their own children

---

[16] I think the respect criterion shows why certain comprehensive doctrines that subordinate women also fail to be reasonable in the broadest conception of reasonableness. I argue for this in *Political Liberalism and Its Feminist Potential*.

[17] For more on the rights of unreasonable citizens, see Quong 2004.

[18] Note that this would be to deny Gutmann's claim that teaching mutual respect is in effect to teach comprehensive liberalism. But Gutmann's conception of mutual respect is a fairly demanding comprehensive conception of mutual respect. I agree with Davis and Neufeld (2007) that a politically liberal conception of respect will be more minimal.

[19] This respect criterion of reasonableness is consistent with defenses of political liberalism's distinctiveness that emphasize the freestanding nature of public political justification and with defenses that emphasize the basic structure restriction. Respecting people as free and equal is one of the more stable considered convictions that form the touchstone of Rawls's reflective equilibrium procedure. Further, the basic structure restriction combined with the respect criterion secure a broad scope for incorporating comprehensive doctrines that differ on how best to respect people as members of religious organizations, as long as the principles of justice protect citizens as free and equal throughout all realms.

are educated, as long as this education does not insulate children from other views.[20] I think the respect criterion of reasonableness could permit wide latitude on this front. In fact, the respect criterion alone is compatible with an education designed to promote the truth of certain comprehensive doctrines.[21] For example, religious schools could be a permissible choice for parents, provided that these schools teach children that all people should be respected as free and equal moral persons and that the terms governing our shared political life should be fair to all, including those who embrace different comprehensive doctrines. This shows that there may be many ways to satisfy the requirement that children learn the respect criterion of reasonableness—including education into comprehensive doctrines that seem quite distant from the larger aim of political liberalism. The important requirement is teaching children to respect their fellow citizens as free and equal, but there are many different ways of meeting this goal. As long as children are taught to respect themselves and all other citizens as free and equal moral persons, their education has met a minimum moral threshold for reasonableness.

Families cannot be permitted to inculcate children with beliefs or practices that undermine their ability to respect themselves or others as free and equal citizens. As Rawls explains, political principles "guarantee the basic rights and liberties, and the freedom and opportunities, of all [members of the family]. ... The family as a part of the basic structure cannot violate these freedoms" (Rawls 2005b, 469). The need to respect the freedom and equality of all is one of our firmly established convictions in contemporary society. An overlapping consensus on this conviction should be supported by any comprehensive doctrine that should qualify as reasonable for the purpose of political justice.[22]

In summary, a civic education designed to teach children to respect themselves and their fellow citizens as free and equal will be widely inclusive. Few of the moral and religious doctrines in society would find reason to reject a civic education designed to promote reasonableness is this sense. Thus, political liberal civic education promoting the respect criterion of reasonableness will not collapse into

---

[20] Ebels-Duggan 2013. It is worth noting that Ebels-Duggan's example to show that non-neutrality is permissible is that a parent or teacher can expose children to the existence and content of racist views while also teaching children such views are wrong (2013, 46). Distinguishing the respect criterion of reasonableness shows clearly why this example actually concerns exposure to an unreasonable comprehensive doctrine. The racist doctrines are unreasonable because they do not respect all people as free and equal moral persons. Thus, this case may not compellingly show that all such instances of exposing children to other views while teaching them the truth of one's own view is a permissible practice for political liberalism. However, the respect criterion alone will not settle this issue.

[21] It is important to emphasize that teaching the respect criterion could be *compatible* with an education promoting the truth of a comprehensive doctrine and *not* that teaching the truth of a comprehensive doctrine is *required* for this purpose. Below, I will argue that teaching the respect criterion is *not sufficient* for political liberal civic education, teaching the burdens of judgment is also required.

[22] Here I use overlapping consensus at a different stage than Rawls does in his defense of *Political Liberalism*, following a strategy similar to Quong (2011, 161–191). However, I use this for illustrative purposes to show the wide consensus on respecting people as free and equal.

comprehensive liberal education. Many moral and religious doctrines could be included on this basis, including those that may reject liberalism.[23]

Inclusive Reasonableness and Civic Education: Teaching the Burdens of Judgment

One might object that simply requiring the state to cultivate the respect criterion of reasonableness is not a distinctively *political liberal* civic education. After all, I have suggested one need not even be a liberal to embrace the respect criterion of reasonableness. For civic education to be distinctive to political liberalism it requires more than simply teaching the respect criterion. The respect criterion is an important minimum threshold for distinguishing between reasonable and unreasonable comprehensive doctrines, but political liberalism also requires respect for the fact of reasonable pluralism. To learn the difference between pluralism as such and reasonable pluralism, children must learn to recognize that people who hold differing comprehensive doctrines are nevertheless capable of being reasonable. For this, learning the burdens of judgment is important. A civic education that teaches children the respect criterion and the burdens of judgment criterion will be distinctive to political liberalism while maintaining the broadly inclusive scope of reasonableness.

In order to respect those who disagree with us as reasonable, we must learn to recognize that citizens who hold different comprehensive doctrines are nevertheless reasonable insofar as they embrace the respect criterion. Teaching children the burdens of judgment is an important way in which PLCE can cultivate this respect for reasonable disagreement.[24] Recall that the burdens of judgment identify the sources of disagreement between reasonable persons. Rawls lists six of the "more obvious sources" of reasonable disagreement: complexity of the evidence, disagreement about the relative weight of relevant considerations, the indeterminacy of political concepts, the way our experience shapes our understanding and weighing of moral and political values, that there are different kinds of normative considerations on

---

[23] Liberalism includes more than simply respecting the freedom and equality of persons. Liberalism often also includes a commitment to the moral priority of individuals over the group and, as a political theory, typically focuses on how states should treat individuals in light of these other commitments.

[24] It is possible that there are other ways in which children could learn to embrace the fact of reasonable pluralism and the reasonableness of their fellow citizens. For example, religious decree that all god's children be respected as free and equal reasoners. Herein I focus on teaching the burdens of judgment as a part of PLCE because I think this is likely the best way to cultivate respect for one's fellow citizens as free and equal reasoners in a way that is compatible with respecting differences between citizens' conceptions of the good. However, I leave open the possibility that some religions could cultivate the appropriate form of respect in other ways. I thank Leif Wenar for pressing me on this objection.

both sides of an issue, and finally, the fact that not every moral and political value can be realized in social institutions (*PL*, 56–57).

Rawls's enumeration of the sources of reasonable disagreement has been widely contested, with commentators arguing that many of these sources are, themselves, reasonably contestable. Callan draws on this controversy to argue that PLCE collapses into CLCE (Callan 1997). Thus, including the burdens of judgment in PLCE may seem inappropriately restrictive. However, regardless of Rawls's list of the sources of disagreement, the essential point behind teaching the burdens of judgment to children is not subject to similar contestation. Focusing on Rawls's motivation for identifying the burdens of judgment helps us see why including the burdens of judgment criterion in PLCE does not threaten collapse into CLCE.

The key point behind learning the burdens of judgment is understanding that those with whom one disagrees can nevertheless be reasonable. Rawls explicitly defines reasonable disagreement as "disagreement between reasonable persons: that is, between persons who have realized their two moral powers to a degree sufficient to be free and equal citizens in a constitutional regime, and who have an enduring desire to honor fair terms of cooperation and to be fully cooperating members" of society (*PL*, 55). The *reasonableness* of persons is defined in terms of their acceptance of the respect criterion—political principles should be fair terms of cooperation among free and equal citizens.[25] The burdens of judgment essentially show that reasonable pluralism is possible. It is possible for people who respect each other as moral equals to nevertheless embrace quite different moral and religious doctrines. To recognize the fact of reasonable pluralism, a person must therefore learn that her fellow citizens who hold different comprehensive doctrines can disagree with her—and that disagreement does not mean that they are either unintelligent or immoral.[26]

Understood in this way, teaching children the burdens of judgment is important for developing the ability to respect one's fellow citizens as not only free and equal moral persons, but also as free and equal reasoners. Differences in beliefs need not impugn the intelligence of one of the parties. We should respect that other people have reasons for their beliefs, even if we disagree. As equals, we should respect one another's freedom to make important choices for oneself and to reason according to one's own lights. We must respect our fellow citizens' rights to embrace different comprehensive doctrines and make different decisions about how best to pursue the good life.

Respecting our fellow citizens' decisions need not imply a smuggled in commitment to comprehensive liberal autonomy. Rawls considers the freedom of citizens

---

[25] I set aside discussion of the two moral powers and full cooperation, as these are the ways Rawls defines persons for the purposes of political liberalism. He defines a person as someone who can be a "fully cooperating member of society over a complete life" and "we ascribe to them the two moral powers … namely, a capacity for a sense of justice and a capacity for a conception of the good" (*PL*, 18–19).

[26] Rawls contrasts reasonable disagreement with unreasonable disagreement. The sources of unreasonable disagreement include being immoral, selfish, prejudiced, irrational, or simply "not very bright" (*PL*, 55 and 58).

to pursue their chosen conception of the good, provided it is reasonable, to be a part of the rational autonomy of citizens, which he considers "but an aspect of freedom" (*PL*, 74–75). But rational autonomy is distinct from both full political autonomy and full ethical autonomy.[27] In Rawls's terms, full ethical autonomy corresponds to the kind of autonomy promoted in comprehensive liberalism. Protecting citizens' freedom to embrace different comprehensive doctrines and pursue what one embraces as valuable does not limit the range of comprehensive doctrines one can embrace.[28] It is perfectly permissible to embrace the doctrine of one's family or community. In fact, those who reject the importance of liberal autonomy could still embrace this right to live according to one's preferred comprehensive doctrine because this right protects the right of those who reject comprehensive liberal autonomy to pursue other shared values. The political conception of justice protects the freedom of individuals to pursue varying conceptions of the good, provided that these conceptions respect all people as free and equal moral persons.

How should PLCE teach children that disagreement need not imply stupidity or immorality? One way to do so is to examine the reasons behind different comprehensive doctrines. Children could be taught some of the basic reasoning behind different major world religions and moral theories, in particular how each contains an account of moral respect for people as free and equal.[29] This could be presented neutrally, without any commitment to ranking the different theories, as it should be in state-run schools. Or, if parents prefer a religious education, neutrality need not be required. One good example of non-neutrality that nevertheless meets the requirements of PLCE is a Catholic school education. Typically, such schooling includes required religion courses. However, religion courses are not simply indoctrination of the Catholic faith. They also include exposure to a wide variety of religions and moral theories even though there is an underlying presumption that Catholicism is the true religion. To me, it seems as if such an education meets the requirements for PLCE even though, since the school is not run by the state, Catholicism is presented as true. Students still learn that other faiths and moral theories are reasonable, and that different moral and religious doctrines still embrace the freedom and equality of all.[30]

---

[27] See *PL*, 72–81 for Rawls's discussion of the contrast between rational, political, and ethical autonomy.

[28] The minimum qualification is that comprehensive doctrines meet the respect criterion.

[29] I believe there are consistent interpretations of all major world religions that include a conception of respect for persons as free and equal. Of course, there are also interpretations that would not meet the respect criterion. With Rawls, I think fundamentalists probably are not reasonable. Likewise, justifications of slavery (regardless of historical attempts to justify slavery by drawing on religious sources) are not reasonable.

[30] History, literature, and philosophy are also subjects that could expose children to the burdens of judgment and the fact of reasonable pluralism. By learning the many ways in which beliefs change over time and vary according to our culture and circumstance, children can start to learn that differences in beliefs are expected given the diversity of people's experiences. Likewise, literature exposes children to alternate ways of living by people who have clear reasons for their actions, aim to live a good life, and, often, desire to be moral. The disagreements between philosophers in any

Restrictive Reasonableness and Civic Education:
The Legitimacy Criterion

In addition to using reasonableness to delineate the scope of reasonable pluralism, Rawls also uses the qualification of reasonableness in a more restricted sense that is tied to the legitimacy of political principles. In this section, I will argue that the use of reasonableness for liberal legitimacy is tied to a different part of the political liberal project and, for the purposes of PLCE, should not be bundled with the other two criteria of reasonableness.

The third criterion of reasonableness holds that one accepts the consequences of the burdens of judgment by using public reason in directing the legitimate exercise of political power. Failure to use public reason constitutes a failure to offer a legitimate justification of coercive power and, for Rawls, a failure to accept "the consequences" of the burdens of judgment. Note the similarities between Rawls's liberal principle of legitimacy and the legitimacy criterion of reasonableness. According to Rawls, the "second basic aspect of reasonableness" is "the willingness to recognize the burdens of judgment and to accept their consequences for the use of public reason in directing the legitimate exercise of political power in a constitutional regime" (*PL*, 54). I think accepting the burdens of judgment can be separated from accepting the use of public reason.[31] I have called the latter the legitimacy criterion of reasonableness because of its resemblance to Rawls's liberal principle of legitimacy. Recall that the liberal principle of legitimacy holds, "our exercise of political power is proper and hence justifiable only when it is exercised in accordance with a constitution the essentials of which all citizens may reasonably be expected to endorse in the light of principles and ideals acceptable to them as reasonable and rational" (*PL*, 217). The basic idea is that the only way for political power to be legitimate is for the basic principles and laws governing our political system to be grounded in terms that all reasonable citizens can be expected to endorse as relevant reasons governing the specific actions or laws.

Educating children to embrace the legitimacy criterion of reasonableness requires teaching all children to use public reason when debating matters of basic justice or constitutional essentials. To meet the legitimacy criterion of reasonableness, children would need to be taught that appealing to the whole truth of one's comprehensive doctrine, when that truth is reasonably contestable, is disrespectful and a way of illegitimately imposing one's own comprehensive doctrine on others. Rawls explains that "insistence on the whole truth in politics [is] incompatible with democratic citizenship and the idea of legitimate law" because political legitimacy is "based on the criterion of reciprocity," which holds that the reasons offered must

---

era are another good source of learning that smart people who aim explicitly at discovering what is just or good, nevertheless reasonably disagree with each other. These kinds of disagreements seem to motivate Rawls's initial turn to political liberalism (*PL*, xiii–lx).

[31] I defend the bifurcation of Rawls's second basic aspect of reasonableness my dissertation, *Political Liberalism and Its Feminist Potential*. Here, I focus on why the separation is important in the context of civic education.

be reasonably acceptable to our fellow reasonable citizens whose comprehensive doctrines may conflict with our own (Rawls 2005b, 446–47). This is far more restrictive than simply requiring that children respect others as free and equal citizens, part of which requires accepting the idea that people could disagree with someone without being immoral or unintelligent (i.e., embracing only the respect and burdens of judgment criteria). The legitimacy criterion also teaches children that the best way to respect reasonable disagreement in political life is the use of public reason.

However, the liberal principle of legitimacy is a distinctive solution to the question of what could make the coercive power of the government legitimate. It is a substantive conclusion with which many who satisfy the respect criterion of reasonableness could disagree. I think this criterion is far too restrictive if included in PLCE as a necessary criterion for reasonableness. While the liberal principle of legitimacy is arguably the best way to respect reasonable disagreement, it is not the only way. Philosophical anarchists, liberal perfectionists, and libertarians all disagree with political liberalism's solution to the problem of legitimacy. Nevertheless, all agree that people should be respected as free and equal. The differences arise in *how* political power can best respect freedom and equality. For example, philosophical anarchists would teach children that there is no such thing as a moral right to be obeyed precisely because it is incompatible with the freedom and equality of persons. This seems like a perfectly acceptable justification of the rejection of legitimate authority and one that is not based on immoral or unintelligent considerations. The anarchist justifies her rejection of legitimate authority by appealing to the very same respect criterion of reasonableness, which holds that citizens should be respected as free and equal moral persons, that lies at the heart of Rawls's conception of reasonable persons.[32] Thus, according to Rawls, the anarchist would qualify in one sense as a reasonable person because she meets the important moral respect threshold for being reasonable. However, using the restrictive sense of reasonableness, defined in terms of the legitimacy criterion—which the anarchist rejects—she would be unreasonable. The question is whether legitimacy-reasonableness should be included as a necessary component of reasonableness for the purposes of PLCE.

I have argued that the respect criterion and burdens of judgment criterion are *necessary* components of the moral qualification of reasonableness and should be included in PLCE. I have also argued that these two criteria preserve the inclusive scope of reasonableness that is tied to Rawls's conception of reasonable pluralism. But if the legitimacy criterion is also a necessary component of reasonableness, then reasonableness becomes far more restrictive—only those who embrace Rawls's liberal principle of legitimacy would qualify as reasonable. This restrictive conception of reasonableness is not appropriate for PLCE.

Civic education that cultivates respect for freedom and equality seems justifiable, even if it has a disproportionate effect on certain comprehensive doctrines. Despite the political liberal's goal of justifying political power in a way that respects deep

---

[32] Recall that in explaining reasonable disagreement, Rawls defines reasonable persons by referencing the respect criterion of reasonableness (*PL*, 55).

disagreement between different comprehensive moral doctrines, the political liberal need not tolerate those views that threaten the very conditions of freedom and equality in a society. But I think it is a further step to argue that those who fail to embrace political liberalism's liberal principle of legitimacy pose the same kind of threat to society. Provided that people embrace the respect criterion of reasonableness, they have recognized the moral status of their fellow citizens as free and equal.

However, there are many different ways that political theories justify or reject the legitimacy of coercive power, including many which also embrace the moral freedom and equality of citizens. As such, justifying the inclusion of the legitimacy criterion as a necessary component of reasonableness in civic education becomes far more difficult. Rawls raises the challenge of children's civic education when considering whether or not political liberalism treats justly those comprehensive doctrines that fair the worst under political liberalism (*PL*, 197–200). Justifying PLCE seems far more straightforward if all that is required in order to cultivate reasonableness in children is a civic education designed to teach respect for the freedom and equality of all people and that disagreement does not mean our opponents are immoral fools. The justification for teaching children one answer to how coercive power could be legitimate seems like a much taller order. It may very well be defensible, but it is a far more restrictive understanding of reasonableness.

If, in order to be reasonable, children should learn to embrace a particular solution to the problem of legitimacy, a political liberal civic education would be as demanding as a comprehensive liberal civic education. This would succumb to the worry Rawls articulated at the outset—that a political liberal civic education would be *in effect if not in intention* to educate children for comprehensive liberalism (*PL*, 199). Even if the justifications for these two forms of education diverge, as Macedo and Costa have emphasized, the practical results would be similarly restrictive (Macedo 1995; Costa 2004).[33]

Furthermore, an education designed to teach children Rawls's liberal principle of legitimacy as a necessary component of reasonableness seems particularly vulnerable to Brighouse's famous challenge to liberal civic education. Recall that within the family of liberal theories of legitimacy,[34] many require the "free and unmanipulated assent of reasonable citizens" (Brighouse 1998, 726). Brighouse argues that civic education tends to condition and manipulate the assent because civic education is specifically designed to promote "loyalties, habits, and beliefs conducive to" the continued stability of the state (*ibid*).[35] Thus, Brighouse argues, civic education seems to undermine the very conditions for liberal legitimacy.

---

[33] What I have called the legitimacy criterion has not been the focus of arguments about civic education. But Rawls's second aspect of reasonableness, taken as a whole to include the recognition of the burdens of judgment and their consequences, have lead many to conclude that political and comprehensive liberalism converge.

[34] There are a number of different approaches to liberal legitimacy beyond Rawls's own favored approach articulated in *Political Liberalism*.

[35] Brighouse argued against Galston's and Gutmann's proposals for civic education and ultimately concluded that more robust training for autonomy and critical scrutiny could mitigate the worries. Brighouse 1998, 734–736, 739. He argues, "civic education can meet the requirements imposed by

Brighouse's challenge can be taken to apply to a Rawlsian who requires that civic education promote a particular solution to the problem of legitimacy as a part of educating children to become reasonable citizens.[36] If one is educated from early childhood that there is one clear solution to the question of what, if anything, could make the coercive power of the state legitimate, this may tilt the scale in favor of a citizenry that is less likely to critique the government's coercive use of power. In all liberal theories of legitimacy, the acceptability of the government to citizens is important.[37] However, if education promotes the acceptance of the legitimacy criterion of reasonableness, then the extent to which legitimacy is freely obtained is threatened. Any education that teaches only one acceptable solution to the problem of legitimacy looks worrisome because there are many competing theories of legitimacy that all claim to be the best way to respect the freedom and equality of citizens—including philosophical anarchism, which rejects the possibility of legitimate authority. Furthermore, including one model of legitimacy in children's civic education is particularly troublesome since civic education is monitored by the very government that seeks to establish its own legitimacy. This could be understood as an instance of the state's coercive use of force to encourage a shared understanding of the best way in which to respect citizens as free and equal.[38]

Education aimed at cultivating only one acceptable approach to establishing the legitimacy of the government demands more than may be justifiably required by a state that seeks to be broadly inclusive. Note the restrictions that accompany the inclusion of the legitimacy criterion of reasonableness in civic education. Only those who embrace Rawls's liberal principle of legitimacy would qualify as reasonable citizens. This would exclude many more citizens as unreasonable. According to Rawls, using public reason when debating matters of basic justice and constitutional essentials is the best way to respect our fellow citizens as free and equal in the context of reasonable pluralism; however, it is not the only way. It is far too restrictive and, as such, has drawn the most vehement criticisms of Rawlsian reasonableness.

Beyond being restrictive, the legitimacy criterion is indefensible as a component of the civic education of children. Following Brighouse, I worry that some forms of civic education could undermine the legitimacy of a government. In particular, if children are taught that there is only one appropriate response to the fact of reasonable pluralism, this may undermine future political debate about criteria for legitimacy. While debate about legitimacy is not foreclosed by including the legitimacy

---

legitimacy only if tied to autonomy-facilitating education, which in turn can be justified on independent grounds" (Brighouse 1998, 744).

[36] Callan 2000 responds to Brighouse's challenge but does so in a way that leans heavy towards comprehensive liberalism. Indeed, the distinction between political and comprehensive liberalism is not at stake in Callan's 2000 essay.

[37] Differences between liberal theories of legitimacy often lie in articulating how this acceptability is obtained (hypothetical consent, normative consent, explicit voluntary consent, etc.).

[38] This looks suspiciously similar to what, in other contexts, Rawls calls "the fact of oppression" (*PL*, 37).

criterion of reasonableness in the civic education of children—it would be significantly curtailed when compared to civic education that teaches children only the
respect and burdens of judgment criteria of reasonableness. If PLCE is modeled
after the inclusive conception of reasonableness that does not consider embracing
Rawls's liberal principle of legitimacy a necessary component of qualifying as reasonable, this opens the door to an education that presents a variety of theories of
legitimacy. Children would learn that there is not only reasonable disagreement
about conceptions of the good, but also reasonable disagreement about the best way
to respect the freedom and equality of citizens in the context of reasonable
pluralism.

In addition, including the legitimacy criterion as a part of PLCE will distract
from some of its more significant educational aspirations. Since Rawls's liberal
principle of legitimacy is widely contested, even among liberals, including the legitimacy criterion as a necessary part of PLCE could lead many to reject PLCE entirely.
In contrast, if PLCE teaches that the first two criteria are the only necessary qualifi-
cations to be considered reasonable, this is both widely inclusive and could establish
an important basis for securing the rights of all citizens.

Focusing on respect for others as free and equal moral persons as the primary
moral qualification for reasonableness highlights the key moral threshold that sets
the limits for which disagreements are reasonable and which are unreasonable. If
reasonable disagreements are disagreements among reasonable persons, they are
disagreements among persons who have met this minimum moral threshold. Beyond
this, there are many conceptions of the good that persons will pursue, given freedom
of conscience and freedom of thought. Furthermore, as I have suggested in this section, there are also many different political proposals that explicitly aim to respect
people's freedom and equality. Teaching children these goals in PLCE could set the
stage for a diverse citizenry that, by learning to respect even those with whom one
disagrees as reasonable, may be less vulnerable to the extreme group polarization
that characterizes contemporary politics in which those who disagree on important
matters are deemed immoral or unintelligent.

Conclusion

A political liberal civic education should aim towards the inclusive scope of reasonableness by cultivating the respect and burdens of judgment criteria of reasonableness. These two criteria should set the minimum moral threshold for qualifying as
reasonable, which is the most important goal of PLCE. If we do this, PLCE will be
far more inclusive of a variety of comprehensive doctrines than any comprehensive
liberal civic education. In so doing, we could make good on Rawls's claim that
PLCE requires far less than CLCE. Nevertheless, this type of civic education would
also be distinctive to political liberalism, as teaching children the burdens of judgment teaches them that political justice ought to respect reasonable pluralism among
its citizenry. However, if PLCE requires cultivating the more demanding acceptance

of the legitimacy criterion of reasonableness, it may risk collapse into comprehensive liberalism—at least in its practical effects. Including the legitimacy criterion in civic education as a component of reasonableness will have the practical effect of making it the case that only political liberals would qualify as reasonable citizens. To preserve a distinctive political liberal civic education, the legitimacy criterion should be bifurcated from the other aspects of reasonableness. Teaching children to embrace a particular approach to liberal legitimacy is not the proper aim of a civic education designed to be broadly inclusive of a wide variety of comprehensive doctrines.[39]

References

Baehr, Amy R. 1996. Toward a new feminist liberalism: Okin, Rawls, and Habermas. *Hypatia* 11(1): 49–66.

Brighouse, Harry. 1998. Civic education and liberal legitimacy. *Ethics* 108(4): 719–745.

Callan, Eamonn. 1996. Political liberalism and political education. *Review of Politics* 58(1): 5–33.

Callan, Eamonn. 1997. *Creating citizens: Political education and liberal democracy.* Oxford: Oxford University Press.

Callan, Eamonn. 2000. Liberal legitimacy, justice, and civic education. *Ethics* 111(1): 141–155.

Costa, M. Victoria. 2004. Rawlsian civic education: Political not minimal. *Journal of Applied Philosophy* 21(1): 1–14.

Costa, M. Victoria. 2009. Justice as fairness, civic identity, and patriotic education. *Public Affairs Quarterly* 23(2): 95–114.

Costa, M. Victoria. 2011. *Rawls, citizenship, and education.* New York: Routledge.

Davis, Gordon, and Blain Neufeld. 2007. Political liberalism, civic education, and educational choice. *Social Theory and Practice* 33(1): 47–74.

De Wijze, Stephen. 2000. The family and political justice: The case for political liberalisms. *The Journal of Ethics* 4(3): 257–281.

Ebels-Duggan, Kyla. 2013. Moral education in the liberal state. *Journal of Practical Ethics* 1(2): 34–63.

Exdell, John. 1994. Feminism, fundamentalism, and liberal legitimacy. *Canadian Journal of Philosophy* 24(3): 441–463.

Fowler, Timothy Michael. 2010. The problems of liberal neutrality in upbringing. *Res Publica* 16(4): 367–381.

Gutmann, Amy. 1995. Civic education and social diversity. *Ethics* 105(3): 557–579.

Hartley, Christie, and Lori Watson. 2010. Is a feminist political liberalism possible? *Journal of Ethics and Social Philosophy* 5(1): 1–21.

Lloyd, S.A. 1995. Situating a feminist criticism of John Rawls's political liberalism. *Loyola of Los Angeles Law Review* 28(4): 1319–1344.

Macedo, Stephen. 1995. Liberal civic education and religious fundamentalism: The case of God v. John Rawls? *Ethics* 105(3): 468–496.

---

[39] Earlier versions of this paper were presented at the 2014 Manchester Center for Political Theory Workshop and at Vanderbilt University's Social and Political Thought Workshop. My thanks to the audiences at both workshops for their thoughtful comments. A special thanks to Marilyn Friedman, Rob Talisse, Larry May, Leif Wenar, and the editors of this volume for their helpful suggestions on earlier drafts of this paper.

Macedo, Stephen. 2000. *Diversity and distrust: Civic education in a multicultural democracy.* Cambridge: Harvard University Press.

Mulhall, Stephen. 1998. Political liberalism and civic education: The liberal state and its future citizens. *Journal of Philosophy of Education* 32(2): 161–176.

Nussbaum, Martha C. 2003. Rawls and Feminism. In *The Cambridge companion to rawls*, ed. Samuel Freeman, 488–520. Cambridge: Cambridge University Press.

Okin, Susan Moller. 1994. *Political liberalism*, justice and gender. *Ethics* 105(1): 23–43.

Okin, Susan Moller. 2004. Gender, justice and gender: An unfinished debate. *Fordham Law Review* 72(5): 1537–1567.

Quong, Jonathan. 2004. The rights of unreasonable citizens. *Journal of Political Philosophy* 12(3): 314–335.

Quong, Jonathan. 2011. *Liberalism without perfectionism.* New York: Oxford University Press.

Rawls, John. 2005a. *Political liberalism: Expanded edition.* New York: Columbia University Press.

Rawls, John. 2005b. The idea of public reason revisited. In *Political liberalism: Expanded edition*, 440–490. New York: Columbia University Press.

Wenar, Leif. 1995. Political liberalism: An internal critique. *Ethics* 106(1): 32–62.

Yuracko, Kimberly A. 1995. Toward feminist perfectionism: A radical critique of rawlsian liberalism. *UCLA Women's Law Journal* 6: 1–48.

Yuracko, Kimberly A. 2003. *Perfectionism and contemporary feminist values.* Bloomington: Indiana University Press.

Chapter 13
"I Can't Tell You *Exactly* Who I am …": The Creation of Childhood and Adulthood in F. Scott Fitzgerald's Short Story *The Curious Case of Benjamin Button*

Nicole Balzer

Abstract This article provides some theoretical impulses for contemporary debates about childhood. Its major part consists of a discussion of F. Scott Fitzgerald's short story *The curious case of Benjamin Button*. It is shown that the Button case not only puts into question common ideas of human development. Rather, it also gives insights into what it requires to live one's life in accordance with the socially and culturally established differentiation between children and adults. It is argued that the crucial characteristic of the development of Benjamin Button's life is to learn to adapt to other people's expectations by means of performing in special ways, if necessary in neglect of his feelings and needs. Finally, it is suggested that any theoretical approach to childhood is intimately connected to the ways in which we refer to and conceive of *adulthood*. Thus, if we want to address political and ethical questions in the terrain of childhood, the study of the meanings and significations of 'adulthood' is indispensable.

Keywords Benjamin Button • Adulthood • Analyses of literature in social theory

The Commonality of Differentiating 'Childhood' and 'Adulthood'

Even if 'childhood' as well as 'adulthood' are "no longer clear and distinct categories in the West" (Walkerdine 2009: p. 118), imagining Western societies beyond the distinction between children and adults is a real challenge for at least three reasons.

Firstly, too much of what we encounter in everyday life is proof of how perfectly natural it appears to us to regard some people as children: There are special chil-

N. Balzer (✉)
Institute of Educational Science, University of Münster, Münster, Germany
e-mail: n.balzer@uni-muenster.de

© Springer International Publishing Switzerland 2016
J. Drerup et al. (eds.), *Justice, Education and the Politics of Childhood*,
Philosophy and Politics – Critical Explorations 1,
DOI 10.1007/978-3-319-27389-1_13

dren's clothes, toys, programmes, books, foods as well as areas, buildings and institutions designed for children. And, not to forget, there are those, at first glance, frequently unnoticed, but no less important information signs that point to child-specific arrangements comprising prohibitions and restrictions as well as beneficial treatments. To name but a few: If you are a child, you won't be sold cigarettes or alcohol, but may be offered special children's meals or drinks; you are not permitted to drive a car, but travel for free or on a cheaper ticket; you may not enter selected public places without accompaniment of an adult, but may visit others for free; you are not allowed to watch a thriller or horror movie, but may have reduced entrance to the cinema.

Certainly, this list could be continued further, but it is similarly important to notice that the differentiation of children and adults, *secondly*, matters enormously because it also has a huge impact on the lives of adults. *On the one hand*, in Western societies not only children, but also those who have a child (or children) receive special treatment: Depending on their home country, they are subject to specific legal provisions, which commit them to take care of their children by performing certain actions and refraining from others, and which also make them profit, for instance from child benefits and tax reduction. *On the other hand*, it is incredibly difficult to relate to adults and adult lives without, however implicitly, referring to ,childhood': Whether we are parents or not, whether we consider childhood as a natural, biologically driven stage of life or as a climax of socialisation, as adults we understand ourselves as well as other adults, to a high degree, both as (more or less straightforward) products of childhood, and as persons, who have, due to having passed through adolescence, left behind (the status of) 'being a child' and who, thus, differ from children.

However, the differentiation of children and adults not only affects how we understand and relate to others and ourselves in everyday life and practice, but it also has, *thirdly*, fundamental relevance for the sciences. In Germany, for instance, differentiating children and adults is of central importance for the field of educational research. *On the one hand*, the juxtaposition of 'child' and 'adult' serves as a basis for the designation of educational subdisciplines (pedagogy in early childhood; adult education); *on the other hand*, 'child' and 'adult' occupy key positions in attempts to conceptualise as well as legitimize education: Even if in the academic study of education, 'childhood' is, by now, in response to the so-called (new) 'sociology of childhood' (cf. James and Prout 1997; Qvortrup et al. 2009; Honig 2009), mostly understood as a 'social construction', and even if quite a lot of educational research focuses on further training and lifelong learning, education, still, is primarily regarded as a matter of *children* being taught and conducted by *adults* (cf. Prange 2005).

Against this background, the starting point for this article was the vague intuition that F. Scott Fitzgerald's short story *The curious case of Benjamin Button* (cf. Fitzgerald 2007/1922) could be of particular interest for a theoretical engagement with 'childhood': Benjamin Button is quite generally at odds with the commonness of age-related differentiations of children and adults, since he, born 70 year-old in September 1860 in a hospital in Baltimore, ages in reverse, and thus, contests the idea that the process of becoming older in years consists in becoming an adult understood as a 'grown-up'. In light of this reversed developmental process, it is very likely that Fitzgerald's short story might cause irritation as well as give productive insights for academic reflections on childhood.

In what follows in the main part of this paper, I will trace the Benjamin Button story in a systematic way, and, in doing so, present some insights the story reveals about 'childhood' and 'adulthood'. In the last section, I will point to implications of the Button case on a more general level. With regard to the problems, references to literary sources frequently involve, my paper, however, starts with some preliminary notes on the role of literature in social theory and a short explanation of the methodological background of my discussion of F. Scott Fitzgerald's short story.

Setting the Course: Preliminary Notes on the Relation of Literature and Social Theory

Ever since the methodological self-understanding of the social sciences as being primarily oriented on the natural sciences, that is towards quantitative criteria and a mathematical description of the social world, the utilisation of fictional literature as empirical (qualitative) material faces the stigma of lacking factual reality and, respectively, a verifiable, testable "reality content" (cf. Suderland 2013). Thus, it is highly controversial, if the inclusion of literary sources in social research is scientifically acceptable, and warnings about a trustful, positivistic usage of literature, for instance in sociological research, are anything but lacking (Kuzmics and Mozetič 2003: pp. 62–63).

Nonetheless, over the last decade quite a few social studies on literary works have been published that aim at dealing with basic social science issues (cf. Kron and Schimank 2004; Koller et al. 2007; Kuzmics and Mozetič 2003). Especially in the educational sciences, intensive and continued efforts have been made to establish analyses of literature as a qualitative method of social research. These efforts are, first and foremost, connected to three anthologies, which were edited by Hans-Christoph Koller and Markus Rieger-Ladich in a book series entitled "Pedagogical readings of contemporary fiction" ("Pädagogische Lektüren zeitgenössischer Romane") (cf. Koller and Rieger-Ladich 2005, 2009, 2013). In light of the general fact that literary works deal with themes that are of central importance for the study of educational practices and processes, in these anthologies educational scientists are not relating to literary texts with the purpose of illustrating either pedagogical issues or educational findings obtained so far. Rather, the contributors are convinced that fictional literature offers material with an analytical quality and, thus, holds a high potential for the *generation* of scientific knowledge (cf. Koller and Rieger-Ladich 2005: pp. 9–10).

Against this background, educational analyses of literature, *on the one hand*, aim at gaining new knowledge and discovering new pedagogical dimensions and aspects to specify and further develop educational theories and concepts (cf. Koller 2005; Müller 2013). *On the other hand*, educational analyses of literature are carried out with the objective of irritation: Based on a scepticism towards all too familiar and beloved figures and forms of educational thinking, the priority here is not a more precise or better understanding of pedagogical phenomena and processes, but a critical academic self-reflection by means of deconstruction and disillusionment of key assumptions and pathos-laden key categories in the field of educational sciences (cf. Liesner 2005; Ricken 2005). However, these deconstructive pedagogical readings of literature not only aim at problematizing and exceeding the presumed definiteness and objectiveness of educational categories and theories. Rather, they are also intended to open up new vistas and insights for the study of pedagogical processes and practices (cf. Ricken 2005: p. 47).

My following discussion of the story of Benjamin Button should be understood against the methodological background of these two approaches to literary sources: Based on the assumption that Benjamin Button is, as mentioned above, a fictitious figure who is subversive to the differentiation of children and adults, I am going to explore the potential of Fitzgerald's story to contribute to the academic discussion on childhood. Thus, I am not regarding and using the story as an 'objective' source of information, as if the Button case provided statements about reality or reflected *truthfully*, for instance, the meanings of childhood in the society he is born into. My objective is not a 'truth seeking' (cf. Koller and Rieger-Ladich 2005: p. 8), nor do I aim at illustrating, specifying or even proving available theories and conceptions of childhood. Rather, my discussion of the Button case is primarily meant to raise questions and hypotheses, which could be relevant for the theoretical discussion of childhood.

A 'Curious Case': Reflections on Benjamin Button

In the following, I will interpret F. Scott Fitzgerald's *The curious case of Benjamin Button* (Fitzgerald 2007/1922) as a story that provides insights concerning the significance of the differentiation between childhood and adulthood. Along these lines, I will interpret the life of Benjamin Button as a life that is focussed on producing Benjamin's 'normality' in accordance with the differentiation between children and adults. The basis for this reading can be found right at the beginning of the story.

The Initial Production of the Child's (Ab)Normality

It is precisely a confusion of childhood and adulthood that is produced in the first two chapters of Fitzgerald's story. Even before the peculiarity of Benjamin is revealed, Fitzgerald not only informs his readers that he is about to set down an "astonishing history" (1), but he also has them witness massive hackles Mr. Roger

Button raises, when he is – "naturally nervous" (2) and hoping "it would be a boy" (2) – on his way to his first encounter with the new-born. The meetings with Doctor Keene, who delivered the new-born, and two nurses at the hospital are characterized by hostility, anger and rage in such a way that the reader immediately becomes aware that the new-born is not only astonishing, but a trial and threatening to those who are exposed to him. However interesting this is, with regard to the question of 'childhood' it is more important to notice that the nurses' acting only suggests that there is something terribly wrong with the new-born, while the doctor's reaction provides early indications that the new-born might not be a 'child': Doctor Keene answers in the affirmative to Mr. Button's question "Is my wife all right?" (3), and in the negative to the question, if the matter were "triplets" (3), but he avoids an answer to the question, if the child is born, by saying: "Why, yes, I suppose so - after a fashion" (3). Likewise Mr. Button's question "Is it a boy or a girl?" (3) remains open: The doctor answers by crying "Here now" (3), and asks Mr. Button "to go and see for yourself" (3).

This initial lack of clarity concerning the identification of the new-born as a 'child' is proceeded throughout the first two chapters by means of diverse forms of addressing. When his peculiarity is first revealed, the new-born is described as follows:

> Wrapped in a voluminous white blanket, and partly crammed into one of the cribs, there sat an old man apparently about seventy years of age. His sparse hair was almost white, and from his chin dripped a long smoke-coloured beard [...]. He looked up at Mr. Button with dim, faded eyes (6–7).

Only some lines after this description, the new-born is initially characterized as "a man of threescore and ten" (7) and then as "a *baby* of threescore and ten, a baby whose feet hung over the sides of the crib in which it was reposing" (7). In the lines that follow, the narrator's addressing of the new-born as a 'man' or an 'old man' is reiterated, whilst the protagonists, verbally as well as mentally, make use of the terms 'child' and 'baby'.

Although it is, thus, right from the beginning of the story not too sure, if the new-born is (to be regarded) a child (or a baby or an old man), in the second chapter the story goes on with Mr. Roger Button leaving the hospital in order to buy some *children's* clothes for his 'child', since "[t]he notion of dressing his son in men's clothes was repugnant to him" (11). Mr. Button ends up finding only a fancy-dress, which he, after his re-arrival at the hospital, forces the new-born to put on. Since "[t]he effect was not good" (14), Mr. Button goes on with 'amputating' "a large section of the [new-born's] beard" (14). Although "even with this improvement the ensemble fell far short of perfection" (14), the father and his son finally leave the hospital.

What is, thus, already suggested in this second chapter is that Mr. Button makes, as Fitzgerald writes at the end of chapter three, a "silent agreement with himself to believe in his son's normality" (20) and is fiercely determined to handle his son's abnormality by producing his normality. Regarding the first part of the story, this means that Mr. Button makes his son look like a 'baby' or at least like a 'child'. Accordingly, "after the new addition to the Button family" (14), Benjamin's hair is "cut short" (14), "dyed to a spare unnatural black" (14–15), his face is "shaved so close that it glistened" (15), and he is "attired in small-boy clothes" (15). Producing Benjamin's normality for Mr. Roger Button, however, not only requires to change his son's outer appearance, but also to treat his son as if he were a child or a baby. At the end of chapter two, right before they leave the hospital, Mr. Button holds out his hand, which his son – addressing him 'father' or 'dad' – takes "trustingly" (14). In line with this, after Benjamin's arrival at the Button family, the father engages a baby-nurse, declares "that if Benjamin didn't like warm milk he could go without food altogether" (15), brings "home a rattle" (15), insisting that Benjamin should play with it, as well as "lead soldiers" (16), "toy trains" (16), "large pleasant animals made of cotton" (16) – and, above all, sends Benjamin to kindergarten when he is five (19).

In doing so, Benjamin's parents, Fitzgerald writes, gradually grow used to her son and – due to the strong "force of custom" (19) – no longer feel "that he was different from any other child" (19). Nevertheless, they produce their son's 'normality' with only little success: *On the one hand*, Benjamin's clothes did not conceal that he was "five feet eight inches tall" (15), and that his eyes "were faded and watery and tired" (15), so that a few "polite" (17) people finally declare "that the baby resembled his grandfather" (17). *On the other hand*, Benjamin, for the most part, does not act and react as his parents wish: He rejects warm milk, keeps falling asleep in the kindergarten, refuses to enjoy play-dates with other children, is uninterested in the toys, and, instead, pores over a volume of the Encyclopedia Britannica, he smokes his father's cigars and sits for hours with his grandfather (15–18).

Against this background, it can be concluded that the production of the young Benjamin's normality not only fails because of his undeniably 'abnormal' bodily condition. Rather, it also fails, because Benjamin fails to behave in accordance with his chronological age and his father's (or parents') expectations based on his chronological age. The reception of Fitzgerald's short story almost exclusively focuses on these failures. In line with many others authors, for instance, Henry Alexander concludes that "how Benjamin Button fails to cope with his peculiar circumstance, how that failure creates confusion and disorientation in his life [...] is the story of his life" (Alexander 2009: p. 4). In clear contrast to this, the following will show that Benjamin Button's life proceeds between failures and success in producing his 'normality' in accordance with the differentiation between children and adults.

Benjamin Button's Life Between Failure and Success in Producing his Normality

The problem that was named in the foregoing, that Benjamin's outer appearance and his physical condition are not in congruence with his chronological age, is a problem Benjamin is faced with again and again throughout the text's progression from his birth to his death – and one of the main reasons, why he occasionally is not able or allowed to participate in selected practices or enter selected institutions.

To mention three incidents: When Benjamin is 18 years old, he passes his examination for entrance to Yale College, but when he is to arrange his schedule at the registrar's office, he is – based on the fact that he couldn't manage to dye his hair before – first taken for his own father, then, due to his insistence on being the expected 18-year old freshman, thrown out as "a dangerous lunatic" (23), and finally followed by "a dense mass of undergraduates" (24) and their "continual succession of remarks" (24), such as, for instance, "Look at the infant prodigy!" (24). In a certain contrast to this incident, Benjamin at the age of 50 successfully enters himself a freshman at Harvard University and even becomes "the most celebrated man in college" (40) due to the fact that he played so brilliantly in the football game with Yale. Nevertheless, this success is not permanent: While Benjamin in his third year is "scarcely able to 'make' the team" (40), in his senior year he does not "make the team at all" (41), since "he had grown so slight and frail" (41). Something quite similar happens when Benjamin, who served 3 years in the Spanish-American War in his late thirties, at the age of 57 receives a letter calling former officers back in to service. Benjamin has a new general's uniform made and proceeds to Camp Mosby, but is considered a playful child, so that, finally, his son Roscoe – born in the 1880s – escorts "the weeping general, *sans* uniform, back to his home" (48).

While these three incidents exemplify that Benjamin fails to do or achieve something due to his bodily condition, it must be stressed that there are as many situations, in which his outer appearance and his physical condition pose no problems at all – or even provide him with advantages. *On the one hand*, after a couple of years in middle age Benjamin reaches "a bodily age equivalent to his age in years" (36). *On the other hand*, there are some situations, in which Benjamin's chronological age is unknown or irrelevant. To mention two incidents: When Benjamin is 20 years old, he and his father are "more and more companionable" (25), they appear "about the same age" (25), and are often mistaken for each other or for brothers. One day, they go out socially and when Benjamin gets to know his later wife, Hildegarde Moncrieff, he decides against enlightening her when she assumes that he is in "the mellow age" (29) of 50 and his father's brother. In a similarly 'conscious' way Benjamin conceals his chronological age as well as the fact that his chronological and bodily ages run in different directions when he enters Harvard: "He did not make the mistake of announcing that he would never see 50 again, nor did he mention that fact that his son had been graduated from the same institution 10 years before" (40).

With regard to the production of Benjamin's 'normality', these two examples are of particular significance. They are both closely connected to the above-mentioned Yale incident. While this is implicitly, but no less obviously the case with Harvard, Benjamin explicitly remembers "his experience at Yale" (28), when he is hesitating if he should enlighten Hildegarde about her mistake in taking him for his father's brother – and decides against it. Thus, it seems that Benjamin had learned to "play dirty" from the fact that he was thrown out of Yale.

The situations, in which Benjamin deliberately conceals his chronological age, are, however, only quite specific examples in view of the fact that Benjamin throughout the story's proceeding more generally begins to see (or 'learn') that it is easier to behave as others see him – which means both to adopt behaviour consistent with other's expectations (which are based on his outer appearance and bodily condition, and/or on his chronological age) and to behave in accordance with the way others behave towards him. Regarding the very first part of the story, this means that Benjamin learns to behave like a baby or a child on the basis of his father's (parent's) behaviour and expectations. Thus, although Benjamin in his young ages is, as mentioned above, hardly meeting his father's (or parents') expectations and wishes, there are, nevertheless, some situations in his younger years where he behaves in compliant (and 'obedient') ways: He makes "an honest attempt to play with other boys" (19), frequently joins "in the milder games" (19), tries "to work up an interest in tops and marbles" (18), jingles the rattle "obediently" (16) – and, finally, he not only manages, "quite accidentally, to break a kitchen window" (18), but, due to the fact that this "secretly delighted his father" (18), even contrives "to break something every day" (18) thereafter. Benjamin, the narrator comments, does these things because "he was by nature obliging" (18), but also "because they were expected of him" (18).

Against this background, it can be argued that Benjamin already in his early years learns to meet other's expectations. Nevertheless, there can be no doubt that his Yale experience constitutes a turning point: From the Yale incident on, what Benjamin *does* – going to work, falling in love, marrying, having a child, going to war and so on –, is, on the surface and to a high degree, in accordance with his chronological age: His life appears as a quite 'normal' life reflecting a standard biography.

This 'normal' proceeding of Benjamin's life, however, holds up only until he is in his late forties, so that there is one more, in a certain way reverse, turning pointing in his life: After having passed middle ages Benjamin is more and more incapable of performing in line with and living up to his chronological age – and thus unable to adapt his behaviour to those people's expectations that are based on the date he was born. One reason for Benjamin's later 'failures' is quite obvious: When Benjamin is born, he can speak, reason, complain, make demands, give in to his father's rudeness, and is in total able to perform in the way 'an old man' would. But when he is growing older, he at first frequently lacks the abilities, skills, capacities and competencies required to meet and cope with the tasks and challenges he is confronted with, then has to be removed from the kindergarten, and, finally, his life ends up with his having the incompetence of a new-born – in a state of unawareness.

However important this decline of Benjamin's abilities, competencies and so on is, explaining Benjamin's later 'failures' only by this fact would overlook that it, at times, is based on the fact that he his acting in accordance with his mental (psychological) condition – that is with what he feels, longs for, likes, dislikes and so on. While the attempt of the ageing Benjamin to return to war is itself a perfect example of his giving way to his feelings in disregard of his chronological age and his outer appearance, Benjamin's first decision to go to war points even more directly to the importance of his (mental) psychological condition: The main reason why Benjamin decides to join the army in 1889 is that "his wife had ceased to attract him" (34), and he gradually loses interest in and is bored of her. Thus, when Hildegarde Moncrief first falls for him, Benjamin is overwhelmed, besotted and reacts physically to her presence. But in his late thirties and early forties Benjamin increasingly feels a discontent and wants to escape his home – maybe hoping that the situation might improve. On his return from the war Benjamin, however, is "depressed" (35) by the sight of his wife, and, after a dispute with her, even wonders "what possible fascination she had ever exercised over him" (37). Thereafter, Benjamin compensates his "growing unhappiness at home for by his many new interests" (38), not only finding "that his thirst for gayety grew stronger" (38), but following his longings as well as his growing "naïve pleasure in his appearance" (39). In doing so, Benjamin acts in accordance with his psychological condition (his feelings) and totally disregards the preceding quarrel with his wife, in which Hildegarde lets him know that he should have "enough pride to stop it" (37) and accuses him as follows:

> You're simply stubborn. You think you don't want to be like any one else. You always have been that way, and you always will be. But just think how it would be if every one else looked at things as you do-what would the world be like? (37).

However, Benjamin, at that time, is not only unable 'to stop it', but also unwilling to act as his wife wishes – precisely because this would mean to ignore his longings.

Conclusions

If we ask, what the Benjamin Button story entails for the theoretical engagement with childhood, our first conclusion can be that the differentiation of childhood and adulthood is determined by the idea of a certain congruence between four threads or lines of a person's life: the chronological age, the physical/biological condition, the psychological/mental condition and the behaviour. As Henry Alexander writes, in Benjamin's case three of these threads are "systematically independent of one another"(Alexander 2009: p. 2): "His years bear little relation to his physical age. His psychological states reflect little, if anything, of his years. Except for his middle years […], there was little congruence between his chronological age, on the one hand, and his physical appearance or his psychological life, on the other" (ibid.).

Certainly, the foregoing has shown that Benjamin frequently gets into trouble because "his chronological age, his bodily age, and his psychological age are seldom congruent and frequently unharmoniously interwoven" (ibid.), that is because his bodily condition and/or his behaviour lacks correspondence with what other people expect. However, while Alexander states that the reason, why Benjamin fails changing his behaviour is that Benjamin is "unable to see himself as others see him" (ibid.: p. 3) and unaware "as to how he comes across to others" (ibid.), the foregoing

has shown, *on the one hand*, that one important reason, why Benjamin fails to fit
other people's expectations is that he, at times, gives into his psychological/mental
condition and behaves in a 'conscious' disregard of other people's expectations. *On
the other hand*, the preceding considerations suggested that one crucial characteristic of Benjamin's life is that he learns to adapt to other people's expectations and
performs himself in accordance with social expectations throughout a quite long
period of his life to a surprising degree of ,success'; he doubles the Button family's
fortune, marries, has a son, makes his father-in-law appreciate him, and so on – and
he is even able to cope with contrasting expectations: While, for instance, when he
is 20 years old, his father wants him to behave like a man of 20, his wife wants him
to behave like a man of 50. However, Benjamin not only learns to act in accordance
with other people's expectations and to reflect, to relate to and engage with the relations he is situated in, but he also, at times, achieves, a certain independence from
the people he is exposed to.

Taking together these different aspects, it can be argued that, although Benjamin
indeed is, regarding his growing physically younger, a *child in the making*, nevertheless, the young Benjamin is an *adult in the making* in that he solves some of the
central adolescent development tasks, which were promoted by developmental psychology in the early twentieth century. The price Benjamin pays for this, however,
is quite high and on a very personal level: *On the one hand*, he has to lie, to pretend
and to perform in disregard of his feelings, longings, needs, and desires – in order
to produce *that* congruence (between his chronological age or his physical appearance and his behaviour), the people who he encounters or lives with expect. Thus,
his ageing process is, last but not least, a process in which he learns to suppress, or,
to put it mildly, to cultivate his feelings – sometimes with more and sometimes with
less success. *On the other hand*, his 'failures' to act in accordance with other people's expectations result in exclusion, accusations or even contempt.

Against this background, our second conclusion with regard to childhood and
adulthood can be that *becoming an adult* encourages or forces us to *perform* ourselves in a way that a certain kind of congruence between our ages, our bodily
condition and/or our outer appearance is achieved – if necessary, in disregard of
what we feel or desire. As long as our longings are not interfering with our performance, whether they fit our performance is quiet irrelevant. On this basis, it is worth
mentioning that no one in the story ever attempts to discover the reason for
Benjamin's condition, nor to accept the strange truth. Instead, Benjamin's father is
embarrassed, his wife, as mentioned above, accusatory – and, in line with his wife,
Benjamin's son condemns his father for behaving "in a curious and perverse manner" (48) – and lets him know the following:

> As a matter of fact […] you'd better not go on with this business much longer. You better
> pull up short […] you better turn right around and start back the other way. This has gone
> too far to be a joke. It isn't funny any longer. You-you behave yourself (42–43).

Although these accusations might seem absurd, they, nevertheless, point to one
remarkable aspect of Benjamin's 'curious case' worth mentioning: Benjamin is not
only unable to meet this son's (or his wife's) expectation to stop his ageing process

of "normal ungrowth" (21). Rather, he is also unable to find the adequate means to tell his story and give a coherent account and explanation of himself. To explain who he is and where he comes from, is an expectation Benjamin is confronted with quite directly after his birth – his father asks him: "Where in God's name did you come from? Who are you?" (8) –, and which he is unable to satisfy: "I can't tell you *exactly* who I am [...] – but my last name is certainly Button" (8). That Benjamin consequently is "as puzzled as anyone else" (18) throughout the story's proceeding, however, is totally ignored by the people around him; instead, they hold him responsible for something that he cannot change. If this points to a third conclusion with regard to childhood and adulthood, is, however, left to the reader.

One Final Note

Certainly, one important lesson to be learned from Benjamin Button is that the categories of childhood and adulthood are indispensably intertwined, so that we are only able to discuss 'childhood' with reference to 'adulthood', that is on the basis of insights into how childhood's counterpart 'adulthood' is constructed and performed. However, although there can be no doubt that 'adulthood' plays an important role for academic reflections on 'childhood', at least insofar as childhood is understood as a separate lifespan that chronologically precedes adulthood, the attempt to scrutinize what kind of role 'adulthood' exactly plays or is supposed to play in empirical research and theoretical reflections on childhood, is a rather complicated task.

Firstly, social theories, in particular in the field of educational research, frequently hold on to the child-adult-distinction without clarifying the underlying idea of adulthood and, thus, lack a theory or, at least, a concept of adulthood. This is, above all, highly problematic from an *ethical* point of view, insofar as at least some classifications of children as somehow deficient or 'curious' are directly connected with normative standards of 'adulthood', to be more precise with the fact that they are regarded as 'adults in the making'.

Secondly, in the 1980s and 1990s, under the heading of a 'new sociology of childhood' (cf. James and Prout 1997), sociologists of childhood precisely criticised (especially developmental) theories of childhood with regard to their presenting children as unfinished or incomplete 'human becomings' in juxtaposition to adults as mature, rational and competent 'human beings' (cf. Tisdall 2012; Qvortrup et al. 1994), and promoted a rethinking of children as active, independent, competent, individual agents.

Since the beginning of the twentieth century, this model of children, however, is, *thirdly*, frequently questioned with regard to its reproduction of an 'adult' conception of the individual as a rational, articulate, knowledgeable, stable, self-controlling being, capable of speaking for herself (cf. Tisdall 2012; Lee 2001; Rose 1999). In this context, not only the notion of children as 'becoming' beings is rehabilitated. Rather, it is also proposed that 'becoming' is an attribute of human existence in general, so that both children and adults are to be seen as 'becoming-beings' (cf. Tisdall 2012; Prout 2005).

Against this background, it can be argued that the theoretical engagement with 'childhood' and 'adulthood' proceeds between two opposite extremes: *Either* childhood is interpreted as absence of and in contrast to adulthood; *or* it is focussed on the common features of children *and* adults in such a way that it seems that there are hardly any differences between children and adults worth mentioning (except for their biological immaturity). In contrast to this, I finally want to argue for a theoretical reconceptualization of the distinction between adulthood and childhood that transcends these dichotomies. Theoretically, we need to advance childhood studies by omitting the question how children and adults *are* (by nature) and ask, instead, how the differentiation of childhood and adulthood is *practiced*, and what, apart from the legal status, the specific rationale and social function behind the attribution of the particular status of being an adult or a child is: For what purpose are we generating ourselves in accordance with different categories of 'adulthood' and 'childhood'?

Addressing these questions might highlight that the differentiation of adulthood and childhood is, at times, not only troublesome to children, but also to adults. Being addressed as an adult first of all means to be addressed as 'being no child', as a person who has passed beyond 'childhood', it means that 'we' as adults should behave ourselves in contrast to children. This may appear like a simple or even trivial point; nonetheless, I argue that performing in accordance with being addressed as a 'non-child', at times, may imply severe restrictions. It may mean – and this is what Benjamin Button's case shows – that we have to negate ourselves, to 'perform ourselves' in contrast to our feelings, emotions, needs, and so on. Questioning the attributions of 'adulthood' and 'childhood' as well as their effects, thus, could mean to produce new possibilities of experiencing life for those who need recognition to live, but who feel restricted by the very parameters that are used for their *recognition as an adult* – ignoring this may have painful consequences, not only for fictitious persons like Benjamin Button.

References

Alexander, H. 2009. Reflections on Benjamin Button. *Philosophy and Literature* 33: 1–17. doi:10.1353/phl.0.0040.

Fitzgerald, F.S. 2007/1922. *The curious case of Benjamin Button*. New York/London/Toronto/Sydney: Scribner.

Honig, M.-S. 2009. *Ordnungen der Kindheit, Problemstellungen und Perspektiven der Kindheitsforschung*. Juventa: Weinheim.

James, A., and A. Prout (eds.). 1997. *Constructing and reconstructing childhood: Contemporary issues in the sociological study of childhood*. London: Falmer.

Koller, H.-C. 2005. Über die Möglichkeit und Unmöglichkeit von Bildungsprozessen. Zu Imre Kertész' Roman eines Schicksallosen. In *Grenzgänge (Pädagogische Lektüren zeitgenössischer Romane, Volume 1)*, ed. Hans-Christoph Koller and Markus Rieger-Ladich, 93–109. Bielefeld: Transcript.

Koller, H.-C., and M. Rieger-Ladich (eds.). 2005. *Grenzgänge (Pädagogische Lektüren zeitgenös-sischer Romane, Volume 1)*. Bielefeld: Transcript.
Koller, Hans-Christoph, and Markus Rieger-Ladich (eds.). 2009. *Figurationen von Adoleszenz (Pädagogische Lektüren zeitgenössischer Romane, Volume 2)*. Bielefeld: Transcript.
Koller, H.-C., and M. Rieger-Ladich (eds.). 2013. *Vom Scheitern (Pädagogische Lektüren zeitgen-össischer Romane, Volume 3)*. Bielefeld: Transcript.
Koller, H.-C., W. Marotzki, and M. Rieger-Ladich (eds.). 2007. Symbolische Gewalt. Zur liter-arischen Ethnographie von Bildungsräumen. *Zeitschrift für Qualitative Forschung* 8(1): 7–10.
Kron, T., and U. Schimank (eds.). 2004. *Die Gesellschaft der Literatur*. Opladen: Budrich.
Kuzmics, H., and G. Mozetič. 2003. *Literatur als Soziologie. Zum Verhältnis von literarischer und gesellschaftlicher Wirklichkeit*. Konstanz: UVK.
Lee, N. 2001. *Childhood and society*. Buckingham: Open University Press.
Liesner, A. 2005. Begrenzte Gänge? Über Schwierigkeiten mit der pädagogischen Lektüre liter-arischer Texte am Beispiel von Doris Lessings Das fünfte Kind. In *Grenzgänge (Pädagogische Lektüren zeitgenössischer Romane, Volume 1)*, ed. Hans-Christoph Koller and Markus Rieger-Ladich, 51–60. Bielefeld: Transcript.
Müller, H.-R. 2013. Produktiv scheitern. Biographische Prozesse und Konfigurationen der Bildung in Jonathan Franzens Roman Freiheit. In *Vom Scheitern (Pädagogische Lektüren zeitgenös-sischer Romane, Volume 3)*, ed. Hans-Christoph Koller, and Markus Rieger-Ladich, 111–132. Bielefeld: Transcript.
Prange, Klaus. 2005. *Die Zeigestruktur der Erziehung. Grundriss der Operativen Pädagogik*. Ferdinand Schöningh: Paderborn u.a.
Prout, A. 2005. *The future of childhood*. London: Routledge/Falmer.
Qvortrup, J., M. Bardy, G. Sgritta, and H. Wintersberger (eds.). 1994. *Childhood matters. Social theory, practice and politics*. Aldershot: Avebury.
Qvortrup, J., W.A. Corsaro, and M.-S. Honig (eds.). 2009. *The Palgrave handbook of childhood studies*. Palgrave: Basingstoke.
Ricken, N. 2005. "Unersetzbar ist das Wort der Dichter ...". Systematische Bemerkungen zum Verhältnis von Pädagogik und Literatur am Beispiel des Romans Mann und Frau von Zeruya Shalev. In *Grenzgänge (Pädagogische Lektüren zeitgenössischer Romane, Volume 1)*, ed. Hans-Christoph Koller and Markus Rieger-Ladich, 35–49. Bielefeld: Transcript.
Rose, N. 1999. *Governing the soul: The shaping of the private self*, 2nd ed. London/New York: Free Association.
Suderland, M. 2013. Review essay: Die Sozioanalyse literarischer Texte als Methode der qualita-tiven Sozialforschung oder: Welche Wirklichkeit enthält Fiktion? [56 Absätze]. *Forum Qualitative Sozialforschung/Forum: Qualitative Social Research* 15(1): Art. 20. http://www.qualitative-research.net/index.php/fqs/article/view/2101/3616. Accessed 15 Apr 2015.
Tisdall, E.K.M. 2012. The challenge and challenging pf childhood studies? Learning from dis-ablitiy studies and research with disabled children. *Children & Society. Special Issue: Researching the Lives of Disabled Children and Young People* 26(3): 181–191. First published online: 16 APR 2012. doi:10.1111/j.1099-0860.2012.00431.x.
Walkerdine, V. 2009. Developmental psychology and the study of childhood. In *An introduction to childhood studies*, 2nd ed, ed. Marie Jane Kehily, 112–123. Berkshire: Open university Press.

Chapter 14
Education for Autonomy in the Context of Consumer Culture

Phillip D.Th. Knobloch

Abstract This article tries to give first indications in relation to the question, which aspects have to be taken into consideration for a concept of education for autonomy in the context of consumer culture. Analyzing the international debates about Education for Sustainable Development, concepts of critical consumer education seem to offer possibilities to support the development of autonomy in relation to the sphere of consumption. Therefore a concept of critical consumer education that works explicitly with the specific concept of consumer culture, and that focuses on sustainable product communication, will be introduced. Although education for critical consumption seems to be a privileged option today, the specific and somehow problematic aesthetic dimensions of critical consumption and sustainability, which play an important role in some related educational concepts, indicate that also forms of general consumer aesthetic education should be taken into consideration. Therefore such an aesthetic concept, also explicitly related to the concept of consumer culture, will be presented. Discussing also the problematic aspects of both concepts, this article concludes that approaches of consumer aesthetic and critical consumer education should be combined for a wider concept of education for autonomy in the context of consumer culture.

Keywords Consumer culture • Consumer critique • Critical consumer education • Consumer aesthetic education • Autonomy

Introduction

Aesthetic and political aspects were closely related in Friedrich Schiller's letters *On the Aesthetic Education of Man* (1795), which introduced the concept of aesthetic education. Art should not only serve to improve and strengthen the human sensorial dimensions, but also the reasoning side; therefore aesthetic education was not thought of as a specific field of education among others, but as education as such

P.D.Th. Knobloch (✉)
Department of Comparative Education, Ruhr University Bochum, Bochum, Germany
e-mail: phillip.knobloch@googlemail.com

© Springer International Publishing Switzerland 2016   221
J. Drerup et al. (eds.), *Justice, Education and the Politics of Childhood*,
Philosophy and Politics – Critical Explorations 1,
DOI 10.1007/978-3-319-27389-1_14

(Koch 2011, 97). It seems plausible to see here also an early concept of citizenship education, because Schiller's idea was to relate the education of the human and the citizen: Whereas the harmonizing aesthetic experience of beauty should make it possible to feel totally human, the complementary energizing aesthetic experience of the sublime is said to remind us that we are moral persons. We can conclude that Schiller presented a specific concept of aesthetic *education for autonomy*, which tried to prevent alienation in a developing modern society on the one hand, offering the possibility for moral judgment and ethical practices on the other. Even if it is undeniable that Schiller's concept cannot serve directly as an actual program of education for autonomy, it is interesting to notice that the relation of aesthetic and political aspects in education is still, or even again increasingly, under discussion today. We can find such discussions for example in relation to the subject of *Education for Sustainable Development* (ESD). It seems worth taking a closer look at this topic, because it opens up new perspectives for discussions about education for autonomy, especially in relation to the context of consumer culture.

The origin of the concept of sustainability can be found in the work *Sylvicultura oeconomica* (1713) by Hans Carl von Carlowitz, who proposed to maintain a balance between the number of chopped down and regrowing trees in forestry to avoid a lack of wood in dependent economic sectors. But even if the origin can be related to this early work, the term sustainability recently gained importance through the work of international committees. One main reference is the report *Our Common Future* (1987) from the Brundtland Commission, where an often cited definition of sustainable development was given: "Sustainable Development seeks to meet the needs and aspirations of the present without compromising the ability to meet those of the future." (WCED 1987, 51) The important role of education for the realization of sustainable development was underlined in the action plan *Agenda 21* of the United Nations, a result of the UN Conference on Environment and Development in Rio de Janeiro in 1992. Another important step to connect education and sustainability was the UN *Decade of Education for Sustainable Development* (DESD) from 2005 to 2014, followed by the actual *Global Action Programme on ESD*. Even if there is no consensus about the concrete meaning of sustainable development and the way in which it can be realized, there seems to be no doubt that this concept is a normative vision and principle, which includes three fundamental dimensions: economic, social and ecological development (cf. Bormann 2011, 5–7). As we can see, culture is not yet a fundamental part of this concept.

But there are UN documents which underline the necessity to connect the ideas of sustainability and ESD with culture, cultural diversity, creativity and arts education. It is said, for example, that cultural diversity "can be seen as a key cross-cutting dimension of sustainable development." (UNESCO 2009, 25) In relation to the Millennium Development Goals adopted in 2000, which did not refer explicitly to culture, and pointing on the creation of a new post-2015 global development agenda, "the importance and power of the cultural and creative sectors as engines of sustainable human development" (Bokova and Clark 2013, 11; cf. UNESCO 2012) is now accentuated by the director-general of UNESCO and the administrator of UNDP. The declaration of the *Third UNESCO World Forum on Culture and Cultural Industries*

(UNESCO 2014a), to give another example, also recommended the integration of culture into sustainable development policies, strategies and educational efforts. Some years before, the *Road Map for Arts Education* already recommended to link arts education with ESD (UNESCO 2006, 19). We can conclude, that there is an innovative and rising tendency to relate political and aesthetic aspects in the case of ESD, or at least to promote such a relation, still missing in many concepts.

Parting from one aspect of ESD, *Education for Sustainable Consumption* (ESC) (cf. UNEP 2011), this article wants to emphasize the necessity to link political and aesthetic approaches in education to sketch the basis for a concept of education for autonomy in the context of consumer culture. In the current *Global Action Programme on ESD* (UNESCO 2014b, 12), the issue of *sustainable consumption and production* (SCP) is defined as an important dimension and learning content of ESD. Focusing on individual and societal transformation, it is said that education should motivate and capacitate the adaptation of sustainable lifestyles. This idea is also clearly expressed in the running programme *Sustainable Lifestyles and Education* (UNEP 2014) and in earlier works from the *Task Force on Sustainable Lifestyles* (TFSL), which was operating from 2005 to 2009. Sustainable consumption and lifestyles are educational topics in which we can see a strong link between political and aesthetic aspects and strategies, because related educational concepts try to connect certain desired rational reflections about consumption and reasonable consumption practices with positive aesthetic experiences. Contrary to a simple economic perspective, factors like "emotions, aspirations, health and happiness" (TFSL 2010, 10) are taken into consideration to promote sustainable consumption. "If we create a thirst for sustainable lifestyles, then policy will be shaped quickly to meet it." (TFSL 2010, 8) Although we can conclude that such programs of ESC, which can be understood basically as a form of political education, include aesthetic approaches, a deeper reflection of the relation of political and aesthetic education is still missing in the analyzed documents.

The cultural and aesthetic dimension of sustainable consumption becomes apparent from a theoretical position based on the concept of *consumer culture*. Studies on this topic emphasize that consumption products cannot be limited anymore to their utility value, because present (affluent) societies can be characterized by the production and consumption of products with cultural meaning. The cultural dimension of products is based for example on connected images, visions, narratives or fictions, and allows diverse aesthetic consumption practices. Appropriate products are provided by a corresponding *aesthetic economy*, which is based on symbols, sensorial experiences and emotions (Reckwitz 2013, 194). Therefore consumption is considered to be an important aspect for identity formation and socialization, not limited just to practices of using or buying products in a narrow sense. As the concepts of sustainable consumption and lifestyles do refer at least implicitly to these topics, these findings seem to suggest, that such concepts are not just responding to ecological and social problems caused by consumer culture, but do also operate within its proper logic. Recent studies, which analyze the role of sustainability in product communication (Gekeler 2012), support this assumption.

It seems to be necessary to take a closer look at the phenomenon of sustainable consumption in the context of consumer culture, to understand in how far ESD can contribute to concepts of education for autonomy today. Overall the cultural dimension of ESD, linked to the promotion of certain lifestyles, puts into question if it is sufficient to rely on just this concept, because recent studies underline that new and problematic forms of social distinction are made possible with these lifestyles. Especially in relation to children we have to ask, if a wider concept of aesthetic education can help to avoid problematic social effects, which are discussed today referring to the term LOHAS, the *Lifestyle of Health and Sustainability*. This article wants to show, that *critical consumer education*, an analog term for education for sustainable consumption, should be combined with *consumer aesthetic education*, as both concepts apparently offer different possibilities to gain autonomy in the context of consumer culture. In this way, the findings presented in this article contribute to the discussion about the integration of cultural aspects into ESD. It is also worth pointing out here, that we can emphasize the importance of (consumer) aesthetic education in reference to the human right to education and cultural participation, expressed by the *Universal Declaration of Human Rights* and the *Convention on the Rights of the Child* (cf. UNESCO 2006, 3–4). Parting from the notion that the concept of consumer culture is very important to understand present societies, we can ask, whether children do have the right, that their education includes a critical and illuminating perspective on consumer culture, opening opportunities of participation, as autonomous as possible. This article wants to open the discussion about children's rights and education in relation to consumer culture, arguing that aesthetic and critical consumption are both central topics, which should be integrated and interrelated in educational debates about global and inter-generational questions of justice and ethics.

Critical Consumer Education

Critical consumption can be understood as a new form of critique of consumption. Whereas conservative and left fundamental critiques of consumption as such were dominant before, contemporary concepts of critical consumption only criticize particular forms of (unsustainable) commodity production and consumption, whereas other forms—which are supposed to be sustainable—are revaluated. These new concepts spread the idea, that the sphere of consumption is a space "where societal learning processes occur, and where responsible consumers exert influence on the economy and on politics by their purchase decisions."[1] (Schrage 2014, 2) Focusing on critical consumption as an aim of education, autonomy cannot be gained here just through negating or criticizing economic influences, or promoting art and (high) culture as the real sphere of education for autonomy. Critical consumer education instead has to focus on learning processes, which enable to distinguish between

[1] All quotations from literature written in German language are traduced by the author himself.

sustainable and non-sustainable products and forms of consumption. But recent studies underline the problems that come with this task. One problem is that critical consumption is a very extensive concept with many different aims, which can come easily into conflict with each other. "Organic grown does not necessarily mean ecologically sustainable, if transport distances are taken into account, healthy and ecologically sustainable food and cosmetics can quite be produced and distributed unfair—the health conscious care of the own body, a way of traveling and consuming which is not harmful for the climate, and the grade of exploitation in the production of goods cannot always be reconciled with each other." (Schrage 2014, 8) Apart from conflicts between different aspects and aims of critical consumption, contradictions between normative ideas and the reality of consumption practices also occur, as it can be difficult to judge unambiguously the moral quality of concrete products or companies. As critical consumers became a specific target group for companies, different marketing strategies are used to promote the sustainable qualities of products; a phenomenon, which also causes critical attitudes towards such strategies among critical consumers. In the following, a study of Gekeler (2012) is used to present some aspects of a concept of critical consumer education, which is situated explicitly in the context of consumer culture, focuses on product communication linked to the term or vision of sustainability, and is based on theories from the area of narratology.

To define the criteria of a sustainable product, Gekeler analyzes the discourse in the field of sustainable design, where he finds six central aspects: *function, materiality, energization, temporality, aesthetics* and *conviviality* (Gekeler 2012, 56–59). Only if a product for example is designed in reference to people's everyday problems, using regenerative materials and energy, having an appropriate life span, being aesthetically and practically attractive and in accordance with human rights and dignity, a product could really be called sustainable in a strong sense (cf. Gekeler 2012, 228). Although the discussion in the field of sustainable design is highly developed, there seem to be very few or nearly no products up to now that fulfill all of these criteria in a strong sense of sustainability. These *narrations* about sustainability are therefore primarily theoretical on the one hand (Gekeler 2012, 51), but do nevertheless offer orientation for the design and the evaluation of products on the other hand.

Referring to the question, how critical consumers can identify products that are *really* sustainable, Gekeler doubts if the term *reality* is appropriate. Parting from constructivist theories, he prefers to talk about *models of reality*, which have to prove their *viability*. Analyzing product communication related to the topic of sustainability, he proposes to differentiate between *fictional* and *factual* narrations. Whereas fictional narrations—similar to those of fictional literature—do not claim to tell real or true stories, factual ones do so. Therefore it might be possible—in some cases and under certain conditions—to prove the viability of information offered via factual narrations in relation to certain models of reality. In contrast to that, fictional narrations can just be valuated in relation to their aesthetic qualities.

To focus on product narrations instead of real qualities seems to be comprehensible, if the topics of critical consumption and sustainable products are situated in the context of *consumer culture*. "Today's products are distinguished for being connected with stories, dreams and fictions" (Gekeler 2012, 10). To analyze the complex structure of sustainable product communication, Gekeler (2012, 45–47) presents a general model where the product itself is placed in the centre, surrounded by an aura that is created by narrations. Parting from the notion that not only producers, consumers or other mediators (for example journalists etc.), but also objects or things themselves can tell stories directly in a certain sense, the product—or its perceivable physical dimension—is conceived to be the nucleus of product communication. But whereas the narrations communicated by producers or consumers can create additional *connotative* meanings and can contribute to form the aura of a product, the perceivable immediate qualities of the product are called *denotative*, offering core meanings. Although the denotative core of a product—for example surface, consistence, smell, function etc.—is widely defined by its design, the consumer can add denotative meanings as well if he or she uses the product in an innovative way. As many qualities related to the idea of sustainability cannot be perceived directly, narratives are necessary to communicate these aspects. "A bicycle is […] more sustainable than a car […]. But the purchaser of a bicycle cannot easily detect, if the bicycle was also produced and transported […] referring to the idea of sustainability." (Gekeler 2012, 40) Therefore most of the communication is indirect and based on further media, including for example all types of advertisement.

Gekeler's analysis indicates that the growing market of products promoted as sustainable can be interpreted as a reaction of companies to the growing skepticism of certain social groups towards fictional product narrations. Socialized in consumer culture, people have learned to understand paratextual and intratextual signals that indicate fictional modes of narration. Therefore advertisement for example is in most cases expected to spread fictional narrations about a product. "The more consumers are conscious about the fictionality of the different brand narratives, the more the urge of the brand authors grows to connect authenticity and credibility with their products" (Gekeler 2012, 41). As market researchers detected a growing group of consumers interested in authentic and credible products and brands— which can serve for what was then called a *Lifestyle of Health and Sustainability* (LOHAS)—, producers focused on offering such products, promoting their specific qualities not only with fictional, but also increasingly with factual narratives. Therefore signals like footnotes, graphics or references are used, to indicate a factual mode of narration. "Whereas it was dominant up until some years ago to connect products with experiences, dreams and visions, products now have to tell credible stories in addition. […] The authentic and credible story is the centre of product communication" (Gekeler 2012, 211).

Gekeler's study provides important ideas for a concept of *critical consumer education* situated in the context of consumer culture. Focusing on product communication related to sustainability, the competence to distinguish fictional and factual product narrations becomes a central aspect of education. The model of product communication might serve as an important tool both for learning processes, which try to offer orientation in consumer culture, and for didactical and pedagogical reflections on this topic. Beyond that, such an education might help to provide competences to criticize fictional narrations of sustainability in reference to their aesthetic qualities on the one hand, and to prove the viability of factual product messages on the other hand. Whereas denotative product elements can be proved only through ones own experiences, specific information—for example from professional test agencies or internet portals—is needed to prove factual narrations (Gekeler 2012, 218–219). Media literacy therefore is a central aspect of this pedagogical concept. Aspects of social learning are important as well, as this idea of critical consumption may include the formation of social groups, which might collect and publish information, or might somehow try to gain critical influence on consumers and producers. This concept is based on the idea, that a complex and developing structure of communication about critical consumption and sustainability could appear, which itself has to be understood as an element of both critical consumption practices and socio-economical development, transforming societies in the direction of the visions proposed originally by the term sustainability. Critical consumer education can be conceived as an important part of a concept of education for autonomy in the context of consumer culture, overall because this concept may help to gain autonomy in reference to consumption decisions and to the valuation of products, which are meant to be sustainable.

Consumer Aesthetic Education

The concept of critical consumer education presented above tends to promote a specific sustainable lifestyle, an aim, clearly expressed also in the mentioned programs on ESD from the UN. In the following, a general concept of consumer aesthetic education is presented, to focus on some problematic aspects of this lifestyle and the related educational concepts, which just concentrate on sustainability. Widening the focus on the aesthetic dimensions of consumption in general might help to gain autonomy also in reference to limiting effects of critical consumption.

Wolfgang Ullrich already presented sketches of a general concept of *consumer aesthetic education*, which can be interpreted as a reformulation of Schiller's theory of aesthetic education in the context of consumer culture. He parts from a distinction between the *utility* and the *fictional value* of products. Focusing on the aesthetic dimension of products and related consumption practices, he compares products with classical, legitimate or high cultural aesthetic objects, like works of fine art, or literature etc. Although, referring to the complexity, density or profundity of the presented fictions, there is obviously a big difference for example between a novel and an ordinary consumption good, both do offer possibilities for aesthetic experiences. One example presented by Ullrich (2009) is the aesthetic use of shower gels. Some shower gels are for example promoted by being said to have a stimulating, others to have a harmonizing effect on the consumer. As these products are also designed to communicate this message on different sensual levels using *multisensory enhancement*, Ullrich claims that an aesthetic use which *really* causes the promoted effects is at least possible. This phenomenon is widely known as placebo effect (cf. Gekeler 2012, 218–224), but it also can be understood as the result of an aesthetic experience.

Ullrich does not only draw an analogy between consumption products like shower gels and literature or works of art, but consistently also between the theatre and the shower cabin (Ullrich 2009, 18), and Gekeler (2012, 35) draws an analogy between the theatre and the supermarket. To relate *economy* and *art* in that way seems plausible, because recent findings emphasize that the former strict opposition between these two fields has disappeared. The sociologist Andreas Reckwitz claims, that "the opposition between economy and art, valid for bourgeois and organized capitalism, was transformed in a structural similarity of economic and artistic practices." (Reckwitz 2013, 145) He presents an alternative history of economy based on the idea, that aesthetics imposed an affective logic on economy. Both the creative production and the aesthetic consumption, characteristic for the actual aesthetic economy, do not refer first of all to economic rationality and rationalization, but to the affective logic of the aesthetic field. Misik (2007, 13) claims, that cultural capitalism can be characterized by two connected phenomena, the *economization of culture* on the one hand, the *culturalization of economy* on the other. Ullrich (2013b, 120) also observes a new form of interaction and mutual interest between economy and art. On the one hand artists recently began to take over aspects of economy, presenting and forming for example the image of the artist as a manager or businessman, or adapting economic practices like teamwork and network organization (Ullrich 2013b, 119). On the other hand, economy seems to be more and more interested in art. Whereas at the beginning companies legitimized the creation of own art collections with social responsibility, and sponsoring in the field of art was understood as an inversion to get a better image, the actual discourse claims, that art can contribute to economic growth and development. It is said that art can motivate employees, support creative processes, improve emotional and rational competences etc (Ullrich 2013b, 115–120). For Ullrich, this type of incorporation of art into economy is possible, because the dominant concept and image of art is very powerful and based on discourses, which underline overall paradox qualities. Referring to the history of the *concept of art* he shows, that unions of paradox characteristics were often used to explain the basic structure of art. An early example is the aesthetic theory of Schiller, where an ideal artwork represents gracefulness and dignity at the same time, causing the paradox effect of both relaxation and energetization at once. Other paradox connections are for example the union of sensuality and intellect, or of liberty and necessity (Ullrich 2013b, 111). For Ullrich, the history of the concept of art can explain, that a certain rhetoric of autonomy, linked to such paradox qualities, created the powerful concept of art still dominant today. Therefore he claims that the enthusiasm for (fine) art is nearly always based on the concept of art, and less on certain works or artists. "Who relies as entrepreneur or manager on art, is loaded in favor of it 'as such'—as a brand—, and the look on images and sculptures is dominated a priori by associations, effected by the word 'art'." (Ullrich 2013b, 122).

One reason for the decreasing difference between economy and art can be seen in the phenomenon, that economy is adapting the "mechanism of the concept of art"

(Ullrich 2013b, 125). Products are designed and promoted for example with paradox qualities as well, following a specific marketing strategy that focuses on *paradessence*, a term introduced by Alex Shakar. Similar to the discourses, which created the image of art, producers try to use these methods to create a specific aura—or a magic, a fiction—of a product. Gekeler's (2012) model of product communication shows, how narrations are used to produce an aura of a product. But beyond these types of *auratizing paradessence*, Ullrich (2013b, 127–128) claims that products and consumption practices may be able to offer a form of paradox experience to the consumer, which art cannot provide. This aesthetic experience is described as a fascinated *affirmation* of an image or a product based fiction, accompanied at the same time by the *negation* of this attitude, expressed by a skeptical distance or an ironic attitude. For Ullrich it seems to be possible, that present consumers can learn to be totally fascinated by a product's image, and critical towards brands and images at the same time (Ullrich 2013b, 128). Therefore the idea of being affected by a product based fiction in an overwhelming way, but at the same time maintaining a critical and ironic distance to this form of *fictionalization*, can be understood as the core of a general concept of *consumer aesthetic education* (cf. Ullrich 2012, 2013a).

If we transfer this concept to the specific sector of critical consumption and sustainable products, it is the *aesthetic dimension of sustainability*, which shifts into the centre of the educational reflections. The concept of consumer aesthetic education suggests that people living in the context of consumer culture have to learn how to deal with product based fictions and product communication in general. From this perspective, *fictions* of sustainability are just a special case of product communication. And product narrations can be conceived to be a special kind of literature, commodity aesthetics can be compared with fine art, and consumption practices with theatre performances. On the one hand the analogy between fine art (or high culture) and consumer culture can help to understand that some kind of aesthetic education is necessary to develop an accurate *taste* for aesthetic consumption practices (cf. Zirfas 2011). It also helps to understand that learning processes might be necessary to get intentionally fascinated by specific fictions in an overwhelming way. But what distinguishes conventional concepts of aesthetic education from those of consumer aesthetic education might be the desired *ironic attitude* towards the fictions and the corresponding aesthetic practices themselves. In our case, this means, that education should help to create not just the taste for sustainable products and the aesthetic competences to indulge oneself with them, but overall an ironic attitude towards fictions of sustainability too—and maybe also towards the fiction of *real* critical consumption.

The necessity of consumer aesthetic education in relation to critical consumption can be illuminated with other findings of Ullrich's study (2013a, 127–149). He points to the phenomenon that sustainable product communication today often indicates that the customer can purchase a *quiet conscience* with these types of products. "The quiet conscience is now for sale. For several years now you can purchase portions of it with products from an organic and natural supermarket or from a worldshop, the same way as with a lot of other brand products." (Ullrich 2013a, 127)

Some problems of this type of *morality consumption* have already been mentioned above in relation to critical consumption in general. First of all the lack of products that are really sustainable, furthermore the problem of conflicting sustainable aims, the contradictions between normative claims and real practices, and the mixing of fictional and factual narrations in product communication. But especially in reference to the consumption of morality and quiet conscience, Ullrich claims that often altruistic and egoistic motives are mixed, for example by people who identify themselves with LOHAS (Ullrich 2013a, 131–135). As it is easier for people with more money to consume critically, Ullrich compares the customers of LOHAS-products with purchasers of letters of indulgence in the Middle Ages. For him it seems to be crucial, that overall people who profit from material prosperity tend to have a bad conscience due to their extensive consumption practices and their privileged social status. Morality consumption therefore offers apparently the possibility to stay rich and privileged without a guilty conscience (Ullrich 2013a, 130).

But the phenomenon of *morality consumption*—and somehow *critical consumption* in general—can also create severe social problems. As the *critical consumer* is a concept that includes sufficient *economic capital* to purchase sustainable products on the one hand, high *cultural capital*—or at least familiarity with the concept and discourse of sustainability—on the other hand, critical consumption can serve as a medium for social processes of distinction and exclusion. A study by Carfagna et al. (2014) shows important changes in the concept of high cultural capital among ethical consumers in the US, which indicate the emergence of what the authors call an *eco-habitus*. Ullrich (2013a, 139–140) sees the danger of the rise of a *consumer bourgeoisie*, whose group identity is based on the distinction both to *ignorant* and *luxury consumers*, two groups also called *consumer proletariat* on the one hand, *nobility of money* on the other. Similar to Ullrich, Carfagna et al. also claim, that "these new HCC consumption strategies may function [...] as a strategy for pursuing distinction" (Carfagna et al. 2014, 175). But they also put emphases on positive effects, because critical consumption could be "a potentially less exclusive locus of cultural authority [...] which can promote awareness of and responses to environmental challenges." (Carfagna et al. 2014, 175).

A study by Hälterlein (2015) on different historic types of *consumption governments*, based on Foucault's theory of governmentality and related governmentality studies, supports the notion that both the discourse and practices of critical consumption have to be analyzed in relation to processes of social distinction. To demonstrate the fundamental historic transformation in the field of consumption governments, Hälterlein compares a historical order about dress codes, published in 1621 by the city of Frankfurt, with a contemporary advertisement from the German brand *Bionade*, where the slogan 'govern yourself' can be read. These examples show different strategies and techniques to govern consumption, using strict rules and punishment on the one hand, or just an appeal referring to the consumer's sense of responsibility on the other. Both try to gain influence on consumption, but are based on different ideas about what type of consumption is right or wrong, and also express different ideas about social order. "Whereas the dress code refers to a hierarchical, divinely legitimized social order due to its differentiation of social estates, the advertising slogan *govern yourself* refers to a society, in which the individual liberty of market participants fulfils the function of a regulative principal." (Hälterlein 2015, 9).

In addition to the presented analysis of historical transformations of governmental regimes of consumption, Hälterlein tries to understand how consumption is governed in the present. He claims that in the German case the creation of a neoliberal society, oriented on free market and economic competition, is directly connected with the concept of critical consumption. Therefore the autonomous, independent consumer who governs him- or herself, concerned with social and ecological problems and conscious of the relation between critical consumption and both individual and social responsibility, is said to be the core element of politics and governmental strategies. Whereas the state hands over social and ecological responsibility by deregulating reforms orientated on the free market and competition, the critical consumer is taking over this role, responsible now for the creation of a better and *sustainable* future. The neoliberal government of consumption therefore is based on a specific form of subjectivity construction, on entrepreneurial and responsible subjects that care about themselves and about others. "What looks like a process of social disintegration from the perspective of classical concepts of morality, appears then as a changed form of government, which ties a bond between the individual and society, not less stable and normative than a moral dualism of the prohibited and the permitted." (Hälterlein 2015, 160) Individualism, hedonism and consumerism therefore are not necessarily dissolving the social, but can even contribute to the construction of a *sustainable* society. "Therefore consumption should be understood both as mode of individualization and as a starting point for the creation of a responsible community. The vanishing point of the neoliberal government of consumption is a society, composed of consumers both entrepreneurial and independent, and socially and ecologically responsible." (Hälterlein 2015, 162) Although people are free to consume whatever they want and can purchase, social responsibility limits this liberty and legitimates *sustainable* consumption. Whereas the discourse on critical consumption spreads the image of a consumer who feels responsible for him- or herself and for society at the same time (cf. Hälterlein 2015, 136–157), discourses on not sustainable forms of consumption demonstrate the opposite (Hälterlein 2015, 123–136). Both discourses can be understood as a fundamental element of the neoliberal government of consumption, *moralizing* in a particular way to support the formation of a specific form of self governing subjectivity. Following Hälterlein (2015, 163), we can conclude that it is important to understand, how critical consumers and sustainable products are involved in present power relations, due to the complex interconnection between critic and power, liberation and subjugation.

Reflecting the social and political implications of sustainable product communication, a general consumer aesthetic education seems an important complement to critical consumer education, as it opens up other important dimensions of education for autonomy in the context of consumer culture. The main difference between both concepts seems to be, that Ullrich parts with the distinction of *utility* and *fictional value*, whereas Gekeler focuses on the distinction of *fictional* and *factual narratives*.

As both forms of narratives can contribute to the fictional value of products, the perspective opened by the concept of consumer aesthetic education offers the possibility of gaining autonomy in reference to the aesthetic dimension of sustainable products and critical consumption as such. In this sense, critical consumption itself can be understood as a fiction. An autonomous attitude towards this fiction can be characterized by the ability to get affected in an overwhelming way through critical consumption practices on the one hand, keeping an ironic distance to this type of aesthetic experience on the other. Whereas it might be comparatively simple to get an ironic distance to fictional narratives, it seems to be a lot more difficult to do so in relation to critical research practices and proved factual narratives of sustainability. Associating the most elaborate forms of critical consumption with other forms of profane consumption might help, to take over this perspective. Such an ironic distance might also help to criticize problematic aspects of critical consumption, which are related to new forms of social distinction.

Conclusion

As a result of the reflections about *education for autonomy* in the context of consumer culture we can conclude, that both analyzed educational concepts offer possibilities of gaining autonomy. Therefore we argue that both concepts should be combined. But we should be careful when we use the term autonomy in this context, because talking about autonomous consumption might cause problematic effects in the sphere of consumer culture as well. Such an effect could be, that both concepts support and orientate consumption practices, which themselves provoke overall an overwhelming *feeling* of autonomy: Whereas the concept of *critical consumer education* bears the danger to connect autonomy directly with concrete practices of critical consumption, the concept of *consumer aesthetic education* bears the danger to connect autonomy with all sorts of affective-ironical aesthetic consumption on the one hand, and with discourses of fundamental critique of critical consumption on the other hand. Even the combination of both educational concepts might not necessarily prevent such effects, because such practices of critical and aesthetic consumption can be combined as well. One result of the reflections about education for autonomy in the context of consumer culture might therefore be the finding, that pedagogical communication about consumption and autonomy can also be part of the consumption processes. From this perspective, the ideas of autonomy connected with critical consumer and consumer aesthetic education can be conceived as specific fictions in the logic of consumer culture. Education therefore should primarily try to prevent, that overall one-sided stable fictions of autonomy are established. Nevertheless we can conclude that autonomy is overall an important fiction, worth to be de- and reconstructed in an ongoing process, to gain in this way at least what somehow might be called *autonomy* in the context of consumer culture.

References

Bokova, I., and H. Clark. 2013. Foreword. In *Creative economy report 2013. Special Edition. Widening local development pathways*, ed. UNESCO, and UNDP, 9–11. http://www.unesco.org/culture/pdf/creative-economy-report-2013.pdf. Accessed 25 Mar 2015.

Bormann, I. 2011. Bildung für nachhaltige Entwicklung. *Enzyklopädie Erziehungswissenschaft*. Online. doi:10.3262/EEO05110161.

Carfagna, L.B., E.A. Dubois, C. Fitzmaurice, M.Y. Ouimette, J.B. Schor, M. Willis, and T. Laidley. 2014. An emerging eco-habitus: The reconfiguration of high cultural capital practices among ethical consumers. *Journal of Consumer Culture* 2: 158–178. doi:10.1177/1469540514526227.

Gekeler, M. 2012. *Konsumgut Nachhaltigkeit. Zur Inszenierung neuer Leitmotive in der Produktkommunikation*. Bielefeld: transcript.

Hälterlein, J. 2015. *Die Regierung des Konsums*. Wiesbaden: Springer.

Koch, L. 2011. Ästhetische Bildung. In *Allgemeine Erziehungswissenschaft II. Handbuch der Erziehungswissenschaft 2. Studienausgabe*, ed. Gerhard Mertens, Ursula Frost, Winfried Böhm, and Volker Ladenthin, 97–124. Paderborn: Schöningh.

Misik, R. 2007. *Das Kult-Buch. Glanz und Elend der Kommerzkultur*. Bonn: Bundeszentrale für politische Bildung.

Reckwitz, A. 2013. *Die Erfindung der Kreativität. Zum Prozess gesellschaftlicher Ästhetisierung*. Berlin: Suhrkamp.

Schrage, D. 2014. Kritischer Konsum zwischen Reflexivität und Popularisierung – zur Einführung. In *Vielfalt und Zusammenhalt. Verhandlungen des 36. Kongresses der DGS in Bochum und Dortmund 2012*, ed. Martina Löw, 1–9. Frankfurt am Main/New York: Campus. CD-ROM.

TFSL. 2010. *Task force on sustainable lifestyles*. http://www.unep.fr/scp/marrakech/taskforces/pdf/SLT%20Brochure.pdf. Accessed 25 Mar 2015.

Ullrich, W. 2009. Über die warenästhetische Erziehung des Menschen. *APuZ* 32–33: 14–19.

Ullrich, W. 2012. *Haben wollen. Wie funktioniert die Konsumkultur?* Frankfurt am Main: Fischer.

Ullrich, W. 2013a. *Alles nur Konsum. Kritik der warenästhetischen Erziehung*. Berlin: Wagenbach.

Ullrich, W. 2013b. *Tiefer hängen. Über den Umgang mit der Kunst*. Berlin: Wagenbach.

UNEP. 2011. *Here and now! Education for sustainable consumption recommendations and guidelines*. http://www.unep.org/pdf/Here_and_Now_English.pdf. Accessed 25 Mar 2015.

UNEP. 2014. *The 10YFP programme on sustainable lifestyles and education*. http://www.unep.org/10yfp/Portals/50150/downloads/SLE_Brochure.pdf. Accessed 25 Mar 2015.

UNESCO. 2006. *Road map for arts education*. http://www.unesco.org/new/fileadmin/MULTIMEDIA/HQ/CLT/CLT/pdf/Arts_Edu_RoadMap_en.pdf. Accessed 25 Mar 2015.

UNESCO. 2009. UNESCO World Report. *Investing in cultural diversity and intercultural dialogue*. Executive summary. http://unesdoc.unesco.org/images/0018/001847/184755e.pdf. Accessed 25 Mar 2015.

UNESCO. 2012. *Culture: A driver and an enabler of sustainable development*. https://en.unesco.org/post2015/sites/post2015/files/Think%20Piece%20Culture.pdf. Accessed 25 Mar 2015.

UNESCO. 2014a. *Florence declaration*. https://en.unesco.org/system/files/Florence%20Declaration_4%20October%202014_EN_3.pdf. Accessed 25 Mar 2015.

UNESCO. 2014b. *Roadmap for implementing the global action programme on education for sustainable development*. http://unesdoc.unesco.org/images/0023/002305/230514e.pdf. Accessed 25 Mar 2015.

WCED. 1987. *Our common future*. http://www.bne-portal.de/fileadmin/unesco/de/Downloads/Hintergrundmaterial_international/Brundtlandbericht.File.pdf. Accessed 25 Mar 2015.

Zirfas, J. 2011. Der Geschmack an der Nachhaltigkeit. Ästhetische Bildung als Propädeutik und Regulativ einer Bildung für nachhaltige Entwicklung. In *Die unsichtbare Dimension. Bildung für eine nachhaltige Entwicklung im kulturellen Prozess*, ed. Gabriele Sorgo, 35–52. Wien: Forum Umweltbildung.

Chapter 15
"My Place"? Catholic Social Teaching and the Politics of *Geborgenheit*

Clemens Sedmak

Abstract In this chapter, the concept of *Geborgenheit,* a German term that expresses a sense of being nested within a sheltering space to which one can open up, is analyzed and its poltical significance highlighted. It is argued that *Geborgenheit* is a key component of a good childhood and the notion is discussed in relation to political questions from the perspective of Catholic Social Teaching. In the first section, Sally Morgan's influential autobiography "My Place" is introduced to motivate how crucial "belonging" and "feeling safe" are for a child's life. In the second section, a definition of *Geborgenheit* is formulated, based on six aspects and it is suggested that it can serve as a valuable hermeneutical and analytical tool for the discourse on the politics of childhood. In the third section, some fundamental aspects of Catholic Social Teaching and its relationship to the concept of *Geborgenheit* are presented. It is concluded that Catholic Social Teaching can contribute to a deeper understanding of *Geborgenheit* as a category to approach normative issues in the politics of childhood.

The Story of Sally Morgan

Sally Morgan's influential 1987 autobiography *My Place* embraces many of the key issues in the discourse on the politics of childhood (Morgan 2012; cf. Sonoda 2009).[1] She expresses longing for as well as grief at having been deprived of a safe family homelife. Her sense of security was threatened by the Posttraumatic Stress Disorder her father was suffering from after returning from the War: "When Dad was happy, I wished he'd never change. I wanted him to be like that for ever, but there was always the war" (MMP 20); she realized that her father was not free, "there were things in his head that wouldn't go away" (MMP 21); he turned to

---

[1] In the following I will be using the abbreviation "MMP" for referring to Sally Morgan's book.

C. Sedmak (✉)
Department of Theology and Religious Studies, King's College London, London, UK

Centre for Ethics and Poverty Research, University of Salzburg, Salzburg, Austria
e-mail: clemens.sedmak@kcl.ac.uk

© Springer International Publishing Switzerland 2016
J. Drerup et al. (eds.), *Justice, Education and the Politics of Childhood*,
Philosophy and Politics – Critical Explorations 1,
DOI 10.1007/978-3-319-27389-1_15

235

drinking with his mates, most of whom were returned soldiers as well, and became "one of the boys", oblivious of wife and children. While her father was incapable of accepting any responsibility,[2] Sally was thrust into taking charge of adult duties such as negotiating with her violent and drunk father whether it was safe for the family to return home after seeking sanctuary in a neighbour's house. Sally Morgan mentions two instances in which she felt sorry for her father, because "he hated himself", and "he was so lost".[3] It is obvious that her childhood had become a stage on which the macro events of World War II were being acted out on the level of micro relationships and individual identity building.

The yearning for a real sense of belonging and safety is vividly described by Sally Morgan in her search for identity as she gradually begins to find out against the resolute resistance of her grandmother and mother that her family roots mean she belongs to the Aboriginals – the aspect that has made this book well known (Renes 2010). In her first attempt to ask the question: "Where do we come from" she is fobbed off with the reply: "Tell them, you're Indian" (MMP 38),[4] after an encounter with her cousins, a "small group of dark children", and her sense of identity is more confused than it was before. One day after school she finds her grandmother weeping about the fact that she is not white. "For the first time in my 15 years, I was conscious of Nan's colouring. She was right, she wasn't white. Well, I thought logically, if she wasn't white, then neither were we. What did that make us, what did that make me? I had never thought of myself as being black before" (MMP 97). The abrupt realization that she is aboriginal is a heavy burden with the social stigma it has attached to it. She begins to retrospectively perceive her childhood as fragmented – having been denied access to her roots; she begins to understand that she cannot excel at school because of certain factors within her self: "The sum total of all the things I didn't understand about them or myself. The feeling that a very vital part of me was missing and that I'd never belong anywhere" (MMP 106). Childhood is supposed to nurture the roots of personal identity; major sources of identity are found in identity-giving groups, groups with the ability to tell their story and enable the individuals within the group to tell their narrative, too; this is an essential step in the experience of recognition (Sedmak 2013, Ch. 2). Access to such sources of identity is a political matter as well since individual identity cannot be separated from the organization of public space and the culture of public and societal perception.

The social framework of her childhood is described by Sally Morgan through the lenses of "poverty" and "institutions": after her husband's death Sally's mother and grandmother raise the five children in poverty. Sally remembers that her mother's packed school lunches, "stand out in my mind as beacons of social embarrassment"

---

[2] "He was just like a child, sometimes, he never mended anything around the house, or took any responsibility. I felt very disappointed in him" (MMP 46).

[3] MMP 21 and MMP 43 respectively.

[4] Her attempts to understand her history are met with the reply: "There's no point in digging up the past, some things are better left buried" (MMP 99).

(MMP 37), she also recalls her father having raided the children's money boxes.[5] Indications of a "culture of poverty" can be seen in the role of the television ("the TV did more for us than warm clothes or extra beds ever could. It gave us a way out"; MMP 53) and in short-term indulgences: "Mum took to indulging us whenever she could. This indulgence took the form of unlimited lollies and fruit, rather than new clothes, toys or books" (MMP 68). Sally complains about the "folk knowledge" that dominated her childhood (e.g. onions are powerful tools to eradicate germs; MMP 85), a knowledge that frequently clashed with what she learned at school. Sally was the only girl in her class not to have a bed of her own which perhaps surprisingly she did not consider a disadvantage but a source of closeness-another indication of the need to feel sheltered and protected. Oscar Lewis' contested thesis of a "culture of poverty" addresses the idea of "mistrust versus institutions"[6] – this is certainly an element that can be identified in Sally Morgan's autobiography with her dark descriptions of hospitals and schools with their regimentation and routine. Sally could not develop a positive relationship with institutions: Looking at her mother and grandmother "I realised that part of my inability to deal constructively with people in authority had come from them. They were completely baffled by the workings of government or its bureaucracies. Whenever there were difficulties, rather than tackle the system directly, they'd taught us it was much more effective to circumvent or forestall it" (MMP 103). It goes without saying that childhood is that crucial stage in a person's life that is deeply influenced by the socio-economic as well as the epistemic situation of "relevant Others" in this life context.

Ultimately, Sally Morgan is telling a story about "belonging" and "feeling safe". After her father's early death she describes the experience of secure family life on evenings in front of the fire: "I'll never forget those evenings, the open fire, Mum and Nan, all of us laughing and joking. I felt secure, then. I knew it was us against the world, but I also knew that as long as I had my family, I'd make it" (MMP 53). Pets play a major role in the cultivation of this sense of "my place" as does her strong sense of imagination: Fairy tales and the discovery of Winnie the Pooh were key factors in Sally's sense of safety.[7] But this idyllic haven is threatened not as one might suppose by strangers but by a family member – to her great surprise and disgust Sally is sexually harassed by an Uncle not expecting members of the extended *family* to pose a threat. She had been warned about strangers, "what no one ever

---

[5] This was a deep breach of trust: "One day, Dad was so desperate he raided our money-boxes. I'll never forget our dismay when Jill and I found our little tin money-boxes had been opened with a can-opener and all our hard-won three penny bits removed. What was more upsetting was that he'd opened them at the bottom, and then placed them back on the shelf as though they'd never been tampered with" (MMP 45f).

[6] "The disengagement, the nonintegration, of the poor with respect to the major institutions of society is a crucial element in the culture of poverty" (Lewis 1966, 21) concerning a critique and discussion of Lewis' claim of a "culture of poverty" see the special issue of *The Annals of the American Academy of Political and Social Science,* Volume 629 (Harding et al. 2010).

[7] Sally writes that Winnie the Pooh: "made me feel more normal. I suppose I saw something of myself in him ... Pooh lived in a world of his own and he believed in magic, the same as me" (MMP 45).

warned us about were friends or relations" (MMP 81). The child is vulnerable, in need of trust and safety; while childhood is open to violence and violation of trust, at the same time childhood needs to provide experiences of sheltered closeness – which brings in the politically relevant concepts of "public protection of the private sphere" as well as "protection of the private from public intervention".

In short we could say that the politics of childhood manifests itself in the permeability of political and societal macro dimensions and personal and individual micro-dimensions. If a key issue in an appraisal of childhood is a "longing for a safe place", a "longing for belonging", we need to explore the politics of this longing.

The Concept of Geborgenheit

There are a number of ways to express what is at stake in childhood in terms of this longing for a special place: We could talk about "sense of belonging", "safe haven", "longing to feel safe and protected", "need to feel needed", "desire for a warm protected place", "experience of being loved, wanted and cared for". All these expressions idiomatically outline the nuances of a philosophically neglected term: *Geborgenheit*. This German noun is etymologically connected with the verb *bergen* (rescue, save, conceal, hide) so that the noun suggests "safety" as well as "privateness". The term "is commonly translated as 'security' but actually evokes an immediately positive sense of sheltered-ness, nested-ness, and well-being." (Hutta 2009, 252) In other words: "The notion of Geborgenheit first and foremost conjures up a sense of being nested within a sheltering space to which one can open up. While the notion of 'safety' tends to be defined in terms of a negation of fears and dangers, 'Geborgenheit' retains a moment of 'security' in a directly positive sense" (Hutta 2009, 256). "Nestedness" and "safety", "being nested" and "being safe" emerge in a first analysis as two key features of the term. If we agree that a key criterion to judge a person's childhood is the question whether there the child is given a sense of *Geborgenheit*,[8] we could discuss the politics of *Geborgenheit* as a key issue for a politics of childhood.

I would suggest to see *Geborgenheit* in two ways – as a value in itself with an intrinsic worth (experiencing Geborgenheit can even be seen as an equivalent to the intrinsic value of *eudaimonia* based on agency). It is good in itself to experience *Geborgenheit*. It is a situation where a person can affirm the situation in a "*bonum est hic esse*"-manner. Because of its element of "safe staying" *Geborgenheit* is also to be seen as an end point, as a goal and destination. On the other hand, *Geborgenheit* can also be seen as a means to end, as a basis from which to tackle difficulties. Janusz Korczak's reminders of the central role of childhood (Korczak 2009, 33 and 42) point to the value of the experience of Geborgenheit as "basis" and "refuge". In this sense *Geborgenheit* is the means to an end, namely agency and responsibility.

---

[8] That is the key concern of Hans-Ulrich Ahlborn's book "Geborgenheit. Wesensmerkmal jeder Erziehung" (Ahlborn 1986).

There is little philosophical material available on the notion of *Geborgenheit*. The German psychologist Hans Mogel describes it as an existential drive that makes us search for a certain condition, also as an existential feeling, a sentiment fundamental to life, a certain disposition vis-a-vis the world, a fundamental attitude (Mogel 1995). One of the few philosophers who has made an in-depth analysis of the concept, is Otto Friedrich Bollnow (1903–1991) who characterized *Geborgenheit* as "givenness of Thou", "robust being", "integrity of things and the world"; he reflected on the importance of "home" and "place" (Bollnow 2011, part II).[9] According to Bollnow "space" and "place" constitute frameworks and foundations for *Geborgenheit* (Bollnow 1976). That is why the question of "where to live" and "how to furnish the home" are existential questions and not just middle-class luxury issues. A "home" is a protected space that is constituted by the difference between "inside" and "outside". Doors are key elements for the cultivation of *Geborgenheit*. The home is a non-agonal sphere of familiarity and peacefulness. "Being at home" means "inhabiting a living space", a space that speaks a familiar language. These ideas resonate with Daniel Miller's studies on the meaning of things in people's households.[10] For there to be *Geborgenheit* at home as a true contribution to a good life, Bollnow calls for a balance between one's life inside and outside of the home, between "home" and "the world". Public life cannot prosper without a proper private sphere; private homes cannot flourish without proper public frameworks. This insight is an indication that *Geborgenheit* is a result of proper public/private interaction. *Geborgenheit* – as any avid reader of George Orwell's *Ninety Eightyfour* will remember – is based on proper political conditions, it cannot happen without these frameworks. James Ludema has described social bonding as a dynamics resulting in a strong sense of *Geborgenheit* (safety, security, protectedness) (Ludema 2001). This means that social dynamics happening in social space leads to the experience of *Geborgenheit*. It is under the conditions of *Geborgenheit* that creativity is fostered, that new knowledge, new conversations, and new ways of understanding things can emerge.

The political dimension of *Geborgenheit* has been convincingly developed by social geographer Jan Simon Hutta. He analyses the public space through its subjective dimension (people's feeling of safety and people's fear of crime) (Hutta 2009). He develops an understanding of *Geborgenheit* that is more closely linked with the public than with the private space. He uses the term to shift the debate on "fear of crime" towards a more existential dimension – "in signifying an immediately positive affective relation, geborgenheit forces what could be called a 'critical différance' (Derrida 1982) in relation to safety – a particular dynamic of differing and deferring regarding the term's hegemonic meaning. Shifting the question from 'How safe do you feel …?' to 'What makes you feel geborgen …?' can help to take

---

[9] Close to Bollnow's phenomenological analysis is Gerhard Kaminski's approach (Kaminski 2003).

[10] Daniel Miller has explored the "things" he found in people's houses of a street in East London; he discovered that most things have a history, are connected with stories, have identity-conferring aspects, mean something to the owner (Miller 2009).

the analytic framework out of its hegemonic order-centred and fear-centred fix and addressing the question of how positive affective intensities come to constitute subjective relations to space". (Hutta 2009, 258) The term serves as a lens and offers an innovative perspective to analyse public space and social interaction. *Geborgenheit* is a way of being at home in public which simultaneously allows for authenticity. It seems that the political dimension of *Geborgenheit* works in at least three ways: (i) the aspect of the necessary political conditions to ensure *Geborgenheit*; (ii) the political impact of *Geborgenheit* within the private home, i.e. a set of repercussions of private safety for public conduct; (iii) the aspect of *Geborgenheit* as a public and political term, as a term to depict a way of inhabiting public space. In this latter sense, *Geborgenheit* is understood to mean "feeling at home in public". Adam Smith famously characterised a non-poor person as one who "can walk about without shame" (cf. Zavaleta Reyles 2007)[11]; by way of analogy we could suggest that the person living in *Geborgenheit*, "can "abide",[12] can "stay without fear". *Geborgenheit* is thus construed as a relational term to include a relationship between subjective attitudes and feelings and a (social) situation including a dimension of spatiality.

It is against this background that I would like to suggest an analysis of the term *Geborgenheit*:

A person P has reasons to experience *Geborgenheit* (has reasons to feel *geborgen*) if

(1) P inhabits S
(2) P experiences S as safe, stable, welcoming
(3) P experiences robust concern and affective care by Q expressed in B
(4) Q is a stable "significant Other" in relation to P
(5) P experiences B as stable and personalized
(6) P develops and preserves P's identity within S and vis-à-vis Q because of (2)–(5).

"P" is a person or a group of persons, "S" is a certain space, "Q" is a person or a group of persons, "B" is a particular type of behaviour expressed in certain actions. The analysis cannot equate these conditions with the experience of *Geborgenheit* because of an irreducibly subjective dimension: traumatized persons may never fully experience *Geborgenheit* as the example of Sally Morgan has shown while others with deeply rooted religious faith like the "Russian Pilgrim" (Bacovcin 1985)[13] will. Nothwithstanding, there are grounds to assume that conditions leading to *Geborgenheit* would in any case be sufficient for having reasons to assume that *Geborgenheit* is constituted.

---

[11] Reyles makes the important point that "humiliation" is a conceptual device to obtain a deeper understanding of the dynamics of being poor.

[12] For a better understanding of "abiding" see Ben Quash' beautiful study on the term (Quash 2012).

[13] The protagonist in this book uses Jesusprayer as a source of *Geborgenheit* under any circumstances.

This analysis would give us three overarching conditions: A "space condition" expressed in (1) and (2), a "care condition" expressed in (3), (4), (5) and an "identity condition" expressed in (6). *Geborgenheit* thus requires a particular kind of space, specifically shaped relations, and the possibility for "being/becoming oneself". These three conditions can be classified further.

The space condition (S-condition): S is a *Geborgenheit*-conducive (G-conducive) space for P iff:

S1 P can appropriate S as "my place"
S2 S is embedded in a safe and stable context
S3 S has the appropriate moral and material infrastructure
S4 S constitutes a distinction between "inner" and "outer" with controlled transition.

G-conducive space is personal and "inhabited", is part of and protected by safe conditions and a safe environment, and properly equipped with material and moral resources, i.e. adequate means to reach the goals of building and protecting safe and warm space. It is a space that creates a world of its own (an "inner"), however with controlled permeability towards an external world.

The care condition (C-condition): P experiences care by Q as *Geborgenheit*-fostering ("G-fostering") iff:

C1 Q "cares" for P, i.e. responds to P's needs by understanding P's self-determined ends, adopting those ends as Q's own[14]
C2 P trusts Q, i.e. believes in and relies on Q's integrity, competence, benevolence, and predictability
C3 Q and P have a "face to face" relationship where Q and P cannot be replaced, i.e. a relationship that extends beyond one person instrumentalising another
C4 P understands B as "caring".

A G-fostering relationship between P and Q is characterised by a caring attitude on the side of Q, an attitude that expresses a commitment ("robust concern") towards as well as affection for P. P and Q have built a personal and trusting relationship that makes both P and Q irreplaceable. P can understand the behaviour and actions of P as translations of Q's caring attitude.

The identity condition (I-condition): P develops and preserves P's identity within S iff:

I1 P has easy access to sources of identity in S, i.e. to recognition, to membership in identity-conferring groups, to practice-relevant access to robust concerns, to the possibility of providing a coherent and unique narrative about P
I2 P has reasons not to expect to be forced to leave S against P's will
I3 P grows within S as a person
I.4 P and Q share a "thin script", i.e. have minimal needs for meta-reflections on role constructions.

---

[14] This echoes Sarah Clark Miller's definition of "care" (Miller 2011, 79).

P's identity ensures that P is recognized as a unique person with the possibility of tapping into major sources of identity. S is a space that enables this access; P can "stay" in S and has a sense of belonging ("at home" status, not guest status); P's relationship with Q is identity-affirming with the possibility of personal growth and development. P can "be herself" without explicitly constructing a role by following an external script.

It is possible to better locate contours of a "politics of *Geborgenheit*" within this framework: P needs to be in a position to inhabit S (Condition 1), which is also a matter of political mandate. An asylum seeker whose application is pending and whose citizen status is unclear will most probably not be in a position to develop a sense of *Geborgenheit* in temporary accommodation (see also I2). Condition (2), a major element of the S-condition, calls for proper political conditions of stability on the macro-level (S2). Furthermore, there have to be appropriate material conditions in place for G-conducive S (S3) which is also a political issue about the allocation of resources. To give an example: a hospital without electricity or food will not be in a position to build *Geborgenheit* even if the relationships are caring as hospitals in New Orleans during the San Catrina Hurricane have shown (cf. Fink 2013). Q as a major element contributing to P's situation can enter a G-fostering relationship only if Q's status is secured. Similarly relevant in political terms is the I-condition: Sally Morgan's autobiography has illustrated the relevance of I1 for personal identity-building; Sally was hindered in her efforts to know who she was by not having access to a coherent narrative about herself; as her account has shown there is a political dimension to the kind of truth she was looking for.

We could add two further dimensions to this political analysis of *Geborgenheit*, namely "G-promoters" and "G-defeaters", i.e. factors fostering and factors hindering the cultivation of *Geborgenheit*: G-promoters would be, for example, political conditions that contribute to the conditions of possibility of G-conducive S and G-fostering care. Lack of political status of P and Q respectively, unsafe macro-conditions, rigidity of space without the possibility of being appropriated and personally inhabited, inappropriate material resources are clearly G-defeaters. More systematically, one could distinguish intrapersonal (based on the psychological setup of a person, eg traumatization), thick-social (relationships with well-known persons), thin-social (relationships with unknown or lesser known persons), infrastructural, local-institutional, and macro-political G-defeaters. G-defeaters could be psychological factors within the person: toxic close or distant relationships, inadequate infrastructure, unsupportive institutional structure, destructive macro frameworks. Similarly, G-promoters can be found on these five different levels. It can thus be shown that there are grounds to develop a "politics of *Geborgenheit*" in the light of the G-conditions. If we accept *Geborgenheit* to be a key term for a hermeneutics of childhood such an analysis would also give us insights into the politics of childhood.

One could, of course, ask the question whether *Geborgenheit* is possible under adverse circumstances as well – can a person alone in her apartment experience it? Or, is it possible to experience it in a prison cell? I would suggest that it is possible to have a caring relationship with one self and (given a larger framework of security)

Geborgenheit is thus possible without caring relationships involving other persons. Virginia Woolf's point about a room of one's own would point in this direction. Furthermore, is *Geborgenheit* in a prison cell or under other adverse circumstances possible? Here again, the answer will be "yes". We could feel reminded of the discussion of the experience of happiness in a concentration camp, famously provoked by Hungarian survivor Imre Kertész who once said: "I experienced my most radical moments of happiness in the concentration camp. You cannot imagine what it's like to be allowed to lie in the camp's hospital, or to have a 10-min break from indescribable labor. To be very close to death is also a kind of happiness." The same line of thought can be applied to an understanding of *Geborgenheit* not as a permanent state ina stable situation, but rather as n island including the experience of a safe and secure space.

Catholic Social Teaching and the Politics of Geborgenheit

Having sketched the political significance of the concept of *Geborgenheit* as a hermeneutical and analytical tool for the discourse on the politics of childhood, I would now like to explore the specific contribution of Catholic Social Teaching to this debate. Catholic Social Teaching, i.e. the Social Doctrine of the Catholic Church, is, in the strict sense,[15] a set of discursive commitments developed in a series of documents, mostly papal encyclicals, since Leo XIIIth encyclical *Rerum Novarum* in 1891.[16] It is quite remarkable to find a coherent theology of the social world developed in a particular religious tradition. Because of the significant percentage of Catholics worldwide and because of the (powerful, but ambivalent) role of religion in children's lives, it may be worthwhile reconstructing Catholic Social Teaching on childhood.

A note of caution may be appropriate: Expecting a contribution of Catholic Social Teaching to the discourse on the politics of childhood may be met with three major objections: (i) The Catholic Church has a shameful history not only of child abuse, but also of (partly systematic) strategies of covering up and suppressing child abuse; (ii) "children" as actor have not played a major role in Catholic Social Teaching documents in which children are "barely visible"[17]; (iii) The context

---

[15] Obviously, the Christian tradition has dealt with social questions before the 19th century; there are grounds to argue for well-established social positions within the Christian tradition, upheld by the Church authorities – this would be the social teaching of the Church in a wider sense (cf. Hengel 1973; Dal Covolo 1995; Padovese 1999).

[16] I will use the following abbreviations for standard documents: CSD: Compendium of the Social Doctrine of the Church; RN: Rerum Novarum; QA: Quadragesimo Anno; GS: Gaudium et Spes; MM: Mater et Magistra; PT: Pacem in Terris; PP: Populorum Progresso; LE: Laborem Exercens; SRS: Sollicitudo Rei Socialis; CA: Centesimus Annus; CV: Caritas in Veritate. I refer to the paragraph numbers as they appear in the English version of the documents as officially published by the Vatican.

[17] This is the result of a recent analysis by Ethna Regan (Regan 2014).

within which children are described by Catholic Social Teaching documents seems to be anachronistic, because of the image of the intact nuclear family and the fact that care-taking responsibilities are primarily assigned to the mothers. These three objections could constitute a constructively critical hermeneutics of suspicion when approaching the documents. I would like to show that Catholic Social Teaching can contribute to a deeper understanding of *Geborgenheit* as a category to approach normative issues in the politics of childhood.

A first indicator for the affinity of Catholic Social Teaching to the *Geborgenheit* discourse is the relationship between micro-structure and macro-structure. The permeability between micro-contexts and macro-structures has been identified as one of the key elements of *Geborgenheit*. This idea is also a crucial dimension for the Social Doctrine of the Catholic Church. Catholic Social Teaching documents advocate that the same moral grammar (values, virtues) permeates the different spheres of society. In other words, the rules we apply when coping with our face to face relationships are not significantly different from the rules we use to coordinate our behaviour with that of strangers in the public sphere. Even more so, the rules that we are required to use in ordering structures and institutions are based on this "personalist" account. The uniformity of and the permeability between the various spheres of human existence are most notably expressed in terms of economics in the third chapter of *"Caritas in Veritate"*. The document is an appeal to re-think the relevance of the categories of "fraternity" and of "gift" for human coexistence and cooperation. Pope Benedict XVI suggests "communion" is a lens through which to look at transactions and interactions, as a third- "civil"- way between market and state.[18] He presents economics and civil virtues as a unity, implementing ideas developed in the civil economy approach (Bruni and Zamagni 2007). "The Church has always held that economic action is not to be regarded as something opposed to society (…). The Church's social doctrine holds that authentically human social relationships of friendship, solidarity and reciprocity can also be conducted within economic activity, and not only outside it or 'after' it. The economic sphere is neither ethically neutral, nor inherently inhuman and opposed to society. It is part and parcel of human activity" (CV 36). That is why economic activities need to be governed by overall principles and must not be separated from ethical imperatives (cf. QA 133f; MM 38).

---

[18] "When both the logic of the market and the logic of the State come to an agreement that each will continue to exercise a monopoly over its respective area of influence, in the long term much is lost: solidarity in relations between citizens, participation and adherence, actions of gratuitousness, all of which stand in contrast with *giving in order to acquire* (the logic of exchange) and *giving through duty* (the logic of public obligation, imposed by State law). In order to defeat underdevelopment, action is required not only on improving exchange-based transactions and implanting public welfare structures, but above all on gradually *increasing openness, in a world context, to forms of economic activity marked by quotas of gratuitousness and communion*. The exclusively binary model of market-plus-State is corrosive of society, while economic forms based on solidarity, which find their natural home in civil society without being restricted to it, build up society. The market of gratuitousness does not exist, and attitudes of gratuitousness cannot be established by law. Yet both the market and politics need individuals who are open to reciprocal gift." (CV 39).

A special place reflecting the import of this principle of permeability, moving towards an explicit consideration of children, is the family. The role of families seems particularly delicate. It is indeed the case that families, as Susan Moller Okin has pointed out in a response to Rawls (Okin 2004, esp. 1540–1542), are not only a source of *Geborgenheit* and a safe haven, but also contexts of threat and destruction (just read Robert Goolrick's autobiography *The End of the World As We Know It*). However, even when acknowledging the ambivalent and even potentially harmful role of families the point that there needs to be a place, as argued by both Rawls and Walzer, where identity forming experiences can be made without the justification of membership and where moral attitudes can be internalized seems to point to the remaining importance of families and family-like contexts.[19] The Catholic tradition can be challenged in terms of "one sided diet of examples", but it would be unwise to dismantle families all together, especially in a context of a trends towards deinstitutionalization of child care and family based child care (Innocenti Research Centre 2003).

Let us then take a benevolent look based on principles of charity at the documents: The family is described as the basis of social and political life, and that "family" as the first school of life prepares children for future citizenship (CSD 210ff); this is the relevance of the family for macro-structures (cf. GS 48; PP 36); on the other hand, macro-structures are called upon to protect and sustain the family, including the payment of wages that make it possible for a family to support itself (RN 13; QA 71; CA 8). If we take a closer look at the discourse on children, we can distinguish three different ways of talking about children within Catholic Social Teaching texts: (1) a universal, (2) a contextual and, (3) a specific one. The universal way of referring to children is in the sense of "all human beings" as "children of God"; the contextual one is situated within the realm of the Roman Catholic Church and addresses "all Catholics" as "children of the Church", whereby the specific approach talks about children in the familiar sense as young human individuals. The first mode of discourse is based on the belief "that all men [all persons] are children of the same common Father, who is God" (RN 25), that all human beings are "members of one great family and children of the same Heavenly Father" (QA 137). This language game is not insignificant since it constitutes (i) an understanding of equality of all human beings, (ii) a sense of prescribed solidarity in terms of the human family idea, (iii) a notion of "being creatures" with all its implications (see Williams 2000). The second language uses the well-known image of the Mother for the Church (cf. Dulles 1987) including expressions such as "the obedient children of the Church" (QA 12) or the invitation "to return to the maternal bosom of the Church" (QA 126). The image of motherhood is an indication of the claim that *Geborgenheit* can be found in and through the Church (although at the price of obedience which can be costly). The specific language game of children as young human beings is the one which is of real interest for the purposes of this paper, hence, deserves special attention that can be read as a preferential option for children. *Quadragesimo Anno* talks about the "special concern for women and children",

---

[19] For this discussion see (Sedmak 2003).

MM 20 establishes the State's duty "to protect the rights of all its people, and particularly of its weaker members, the workers, women and children". EV 8 provides a list of "society's weakest members" that mentions children after "the elderly, the infirm, immigrants". EV 10 calls for a special attention to children particularly with regard to violence. Unsurprisingly, children are characterized by a particular vulnerability that constitutes a need for protection: QA 71, MM 13 and CA 8 warn against the work-related abuse of years of childhood and inhumane working conditions, QA 121 cites the vulnerability of children with regard to (socialist) propaganda. Because of their special vulnerability, they need special care (GS 52: "The children … need the care of their mother at home"; LE 19: Children need "care, love and affection"). We could read RN 42 as identifying early exploitation as a defeater of *Geborgenheit*,[20] other G-defeaters include poverty (SRS 13) and materialistic thinking (EV 23).

The documents of Catholic Social Teaching see children as agents who contribute to the common good of the family as well as to the well-being and development of their parents – this is especially explicit in *Gaudium et Spes*, a key document of the Second Vatican Council: "As living members of the family, children contribute in their own way to making their parents holy. For they will respond to the kindness of their parents with sentiments of gratitude, with love and trust" (GS 48); children "contribute very substantially to the welfare of their parents" (GS 50). One could interpret this as a contribution to a cultural of family-*Geborgenheit*.

In fact *Geborgenheit* can be seen as a key concern of family life since metaphors of "family hearth" (GS 48) or "bosom of the family" (GS 52) are used in Vatican II language. The fostering and nourishing of *Geborgenheit* follows a particular order, especially the special authority of parents that is expressed in numerous places throughout the documents of Catholic Social Teaching (PT 37). *Geborgenheit* is brought about through efforts; there is, one could say, "G-labour", specific labour in order to build and preserve *Geborgenheit*; this labour involves sacrifice (cf. MM 195) and moral effort (fidelity of the spouses: GS 48). Because of the real labour involved, care work needs to be properly recognized (LE 9).

Geborgenheit is not an end in itself according to Catholic Social Teaching, but serves as the basis for personal development as a moral agent and as a social being (GS 48, GS 52, LE 19, CA 39). The cultivation of *Geborgenheit* requires appropriate conditions (GS 68, CA 49) and legal frameworks (QA 28, GS 52). A special framework for child-relevant *Geborgenheit* in a family setting are the "bonds of marriage" (GS 48). The understanding of *Geborgenheit* in the Catholic social tradition can be reconstructed as comprising three dimensions: a material dimension that is based on an understanding of just wage (family wage: PT 20, CV 63), the right to ownership and private property (RN 13) and the possibility to make (some) savings (RN 46). The moral dimension is rooted in the idea that it is a sign of self-respect if parents can provide *Geborgenheit* for their children (cf. RN 13), that *Geborgenheit* is fostered within an appropriate moral environment (CA 47) and that the cultivation of *Geborgenheit* requires generosity (EV 26). The spiritual dimension of

---

[20] "With regard to children, great care should be taken not to place them in workshops and factories until their bodies and minds are sufficiently developed" (RN 42).

Geborgenheit can be primarily expressed in the proper communication of divine providence and the fostering of a culture of trust in God's providence (MM 195).

This reconstruction has given us the following claims about an understanding of the concept of *Geborgenheit*: (i) Children are in special need of *Geborgenheit* because of their particular vulnerability; (ii) this vulnerability justifies a preferential option for children; (iii) Children are not only G-recipients, but also G-agents; (iv) *Geborgenheit* is constructed within a particular order which implies legal, political, societal and moral conditions; (v) *Geborgenheit* is based on G-labour; (vi) There are G-defeaters such as exploitation, poverty, insufficient material conditions, and materialistic thinking; (vii) *Geborgenheit* is not an end in itself, but a basis to enable personal growth as a moral agent and a social being; (viii) *Geborgenheit* is poly-dimensional with a material, a moral, and a spiritual dimension. These claims – especially (iv), (vi) and (viii) – point to the political dimension of the cultivation of *Geborgenheit* once again.

Conclusions

The discourse on children within Catholic Social Teaching documents can be critically questioned – especially with regard to role allocations to men and women, the understanding of authority and obedience, the rather narrow understanding of a proper family. These avenues of criticism would have an impact on the discourse on *Geborgenheit* within Catholic Social Teaching. "Caring relationships" can be distorted or undermined through gender stereotypes and misleading ideas of authority. It goes without saying that Catholic Social Teaching is struggling with credibility. There is the challenge of an "esoteric language" that is not open to outsiders, there is the lack of real life examples, the one-sided diet of images, the separation between form of life and moral expectations especially with regard to family issues, there is the challenge of the minimal role of participation of children in significant Church contexts including the challenge of decision making processes dominated by celibate men.

However, there are also some important new points concerning the politics of childhood. Catholic Social Teaching allows for a deeper understanding of *Geborgenheit* by supporting ideas of "G-labour", "G-order", and "G-multidimensionality". The S-condition mentioned above is deepened by terms such as "climate of mutual interaction and enriching communication" (EV 94), "moral environment conducive to the growth of the child's personality" (CA 47), the importance for children of not "being uprooted from their natural environment" (EV 93). The understanding of the C-condition has been enriched by the terms "attentive and loving care" (EV 93), by "love and affection" and "educating them [the children] in accordance with their needs, which vary with age" (LE 19). The I-condition is complemented by insights into capacity-building and moral identity formation during childhood (cf. MM 195, GS 52, GS 61, CA 47, EV 92) with the idea of providing *Geborgenheit* in order to afford a basis for personal, moral and social maturity. The significant insights into *childness* gained from a Catholic Social Teaching perspective are the necessity of special attention to and even preferential treatment of children; the idea that children are agents of *Geborgenheit*, and the emphasis on the moral and spiritual dimension of childhood and child care.

Further insights into the discourse on childhood can be found in the 1986 Pastoral Letter "Economic Justice for All" (EJA) by the United States Conference of Catholic Bishops. This is an expression of regional Catholic Social Teaching not with the same level of ecclesial authority as papal documents but still normatively relevant. The document is an influential Pastoral Letter on "Catholic Social Teaching and the U.S. Economy".[21] The document talks about the struggle to secure a better future for children (EJA 11) thus lending weight to the idea that *Geborgenheit* is not an end in itself; parents are invited "to guide their children to the maturity of Christian adulthood and responsible citizenship" (EJA 85) thus bringing a political dimension into a *Geborgenheit*-based upbringing. The document underlines the political scope of childhood by raising the question: "How do my economic choices contribute to the strength of my family and community, to the values of my children?" (EJA 23). In line with the preferential treatment of children as well as the poor, special emphasis is laid on poverty as a *Geborgenheit*-defeater: children living in poverty are placed at the centre of the ethical appraisal of the economy (EJA 176ff). Political claims are connected with that analysis: "We affirm the principle enunciated by John Paul II that society's institutions and policies should be structured so that mothers of young children are not forced by economic necessity to leave their children for jobs outside the home"(EJA 207), and similarly: "For those children whose parents do work outside the home, there is a serious shortage of affordable, quality day care"(EJA 208). These points refer to conditions S2 and S3 from the analysis above.

Finally, it should not be forgotten that Catholic Social Teaching is primarily not a philosophical but a theological contribution to the debate on social ethics (cf. CSD 66, 73–75), and there is a deep message in the idea that children have a prophetic voice. Children are not only G-agents, they are also *redemptive* agents. EV 45 states this point as follows: "The value of the person from the moment of conception is celebrated in the meeting between the Virgin Mary and Elizabeth, and between the two children whom they are carrying in the womb. It is precisely the children who reveal the advent of the Messianic age: in their meeting, the redemptive power of the presence of the Son of God among men first becomes operative". The language may sound alien to non-Catholics, but there is deep sense of the importance of the child as a witness to an ethically inspiring and normatively important possible world: the world of the "Kingdom of God". Children are depicted as epistemic agents in the account of Jesus' encounter with children in the synoptic gospels. The passage is well known: people are bringing little children to Jesus; the disciples try to prevent this happening, but Jesus says: "Let the little children come to me; do not stop them; for it is to such as these that the kingdom of God belongs ... whoever does not

---

[21] The official document can be found on the US Catholic Bishops' Website; for a theological discussion see (Allman 2012).

receive the kingdom of God as a little child will not enter it."[22] The child is not only "agent", but also "witness" and "model". If we take the idea of the Kingdom of God as a model of *Geborgenheit* (see Is 65:25) with a political dimension – Kingdom as being "among us" according to Lk 17,20-21 with its imperative of liberation (Gonçalves 2009) – , we can see the unique contribution of the Christian tradition to the moral status of the child (as witness, model and redemptive agent) and to the politics of *Geborgenheit*.

One of the key components of a good childhood which is one of the key ideas of a "Kingdom Theology" is the idea of *hope*. In her autobiography, Sally Morgan mentions her mother's failed attempts to give a message of hope to their poverty or her husband's health to the children: "I knew that tone of voice, it was the one she always used whenever she spoke about Dad getting better. I knew there was no hope" (MMP 17). "Hope" is a precious moral (and spiritual) good that is also a constituent part of *Geborgenheit* (cf. conditions C2 and I2 in our analysis). Hope has a political dimension which has been beautifully expressed by Ernst Bloch. *Geborgenheit* seems to remain a utopia, but a politically powerful one. Ernst Bloch famously ends his *Principle of Hope* with the statement: "Once [we have] established [our] own domain in real democracy, without depersonalization and alienation, something arises in the world which all men [sic] have glimpsed in childhood: a place and a state in which no one has yet been. And the name of this something is home (*Heimat*)" (Bloch 1995, 3:1376).

References

Ahlborn, Hans-Ulrich. 1986. *Geborgenheit: Wesensmerkmal Jeder Erziehung*, 1st ed. Bad Heilbrunn/Obb: Klinkhardt.
Allman, Mark J. (ed.). 2012. *The almighty and the dollar: Reflections on economic justice for all*, 1st ed. Winona: Anselm Academic.
Bacovcin, Helen, trans. 1985. *The way of a pilgrim, and the pilgrim continues his way*, 1st ed. New York: Doubleday.
Bloch, Ernst. 1995. *The principle of hope*, Studies in contemporary German social thought, vol. 3, 1st ed. Cambridge: MIT Press.
Bollnow, Otto Friedrich. 1976. Die Erzieherische Bedeutung Der Geborgenheit Im Hause. *Vierteljahresschrift Für Heilpädagogik Und Ihre Nachbargebiete* 45(2): 149–158.
Bollnow, Otto Friedrich. 2011. *Neue Geborgenheit: Das Problem Einer Überwindung Des Existentialismus*, Schriften/Otto Friedrich Bollnow 5, 1st ed. Würzburg: Königshausen & Neumann.
Bruni, Luigino, and Stefano Zamagni. 2007. *Civil economy: Efficiency, equity, public happiness*, Frontiers of business ethics 2, 1st ed. Bern: Peter Lang.
Dal Covolo, Enrico. 1995. Dottrina Sociale Della Chiesa E Studio Dei Padre. *La Società* 5(3): 674–678.
Derrida, Jacques. 1982. Différance. In *Margins of philosophy*, 1–27. Chicago: University of Chicago Press.
Dulles, Avery. 1987. *Models of the church*, 1st ed. New York: Bantam Doubleday Dell.

---

[22] Mk 10,14-15 (NRSV).

Fink, Sheri. 2013. *Five days at memorial: Life and death in a Storm-Ravaged Hospital*, 1st ed. New York: Crown Publishers.

Gonçalves, Alonso. 2009. The kingdom of god and pastoral praxis. An approach using Jon Sobrino's theology. *Ciberteologa. Journal of Theology & Culture* 23(3): 29–34.

Harding, David J., Michèle Lamont, and Mario Luis Small (eds.). 2010. *The ANNALS of the American Academy of Political and Social Science*, vol. 629, Special Issue.

Hengel, Martin. 1973. *Eigentum Und Reichtum in Der Frühen Kirche; Aspekte Einer Frühchristlichen Sozialgeschichte*, Calwer Paperback, 1st ed. Calwer: Stuttgart.

Hutta, J. Simon. 2009. Geographies of Geborgenheit: Beyond feelings of safety and the fear of crime. *Environment and Planning D: Society and Space* 27(2): 251–273.

Innocenti Research Centre. 2003. *Children in institutions: The beginning of the end? The cases of Italy, Spain, Argentina, Chile and Uruguay*, Innocenti Insight 8. Florence: Innocenti Research Centre. http://www.unicef-irc.org/publications/pdf/insight8e.pdf.

Kaminski, Barbara. 2003. *Geborgenheit und Selbstwertgefühl*, 1st ed. Frankfurt am Main: Haag + Herchen.

Korczak, Janusz. 2009. *The child's right to respect*. Strasbourg: Office of the Commissioner for Human Rights. http://www.coe.int/t/commissioner/source/prems/PublicationKorczak_en.pdf.

Lewis, Oscar. 1966. The culture of poverty. *Scientific American* 215(4): 19–25.

Ludema, James D. 2001. From deficit discourse to vocabularies of hope: The power of appreciation. In *Appreciative inquiry: An emerging direction for organization development*, 1st ed, ed. David L. Cooperrider, Peter F. Sorensen, Therese F. Yaeger, and Diana Whitney, 443–466. Champaign: Stipes Publishing.

Miller, Daniel. 2009. *The comfort of things*, 1st ed. Cambridge/Malden: Polity.

Miller, Sarah Clark. 2011. *The ethics of need: Agency, dignity, and obligation*, Studies in philosophy, 1st ed. New York: Routledge.

Mogel, Hans. 1995. *Geborgenheit: Psychologie eines Lebensgefühls*, 1st ed. Berlin: Springer.

Morgan, Sally. 2012. *My place*. London: Virago Press.

Okin, Susan Moller. 2004. Gender, justice and gender: An unfinished debate. *Fordham Law Review* 72(5): 1537–1567.

Padovese, Luigi. 1999. La Dimensione Sociale Del Pensiero Patristico: Considerazioni Generali. *Studia Moralia* 37(2): 273–293.

Quash, Ben. 2012. *Abiding: The Archbishop of Canterbury's 2013 Lent book*, 1st ed. London: Bloomsbury Continuum.

Regan, Ethna. 2014. Barely visible: The child in catholic social teaching. *The Heythrop Journal* 55(6): 1021–1032. doi:10.1111/heyj.12207.

Renes, Martín. 2010. Sally Morgan: Aboriginal identity retrieved and performed within and without my place. *Estudios Ingleses de La Universidad Complutense* 18: 77–90.

Sedmak, Clemens. 2003. Gerechtigkeitstheorien Und Familienbegriff. *Zeitschrift Für Familienforschung* 15(1): 55–73.

Sedmak, Clemens. 2013. *Innerlichkeit Und Kraft: Studie Über Epistemische Resilienz*, Forschungen Zur Europäischen Geistesgeschichte 14, 1st ed. Freiburg im Breisgau: Herder.

Sonoda, H. 2009. A preliminary study of Sally Morgan's my place. *The Otemon Journal of Australian Studies* 35: 157–170.

Williams, Rowan. 2000. On being creatures. In *On Christian theology*, Challenges in contemporary theology, 1st ed, ed. Rowan Williams, 63–78. Oxford/Malden: Blackwell Publishers.

Zavaleta Reyles, Diego. 2007. The ability to go about without shame: A proposal for internationally comparable indicators of shame and humiliation. *Oxford Development Studies* 35(4): 405–430. doi:10.1080/13600810701701905.

About the Authors

Alexander Bagattini is lecturer at the department of philosophy of the University of Düsseldorf, Germany. His areas of specialization are: Normative ethics, applied ethics and social philosophy.

Nicole Balzer is working as a post doc at the Institute of Educational Science at the Westfälische Wilhelms-University Münster. Her research activities focus on educational theories and theories of ,Bildung', anthropological and philosophical foundations of educational theory, theories of recognition, subjectivation and power, as well as qualitative educational research.

Mar Cabezas is a postdoctoral researcher at the Centre for Ethics and Poverty Research (University of Salzburg) working as member of the project "Child Poverty and Social Justice". PhD in Philosophy specialized in the role of emotions in moral reasoning by the University of Salamanca (Extraordinary doctorate Award 2013) and Expert in Children Mistreatment (UNED 2011), her work focuses on building bridges between practical philosophy and moral psychology.

Johannes Drerup works as a postdoctoral researcher at the Institute of Educational Sciences of the University of Münster and holds a temporary professorship at the University of Koblenz-Landau. His major research interests include educational theory, philosophy of education and applied ethics. Recent publications are: Paternalismus, Perfektionismus und die Grenzen der Freiheit. Paderborn, München, Wien, Zürich: Ferdinand Schöningh, 2013 (ISBN: 978-3-506-77298-5); Autonomy, Perfectionism and the Justification of Education. In: Studies in Philosophy and Education, 2014 (doi: 10.1007/s11217-014-9426-3).

Elizabeth Edenberg is a Postdoctoral Teaching Fellow at Fordham University. She received her PhD in Philosophy from Vanderbilt University, under the direction of Marilyn Friedman. Elizabeth specializes in Political Philosophy, Ethics, and

© Springer International Publishing Switzerland 2016

251

J. Drerup et al. (eds.), *Justice, Education and the Politics of Childhood*,
Philosophy and Politics – Critical Explorations 1,
DOI 10.1007/978-3-319-27389-1

Feminist Philosophy. Her article, "Unequal Consenters and Political Illegitimacy," co-authored with Marilyn Friedman, was published in *The Journal of Political Philosophy*. She has also co-edited a book with Larry May on *Jus Post Bellum and Transitional Justice* (Cambridge University Press, 2013).

Allyn Fives is a Lecturer in Political Science and Sociology, NUI Galway. He holds a PhD in Political Theory from Edinburgh University. His political philosophy publications have been in the areas of political reason, welfare theory, the political thought of Rawls and MacIntyre, and parental authority and children's agency. His social science publications have been in the areas of children's reading self-beliefs, the role of random allocation in RCT studies, researching hard-to-reach child populations, and young carers. He teaches in the areas of political theory and research ethics. He is also Chair of the University's Research Ethics Committee.

Gunter Graf is a postdoctoral researcher at the Center for Ethics and Poverty Research, where he works in the project group for 'Social Justice and Child Poverty'. He is also a Research Fellow at the International Research Centre for Social and Ethical Questions in Salzburg. He mainly works in political and social philosophy, with a focus on the capability approach and its relation to poverty and children.

Phillip D.Th. Knobloch graduated from the University of Würzburg, in Philosophy of Education and Special Needs Education. He obtained a doctorate in Philosophy at the University of Cologne. He was research assistant at the University of Cologne, staff scientist and lecturer in Education at the University of Bayreuth. Currently he is lecturer in Comparative, International and Multicultural Education at the Ruhr-University of Bochum. He realized research and field studies in Latin America. A central focus of teaching and research is Postmodern and Postcolonial Education in the context of globalization, internationalization, plurality and diversity.

Lars Lindblom is a senior lecturer at Umeå University. His research takes place at the intersection of political philosophy. He has written on workplace ethics, evaluation studies, risk regulation, and the relationship between economic theory and political philosophy. At present, he works on one project on equality in schooling and another project on unions and justice.

Colin M. Macleod is Associate Professor of Philosophy and Law at the University of Victoria in Canada. His research focuses on issues in contemporary moral, political, and legal theory with a special focus on distributive justice and equality; children, families, and justice; and democratic ethics. He is the author of *Liberalism, Justice, and Markets* (OUP 1998), coeditor with David Archard of *The Moral and Political Status of Children* (OUP 2002) and co-editor with Alexander Bagattini of *The Nature of Children's Well-Being: Theory and Practice* (Springer 2014).

Nicholas John Munn Nick is a Senior Lecturer in Philosophy at the University of Waikato, where he has worked since 2012. His research interests are primarily in democratic theory and applied ethics, with a focus on political exclusion and the means through which we overcome it.

Josephine Nielsen is a PhD candidate at Queen's University in Kingston, Canada currently working under Will Kymlicka. Her dissertation focuses on the rights of parents, children, and cultural minorities within liberal multiculturalism.

Christoph Schickhardt is post-doc researcher and scientific coordinator in biomedical ethics at the National Center for Tumor Diseases, Heidelberg University Hospital. He studied philosophy and was awarded a PhD degree in Ethics for a book on children in ethical theory by the University of Düsseldorf in 2011. He teaches philosophy at the universities of Heidelberg and Bamberg (Germany).

Christina Schües is Professor for Anthropology and Ethics in *the Institute for the History of Medicine and Science Studies* at the University of Lübeck, and Adjunct Professor for Philosophy in the *Institute for Philosophy and the Science of Arts* at the Leuphana University of Lüneburg. Her areas of research are devoted to anthropology, ethics, epistemology, phenomenology, and political philosophy. Presently she is working on a project about the *precarious well-being of children.*

Gottfried Schweiger works at the Centre for Ethics and Poverty Research, University of Salzburg, where he is currently the Principal Investigator of a 3-year research project on "Social Justice and Child Poverty", funded by the Austrian Science Fund (FWF). During the winter semester 2014 he is visiting researcher at the Department for Philosophy, University of St. Gallen.

Clemens Sedmak is a philosopher and theologian. He holds the F.D. Maurice Chair at King's College London and the Franz Martin Schmolz OP Visiting Professorship for Social Ethics at the University of Salzburg. He is Head of the Centre for Ethics and Poverty Research at the University of Salzburg and President of the International Research Centre for Social and Ethical Issues (ifz Salzburg). His research interests include poverty research, social ethics, epistemology, and philosophy of science.

CPSIA information can be obtained at www.ICGtesting.com
Printed in the USA
BVOW06*0214070416

443346BV00004B/18/P

9 783319 273877